THE LONG FUSE

BOOKS BY DON COOK

The Long Fuse

Forging the Alliance:
NATO, 1945–1950

Charles de Gaulle: A Biography

Ten Men and History

The War Lords: Eisenhower
(Essays Edited by Field Marshal Lord Carver)

Floodtide in Europe

The
LONG FUSE

How England Lost the
American Colonies, 1760–1785

DON COOK

THE ATLANTIC MONTHLY PRESS
NEW YORK
•

Published simultaneously in Canada
Printed in the United States of America

Library of Congress Cataloging-in-Publication Data

Cook, Don, 1920-1995
The long fuse: How England lost the American colonies.
1760-1785 / Don Cook.
Includes bibliographical references and index.

ISBN-13: 978-0-87113-661-9

1. United States—Politics and government—1775–1783. 2. United States—
History—Revolution, 1775–1783. 3. Great Britain—Politics and
government—1760–1789. 4. Great Britain—Colonies—America—
History—18th century. I. Title.
E210.C665 1995 973.3—dc20 94-43632

Design by Laura Hammond Hough

Atlantic Monthly Press
an imprint of Grove/Atlantic, Inc.
841 Broadway
New York, NY 10003

Distributed by Publishers Group West

www.groveatlantic.com

11 12 13 14 15   12 11 10 9 8

We lost the American colonies because we lacked the statesmanship to know the time and the manner of yielding what it is impossible to keep.

But the lesson was learned. In the next century and a half, we kept more closely to the principles of the Magna Carta, which has been the common heritage of both our countries.

We learned to respect the right of others to govern themselves in their own way. This was the outcome of the experience learned the hard way in 1776. Without that great act in the cause of liberty performed in Independence Hall two hundred years ago, we could never have transformed our Empire into a Commonwealth.

Queen Elizabeth II
Independence Bicentennial
Philadelphia, Pennsylvania
July 6, 1976

Magnanimity in politics is not seldom the truest wisdom; and a great Empire and little minds go ill together.

Edmund Burke
House of Commons
March 22, 1775

Contents

AUTHOR'S NOTE   xi

Chapter 1 ENGLAND VICTORIOUS   1

Chapter 2 PITT DEPARTS, BUTE LIGHTS THE FUSE   21

Chapter 3 FRANKLIN IN LONDON   38

Chapter 4 THE STAMP ACT   51

Chapter 5 THE CRISIS   70

Chapter 6 FRANKLIN TESTIFIES, ROCKINGHAM REPEALS   88

Chapter 7 THE CHATHAM FIASCO   106

Chapter 8 THE TOWNSHEND CRISIS   119

Chapter 9 ANOTHER REPEAL   133

Chapter 10 THE KING FINDS A PRIME MINISTER   147

Chapter 11 LORD NORTH'S TEA PARTY   163

Chapter 12 "BLOWS MUST DECIDE"   179

Chapter 13 FRANKLIN'S LAST TRY   201

Chapter 14 ENGLAND AT WAR   219

Chapter 15 THE HOWE BROTHERS TRY WAR AND PEACE   240

Chapter 16 THE ROAD TO SARATOGA   262

Chapter 17 A NEW WAR FOR ENGLAND   283

Chapter 18 THE SOUTHERN STRATEGY   304

Chapter 19 THE ROAD TO YORKTOWN   319

Chapter 20 THE KING FIGHTS ON   340

Chapter 21 THE PEACE PROCESS   360

EPILOGUE   382

SOURCE NOTES   389

SELECT BIBLIOGRAPHY   397

INDEX   403

Author's Note

In my ten years as a newspaper correspondent in London, covering Parliament, politics, and the Foreign Office, I found much that stirred reflections on what political life would have been like in England under King George III at the time of the American Revolution.

How was it that Great Britain at the height of its eighteenth-century power, victorious around the globe after the Seven Years' War with France, politically mature with a stable government in a free-speaking democracy, made such a remorseless succession of blunders that ended in an unnecessary and unwinnable war and lost King George the greatest of his empire's possessions?

When I began to assemble and distill the abundance of historical and biographical material for this book, I was soon caught up in this great drama of England's political failure. Here was the other side of the story of the American Revolution, which American histories generally only summarize in passing. But London in those days was alive with a strong cast of figures, not only those in Parliament, but also writers, scientists, preachers, and artists. They left a record of ringing oratory and a wealth of written documentation attesting to their follies and frustrations. The story of England and the American Revolution was there, told by the participants in their own words.

One of the most indefatigable of writers was King George himself; he dominated his government, determined not merely to reign but to rule, an autocrat who scorned anyone who dared speak in opposition to his will. He was one of the hardest-working monarchs of English history, writing endlessly in his own clear hand and usually recording not only the date but the exact time of day on his ceaseless flow of instructions, letters, and comments.

Six large volumes of *The Correspondence of King George III* were edited by Sir John Fortescue and published in the 1920s. They record in vivid detail the king's direct involvement in American affairs at virtually every turn of the way, from the Stamp Act in 1765 to the Battle of Yorktown in 1781. It was the king who prodded governments into acts that led to war and the king who kept the war going, refusing all thoughts of conciliation or compromise with the colonies.

Along the way were some of the great parliamentary debates of English history: William Pitt, Edmund Burke, Charles James Fox, Lord North, George Grenville, Colonel Isaac Barré, Lord George Germain, Alexander Wedderburn, the earl of Dartmouth, Charles Townshend, and others tangled repeatedly over the American question. The opponents of the king's policies had many voices—but they did not have the votes. And as the king refused to compromise, the march of folly went on.

Benjamin Franklin watched all this unfold during his sixteen years in London as colonial agent for Pennsylvania and the voice of American interests. His vast correspondence and lucid political writings of those years are an integral part of the history of England and the American Revolution. A devoted Anglophile when he arrived in London on his first tour, in 1757, Franklin worked assiduously to try to shape a political understanding that would keep America in the British Empire. The English, certainly those who were running the government, would not listen. He departed on the eve of war in 1775, now a determined revolutionary, sick and tired of "this old rotten state, it will only corrupt and poison us also."

Perhaps Franklin's finest hour in London was his extraordinary appearance before the full House of Commons to testify against the Stamp Act in February of 1766. Watchers of televised American congressional hearings in Washington or sessions of the House of Commons in London will find Franklin's testimony as fresh and vigorous as anything that goes on in legislative proceedings today.

When the war began, so did querulous military dispatches from the overrated British generals in America who were operating at the end of tenuous three-thousand-mile supply lines. Back came confusing orders from the egregious Lord George Germain, who was directing the war from London.

Lord North, the king's prime minister for twelve decisive years, from 1770 to 1782, bobbed like a cork in this troubled sea. An amiable man, a skilled parliamentarian with many political friends and few enemies, he had none of the ruthless will needed to lead a country in war, and he knew it. He saw disaster building but, loyal to the stubborn king, he could do very little about it. Frustrated, he tried repeatedly to resign, but the king would never let him go. Somehow he managed to remain amiable to the end.

Ultimately, the American colonies were lost as much through the inexorable missteps in London as they were by Burgoyne at Saratoga and Cornwallis at Yorktown.

Philadelphia
November 1994

THE LONG FUSE

Chapter 1

ENGLAND VICTORIOUS

King George III acceded to the throne of England in October of 1760, a fortuitous time in the history of his nation. England was reaching the apogee of her eighteenth-century power with a remarkable string of global victories over France in the Seven Years' War. The French had already been ousted from Canada and America, and by the end of the war the Union Jack flew secure from the Caribbean to the Mediterranean, from Senegal in Africa to Madras in India and later on to Singapore, Sumatra, and Manila in the Pacific.

Horace Walpole, that inveterate letter writer and chronicler of English life and politics, wrote in jubilation, "Victories come so tumbling over one another from distant parts of the globe that it looks like the handiwork of a lady romance-writer. . . . The park guns will never have time to cool. We ruin ourselves with gun-powder and sky-rockets." And to another friend he exulted, "The Romans were three hundred years conquering the world. We subdued [it] in three campaigns. . . . Our bells are worn threadbare with the ringing for victories."

But fifteen years later, Walpole looked back not on victories but on a period of English decline. He despaired of looking forward. The American colonies were in growing revolution. King George

III's government was stumbling, bewildered about what to do to preserve the empire. Before the first shots were fired at Lexington and Concord, Walpole wrote to his friend Sir Horace Mann:

> The next Augustan age will dawn on the other side of the Atlantic. There will be, perhaps, a Thucydides at Boston, a Xenophon at New York, and in time a Virgil at Mexico and a Newton at Peru. At last some curious traveller from Lima will visit England, and give a description of the ruins of St. Paul's, like the edition at Balbec and Palmyra.

The Seven Years' War ended officially with a treaty signed in Paris on February 10, 1763. Twenty years later, English ambassadors were back in France to conclude another treaty of peace. This one, signed on September 3, 1783, ended the eight-year war with the colonies and recognized the independence of the new United States of America. With invaluable help from France, the Americans had broken the British Empire. For hitherto victorious England, the world had turned upside down.

The end of the Seven Years' War set the stage on both sides of the Atlantic for the American War of Independence. The British Army had routed the French from Canada and the American colonies, but sizable English forces stayed behind, ostensibly to guarantee the peace. In London, a lax and benevolent attitude toward the colonies was changing, under the new king, to one of stern and tightening imperial rule and control. England emerged from the Seven Years' War sure of her power in the world and determined to run the British Empire as she damn well pleased.

The American colonies, on the other hand, emerged from the war with their western frontiers secure, free of any threat from a foreign power now that the French were gone. The Indians were mostly subdued, and a vast continent was open and inviting exploration and settlement. There was not the slightest doubt at that time about the overwhelming loyalty of the colonial population to King George III. Some twenty-five thousand Americans had joined militias to fight alongside the English in the war. But America was also imbued with a heightened sense of independent political and economic strength and a vision of expansion and destiny. The colonies simply wanted to be left alone to run their own affairs and to grow and expand on their own—nevertheless, as a loyal part of the British Empire.

Thus the Seven Years' War laid the long fuse that would eventually splutter into revolution.

The peaceful allegiance of the American colonies to the English Crown was largely the fruit of a wise and benevolent policy laid down early in the century by Sir Robert Walpole, the great Whig prime minister under King George I. Walpole took the enlightened view that if the colonies were left to run their own local affairs with minimal interference from London, they would produce more wealth and commerce, prosper, and give less trouble. They were securely tied to England by navigation acts, which ensured a virtual British monopoly on trade. England's mission was simply to provide protection, peace, and commerce, ensure law and order and domestic tranquillity, and send the ships that carried necessities and brought settlers to swell the ranks of loyal English customers. Walpole described his policy succinctly as one of "salutary neglect."

It had worked well for both countries. America grew from a tiny outpost at Jamestown to a population of a million and a half by 1760. By the time of the Revolution, the population had swollen to nearly three million. Philadelphia was the second largest city in the British Empire after London itself, with a population of thirty-four thousand—larger than either Bristol or Dublin.

One English historian wrote that America was "an anarchy of local autonomy," but the system suited the people. Each colony had its own individual royal charter from England, each one different from the other. Each had its own legislature, ran its own civil affairs, and collected its own taxes. While the royal governors exercised the ultimate authority in the name of the king, they used their powers sparingly. They could veto legislation, dismiss and appoint officials, and decide on judicial appeals. But they were not Spanish viceroys. They were there to keep the peace and avoid trouble. As Benjamin Franklin observed, "The colonies cost England nothing in forts, citadels, garrisons, or armies to keep them in subjugation. They were governed at the expense of a little pen, ink, and paper."

England had not sought confrontation with other powers in the push to plant the English flag in North America, but friction could scarcely be avoided. There had already been more than a century of miscellaneous conflicts in Europe between England and France . . . and Spain . . . and Holland . . . and the German states. English colonies sprang up on the Atlantic coast because it was closest to "home," with good harbors for trade.

As English possession of the Atlantic seaboard expanded, the French and Spanish kings sent military missions up the great rivers into the American interior to lay claim to the western lands. The French traveled up the St. Lawrence into Canada, then across the Great Lakes to Detroit and into the Ohio Valley to Fort Duquesne (present-day Pittsburgh). The Spanish moved up the Mississippi and then headed west across Texas and Arizona and down into Mexico.

In 1749, a French military commander, Commandant Céloron, laid claim to the entire Ohio Valley for the French king and warned English settlers that "should they make their appearance on the Beautiful River they would be treated without any delicacy." The French found ready allies against the settlers among the Indian tribes of western Pennsylvania. In 1754, the French and Indian War began, the American prelude to England's participation in the Seven Years' War.

Local autonomy and salutary neglect had extended even to the military. When the frontier fighting began, there were only five companies of English soldiers—with about one hundred men in each—in all of America: two in New York, one in New Jersey, and two in the Carolinas. England had left it to each colony to raise, equip, and train its own militia for whatever protection it believed was needed against the Indians.

But England was challenged by France. Finally, in 1755, some six thousand British troops were dispatched to Canada and the colonies under Major General Edward Braddock. In June of 1755, Braddock suffered a severe defeat when a British force of some fifteen hundred was virtually wiped out in a savage ambush by French and Indians as the troops approached Fort Duquesne. Braddock himself was killed in the battle.

England delayed declaring war on France until 1756. Things continued to go badly. At last, in 1757, the great William Pitt joined the Whig government to take charge of the military strategy and the diplomacy of what had turned into a global conflict. The tide quickly began to turn. Pitt judged correctly that defeat of the French in North America was the key to ultimate victory. Troops were dispatched to seize two strategic objectives that were held by the French: Quebec City and Montreal.

The first decisive victory came when Major General James Wolfe defeated Montcalm and the French on the heights of Quebec in September 1759. Both commanders were killed in a battle that lasted little more than ten minutes. Major General Jeffrey Amherst then captured Fort Duquesne, where Braddock had been killed, and took his troops up through western Pennsylvania, into New York to Fort Ticonderoga, and on to Canada. With victory at Montreal in September 1760, Amherst completed the rout of the French from North America.

Thus, on a wave of victories, in October, upon the death of his grandfather, King George III took the throne.

George III was twenty-two years old when he began a history-laden reign that would last for sixty years. He was headstrong and obstinate, full of youthful prejudices, lacking in humility, wisdom, or vision, with little interest in the opinions of others. But he was also hardworking, prudish, religious, and moral. He came to the throne determined not merely to reign but to rule. To do so, he would have to bring his own Loyalists to power and open a new political era after a half century of dominance by the Whigs. He judged that England was war-weary and overburdened with debt. He wanted peace, and he took no great pride in Pitt's faraway victories in the American colonies or other parts of the globe. American trade was booming, there were no signs of trouble, and all seemed well.

George soon surrounded himself with successive governments of inexperienced, inward-looking, narrow-minded men. Governments came and went in what seemed like a game of musical chairs. There were five different prime ministers during the first ten years of the reign. With the king's full blessing, these successive governments began imposing new English controls over the colonies. Far from being left alone to find their own destiny, the Americans found that the days of salutary neglect were over. Imperial power was tightening. King George would rule in all parts of his empire.

"A great Empire and little minds go ill together," Edmund Burke declared in the House of Commons in March 1775, just before Lexington and Concord. The governing minds of England could not understand how Americans, largely of English stock and professing loyalty to King George, had become a different people, how the very vastness of America was shaping the politics of independence and a new nation. It was beyond British upper-class comprehension how colonials could claim the same rights as Englishmen or could declare that the English Parliament had no right to impose taxes on them from London.

Americans were prepared to solve their problems with England and remain within the British Empire as a self-governing entity, but the "little minds" of England would not have it. England lost the American colonies as much through political mistakes in London as by military defeats at Saratoga and Yorktown. Historians generally contend that once the British Army had cleared the French out of North America and the colonies were no longer threatened by this outside power, American independence became inevitable. Perhaps this would be so, . . . but it was not inevitable when George III began his reign.

Shortly after seven o'clock on the morning of Saturday, October 25, 1760, a royal page at Kensington Palace knocked gently on the door of the chambers of seventy-seven-year-old King George II and entered with a tray of hot chocolate. He parted the bed curtains, and the king roused comfortably, inquiring about the winds, anxious for mail from his beloved Hanover, delayed in Holland. The king rose and opened a window looking out onto Kensington Gardens. He remarked that it seemed a fine day and he would take a walk. Then he retired to his toilet (he had long been a sufferer of constipation). The page bowed and turned to leave.

As the page reached the door, he "heard a deep sigh, immediately followed by a sound like the falling of a billet of wood from a fire." He rushed back to find the king fallen from his commode and stretched out on the floor as if trying to reach the servant's bell. To the startled page, the king murmured, "Call Amelia," and then lapsed into unconsciousness. He had reigned for thirty-three years.

While the king's daughter Amelia and his doctor and court officials were being summoned to the bedchamber, his German valet, Schreider, left and rode fast for Kew Palace, seven miles away, to carry the news to the king's grandson and heir to the throne, the twenty-two-year-old George William Frederick, Prince of Wales. At Kew Bridge, Schreider encountered the prince and his attendants riding into London. Told that the king had been stricken, probably fatally, the prince instructed Schreider to return to Kensington Palace at once "and to say nothing further" to anyone. The prince then turned back to Kew Palace, telling his attendants brusquely that his horse had gone lame. Soon after his return, a messenger arrived with a brief note from his aunt, Princess Amelia, addressed formally "To His Majesty," informing the prince that he was now, on the death of his grandfather, the king.

A carriage was ordered at once, with outriders and attendants providing a royal escort for the new king's entry into London. As his party neared Kew Bridge, George was once again intercepted, this time by a coach-and-six trotting out from London. The grooms were dressed in the striking blue-and-silver livery of the great William Pitt, secretary of state and the most powerful figure of his time. When news of the death of George II reached Pitt from Kensington Palace, he had set out promptly for Kew Palace to be the first to make formal obeisance to the new king.

Thus began the long reign of George III, a rich and formative up-and-down period of English history. In the first decade of his reign, the king stumbled and fumbled through weak and changing governments, each one of which made matters worse with the American colonies. In the second decade, England marched blindly into the unnecessary and unwinnable war with America. In the third decade, after the empire had been broken by an ignominious defeat, true national leadership would be restored under the younger William Pitt. During the fourth decade, England survived the Napoleonic challenge with exemplary success, entering the nineteenth century with a renewed empire. For the next century and a half, England firmly occupied a position of world supremacy and power. But King George III, during the last ten years of his reign, would disappear behind the walls of Windsor Castle, shrouded in the mists of insanity, never again to be seen in public.

George III was scarcely a great man, even less a great king, but neither was he an evil man or a ruinous despot. He was a constitutional monarch devoted to his duty in an age when sovereigns were more noted for their lax morals, extravagance, and selfish weakness.

No moral aspersions were ever cast upon George III, and no scandal ever shadowed his prudish court.*

The future king was born on June 4, 1738, in a brick mansion on St. James's Square in the heart of London. His father, Prince Frederick Louis, was the firstborn son of King George II. The king hated his son, and his temper and arrogance were notorious. It was said that "he looked upon all men and women as creatures he might kick or kiss for his diversion." George II called Prince Frederick Louis "the greatest liar, the greatest canaille, the greatest ass, the greatest beast in the whole world and we heartily wish him out of it." This venomous wish was granted when Frederick Louis died suddenly, in 1751. The king took final revenge by refusing to pay his son's not inconsiderable gambling debts.

The thirteen-year-old grandson, George William Frederick, now became Prince of Wales and heir to the throne. His grandfather immediately decided to take charge of the prince's education and removed him from the custody of his mother, the Princess Augusta of Saxe-Gotha. The princess was a woman of virtuous character and strong emotions but of only a limited intelligence. The prince was sent to live at Hampton Court, where his grandfather, with an unloving eye, chose new tutors for him and imposed new routines on his upbringing. Not surprisingly, the forced separation from his mother and family and the harsh disciplines dictated by the king aroused deep resentments and hatreds in the adolescent prince. The king's intention was to educate and train his heir to respect the Whigs and other ruling political leaders he would inherit. Not only did this not work, but it only deepened the prince's prejudices.

The king placed Lord Harcourt in charge of the royal pupil. The diarist Horace Walpole described Harcourt as "a man of quality but little brain, a civil sheepish peer in need of a governor himself." Harcourt was assisted by Dr. Hayter, bishop of Norwich, a man whom George characterized as "an intriguing, unworthy man more fitted to be a Jesuit than an English bishop."

The tutors were soon squabbling among themselves. The king

---

*His firstborn son, later George IV, was quite the opposite, a rake and a rebel of extravagant taste in everything from clothes to gambling to food and drink—and women.

brought in Earl Waldegrave and put him in charge. George called the earl "depraved and worthless"; the earl, for his part, found the young Prince of Wales "uncommonly full of princely prejudices contracted in the nursery and improved by bedchamber women of the backstairs." The king himself began muttering that his grandson "lacked the desire to please"—probably an understatement, given the circumstances of his separation from his mother and his miserable life at Hampton Court.

As a student, the prince was apathetic, sleepy, dull, and backward, unable to read properly until he was eleven. But none of this was reflected in his later life. Perhaps it was the prince's reaction to second-rate tutors and circumstances and conditions he resented. Later in his life, he complained that "through negligence, if not wickedness," he had not been given "that degree of knowledge and experience" from his tutors that he had the right to expect. But he needed no educating in how to be headstrong and opinionated. When, at the age of sixteen, the king permitted him to return to his mother's household, his surroundings may have improved—but his educational horizons did not. Princess Augusta, prim, censorious, was determined that her children would grow up virtuous and uncontaminated. Thus they were maintained in a state of social quarantine.

Into the life of this nearly friendless, unhappy, and rather lazy prince entered the enigmatic and ambitious earl of Bute, who soon became the dominant influence, the father figure of George III's early manhood.

Lord Bute was cultured and intelligent but a man of complex and peculiar temperament. He was a Scottish peer—and Scottish peers in those days were treated as social and political inferiors by English peers. Bute was therefore an outsider as far as the Whig leadership was concerned, and he resented it. But he was ambitious and gravitated toward what was called the Leicester House set, oppositionists who had gathered regularly at the home of Prince Frederick Louis. After the prince's death, Bute had continued his visits to Leicester House to call upon Princess Augusta, visits that inevitably gave rise to gossip that perhaps the relationship went beyond friendship.

London has always been titillated by royal gossip—but in this case, gossip it remained. It would have been out of character for either of these straitlaced people to carry on an affair—Bute was married to a wealthy heiress who provided him with a large country estate north of London. But Bute and Augusta did, certainly, find comfort in their shared prejudices, political dislikes, frustrations, and contempt for King George II. And Bute could have found no better way of satisfying his own social and political aspirations than by pursuing a sympathetic association with the dowager princess and, through her, with the future king.

Princess Augusta may have doted on Bute's company, but others did not. The earl of Shelburne, Bute's contemporary in politics, wrote in his autobiography this unflattering appraisal:

> His bottom was that of any Scotch nobleman, proud, aristocratical, pompous, imposing with a great deal of superficial knowledge and very false taste in everything. He had a very gloomy sort of madness. . . . He read a great deal, but it was chiefly out of the books of science and pompous poetry. He was insolent and cowardly, at least the greatest political coward I ever knew. He was rash and timid, accustom'd to ask advice of different persons, but not sense and sagacity to distinguish and digest, with a perpetual apprehension of being govern'd, which made him, when he followed any advice, always add something of his own in point of matter or manner, which sometimes took away the little good which was in it, or changed the whole nature of it. He felt all the pleasure of power to consist either in it punishing or astonishing. He was ready to abandon his nearest friends if attacked, or throw any blame off his own shoulders. He excelled, so far as I could observe, in managing the interior of the court with an abundant share of art and hypocrisy.

Shelburne's own political prejudices were those of a Whig, devoted to William Pitt, which no doubt sharpened his caustic assessment of Bute. But he was not alone in his opinion. Lord Chesterfield wrote of Bute:

> He interfered in everything, disposed of everything, and undertook everything, much too soon for his inexperience in business and for at best his systematic notions of it, which are seldom or never reducible to practice. . . . Every man who is in business is at first either too rash or too timorous, but he was both. He undertook what he feared to execute, and what consequentially he executed, ill. He had honour, honesty and good intentions. He was too proud to be respectable or

respected; too cold and silent to be amiable; too cunning to have great abilities; and his inexperience made him too precipitately to undertake what it disabled him from executing.

What Lords Shelburne and Chesterfield saw in Bute was not apparent to the limited mind of Princess Augusta. In 1755, she appointed Bute as her son's tutor, imploring him to "imprint your great sentiments in him and so make mother and son happy." As he prepared to take charge, Bute wrote an effusive letter to the young prince:

> And now, my Prince, let a friend, who most sincerely loves you, be happy enough to think that you will give attention to these abstracts. . . . Next to your own family you have condescended to take me into your friendship, don't think it arrogance if I say I will deserve it. The prospect in forming your young mind is exquisitely pleasing to a heart like mine. I have not a wish, a thought but what points to your happiness alone.

In no time, the emotionally starved, intellectually empty George was pouring out his heart to Lord Bute and filling up his mind with Bute's teaching. Just as the prince was coming into manhood, Bute dominated his life. George began a correspondence with Bute of cloying affection and a self-abasement that was as pathetic as it was passionate. At the end of his first year under Bute's tutelage, the prince wrote to the man he was now calling "my dearest friend":

> I have had the pleasure of your friendship during the space of a year, by which I have reap'd great advantage, but not the improvement I should if I had follow'd your advice; but you shall find me make such progress in this summer that shall give you hopes that with the continuation of your advice, I may turn out as you wish. . . .
>
> I hope, my dear Lord, you will conduct me through this difficult road and still bring me to the gole. I will exactly follow your advice, without which I shall inevitable sink. I am young and inexperienc'd and want advice. I trust in your friendship which still assists me in all difficulties. I know few things I ought to be more thankful for to the Great Power above, than for its having pleas'd Him to send you to help and advise me in these difficult times.

In his letters to Bute, the Prince of Wales berated himself constantly for "that incomprehensible indolence, inattention and heedlessness that reigns within me." He talked of his duty "to restore my much loved country to her antient state of liberty . . . free from her present load of debts and again famous for being the residence of true piety and virtue." He implored Bute "to be persuaded that I will constantly reflect whether what I am doing is worthy of one who is to mount the throne, and who owes everything to his friend."

Bute had his own ambitions. Perhaps emboldened by his insider role as tutor to the prince, he made an indirect approach, in 1758, to William Pitt for a government position. He got a stiff brush-off. Pitt informed Bute, via an intermediary:

> I will not be rid with a check rein. . . . It is impossible for me to act in a responsible ministerial office with Lord Bute. . . . He gives hourly indications of an imperious nature, I can't bear a touch of command, my sentiments in politics, like my religion, are my own, I can't change them.

After this rebuff, Bute's education of the prince included denigration of Pitt. The prince was more than ready to absorb this, along with Bute's many other prejudices. The political dominance of Pitt, Newcastle, and the Whigs, systematically diminishing the power and prestige of the Crown, became a constant leitmotif of Bute's tutorials. And the prince's contempt for his grandfather turned to hatred. In letters to Bute, he referred to the king as "a shuffling devil," declared that the king was "unworthy to be a British monarch," and asserted that "the conduct of the old K. makes me ashamed of being his grandson; he treats me in the same manner his knave and counselor the Duke of Newcastle does all people."

Even England's victories were sour news for the prince. When word reached London of Amherst's capture of Montreal, the soon-to-be-king George wrote to Bute:

> I wish my Dearest Friend joy of this success; but at the same time I can't help feeling that every such thing raises those I have no reason to love. . . . I hope this nation will open her eyes and see who are her true friends, and that her most popular man [Pitt] is a true snake in the grass.

In another letter, he wrote that "Pitt treats both you and me with no more respect than he would a parcel of children. He seems to forget that the day will come when he must be treated according to his deserts." Again, he called Pitt "the blackest of hearts, the most ungrateful and in my mind the most dishonourable of men. I can never bear to see him in any future ministry."

Such was the mood and temper of King George III when he came to the throne. He was utterly and obstinately convinced that the dominance of the Whigs had to be broken if the prestige of the monarchy was to be restored. All else was peripheral to this objective.

But in listening to and taking advice solely from the earl of Bute, George still had no clear idea about how to replace the Whigs or what he wanted to accomplish for England. He could dismiss the old, experienced leaders who had made England victorious, but where were the new leaders? Where the new wisdom and direction that could replace them?

"George, be a King," admonished Princess Augusta—frequently. And George, upon becoming king, immediately cast off all the self-doubts he had expressed to Lord Bute. Far from being indolent, he seems never to have stopped working. Far from being indecisive, he produced a ceaseless stream of orders, instructions, commands, approvals, disapprovals. It was as if, in his newfound power, he had found a way to obliterate his self-perceived weaknesses.

He had one great advantage over his Hanoverian predecessors: He spoke and wrote English exceedingly well. From the first hour he became king, George III wrote messages constantly, in his own free-flowing hand. He meticulously dated all his writings; almost all bore the day and hour of their composition. There are literally thousands of documents written by George III in the Windsor Castle archives, six thick volumes of which were edited and published by Sir John Fortescue in the 1920s. Because the king held the ultimate control and final say over the affairs of an empire, these documents deal with every detail associated with running the state, the Church of England, the judiciary, the peerage, the diplomatic service, the British Army, and the Royal Navy.

The king was hardly an intellectual; he had no great depth. He was much more a day-to-day tactician than a strategist in politics, war, or diplomacy. He enjoyed music; he played both harpsichord and flute and even tried the violin. True to Germanic tradition, he loved Handel's music; he invited the young Mozart to perform twice for the royal family during his visit to London; and during the long stay in which he composed the London symphonies, the king welcomed Haydn. The king also took an interest in art and artists, founding the Royal Academy in 1768. The Philadelphia painter Benjamin West was one of George's favorites; in 1772, he made West historical painter to the court at a handsome stipend of one thousand pounds and had several portraits painted by him.

He was strongly—and genuinely—a religious man, influenced in this not only by his mother but also by a pious aversion to the scandalous behavior of his Hanoverian predecessors. He took his role as head of the Church of England very seriously. He attended services regularly in his private chapel and was faithful and devoted to his bride, Queen Charlotte, all his life.

As head of the Church of England, King George III had the added conviction that his judgments were fulfilling God's appointed tasks. He acted more like a conscientious bull in a political china shop, as extracts from his letters and instructions show:

> I know I am doing my duty, and therefore can never wish to retreat.

> Men of less principle and honesty than I pretend may look on public measures and opinions as a game. I always act from conviction.

> It has ever been a certain position with me that firmness is the characteristick of an Englishman.

> I begin to see that I shall soon have enfused some of that spirit which I thank Heaven ever attends me under difficulties.

> I will rather risk my Crown than do what I think personally is disgraceful, and whilst I have no wish but for the good and prosperity of my country, it is impossible that the nation shall not stand by me: If they will not, they shall have another King.

King George was very much the epitome of the English country gentlemen over whom he reigned. These wealthy owners of vast acres of farms and farm cottages and whole villages were intensely conservative and autocratic, limited in intellectual interests and ability, and possessed of the absolute knowledge that they were God's chosen, destined to rule over England's less fortunate mortals. They were oblivious to the economic and social changes that were beginning to take hold in England, to the early stirrings of the Industrial Revolution—and to the changes and political ferment that had begun to rumble through the American colonies.

For all its ostentatious wealth and easy living, England's upper class delighted in boorish practical jokes, bawdy conversations, brutal behavior, wild gambling, indelicate taste, and heavy drinking. In their country homes, the wealthy were isolated from squalor, but not in London. Samuel Johnson, soon after his arrival from Lichfield, described London as "a city famous for wealth, commerce and plenty, and for every kind of civility and politeness, but abounds with such heaps of filth as a savage would look on with amazement."

With a population approaching 700,000, London was by far the largest city in the world (and would remain so for another century and a half). While thousands lived in appalling conditions, surrounded by crime and violence, drunkenness and brutality, London was nevertheless a vibrant, cultured city, pulsing with activity and absorbing interests and entertainment to suit every whim of vice or virtue. The Haymarket Theatre opened in 1720 and Covent Garden in 1733. There were coffeehouses and clubs for the upper classes and aristocracy; losses of ten thousand pounds in an evening of whist, piquet, brag, loo, and other card games were common. For the working class, for whom a wage of one pound a week meant a good income, there were taverns that offered plenty of cheap gin, cockfights, dogfights, and badger baiting. Boxing matches, just then going public, were more like brawls in these days before the Queensberry rules were established. The most popular public entertainment was the hangings at Tyburn Tree.

While England was predominantly an agricultural nation, her greatness lay in trade. At the end of the Seven Years' War, her merchant fleet totaled some 500,000 tons of sailing ships. Bristol, located on the west coast close to the main sea routes to North America, was the largest city in England after London, with about thirty thousand inhabitants. Small ports thrived, from Newcastle on the North Sea to Plymouth on the English Channel. A contemporary observer wrote of London, "The whole surface of the Thames is covered with small vessels, barges, boats, wherries, passing to and fro, and below the three bridges [Westminster, Blackfriars, and London] such a prodigious forest of masts, for miles together, that you would think all ships of the universe were here assembled."

The age of canal building was under way, greatly improving commerce and communications among the smaller towns to the north of London. Coal and iron mining was beginning to make even greater fortunes for the already wealthy landowners. At the same time, in industry, larger units of production had begun to replace small pig-iron furnaces and forges. Mechanical looms and spinning jennies were changing the textile industry. And major landowners were enclosing their farmlands to improve drainage systems and increase productivity—much to the distress of small tenant farmers, who were being driven from the communal pasturelands.

In small villages, isolated from the commercial hurly-burly of London, life centered on the squire's manor house, the church, and the village pub. The squires were local despots. While they didn't have the titles and the wealth of the great landowning aristocracy, they did have the same arrogance and powerful hold over the locals. But villages were nonetheless home to a multitude of small producers—furniture makers, blacksmiths, cabinetmakers, clockmakers—artisans and craftsmen of all kinds.

Whatever its oligarchy, England was a democracy of free speech and boisterous public opinion. Critics of the king and the government were both numerous and noisy; political debate was plentiful in Parliament, coffeehouses, and countryside. The people could demonstrate, write what they thought, and say what they liked. And they did. But they could not vote. The right to vote was restricted to a minority of male property owners, which effectively disenfranchised the entire working class, tenant farmers and farm laborers, and the growing middle class. "Democracy" was controlled by England's upper class, wealthy, landowning aristocrats. They, in turn, insulated the king from political, public, and social ferment. For half a century, government power had rested unchallenged in the hands of long-serving Whig prime ministers.

Neither George I, fresh from Hanover in 1714 and speaking almost no English, nor George II had found reason to challenge Whig prime ministers or seek political change. But it would be different under George III, influenced by his youth, his ambition to rule, his prejudices—and the earl of Bute's tutelage, his sole preparation for the throne. But regardless of his ambitions, George III was a constitutional monarch; he could not operate in a vacuum. The question was, How might he use the machinery of royal power and the political system he was inheriting to achieve his own political ends?

Ideas of compromise, accommodation, or attention to others' views were not part of the king's political nature. He was utterly disdainful of political opposition and resisted coming to any political "arrangement" with opponents. Consistency—which in his case translated into being unyielding and stubborn, sticking with his own opinions regardless—was one of the king's strongest characteristics. It was also his major weakness, for it became a convenient way to avoid admitting mistakes and to refuse to reexamine a policy or problem. It served as a ready cover for a lack of vision and wisdom, a way for the king to appear strong while avoiding difficult judgments.

It was this determined "consistency" that took the king and England through a succession of political blunders all the way to Yorktown. The king was successful in breaking the power of the Whigs and installing his own Loyalist ministers, and his governments consistently enjoyed majorities in the House of Commons of four to one over the ousted Whigs. Thus, immune from political opposition, secure in parliamentary majorities, possessed of a self-righteous certainty of his own judgment, George III never wavered on the American question.

Six months after the Battle of Yorktown, the king's government was about to fall. Charles James Fox, standing before a packed, sober, and silent House of Commons, pronounced an epitaph:

There is one grand domestic evil from which all other evils, foreign and domestic, have sprung: The influence of the Crown. To the influence of the Crown we must attribute the loss of the army in Virginia. To the influence of the Crown we must attribute the loss of the thirteen provinces of America; for it was the influence of the Crown in the two Houses of Parliament that enabled His Majesty's ministers to persevere against the voice of reason, the voice of truth, the voice of the people.

* * *

English historians have scarcely been any kinder than Americans in their historical and emotional judgments of King George III. Sir George Otto Trevelyan wrote of him in 1909 that "he invariably declared himself upon the wrong side of every conflict." William E. H. Lecky judged him to be "a sovereign of whom it may well be said without exaggeration that he inflicted more profound and enduring injuries upon this country than any other modern English King." (Without exaggeration?) More recently, J. H. Plumb, Cambridge University scholar and author of *The First Four Georges,* wrote that "to ordinary men he remains one of England's most disastrous Kings, like John and the two Jameses."

More than two centuries after the American Revolution, judgments on George III have become more tempered, but it is still a prejudicial task to attempt any balanced assessment of his place in history. The mind-set of King George toward the American colonies was also the dominant mind-set of England toward its empire in that era. Had the king possessed greater imagination, perception, intelligence, or leadership, he might well have steered England away from the disastrous policies of confrontation with America—but he did not.

Judgments have also been clouded by the "madness" business, particularly those of nineteenth-century historians and biographers. In past years, writers have had no difficulty equating the king's behavior from childhood through adolescence to his adult conduct on the throne with that of a man possessed of an unbalanced mind. For two centuries, it was generally assumed that George III was, in modern terms, a manic depressive who verged on insanity. The American historian George Bancroft even concluded that the king was temporarily insane when the Stamp Act passed Parliament, in 1765. Therefore, he could not be held responsible for legislation that, more than any other single incident, precipitated the Revolution. In 1857, Bancroft wrote in his *History of the United States:* "Be every sentiment of anger towards the King absorbed in pity. At the moment of the passing of the Stamp Act, George was crazed."

This judgment was echoed for many generations. But in 1966, the *British Medical Journal* published an article of extraordinary medical and historical research conducted by two London doctors of psychological medicine. Ida Macalpine and Richard Hunter had searched out and sifted through the very considerable original medical records kept by the king's doctors across sixty years. Their conclusion was that George III was not a manic depressive, nor had he suffered from any inherited mental disorder. He was a victim of a rare disease, unknown until it was finally diagnosed, in the 1930s, and called porphyria. It is a metabolic disorder that in its early stages acts like a persistent cold accompanied by colic, constipation, nausea, acute chest and stomach pains, cramps, fast pulse, and fever. Attacks come and go without warning. Eventually, over a period of years, porphyria worsens and attacks the brain.

Once it was clinically identified and diagnosed, porphyria could be treated effectively with modern drugs. "This study," the English doctors wrote in 1966,

> allows the certain conclusion that George III's malady was not "mental" in the accepted sense, in whatever old or modern terms it may be couched. The assumption that the King was "neurotic" will also have to be revised, since porphyria may render its victim restless, hurried, agitated and impulsive, especially in milder attacks which go unrecognized. Finally, this diagnosis clears the House of Hanover of an hereditary taint of madness, imputed by the erroneous interpretation of George III's illness.

The king's first identifiable attack of porphyria did indeed occur at the time of the Stamp Act's passage, in 1765. He was then not yet twenty-seven years old and disappeared from public duties from January to April with no other explanation than that he was "unwell." But he was still transacting state business and signing papers. The prime minister of that time, George Grenville, saw the king several times and made no mention in his diaries of any derangement. It was Grenville's conclusion, also reflected in Horace Walpole's letters and diaries, that the king was suffering from a form of pleurisy that he could not throw off. He was a very sick man, and his doctors were baffled.

But when the porphyria receded in April of 1765, the king returned to full duties and remained in good health. He had no illness, mental or otherwise, until a second flare-up in 1788, long after the American war had ended. The king was then fifty, and this time the attack was much more serious and long lasting. But in March of 1789, he was again able to resume full royal duties, though he wrote to the bishop of Worcester that "I cannot boast of the same strength and spirits I enjoyed before." For the next twelve years—so decisive in English history, embracing the French Revolution and the rise of Napoléon—George III was in normal health.

In February and March of 1801, the porphyria flared up again, and his descent into madness began. He was finally confined, in 1812, to Windsor Castle, under medieval treatment almost more insane than he was. There he remained for the rest of his days.

Another war, this one in 1812, was fought with America and lost. But the king was in the mists of his decline. After the American Revolution, George III and the monarchs who followed him found it wiser and safer for sovereigns to reign and leave it to others to rule.

Chapter 2

PITT DEPARTS, BUTE LIGHTS THE FUSE

The first day of the new king's reign played out like the opening scenes of a latter-day Shakespearean drama, with simple matters of protocol setting the stage for a new era of kingly power.

After receiving the news of his grandfather's death, the first thing young George III did was to dash off a timorously worded note to Lord Bute:

> I thought I had no time to lose in acquainting my dearest friend of this. I have order'd all the servants that they were to be silent about what had passed as they value their employments, and shall wait till I hear from you to know what further must be done. I am coming the back way to your house, the coach will soon be ready.

The king set out for London, heading not to his own residence at Savile House but to his mother's at Carlton House, where he assumed Lord Bute would by now be waiting.

The three had been anticipating this moment for a long time. Now, under Bute's guiding hand, they began drafting a statement for the king to read at the Privy Council meeting that would be assembled later that day. This meeting would mark George's formal accession to the throne. Next, the king elevated Lord Bute to Privy Council membership so that he could attend the gathering of this elite.

Meanwhile, word of the old king's death was spreading throughout London—and there was confusion as to the new king's whereabouts. The Privy Council was finally notified that its first meeting
of the new reign would be held at Carlton House. The significance
of this meeting at the home of the king's mother was not lost on the
Whigs. Change was coming rapidly.

They arrived, led by the prime minister, the duke of Newcastle,
and William Pitt, secretary of state and the dominant figure of both
government and Parliament.

The councillors assembled. The king entered the room. He was
approached by a deferential Pitt, who proffered him a draft of remarks that he thought suitable to the inauguration of a new reign.
The king thanked Pitt courteously but informed him that he had
already prepared an address. Had this been an opening of Parliament, the king would have been obliged to read a statement written
by his ministers, but as it was, he was quite within his constitutional
rights to address his first Privy Council in his own words.

George III's first remarks were scarcely notable. He began with
the customary expression of grief at the loss to the nation of his
grandfather. He followed with an appropriate allusion to his own
inadequacies and a declaration that it would be his goal "to promote
the glory and welfare of the Empire." Then came an unexpected
statement that stung Pitt: "As I mount the throne, in the midst of a
bloody and expensive war, I shall endeavor to prosecute it in the
manner most likely to bring an honourable and lasting peace."

The king's listeners could not possibly mistake the royal dig at the
great war minister. England was in the fifth year of what would be
called the Seven Years' War. The king's remarks were certainly a
reflection of the country's growing war-weariness. Even the powerful Whigs were tiring of the disruptions to trade, commerce, the
economy in general. England was buried in debt, borrowing more
money than it had in all its past history. The war was straining the
manpower of a population little more than half that of its enemy,
France. The people were restive, asking with increasing fervor when
Pitt's great string of victories would bring peace.

Pitt, however, was never a man to weary of war. He was incensed
that the king should construe his victories as "bloody and expensive" and talk openly of seeking peace without even mentioning
Prussia and England's other allies in the conflict.

When the king left the room and the Privy Council had ended, Pitt immediately sought out Bute. He insisted that the offending wording be changed in the formal written record of the meeting. After some altercation, Bute finally agreed to make Pitt's views known to the king.

The following afternoon, the king acquiesced, reluctantly. He was formally recorded as having said, "As I mount the throne in the midst of *an expensive but just and necessary war,* I shall endeavor to prosecute it in the manner most likely to bring an honourable and lasting peace *in concert with my allies*" [emphasis added]. Thus, in the first hours of the reign of George III, William Pitt directly challenged the sovereign, forcing him to change a passage in his first formal statement from his throne, one that he had drafted in his own hand. Pitt's victory was a hollow one, for it only hardened the king's attitude against him. A few days later, he wrote to Bute, saying that Pitt was "a man who from his own ambitions, pride and impracticability, means to disturb my quiet and (what I feel much stronger) the repose of my subjects." It was the beginning of Pitt's downfall.

But the king ascended the throne on a wave of popular enthusiasm, for he held the promise of youth and vigor and had an openness of manner that came as a welcome relief after the two ponderous Hanoverians who preceded him. Moreover, after a half century of German-speaking monarchs, England finally had a native-born king, who spoke in the clearest, most correct drawing-room English. Horace Walpole wrote, after attending one of the first levees of the new reign:

> The King himself has all good-nature, wishing to satisfy everybody. All his speeches are obliging. I saw him again yesterday and was surprised to find the levee-room had lost entirely the air of the lions den. This sovereign doesn't stand in one spot with eyes fixed royally on the ground and dropping hints of German news. He walks about and speaks to everybody. He is graceful and genteel with dignity and reads speeches well.

The Newcastle-Pitt government had been in office for about three years when George III came to the throne. Initially, it continued in what appeared to be unruffled calm. But behind the scenes, the earl of Bute used his role as the king's closest confidant to burrow away at Newcastle. Bute needed a seat in the cabinet so that he might carry out the king's wish to get rid of William Pitt and break the power of the Whigs.

Outwardly, the Newcastle-Pitt coalition seemed strong and successful. Inwardly, it was a quarrelsome relationship, a coalition of political necessity in which there was little friendship, nor much trust.

Newcastle epitomized the social hierarchy of Whig power. He was the head of one of the oldest, wealthiest, most powerful English families. He had been in every government since the days of Robert Walpole. As controller of Whig patronage and prime minister, he had power that exceeded his qualities of intellect and his leadership. He was an experienced, powerful, and skillful political hack. Because of his own inadequacies in conducting the war, he had been forced to take Pitt into his government and make him a coequal.

Pitt, on the other hand, came from a family of untitled, moderately wealthy country landowners, a class known as yeoman farmers. His grandfather had dominated the family. The elder Pitt was a hard-driving, uncouth, rough-spoken, ambitious man who left his Dorsetshire farm early in the 1700s to enter the shipping trade as a freebooter ready for just about any piracy. He settled down for some profitable years in India, where he served as a local governor for the East India Company. In the then normal fashion of company operations, he was able to skim off comfortable wealth for himself.

He returned to Dorset to buy up more land, hoping that property and wealth would bring him a title, perhaps even open the doors to political society. They did not. His landholdings were extensive enough to give him control of several "pocket borough" seats in the House of Commons, but as far as Whig society was concerned, he was still a self-made, ostentatious, rather vulgar man. The doors of society remained closed.

William Pitt was born in 1708 and grew up under his grandfather's influence. He went off to Eton and Oxford, but he wasn't much of a scholar, and he resented the snobbery of the aristocrats with whom he was studying. He left Oxford after only a year, seeking more interesting educational horizons at the prestigious university at Utrecht in Holland. He returned to England in 1727, around the time of his grandfather's death, and joined the army as a cornet (the equivalent of a lieutenant) in a cavalry regiment. He spent five and a half years in the army. One of those years was passed in France, where he polished his written and spoken French to a fluency that he retained for life. He also deepened a visceral enmity for that nation.

In the great agricultural counties such as Pitt's, gentleman farmers routinely passed on House of Commons seats from one family member to another. So, in 1735, one of the pocket-borough seats controlled by the Pitt family was "placed at William's disposal." He was twenty-seven when he entered Parliament. Walpole was prime minister, but Pitt was too resentful of aristocratic snobbery to attempt to curry favor with the Whigs. Instead, he made his mark in Commons by speaking out, actively and determinedly, on his own. He made his views known with intelligence; he was possessed of ability and growing authority.

In 1743, Henry Pelham succeeded Walpole as prime minister. Pelham was a Whig of notable ability and great common sense. He recognized Pitt's abilities and brought him into the government in the secondary but important administrative post of paymaster general of the forces. Pitt held the office for eight years; where his predecessors had indulged in shameless graft and private profit, Pitt set a new standard for honesty and efficiency.

Affairs in the American colonies figured scarcely at all in the debates and politics at Westminster in the 1750s. But in 1754, fighting broke out on the western frontiers of Pennsylvania and Virginia. As the fighting in America intensified, Henry Pelham died. He was succeeded by his brother the duke of Newcastle. In 1755, Newcastle shuffled his government and dismissed Pitt from his post as paymaster general.

Bad news came from America: Braddock's defeat and death at Fort Duquesne. England now had a war with France on its hands. But Newcastle shied away from declaring war until May of 1756. By then, it was war in the Caribbean, the Mediterranean, the Atlantic and on the European continent as well as North America. As the situation worsened under Newcastle's ineffectual leadership, Pitt was declaring loudly that "I can save this country and no one else can." Pitt's popularity was high. The House of Commons believed him.

By June of 1757, the Newcastle government was close to collapse. The duke finally agreed to bring in Pitt to form a coalition. Pitt would become secretary of state, in full charge of the army and the Admiralty. He also took the responsibility for diplomacy and foreign policy in directing the war. Newcastle would continue as prime minister, looking after finances and the Exchequer as well as government patronage for the Whigs. Pitt, the popular Great Commoner, would gain the plaudits for all that was decent and patriotic, honorable and victorious. Newcastle handled all the tawdry politics in that most venal, corrupt period of English government.

Pitt had risen not through social pedigree but on the strength of his own abilities—his intellect, his fierce drive, his powers of oratory in the House of Commons. He had strength all his own, a maverick loner amongst the Whigs.

Under Pitt, the turnaround in the fortunes of war was swift. Thus, when George III ascended the throne, Pitt was at the height of his career. The historian Thomas Babington Macaulay wrote:

> War had made him powerful and popular. With war, all that was brightest in his life was associated. For war, his talents were peculiarly fitted. He had at length begun to love war for its own sake, and was more disposed to quarrel with neutrals than to make peace with enemies.

But there lay the two weaknesses in Pitt's position. He had "begun to love war for its own sake" while the sentiment of both king and country was for peace. His second weakness was the duke of Newcastle, no friend of his. Superior in title but inferior in ability, Newcastle was prepared to play any political game to stay in power. With the king opposed to Pitt and anxious for peace, Newcastle soon saw Pitt as a liability to Whig rule rather than as the national asset of war leader.

So the game got under way. The king's prejudices colored his judgment. Bute was motivated by ambition. Newcastle wanted to cling to power and the control of patronage.

Pitt, buoyed by success, was unwittingly vulnerable.

In March of 1761, five months into the new reign, the outward calm of the Newcastle-Pitt government broke. Newcastle bowed to the persistent pressure from Lord Bute for a place in the cabinet. Another member of the cabinet, Lord Holderness, was persuaded by the offer of a higher rank in the peerage to give up his seat as one of several secretaries of state. Bute would take his place, thus attaining a cabinet rank equal to Pitt's. He was now able to monitor cabinet business from the inside and report directly to the king—particularly on how Pitt was dealing with the slow-moving process of ending the war. Pitt's powerful position was beginning to erode.

In March 1761, general elections were held for a new House of Commons that would sit for seven years. It would, among other things, pass the Stamp Act legislation, setting England on the course that would result in the War of Independence.

In the mid-eighteenth century, England's House of Commons was far from the citadel of democracy it would become a century later. The right to vote was based on the ownership of property. This excluded the working class, farm laborers, and all but a tiny percentage of the people from ever getting anywhere near a ballot box. Out of a total population of more than 8 million in England, Scotland, and Wales in 1761, a mere 215,000 adult males were eligible to vote. Further, the way in which the voting districts were drawn meant that wealthy landowners could dictate who would stand as candidates and who would be elected. Nominations for assured election were routinely bought and sold. The wealthy thus elected representatives to sit in Parliament in much the same way they admitted members to their private clubs.

The English historian Sir Lewis B. Namier, in his important 1930 work, *England in the Age of the American Revolution,* recorded that in the whole of Devonshire from 1688 to 1761, only fifteen different men were elected to the House of Commons. Ten of those fifteen came from only three different families. Moreover, for nearly eighty years, those fifteen members "made no speeches, held no office, achieved no distinctions of any sort, and whenever it was known that they recorded a vote, it was against the government then in office."

These elected representatives of the rural counties of England were stubborn, independent-minded men who were outside the aristocratic, titled Whig oligarchy. They owed their allegiance only to their families and their land. On average, there were about a hundred such members in every Parliament, and they formed the core of Tory opposition to the dominant Whigs. Since they numbered less than a fifth of the total Commons membership, they were hardly a threat to Whig power. But they were ready to support King George III when he moved to break the long rule of the Whigs.

Namier also found that of the 558 men elected to the House of Commons in that March of 1761, at least 270 were on the government payroll or operating as government contractors. He listed 50 court officials of the royal household, 57 officers of the British Army and the Royal Navy, 50 government ministers and civil servants, 57 suppliers or contractors to the government, 50 who held sinecures, and 10 who were either on pensions or being paid out of secret government funds.

As both a historical curiosity and an irony, there were five Americans who sat in the House of Commons for varying lengths of time between 1763 and 1775. As English subjects, if they could be nominated to a constituency and elected, they had every right to sit in Parliament. And so they trickled in through by-elections as odd seats became vacant: Barlow Trecothick, a merchant from Massachusetts; John Huske and Paul Wentworth from New Hampshire; and Henry Cruger and Staats Long Morris from New York. Trecothick served the longest, from 1768 to 1774, and even became lord mayor of London. Paul Wentworth, an out-and-out Loyalist, went on the payroll of the British secret service. He became a not so secret agent for the British, dealing unsuccessfully with Benjamin Franklin in Paris after the Battle of Saratoga.

In all, with nearly half its members either directly or indirectly on the government payroll, obtaining a pro-government Whig majority in the House of Commons should have been easy. But it wasn't that simple. The Whigs were never more than a collection of factions; to hold these factions together from one major vote to the next meant buying them off constantly, using patronage favors or even open bribery from secret government funds.

The patronage system was one big honeypot for those who could get to it. Civil expenditure and the government payroll were covered by a single large annual supply-bill appropriation, which in 1761 amounted to £800,000. This sum funded the expenses of the king's court; pay for all civil servants; financing of diplomatic missions; secret funds, much of which went for straight parliamentary bribery; and the purchase of government supplies—plus payoffs and bribes. Military and naval appropriations were voted separately but were rife with the same system of rake-offs and bribes. Accounting and accountability were not merely lax; they were virtually nonexistent.

Moreover, the factional voting in the House of Commons was

largely controlled by the grandees in the House of Lords. These great property owners, men of enormous wealth and social prestige, were able to name their own slates for election to the House of Commons from the constituencies they controlled. These members were known as placemen, selected to sit in their places and vote as they were told. According to Namier, after the election of 1761, the duke of Newcastle controlled the votes of forty-nine members of the House of Commons; the duke of Bedford, ten; Lord Bute, a largely Scottish bloc of seventy-six; the earl of Hardwicke, eleven; the duke of Dorset, eight; the marquess of Rockingham, six; the duke of Devonshire, five—and so on.

In July of 1761, the hitherto neutral King Charles III of Spain took the stage in the Seven Years' War. Pitt had long feared that Spain might be tempted to join the side of France. The English secret service then intercepted diplomatic letters between the Spanish ambassadors in London and Paris that provided direct information that such an alliance was indeed nearing completion. Once he was certain of Spain's intentions, Pitt characteristically chose to strike first.

But he would have to have the approval of the king to enlarge the war, and the king had other things on his mind—his marriage and coronation. He did not want a new war putting a blot on these festivities, which were scheduled to take place in late September.

Before ascending the throne, George III had carried on a brief and decorous distant courtship with a suitable young beauty of the English aristocracy, Lady Sarah Lennox. But when he came to the throne, this possible choice of his heart was overruled by Lord Bute and the king's mother. He was told quite firmly that for reasons of state, a bride had to be found somewhere in the German principalities. So an army colonel from the royal household was dispatched to seek out fifteen-year-old Princess Charlotte Sophia of Mecklenberg-Strelitz, "accomplished in music and of amiable temperament." She was approved and dispatched to England, arriving in early September of 1761. She went straight to the altar and married George. Two weeks later, on September 22, she was crowned Queen of England. She went on to bear the king fifteen children. If this was not a marriage made in heaven, it was certainly made in bed.

Two weeks after the coronation, an impatient Pitt moved in the cabinet to go to war with Spain. But Lord Bute signaled the wishes of the king. The cabinet voted against Pitt, who immediately turned in his seals of office and left the government he had dominated for five victorious years.

Almost exactly one year after coming to the throne, King George was rid of William Pitt. The duke of Newcastle, still prime minister, held the reins of Whig power, but Lord Bute assumed Pitt's role in charge of war and foreign policy. Newcastle's days were numbered.

Bute began by maneuvering to try to avoid the war with Spain that Pitt had forecast. Pitt wisely had alerted the Royal Navy to be prepared to fight. The Spanish ambassador was recalled to Madrid on January 1, 1762, and three days later England declared war on Spain. Thanks to Pitt's strategic foresight, the war itself was more successful than Bute's diplomacy. But while the sea battles went on, the king prodded Bute to get rid of the duke of Newcastle.

England for seven years had been paying a large subsidy to King Frederick the Great of Prussia to finance the Prussian army in the war against France. But in April of 1762, King George abruptly informed Bute that "the more I consider the Prussian subsidy the more objections arise in my mind against it." Bute was not slow to take the royal hint. Here was a chance to get rid of the Prussian subsidy and the duke of Newcastle. He moved in the cabinet to cut the payments to Prussia, and Newcastle strongly opposed. On a cabinet vote, only one member of the government supported the prime minister, who promptly resigned. Newcastle joined Pitt in defeat on May 26, and Lord Bute promptly took over as prime minister. Whig power had ended at last.

In September, Bute sent the duke of Bedford to Paris to seek peace. The French by now were as weary of the war as the English, and the alliance with Spain was proving more of a liability than a military asset. In December, peace terms emerged that largely ratified the victories England had gained. She would keep all of Canada, and France would give up her claims to the Ohio Valley and the western reaches of the American colonies.

But whatever the terms of the peace agreement, Lord Bute would face a major parliamentary battle to win its approval from the embittered Whigs. Bute had few political friends to help him and neither the skills nor the experience of his own for the battle ahead. He turned to one of the more unsavory political characters of the time for help—Henry Fox. With a mixture of threats and bribery, Fox managed to produce a vote of 319 to 65 to approve the treaty, with 174 members, mostly Whigs, either absent or abstaining.

The political aftermath against the Whigs from the king himself was draconian and swift. He wrote to Bute that any officeholder who had not supported the government "at a time like this must be made an example of." A major purge of the patronage roles began at once, with Fox planning the details and Bute wielding the sword.

Beginning at the top, the dukes of Newcastle and Grafton and the marquess of Rockingham were stripped of their honorific appointments as lord lieutenants of various English counties. Newcastle appointees such as the customs officer at Rochester, the surveyor of riding officers in Kent, the inspector of accounts at Dover, and the collector of the subport of Rochester were tossed out of office. In a letter to his Whig friend Lord Hardwicke, Newcastle wailed:

> I never expected any regard would be paid to myself for having spent my time and all my fortune in support of this royal family; *that* I suppose is my *crime*. . . . Mr. Fox declares he will not spare one single man. My heart is almost broke for all the cruelties with which they are treating poor innocent men in order to be revenged on me. . . . My cousin Henry Pelham to be turned out of the customs. There is to be quite a new Admiralty. . . . Poor Wilkinson, the only man in the ordnance turned out.

Whig rule was not merely over. Whig power was completely shattered.

Henry Fox got his prompt reward—a peerage he desperately wanted. He went to the House of Lords as Baron Holland, a wealthy man whose only remaining ambition was to spend the rest of his days indulging whims of pleasure.

In September of 1762, before the peace negotiations had even got under way in Paris, King George III sent an important memorandum to Lord Bute: "I have been some days drawing up a state of the troops for the Peace, and hope to send it this evening, by which ten regiments raised at the beginning of the war remain, and yet the

expense will be some hundred pounds cheaper than in 1749."
George III worked intermittently for another four months on his
blueprint for the future size and cost of the British Army. Lord Bute,
dedicated to carrying out the king's wishes, undertook to prepare in
early 1763 the government's first peacetime armed forces budget in
more than seven years. The decisions that Bute made—with very
little discussion or parliamentary debate—would shape the size and
strategic deployment of England's land and naval forces for the next
decade and have unanticipated historical effects, particularly on the
American colonies.

Since England had no real strategic worries about an invasion of
its island fortress or fighting a war on English territory, it had never
maintained a large standing army at home in peacetime, as France
and the other continental powers had found necessary. If England
went to war, she would raise the troops that were necessary and
discharge them when they came home after the fighting was over,
keeping only a small standing army at the ready for national defense.
Preference was always given to the Royal Navy, which was supposed
to be kept at a high state of readiness as the first line of defense
against any threat of war and to keep the sea-lanes of commerce
open to the expanding empire.

But the Seven Years' War had greatly altered the global-strategy
picture for England. In the first half of the eighteenth century, England had little need for ships or soldiers to police and protect her
largely peaceful, mercantile empire. Merchant ships, trading ties,
commerce, and handfuls of troops here and there held the empire
together. Sea-lanes were threatened mainly by piracy, not naval war.
In the American colonies, there had been only about five hundred
English redcoat regulars when the French and Indian War broke
out, in 1754. By the end of that war, in 1763, all this had greatly
changed.

Pitt's victories had vastly enlarged the British Empire. Instead of
just the Atlantic seaboard of North America, England now claimed
colonial territories west to the Mississippi and areas around the
Great Lakes to the Missouri River. All of Canada was under English
rule, including the French-speaking Catholic colony of Quebec City
on the strategic heights above the St. Lawrence River. New island
possessions had been added in the Caribbean, and Florida had been
taken from the Spanish.

The British Empire was no longer a collection of far-flung, peaceful trading posts. It formed a web of global power, militant rather than mercantile. The expanded empire and new militancy posed new strategic problems for both the Royal Navy and the British Army. By the end of the Seven Years' War, the army numbered about 120,000 men; there were 70,000 seamen in the Royal Navy, and some 60,000 mercenaries, hired from German principalities, under English command. But there was a much larger empire to be defended.

As Lord Bute worked on plans for the British forces, he was also taking into account the personal interest the young king was showing in the British Army rather than the Royal Navy. For continental rulers, armies were both the symbol and the reality of power. English monarchs could not rent out British soldiers as mercenaries for foreign princes—but the army did provide useful patronage for the king to dispense. It was the king who authorized the raising and recruiting of army regiments. He personally chose the regimental commanders and passed on all promotion lists. He monitored troop movements and military maneuvers, handed out medals and awards and knighthoods, found safe seats in the House of Commons for senior generals, and passed out such comfortable posts as constable of the Tower of London and governor of Gibraltar. Of course, the king also controlled all the Royal Navy's senior promotions, but ships at sea did not offer the same patronage possibilities as land-based army regiments. Hence the king's preferential interest in how many regiments and military appointments would be at his disposal in peacetime rather than how many ships.

North America would continue to be the strategic focus of the British Empire in peacetime. How much defense would it require? The French were gone, and no other outside power appeared to threaten, but there were still hostile Indian tribes that could make trouble in colonial frontier country. The French-speaking colony of Quebec City and the wilderness to Montreal and beyond all had to be gathered under English rule. The Royal Navy maintained a major station that had to be secured at Halifax, Nova Scotia. There were already some eight thousand British troops in North America, . . . but how large should a permanent garrison be?

Along with immediate strategic considerations, English officials in America, as well as civil servants in London who were dealing with colonial affairs, were beginning to express apprehensions about a hitherto unthinkable possibility: American independence. Although no such thing as an overt independence movement was as yet even remotely discernible in the colonies, it was prudent for officials to report rumblings, no matter how faint, to London. Governor William Shirley of Massachusetts had written to London at the early stages of the French and Indian War, urging the permanent stationing of troops in America:

> Apprehension has been entertained that they [the colonies] will in time throw off their dependency upon their mother country and set up one general government among themselves. Whilst His Majesty hath seven thousand troops kept within them, it seems easy, provided his governors and principal civil officers are commonly vigilant, to prevent any step of this kind being taken.

In London, William Knox, a former colonial official in Georgia who was working in colonial administration at the Board of Trade, submitted a policy recommendation in 1763, urging that troops be left in the colonies and stating flat out that "the main purpose of stationing a large body of troops in America [would be] to secure the dependence of the colonies on Great Britain."

The American colonies, therefore, gave Lord Bute ample political and strategic reasons to follow the wishes of King George and keep the British Army at the highest peacetime level in its history. Of course, the army would have to be reduced drastically to save money—from 120,000 men to 30,000. In order to provide the king with sufficient royal patronage, the troops would be spread thinly across seventy regimental formations. Each regiment would have a full complement of officers, commissioned by the king, but fewer troops than at wartime strength. This would facilitate wide deployment of the army at islands, forts, garrisons, and strategic towns and cities throughout the British Empire. In North America, Bute's new long-term plan called for the permanent deployment of fourteen infantry regiments with artillery and supporting troops. This would amount to 10,000 men, or one third the total strength of the planned peacetime army.

Finally, when the plans were announced in the House of Commons in February of 1763, the secretary at war, Welbore Ellis, informed Parliament—almost as an afterthought—that "[t]he army *stationed in America will be supported in the first year by England, afterwards by the colonies"* [emphasis added]. Thus it was decreed by the earl of Bute that by 1765, the Americans would be billed for ten thousand British troops to be stationed in their midst on permanent peacetime duty. The size of the bill and the method of taxing would be decided at a future time. If there was any voice raised in Parliament against the policy, it was not recorded. Nor was such a voice likely, for it probably all sounded logical and reasonable to English taxpayers, who were still paying for the burden of a long war. Why indeed shouldn't the Americans pay for British troops sent to defend them?

It may have seemed like a routine, insignificant decision. Nobody seemed to realize that Lord Bute was lighting the long fuse that would finally explode in the American Revolution.

Six weeks after completing the far-reaching plans for the future of the British Army and the American colonies, Lord Bute suddenly turned in his seals of office to King George and stepped down as prime minister. He was a proud man, but by now the Whigs had made him one of the most hated men in England, jeered in theaters and stoned in public for the ousting of William Pitt. He had never before held any government office and never had any active experience in Parliament. As the king's confidant, he had practiced only drawing-room politics; he had no stomach for the real politics of governing. He had done all he could for the king, but politics had made his life miserable. He was out of his depth and crushed by his own inadequacies; resignation saved him further obloquy.

The king did not grieve long at the loss of his "dearest friend." Soon after Bute had gone, the king remarked that "I found him unhappily deficient in political firmness."

In May of 1763, only days after Lord Bute's departure, Indian fury broke out, taking by surprise an ill-prepared British Army in America. If protection of the colonies against Indian attack was supposed to be one of the reasons to deploy a large, permanent force of English soldiers in America, it was put to a swift and bloody test in what became known as Pontiac's War. This savage insurrection, which took the British forces and American militias eighteen months to bring under control, was largely caused by the political blundering and poor military judgment of the British commander in chief in America, Major General Jeffrey Amherst.

General Amherst had been made British commander in chief in North America after his victory over the French at Montreal, in 1760. He was, in the words of an officer who served with him, a man of "stoic apathy," a commander whose military talents were managerial rather than tactical. He despised Indians. He was almost equally contemptuous of the American colonists, about whom he wrote in his diary, "They are sufficient to work our boats, drive our waggons, to fell trees and do work that in inhabited countries are performed by peasants. If left to themselves they would eat fryed pork and lay in their tents all day." Not surprisingly, General Amherst had neither flair nor imagination for fighting Indians in wilderness country.

The leader of the Indian uprising was Pontiac, chief of the Ottawas, whose tribal homeland was in northern Michigan. The attacks began in early May with a ferocity, coordination, and military skill never seen before in the colonies.

A band of Chippewas surprised a small detachment of British soldiers and sailors taking soundings on Lake St. Clair, near Detroit. All of the English were either killed or marched away as Indian prisoners. Two days later, the Ottawas, under Pontiac, struck directly at Detroit, and by May 14 it was under siege by at least six hundred warriors. Smaller forts began to fall like tenpins. By the end of 1763, after more than six months of fighting, it was estimated that two thousand settlers had been killed or captured, with thousands more driven from their homes and frontier outposts back to the security of more settled areas.

Meanwhile, as the British Army was reeling from the early attacks of the uprising, the authorities in London issued a major decree in an attempt to buy peace with the Indians. A royal proclamation, on October 7, 1763, reserved for the exclusive use of the Indians almost all of the western territory that had been ceded to King George by the French in the peace of February 1763. This sweeping declaration, "for the present and until further pleasure of His Majesty be known," excluded white settlers from the *whole* of the present states of Ohio, Indiana, Illinois, Michigan, Wisconsin, Kentucky, and Tennessee; from parts of Minnesota, New York, Pennsylvania, Maryland, West Virginia, North and South Carolina, Georgia, Alabama, and Mississippi; and from the Canadian territories of Ontario and Quebec.

Having failed to protect white settlers in the frontier country, the British would now attempt to solve the problem by keeping the settlers from penetrating beyond the Appalachian mountain range, all the way from Canada to the Carolinas.

In London, the Board of Trade devised a further rationale for this exclusion. A memorandum to the Privy Council urged "keeping the colonists as near as possible to the Ocean," dependent on trade with England. The interior of America should be kept "as wild and open as possible for the purposes of hunting."

Thus, by the end of 1763, the French were gone from America, the Seven Years' War formally ended, and a major Indian uprising was dying down. But a large British Army, deployed as a permanent peacetime force in the colonies, was deemed by the British to be more necessary than ever. The imperial rule was tightening. Peace would not bring tranquillity to America.

Chapter 3

FRANKLIN IN LONDON

During a long and extraordinarily full life, Benjamin Franklin lived in London and Paris almost continuously from 1757 to 1785. In those twenty-eight years, he spent less than four at home in Philadelphia. His first mission to London, as Pennsylvania's colonial agent, lasted from 1757 to September of 1762. He returned to London in October 1764, shortly before the passage of the Stamp Act, and remained there until the eve of the Revolution, in March 1775. In October 1776, soon after signing the Declaration of Independence, he left secretly on his important diplomatic mission to France. He remained in Paris until 1785, two years after signing the peace agreements with England. He took part in the drafting of the Constitution in 1787, and died, aged eighty-four, on April 17, 1790.

Franklin was fifty-one when he began his long sojourn abroad. He was in his prime, full of physical and intellectual vigor, successful in an amazing range of commercial, journalistic, scientific, educational, philosophical, military, and political pursuits: As a young man, he started his own printing business in Philadelphia; either founded or helped found an insurance company and a fire company, the first public library, the first public hospital, the University of Pennsylvania, a colonial postal service, and a rudimentary public health system; and he authored *Poor Richard's Almanack* and many other writings. He dabbled constantly with scientific experiments—with electricity in particular—and invented such diverse things as bifocals, an improved iron heating stove, and the glass harmonica. He was the preeminent First Citizen of the American colonies, foremost in authority and political experience, possessed of a broad knowledge of the colonies and their political leaders, gained during his travels as organizer of the infant postal service. He was a generation older than the men who would become famous during the Revolution: In 1757, Washington was twenty-five; John Adams was twenty-two; John Hancock, twenty. Thomas Jefferson was only fourteen; John Jay, twelve. James Madison was a child of six, and Alexander Hamilton was only a baby.

When Franklin went to London in 1757, he was returning to a city he already knew well. He had spent nearly two years there (1725–26) as an apprentice, learning the printing trade. Back in London, his reputation as a scientist had preceded him, especially the reports of his experiments with electricity. And he was a lifelong friend of scientist and physicist Joseph Priestley, the discoverer of oxygen. Franklin, in recognition of his scientific experiments and writings, had already been elected a member of the prestigious Royal Society in London, an exclusive honorary group of men of intellectual and scientific repute. And so he settled into life in London quickly and comfortably, joining at least six private clubs in addition to the Royal Society.

Like most colonials of his time, Franklin was an Anglophile and loyal to the British Crown. The Seven Years' War was then at its height and at no time did thoughts of revolution cross Franklin's mind. From the time he arrived in London, he worked hard, and with great patience, skill, and intelligence, to avoid the Revolution. He remained loyal to the Crown until the English themselves made it impossible for him to continue to do so. As a revolutionary, with his clear vision of the basic principles and issues at stake, he used his diplomatic skills (and his considerable social graces) to enlist the French in the American cause.

His first order of business, on his arrival in 1757, was to lodge an appeal with the Privy Council on behalf of Pennsylvania. The descendants of William Penn had refused to allow their vast personal landholdings to be taxed like those of any other citizen. The Penn family, which had become absentee landlords living in London, held a hearty dislike for Franklin's political activities aimed against them. Thomas Penn, oldest of the surviving sons of William, had written to the provincial secretary in Philadelphia, Richard Peters, that "Mr. Franklin's popularity is nothing here. . . . He will be looked very coldly upon by great people. There are few of any consequence that have heard of his electrical experiments, those matters being attended by a particular set of people."

Franklin arranged to make his first official call in London to Lord Granville, president of the Privy Council. But Thomas Penn had thoroughly briefed Granville on the tax problems with Franklin and the Pennsylvania Assembly. Granville gave Franklin a very cool welcome. Immediately after the meeting, an alarmed Franklin wrote in a letter to Isaac Norris, speaker of the Pennsylvania Assembly:

> He received me with great civility; and after some questions respecting the state of affairs in America and discourse thereupon he said to me: "You Americans have wrong ideas of the nature of your constitution; you contend that the King's instructions to his governors are not laws, and think yourselves at liberty to regard or disregard them at your own discretion. But these instructions are not like the pocket instructions given to a minister going abroad, for regulating his conduct in some trifling point of ceremony. They are drawn up by judges learned in the laws; they are then considered, debated and perhaps amended in council, after which they are signed by the King.
>
> "They are then, so far as they relate to you, *the law of the land* for the King is the LEGISLATOR OF THE COLONIES."
>
> I told his lordship that this was new doctrine to me. I had always understood from our charters that our laws were to be made by our Assemblies, to be presented indeed to the King for his royal assent, but that being once given the King could not repeal or alter them. And as the Assemblies could not make permanent laws without his assent, so neither could he make a law for them without theirs. He [Granville] assur'd me that I was totally mistaken. I did not think so, however, and his lordship's conversation having a little alarm'd me as to what might be the sentiments of the court concerning us, I wrote it down as soon as I returned to my lodgings.

Franklin had every right to be concerned. Lord Granville had thrown down a political gauntlet, even though it would be nearly two decades before the English pushed this determination into revolution.

A few days after his meeting with Granville, Franklin had an even angrier conversation with Thomas Penn himself. The two men began by exchanging mutual complaints about political issues in Philadelphia. When they got down to cases, their meeting rapidly turned hostile. Franklin declared that William Penn's charter to the colony gave the assembly "all the powers and privileges of an assembly according to the rights of free-born subjects of England, and as is usual in any of the British plantations in America." Franklin then recorded this exchange:

> "Yes," says he, "but if my father granted privileges he was not by royal charter empowered to grant, nothing can be claimed by such grant." I said: "Then if your father had no right to grant the privileges he pretended to grant, and published all over Europe as granted, those who came to settle in the province on the faith of that grant, and in expectation of enjoying privileges contained in it, were deceived, cheated and betrayed."
>
> He answered that they should have themselves looked to that; that the royal charter was no secret; they who came into the province on his father's offer of privileges, if they were deceived it was their own fault. And he said with a kind of triumphing, laughing insolence, such as a low jockey might do when a purchaser complained he had been cheated on a horse. I was astonished to see him thus meanly give up his father's character, and conceived at that moment a more cordial and thorough contempt for him than I ever felt for any man living.

Franklin later noted to Isaac Norris, "When I meet [Thomas Penn] anywhere, there appears on his countenance a strange mixture of hatred, anger, fear and vexation." This was not exactly an auspicious start for Franklin's mission.

Franklin was genuinely surprised at encountering these attitudes toward the constitutional rights of the colonies and the powers of the king to control those rights. Nevertheless, he expected that the business with the Privy Council would take only a year or so to conclude. It was, in fact, three years before he finally got a decision that at least partly resolved Pennsylvania's problems.

Meanwhile, Franklin was happily ensconced in London. He had

brought with him his legitimized son William, and together they lived in a four-room flat at 36 Craven Street.*

As a lobbyist on an expense account, Franklin charged nearly everything to the Pennsylvania Assembly. His expenses became an increasing irritant to the frugal Quakers and other thrifty citizens of Philadelphia. He hired a horse and carriage to be at his disposal full-time, established himself with an excellent London tailor, and enjoyed the best of wine with foods prepared by his landlady, a Mrs. Stevenson.

Franklin, effective lobbyist that he was, enlisted the services of a well-placed local lawyer, Richard Jackson, with whom he had been in correspondence. Jackson was a respected Inner Temple barrister, a dashing young bachelor of wealth and wide social and political contacts, known for his lively intelligence and conversation. The eminent curmudgeon of the London coffeehouses and club life, Dr. Samuel Johnson, had bestowed upon him the nickname Omniscient Jackson. He was a popular insider, and he quickly became a close collaborator in Franklin's lobbying activities. Not least of all, he specialized in the legalities of the various royal charters of the colonies and of common-law rights.

Franklin also turned to his friends in the publishing world for help in airing his case. One of his first contacts was William Strahan, publisher of the works of Edward Gibbon, Samuel Johnson, Oliver Goldsmith, and many others. Franklin's Philadelphia publishing establishment had been a principal American outlet for Strahan; the two men had corresponded for some fifteen years. Strahan not only introduced Franklin into an ever-widening circle of literary, social, and political contacts. He also printed many of Franklin's letters in the *London Chronicle,* one of London's most widely read, influential newspapers, of which he was the principal shareholder and "printer," as publishers were called in those days.

There was no systematic news gathering in the eighteenth century. The news content of most papers consisted of paragraph items of coffeehouse gossip, letters from overseas capitals, items passed along by merchants or lawyers or sea captains. Further, until 1780,

---

*This building still exists today. It is located just off the Strand, behind Charing Cross Station.

reports on anything that happened in Parliament were not allowed to be printed. While there was no official censorship of the press, there were libel laws, and newspaper owners did have to be cautious in handling sensitive subjects. There were no editorials per se. Thus the letters to the press, which were not subject to any oversight, were the most provocative and hence the most widely read part of each issue—the mainstay of circulation. Printers vied with one another for controversial letters, which were always signed with either a pseudonym or initials.

The London press was a journalistic heaven for Franklin, who through his Philadelphia publications, was already a past master of the art of the anonymous letter, literary practical jokes, and hoaxes that would stir up reader interest. He relied heavily on the press to advance his lobbying efforts. In his years in London, he wrote more than three hundred different letters to the press, signing them with twenty-two different names.*

In general, the American cause got a surprisingly full and sympathetic airing. Before the passage of the Stamp Act, the main interest in the colonies had been in the battles with the Indians (including a six-page account of the Conestoga Indian massacre in Lancaster County, Pennsylvania, which was probably written by Franklin). The Stamp Act (1765), the riots that followed in America, the disastrous economic impact on England, and then the abrupt repeal of the act brought a marked increase in news and comment on America.

Soon after Franklin's arrival in London, William Strahan felt impelled to address a friendly letter of advice to Deborah Franklin, Benjamin's wife, in Philadelphia:

I never saw a man who was, in every respect, so agreeable to me. Some are amiable in one view, some in another, he in all. Now,

---

*In an extraordinary piece of literary detective work by Verne W. Crane, Franklin's London correspondence was identified and collected as *Benjamin Franklin's Letters to the Press, 1758 to 1775,* and published in 1954. Among the signatures Franklin used were Pacificus Secundus, A Traveller, Homespun, A Londoner, F. B., B. F., A New Englandsman, A Friend to the Poor, and on one occasion, A Well-Wisher to the King and All His Dominions.

Madam, as I know the ladies here consider him in exactly the light as
I do, upon my word I think I should come over with all convenient
speed to look after your interest. Not but that I think him as faithful
as any man breathing, but who knows what repeated and strong
temptation may in time, and while he is at so great a distance from
you, accomplish.

Deborah had no illusions about her husband being "as faithful as
any man breathing," but she had a deep fear of sea voyages and
would not contemplate stirring from her Philadelphia home. She
was a simple woman, plain, of no great intelligence, barely literate.
Franklin probably had an affair with her while he was boarding at
her parents' house before he left to learn the printer's trade in London in 1725. Upon his return, he found that she had married but
had subsequently been deserted by a wastrel husband.

"I piti'd poor Miss Read's unfortunate situation," Franklin wrote
in his *Autobiography*. "I considered my giddiness and inconstancy
when in London as in a great degree the cause of her unhappiness. . . . Our mutual affection was revived, but there were now
great objections to our union. . . . We ventured, however, over these
difficulties, and I took her to wife, September 1st, 1730."

The "difficulties" were Deborah's first husband's debts and her
uncertainty as to whether he was alive or dead. A common-law
union was their solution. It was a marriage of convenience to which
both agreed with a dutiful degree of affection. In London, Franklin
remained undisturbed by his friend Strahan's concerns. Deborah
remained in Philadelphia.

Accompanying Franklin to London to study law was his son, now
legitimized, William. "My son was of much use to me", the elder
Franklin wrote, and for more than thirty years of their lives that was
certainly so. But soon William Franklin—twenty-eight years old in
1759, lively, virile, intelligent, and handsome—began to move out
from under the rather heavy paternal and political shadow of his
father.

While waiting for action from the Privy Council on the Pennsylvania tax case, the two made a six-weeks' carriage journey to Scotland in September of 1759. They traveled all the way north to Perth,
where Franklin received an honorary degree from St. Andrews University. But a guest at one of the many Scottish dinners given for

them, Dr. Alexander Carlyle, who was head of the Edinburgh Philosophical Society, recorded "a certain unpleasant undercurrent in the room" between father and son: "Franklin's son was open and communicative and pleased the company better than his father, and some of us observed indications of that decided difference of opinion between father and son which, in the American war, alienated them altogether."

Benjamin Franklin had his own concept of loyalty to England, which he was always at pains in conversation and writing to make clear to the English. It was not a loyalty to English rule or to laws and taxes passed by Parliament in London. To one of his hosts in Scotland, Lord Kames, an Edinburgh judge, he wrote on his return to London:

> I have long been of the opinion that the foundations of the future grandeur and stability of the British Empire lie in America; and though, like other foundations, they are low and little used, they are nevertheless broad and strong enough to support the greatest political structure human wisdom ever yet erected.

In 1760, Franklin published a major pamphlet to explain and define fully his concept of an expanding America as the strategic and economic cornerstone of the future of the British Empire. The pamphlet carried the lengthy title *The Interest of Great Britain Considered with Regard to Her Colonies and the Acquisition of Canada.* It was occasioned by a lively public debate going on in London with the sugar merchants calling on William Pitt to make peace with France by returning Canada to the French in a swap for the Caribbean sugar island of Guadeloupe, which had been captured by the English in 1759.

Under the cloak of anonymity (which virtually guaranteed attracting more attention than anything signed), Franklin wrote not as an American but in the style of an Englishman well versed in both American affairs and imperial strategy. He probably had some help from Omniscient Jackson, but much of the pamphlet, written in Franklin's own hand, is preserved today at the Historical Society of Pennsylvania.

The idea that England should swap the Canadian wilderness for a sugar-rich Caribbean island seemed less ridiculous in 1760 than it does today. Franklin dismissed it as a strategic stupidity. North

America was not only a thriving market; it was also the western frontier of the British Empire. It was imperative, Franklin wrote, that
Canada remain English in order to secure all of North America to
the benefit of the empire:

> The present war teaches us that disputes arising in America may be an
> occasion of embracing nations who have no concerns there. And two
> great nations can scarcely be at war in Europe but some prince or
> other thinks it a convenient opportunity to revive some ancient claim.
> Flames of war once kindled spread far and wide and the mischief is
> infinite. All kinds of security are obtained by subduing and retaining
> Canada.

He then sketched out a vision of North America as a part of an
empire that would expand in riches, power, and splendor until one
day there would be more Englishmen in America than in England
itself. Where land was free and easy to acquire, Franklin forecast in
1760, "America might one day number a hundred million people."
Franklin dismissed the possibility of this populous and distant
land ever being in revolt against England:

> If they [the colonials] could not agree to unite for their defense
> against the French and Indians who are harassing their settlements,
> burning their buildings and murdering their people, can it reasonably
> be supposed there is any danger of their uniting against their own
> nation, which protects and encourages them, with which they have so
> many connections and ties of blood, interest and affection.

He finished by saying that "I venture to say that an union
amongst them for such a purpose is not merely improbable; it is
impossible."
But he was prudent and prescient and worried enough about the
attitudes he was encountering in London not to end his discourse
on too high a note of optimism:

> When I say such an union is impossible, I mean without the most
> grievous tyranny and oppression. People who have property in a
> country which they may lose, and privileges which they may endan-
> ger, are generally disposed to be quiet, and even to bear much rather
> than hazard all. While the government is mild and just, while impor-
> tant civil and religious rights are secure, such subjects will be dutiful
> and obedient. *The waves do not rise but when the wind blows.* [Empha-
> sis added.]

Although it would be another two years before he actually packed his bags and went home to Philadelphia, the pamphlet was something of a political valediction for Franklin's first mission to London. By the time he left, the winds were not yet blowing, but they were picking up speed.

During this stay in London, Franklin submitted to the Privy Council for approval by the king nineteen laws that had been passed by the Pennsylvania Assembly. The Penns managed to get six of the laws vetoed, but Franklin prevailed over the Penns' objections, and the other thirteen laws were upheld.

In the mid-eighteenth century, the Privy Council functioned as the ultimate appeal on legislation passed by colonial assemblies and later contested—as the Penns were contesting the right of the Pennsylvania Assembly to tax their lands. The case was the most important, both politically and constitutionally, that Franklin handled.

A preliminary committee hearing at first recommended in favor of the Penns, but when the case reached the Privy Council for a final decision, on August 27, 1760, the hearing suddenly took a different turn. Presiding over the case was the lord chief justice of England, Lord Mansfield, with whom Franklin and his son had stayed during their trip to Scotland the year before.

Lord Mansfield proved to be sympathetic. On the second day of the hearings, Franklin relates:

> Lord Mansfield rose, and beckoning me into the clerk's chamber while the lawyers were pleading, and asked me if I was really of the opinion that no injury would be done the proprietary estate in the execution of the act. I said certainly. Then, says he, you have little objection to enter into an engagement to assure that point. I answer'd, None at all. He then called in Paris [the lawyer for the Penns] and after some discourse his Lordship's proposition was accepted by both sides.

Mansfield ruled that surveyed lands (lands that had been mapped for development and sale) owned by the Penns would be taxed no higher than similar properties privately owned, but their unsurveyed lands would not be taxed.

In Philadelphia, this compromise was greeted as a triumph for Franklin. Pennsylvania, and by extension all of the other colonies, had at last established a fundamental right to tax all property within its boundaries. No exceptions would be made for "feudal" ownerships.

Franklin's basic mission had now been accomplished, but he was in no hurry to leave. He was enjoying a stimulating life in London too much to tear himself away. In any case, the long-anticipated death of King George II and the accession of George III, which occurred shortly after the Privy Council's ruling, gave Franklin a good excuse to stay on: Clearly, the transition to a new reign would bring important political changes.

As the eclipse of William Pitt and the Whigs began, friends of Lord Bute emerged from the shadows and quickly moved to the center of the social stage. Benjamin Franklin's social life slackened while his son's accelerated. In late September of 1761, when George III was crowned in Westminster Abbey, William Franklin, through the duchess of Northumberland, a friend of Bute's, had a seat inside. His father, merely agent for Pennsylvania, was given a ticket to a seat in a booth overlooking the coronation-parade route.*

Franklin returned to Philadelphia at the end of the summer, 1762. It was a long, slow voyage, escorted by a convoy of Royal Navy frigates, that stopped in Madeira to take on supplies and took ten weeks to cross the Atlantic.

It was high time Franklin got home. Although he had been re-elected regularly to the Pennsylvania Assembly while he was in London, his popularity had slipped. The political, religious, and ethnic demographics of Pennsylvania had changed considerably in the five years he had been abroad.

Further, the Penns, stung by their setback in the Privy Council, had retaliated by dispatching John Penn, Thomas's nephew, to be Pennsylvania's governor. Until then, the Penns had made only brief, occasional visits to the colony. William Penn's descendants had all but abandoned any Quaker sense of benevolence toward Pennsylvania. With John Penn sitting in the governor's chair, the political

---

*Lord Bute, in 1762, recommended to the king the appointment of William Franklin as royal governor of New Jersey.

mood of the colony soured, becoming increasingly combative. And of course, John Penn was not averse to criticizing Franklin's expense account and stirring up whatever other troubles he could that would reflect badly on Franklin.

Then, in the summer of 1763, Pontiac's War swept like wildfire out of western Pennsylvania. Indians pillaged and killed isolated settlers all the way east into the Lehigh Valley, through rich Lancaster County, up to the edge of Philadelphia itself.

John Penn chose this most difficult moment to lock horns yet again with the legislature over the same tired issue of the taxation of Penn family lands. The assembly had passed two bills to meet the Indian emergency, one to raise a militia, the other to raise the taxes to pay for it. Penn vetoed both bills. He insisted that as royal governor, he should appoint all militia officers; they should not be chosen by the militiamen, as had happened when Franklin was elected to command the Pennsylvania militia in 1756. Penn certainly didn't want Franklin taking charge of anything. And he contended that the tax bill did not conform to the intent of the Privy Council compromise obtained by Franklin. He maintained that according to the Privy Council ruling, Penn lands had to be assessed at the lowest rate and could not be taxed any higher whether or not they had increased in value or been built on.

The assembly was outraged by these vetoes and passed a resolution to consult voters on whether to submit a petition to King George that "he take the people of this province under his immediate protection and government" and end the Penns' proprietary charter. John Penn dashed off a letter to his uncle Thomas: "There will never be any prospect of ease and happiness while that villan [Franklin] has the liberty of spreading about his poison of that inveterate malice and ill-nature which is deeply implanted in his own black heart."

A general election was due to be held for the assembly in October 1764. It was a nasty, hard-fought campaign marked by strong religious infighting among Presbyterians (who claimed that if the Penns were ousted, King George would make the Church of England the supreme religion in the colony), Methodists, German Moravians, Catholics, and just about everybody else with a voice. Of course, Franklin's expense account and William's illegitimacy received considerable attention.

Polling began at nine in the morning at the State House (present-day Independence Hall) in Philadelphia. Voters streamed in all through the day and evening and into the early morning hours. At 3:00 A.M., the New Ticket faction backing Governor Penn wanted to close the polls, but Franklin's Old Party workers were still bringing in voters from Germantown, eight miles away, and insisted on keeping the polls open. Voting went on till three o'clock the next afternoon. When the count was completed, Franklin's Old Party had kept control of the assembly—but Franklin himself had lost his seat, by a mere twenty-five votes out of the nearly four thousand cast.

John Penn's jubilation at Franklin's unseating was short-lived. The assembly voted, on October 26, 1764, to send Franklin back to London as colonial agent, along with the petition to oust the Penns and make Pennsylvania a crown colony.

Franklin wasted no time in getting under way. Two weeks after the vote, he set out by carriage from Philadelphia, accompanied by some three hundred friends and well-wishers. His escort rode alongside him as far as Chester, fourteen miles south on the Delaware River, where a packet was waiting to sail for England.

His wife, Deborah, and a few of his friends stayed aboard and dined on turtle. At New Castle, near Delaware Bay, they disembarked. Franklin would never see his wife again. He wrote to her from the Isle of Wight on December 6, 1764: "Tell our friends that dined with us that the kind prayers they put up for thirty days' favorable wind for me was favorably heard and answered, we being just thirty days from land to land."

But the political winds were far from favorable when he settled in once again at 36 Craven Street.

Chapter 4

THE STAMP ACT

There were many causes for the growing irritation in the American colonies, but the measure that turned discontent into incipient revolution was the Stamp Act of 1765. The author-perpetrator was the king's third prime minister, George Grenville.

Thomas Babington Macaulay, a historian of many words and strong opinions, wrote this blunt appraisal of Grenville in 1844:

> The worst administration which governed England since the Revolution [of 1688, which ended the Stuart dynasty] was that of George Grenville. His public acts may be classed under two heads, outrages on the liberty of the people, and outrages on the dignity of the Crown. . . . With the Stamp Act on America, he proposed a measure destined to produce a great revolution, the effects of which will be remembered as long as the globe lasts.

Subsequent judgments of Grenville have not been tempered by time or historical hindsight. A century after Macaulay, O. A. Sherrard, biographer of William Pitt, described Grenville (who was Pitt's brother-in-law) as "intolerably conceited, and to make matters worse added to his conceit an excessive measure of those faults that often go with it—obstinacy, rancour, resentment, an implacable temper, an inability to forget or forgive." In 1960, the Oxford historian J. Steven Watson, in his book *The Reign of George III*, added this unflattering picture:

> George Grenville's mind had no great depth, his speeches no elo-quence, his methods no finesse. His greatest strengths lay in his busi-nesslike methods, his care for detail, and the clarity of his mind. This clarity was the result of a lack of vision of anything but the point nearest ahead of him. But it did, with his strength of will, enable him to defeat men of greater natural talents.

The king himself was contemptuous of Grenville, whom he de-scribed as a man "with the mind of a counting-house clerk." Gren-ville was inclined to be long-winded, something the king deplored: "[He] would talk for an hour and look at his watch and then go on for another half-hour." Only a few months before appointing him to high office, the king had written to Bute that "Grenville is very far out if he thinks himself capable for a post where either decision or activity are necessary; for I have never met a man more doubtful or dillitory." It would have been better for England and the colonies if the king had held to his judgment, but when Bute abruptly quit his office of prime minister in 1763, the king found himself with little choice but to turn to Grenville, the highest ranking secretary of state in the Bute cabinet. So it was that a man of little mind, blinkered judgment, obstinacy, and bad temper came to be prime minister and set his nation on a course that would cost it dearly.

Grenville, like Bute before him, owed his elevation to high office solely to the king—not to his own political strengths, nor to any support in Parliament, nor to any popular following. He had, in his rise to power, broken with his brother-in-law William Pitt and the Whig leadership; thus, he could command no backing from them. A prime minister without a base of political support is bound to be weak—as the king had already learned with Bute. By choosing Grenville as Bute's successor, George III was not providing kingly leadership but, rather, ensuring the continuation of weak and often-changing governments.

As secretary of state in Bute's government, Grenville had enthusi-astically supported the decision to station ten thousand British troops in the American colonies—and to tax the Americans to pay for those troops. It now fell to him, as Bute's successor, to determine when and how much the Americans would be required to pay and how this revenue would be raised.

There was nothing new about London imposing taxes and regulations on the colonies to control trade, but so far none of the taxes that had been imposed was designed solely to raise revenues. They were indirect taxes, such as customs duties and other charges relating to trade. When it came to taxing citizens to raise money to meet government expenses, it was a well-established principle that the colonials would tax themselves through their own legislatures. They had raised the money themselves to support the British during the Seven Years' War; they continued to raise money themselves to pay the salaries of royal governors, royal judges, and other government officials appointed by the Crown.

Customs duties and trade regulations imposed by London had largely been accepted as the normal practice of a nation engaged in the colonization and building of an empire. Whatever irritations those tariffs and regulations might arouse, they were hardly cause for rebellion.

In 1704, an act required that the colonies limit their export of rice and molasses as well as tar, turpentine, hemp, and other naval stores to England alone. In 1721, another act prohibited importation of any tea, pepper, spices, drugs, silks, and cotton fabrics except through England and the East India Company.

In 1722, the White Pines Act restricted New Englanders from felling trees beyond a certain circumference. These trees were valuable as ships' masts, and were therefore declared Crown property, to be cut only under the supervision of Crown agents and shipped to England to be used by the Royal Navy and England's merchant fleet.

After the 1730s, the colonies were forbidden to levy any import duties on English products; this prevented the Americans from raising protective tariffs to encourage their own domestic industries. But of course, the English could and did raise tariffs in America on the import of non-English goods.

In 1732, a Board of Trade regulation prohibited the export of American-made felt and felt hats, even from one colony to another. Further, no felt hats could be manufactured in the colonies by any hatmaker who had not served an apprenticeship of at least seven years in England. That same year, the colonies were banned from exporting hops for beer making to Ireland. This prevented them from undercutting the English hop growers.

In 1733, the Molasses Act imposed on the colonies a sixpence-per-gallon duty on all molasses imported from the French Caribbean. Molasses imported from the British Caribbean was tax-free.

In the 1750s, a tobacco tax in Virginia became a matter of ongoing conflict between the colonial government and the Board of Trade.

England also hobbled American industry. In 1750, Parliament prohibited the building of any new mill in the colonies for the rolling or plating of iron ore and of new furnaces for making steel. Pig iron could be exported only to England.

By the 1760s, these and many other trade restrictions and prohibitions were in place, but they had not greatly changed the attitude of salutary neglect. Each colony still ran its own internal affairs, and collectively the colonies enjoyed English protection against the French and their Indian allies. Colonial trade was booming, and the colonies profited from preferential access to the English market.

Moreover, the English were quite lax about enforcing their own restrictions. In truth, smuggling to avoid customs and other trade regulations was widespread, even rampant, on the long, porous American coast. This was particularly true for molasses from the French Caribbean, which was turned into fiery, high-quality rum in New England distilleries. Nor was it possible for a handful of English authorities to find every hatmaker or forge operator in the widely scattered towns and tiny settlements of the thirteen colonies. During the 1760s, there were only about two hundred English customs officers to cover an area that stretched from Nova Scotia to Barbados. That handful found it more profitable to make money by turning a blind eye to smugglers than by collecting a legal percentage of the meager duties.

So the practical effects of all the restrictions were not onerous, and business was good. The colonial economies were growing, and their preference for English goods continued unabated.

With a new king on the throne and war with the French receding, this situation changed. Laxity in matters of trade, revenue, and governance was soon to pass.

*   *   *

While there were many reasons for the king and others to dislike George Grenville, he was hardworking, a thrifty and conscientious administrator who had a good head for business. His good qualities, however, were easily overlooked.

Grenville had a prickly, abrasive relationship with the king from the outset. Given the king's youth and headstrong personality and his determination to reign and to rule, a wise new chief minister might have been careful about challenging his royal master. But Grenville was neither wise nor prudent nor tactful, and his political insecurity made him all the more determined to assert himself vis-à-vis the king. Grenville also feared that Bute, his particular bête noire, would continue to exploit his personal relationship with the king by working as éminence grise, the power behind the throne.

Grenville began his troubled tenure in office by directly challenging the king over how to run the government, declaring that he must be the king's only channel for conducting the nation's business. In the king's indignant words, "he had the insolence to say that if people presum'd to speak to me on business without his previous consent, he would not serve an hour."

Grenville also insisted that the king's erstwhile "dearest friend" Bute should be banished from London, forced to retire to his country home, and "give up all business and absent himself from the King until an administration firmly established should leave no room for jealousy about him." The king, angry with Grenville, nevertheless asked Bute to resign his last royal appointment, keeper of the privy purse.

The king came to hate having to do business with Grenville, who invariably mixed his irritating, jealous importunings with tedious lectures about public business and matters currently before Parliament. The king became so desperate that in August 1763, after only five months of Grenville, he held a secret, three-hour meeting with that "blackest of hearts," William Pitt. If he wanted a broad-based government, he would have to reenlist some Whig support. But the overture to Pitt was unsuccessful: the king found that Pitt's demands and conditions for returning to office would be even more of a burden than putting up with George Grenville.

So Grenville pushed ahead with what he liked to do best: acting as countinghouse clerk, cutting spending, raising taxes, balancing the books. No expense was too small to escape his notice (he turned down a proposal to institute a police horse patrol from London's Tottenham Court Road police station), nor was any influential request too large to deny (the king himself was refused a twenty-thousand-pound grant to enlarge the grounds around Buckingham House). The *Public Advertiser* declared that Grenville considered "a national saving of two inches of Candle a triumph greater than all Mr. Pitt's Victories."

The Royal Navy suffered the most from Grenville's penny-pinching. Ships returning from victories in the West Indies, the Indian Ocean, the Mediterranean, the far Pacific, and the North Atlantic were laid up to rot in the docks at Portsmouth, Plymouth, and Chatham. Not a shilling was allowed for maintenance; crews were dismissed and dispersed. The number of Royal Navy dockyard workers dropped to the low level that had left England so ill prepared for the Seven Years' War. Lord Egmont, first lord of the Admiralty, warned Grenville that the French would soon be superior at sea, that "we have not now, guardships [reserves] included, in Great Britain, seventeen ships of the line complete." Grenville replied that surely further economies were possible in that year's naval-supply bill of £1.5 million.

At the end of the Seven Years' War, England's national debt had soared to the enormous (for those times) sum of £140 million and was burdened with £5 million a year in interest charges. The per capita debt in England amounted to eighteen pounds; in America, it was estimated to be a mere eighteen shillings. These numbers loomed large in the countinghouse clerk's mind. Few in Parliament disagreed with the idea that Americans should be required to pay for their own defense. So George Grenville made the break with the past and set out to raise revenues in the colonies. None of his ensuing measures struck either the English politicians or public as particularly onerous, unreasonable, or provocative. Few—least of all Grenville himself—tried to anticipate the possible consequences. The long fuse now began to burn.

Benjamin Franklin, meanwhile, was still back home in Philadelphia, mending his political fences. He learned of the new policy in a March 10, 1763, letter from his friend Richard "Omniscient" Jackson, who had taken over as acting agent for Pennsylvania. Jackson informed Franklin of Bute's decision to station fourteen battalions in North America and that Americans would be taxed to provide the money to pay for the troops. Franklin replied with a verbal shrug: "You mention a proposal to charge us here with the maintenance of 10,000 men. I shall only say, it is not worth your while. All we can spare from mere living goes to you for superfluities. The more you oblige us to pay here, the less you can receive."

By the time Franklin's letter reached Jackson, Grenville had replaced Bute. And Jackson, who was an extraordinary political operator, had added to his portfolio of responsibilities: He was already a member of Parliament and acting agent for Massachusetts and Connecticut as well as for Pennsylvania. Now he was also Grenville's private secretary, probably in recognition of his considerable knowledge of colonial affairs and the evolution of colonial law under royal grants and charters. If Jackson saw any conflict of interest in all this, it doesn't appear to have bothered him.

He wrote to Franklin in January of 1764 with the news that Grenville planned to introduce tax measures to raise £200,000 from the colonies. These, he told Franklin, would include "inland duties," that is, some form of direct taxation in addition to customs duties on trade and commerce. Grenville would begin with a revision of the 1733 Molasses Act, which had been so conspicuously ignored by smugglers and customs agents alike.

Once again, Franklin was indifferent, replying to Jackson on February 11, 1764:

> I am not much alarm'd about your Schemes of raising money from us. You will take care for your own sakes not to lay greater burthens on us than we can bear; for you cannot hurt us without hurting your selves. All our profits center on you, and the more you take from us, the less we can lay out on you.

By this time, George Grenville was well under way in the first stage of his revenue policy, tightening English customs controls on smuggling. But Franklin did not see these initial actions as portents of greater difficulties to come. He was, perhaps, too convinced that the English would not be so foolish as to take actions that would damage their greater interests—especially when those interests included the economic benefits they were enjoying in the expanding

American market. Franklin did not understand Grenville's obstinate temperament and political will—or the English capacity for sticking with mistakes.

Besides, Franklin had other things on his mind: the renewed controversy between the Pennsylvania Assembly and the new governor, John Penn, over taxes; his relations with his ultra-Loyalist son, William, now governor of New Jersey; and Pontiac's War, which had reached the outskirts of Philadelphia. Franklin was also concerned for his own political fortunes. The king could suspend at any time his royal appointment as assistant postmaster general for the colonies, which carried a stipend of three hundred pounds per year. Franklin was usually inclined toward caution and prudence anyway. Since news took quite a while crossing the Atlantic, he played "wait and see," believing that compromise was always possible, that reason and logic could prevail.

This indifference did not endear Franklin to the hard-liners, the ultrapatriotic Sam Adams, John Adams, John Hancock, and others. Franklin's personality and his penchant for playing the diplomat made the impatient younger men suspicious of him, thinking him timid, lacking in the forcefulness necessary to defend American interests. It was not until after his return to London late in 1764 that Franklin abandoned his laissez-faire attitude toward the Stamp Act.

The condition of the English customs service in 1763 would have agitated any prime minister, let alone a penny-wise George Grenville. The Board of Trade estimated that approximately £700,000 of merchandise was being smuggled into the American colonies annually without a cent of duty being collected. A summary of duties raised by the Molasses Act of 1733 showed that in thirty years, up to 1763, the sixpence-per-gallon duty collected came to £21,652, a mere £700 per year.

Worst of all, when the Treasury totaled up the cost of the customs service in America, it discovered that the agents' salaries came to about eight thousand pounds per year—but annual collections amounted only to some two thousand pounds. In George Grenville's eyes, this situation was completely out of control.

Grenville quickly found one reason for all this: The customs service was part of the patronage system. Once safely ensconced on the royal payroll, men who had been appointed to the American colonies settled down comfortably—in England. They drew their pay and delegated their duties on the other side of the Atlantic to subordinates, who were described by the London *Public Advertiser* as "needy wretches who find it easier, and more profitable not only to wink but to sleep in their beds; the Merchants' Pay being more generous than the King's." Grenville took short, sharp action. He corrected the situation by ordering British placemen to get to their posts in America or get off the patronage payroll.

Grenville issued a flock of new regulations. Shipowners, shipmasters, and merchants were all enmeshed in a web of red tape to improve customs controls. There were new requirements for certificates, affidavits, warrants, bonds, clearance orders. Owners must now post bond on a cargo *before* it left harbor, not after, lest they "forget" to pay customs. The Royal Navy was dispatched to patrol the American coast, particularly New England, to assist the customs service. The *Boston Gazette* groaned, "Men of war, cutters, marines with their bayonets fixed, judges of admiralty, collectors, comptrollers, searchers, tide waiters, land waiters, and a whole catalogue of pimps are sent hither not to protect our trade but to distress it."

Perhaps the greatest wave of indignation in the sea of Grenville edicts came over an order that enlarged the authority of the Admiralty Court. The court could now try smugglers, customs evaders, shipowners, and others accused of violating commercial regulations. Under English law, such cases were decided by a judge alone, without a jury; and the judge received a 5 percent commission on all fines and condemnations collected. Moreover, the Admiralty Court for North America was located at Royal Navy headquarters in Halifax, Nova Scotia, to which violators were to be transported.

In actual fact, few Americans were ever transported—but this did not lessen colonial outrage. The *Boston Gazette* groaned some more over the fate of those who had been "seized by numerous swarms of horse-leeches who never cease crying Give! Give!, thrown into a prerogative court, a court of Admiralty, there to be judged, forfeited and condemned without a jury."

Tempers were rising among the shipowners and merchants in the ports—and now, along came Grenville's revision of the Molasses Act.

*　　*　　*

The making of rum was an enormous, profitable, and thoroughly nefarious business in America and a major element in the Triangular Trade. In the first leg of the triangle, Americans exported timber, fish, cotton goods, and some light manufacturing to the French Caribbean. (These islands were, at the time, more prosperous and heavily populated than the British West Indies and constituted a very good market.) Then, using the profits from these sales, Americans bought molasses from the French sugarcane planters. (To protect French cognac from competition, the planters were forbidden by the French authorities to operate rum distilleries.) So the French molasses was shipped to the colonies. Now, with a wink and a bribe to the customs officers, the molasses was distilled into high-quality rum. Some was sold on the domestic market, some was bartered to the Indians. But the real profit came from sales to slave traders, who brought their human cargo from Africa to sell in the southern colonies and the Caribbean. Having disposed of their cargo, they would stock up with American rum for the voyage to Africa, where it would be used to stupefy native blacks and lure fresh cargoes onto the slave ships. The traders would pay for the rum with deposits to American bank accounts in London; the profits would pay English merchants for goods shipped across the Atlantic to the colonies.

Rhode Island was a prime example of the economic importance of the Triangular Trade. With a 1763 population of about forty-eight thousand, Rhode Island operated more than thirty rum distilleries—one for every sixteen hundred of its citizens. The colony imported or smuggled an impressive total of fourteen thousand hogsheads of molasses annually and from this produced a million and a half gallons of rum. The Rhode Island legislature itself offered these figures to the London Board of Trade, pointing out that the colony's imports from England were valued at £120,000 annually— about £25 per person. With little understatement, the colony's memorandum declared that distilling rum "was the main hinge upon which the trade of the colony turns."

Word came that Grenville was considering changing the Molasses Act and reducing the tax from sixpence to threepence per gallon. But the new version would also apply to the previously untaxed molasses from the British West Indian islands. There was an uproar. In

August 1763, the chief justice of Massachusetts, Thomas Hutchinson, wrote to Omniscient Jackson that

> To reduce the duty to a penny per gallon I find would be generally agreeable to the people here, and the merchants would readily pay it. . . . But do they see the consequences? Will not they be introductory to taxes, duties and excises upon articles, and would this consist with the much esteemed privilege of English subjects—the being taxed by their own representatives?

Hutchinson came from one of Massachusetts's oldest families, and he was well respected. He was, nevertheless, a loyal and ambitious servant of King George III. He attempted to alert George Grenville to the battle cry that would soon sweep the colonies: "No taxation without representation!"

But Grenville was unswerving in his belief that England had the constitutional right of full sovereignty to tax her possessions as she chose. He told the House of Commons, "I hope that the powers and sovereignty of Parliament over every part of the British dominions *for the purpose of raising or collecting any tax* would never be disputed" [emphasis added].

And no one in Parliament disputed his statement—at that time. His error lay not in his interpretation of constitutional rights but in his lack of political wisdom. Hutchinson's message—that the colonists would grumble but in the end pay the duty—was what Grenville wanted to hear. Omniscient Jackson, acting in a dual capacity as agent for Massachusetts and Grenville's secretary, lobbied for lowering the intended duty to a penny and a half per gallon. But Grenville could see no trouble ahead, only grumbling, and there was already plenty of this in England.

In March 1764, Grenville was ready to introduce the first of his tax measures to the Americans—the Sugar Act, to replace the Molasses Act. His peers considered it sweet reasonableness itself. He would cut the tax on molasses, but by extending the tax to all molasses, Grenville would increase revenue from the Americans. The Royal Navy and the now rejuvenated customs service were supposed to ensure the collection of the new duties. The Sugar Act was nodded through Parliament on April 5 on a voice vote and was scheduled to take effect six months later.

So Grenville was over his first hurdle in raising money from the colonies. Now he was ready to go on with the Stamp Act, and a complaisant Parliament was ready to follow him along this road to disaster.

After the Sugar Act breezed through Parliament, Grenville informed the House of Commons that it would be necessary to raise further revenues in the colonies. A stamp tax was a tax collector's dream act: It was largely self-enforcing since it made impossible the conduct of business or the business of life—registering a birth, graduate certification, marriage, death, or will—without first purchasing a stamp.

Meanwhile, with the Sugar Act about to take effect in October, combined with advance warning of the Stamp Act, alarm bells began to sound in America. Official protests began arriving in London from the colonial capitals. Some of these objections were addressed directly to the king, others to the House of Commons. Yet others took the form of instructions that required colonial agents in London to make known to the Board of Trade and other responsible authorities the views of the colonial governments.

One of the most forthright of these protests was lodged by the New York Assembly, which passed a resolution in October 1764 titled Rights and Privileges. In this resolution, the assembly declared that colonial rights included "an exemption from the burthen of all taxes not granted by themselves which, even if a mere privilege, could not, unless abused, be justly taken from the people, and in fact there has been no abuse."

South Carolina was equally direct, instructing its agent "to oppose the passing of the bill for laying a Stamp Duty or any other tax on this colony," declaring that such action would be "inconsistent with the inherent rights of every British subject not to be taxed but by his own consent or that of his representatives."

Massachusetts and Connecticut passed resolutions affirming the right of Parliament to levy *external* taxes, such as customs duties, but disallowing *internal* taxes, such as the Stamp Act. Pennsylvania took a softer line, instructing Omniscient Jackson to prevail upon Parliament to repeal the Sugar Act and not create taxes that would harm trade with England. North Carolina, New Jersey, and Rhode Island also sent protests to their agents, against both the Sugar and the Stamp acts.

Grenville paid scant attention to this chorus of protests. He was convinced of Parliament's *right* to tax the colonies, and he was determined to press on down his chosen path.

In England, an island with a concentrated population, a stamp act was easy to enforce. Grenville simply did not understand that America was a different country. He never attempted to examine the differences in geography, distance, and population density in America, nor did he stop to consider the political repercussions of imposing such an act. England had been wise enough not to try to export its stamp-tax system to Ireland, just a short boat ride across the Irish Sea—but Grenville was ready to ship it to America, three thousand miles across the Atlantic.

The new law was supposed to be simple to apply and administer. Grenville would appoint stamp-tax officers for each of the thirteen colonies, and these officers would be empowered to open suboffices in towns and villages. The system would work just as it did in England. All official papers—birth and death certificates and marriage licenses, for instance—would have to be taken to the stamp office where, on receipt of the legal stamping fee, they would be embossed with a stamp or receive an ink stamp similar to a postal cancellation. Printed revenue stamps of varying denominations could be purchased at the stamp office and affixed to documents to indicate that the proper tax had been paid. Documents without stamps were illegal; no court case could proceed until all pertinent documents bore the correct stamps. And there were, of course, fines and penalties for failure to have the proper stamps or attempts to avoid the stamp tax.

The legal machinery for the Stamp Act began to turn in August 1764, when Lord Halifax, the secretary of state for the Southern Department in charge of the Americas, addressed a circular letter to the colonial governors. In it, he directed them to send on without delay "all instruments made use of in public transactions, law proceedings, grants, conveyances, securities of land or money within your government." These would be cataloged by the Board of Trade and the Treasury and used for drafting the Stamp Act. The authorship of the act was entrusted to Thomas Whately, joint secretary of the Treasury. He completed the draft, which was approved by the Treasury on December 17, 1764.

Whately seems to have taken his assignment as an opportunity to impose retribution on the obstreperous and ungrateful Americans. One of his recommendations read:

> On admission to any of the professions or to university degree, stamp duties should certainly be as high in America as in England. It would indeed be better if they were raised here and there considerably, *in order to keep mean persons out of those situations in life which they disgrace.* [Emphasis added.]

So Americans who wanted to go to a university had to pay two pounds for a matriculation certificate and another two pounds in stamp tax on a diploma (in England, the comparable tax was only two shillings). For admission to the bar, Americans would pay ten pounds (English lawyers paid six pounds). Stamp taxes would be levied on the probate of wills, liquor licenses, deeds, leases, mortgages, insurance policies, bonds, ship charters, bills of lading, customs clearances, newspapers, pamphlets, books, almanacs, advertisements, playing cards, dice. Without the stamp, no legal document was admissible in court. Heavy penalties were imposed on lawyers who attempted to proceed without the proper stamps and on vendors who sold untaxed newspapers. Moreover, such cases were to be tried in Admiralty Courts, not civil courts.

While the legislation was being written, the English Treasury ordered large printings of revenue stamps shipped to America. There were one-penny stamps for newspapers and pamphlets, which cost could be passed on to the purchaser; four-penny stamps for books and almanacs; and stamps of larger denominations for more important documents and transactions. Special dies were designed for embossing these stamps.*

Thus it was that the Stamp Act fashioned by George Grenville was a revenue measure that would reach into the pocket, life, and livelihood of every citizen in even the remotest frontier settlement. It affected every court of law, every school, every ship and boat—and the harbor itself. It was, to the Americans, not just a tax measure but an iniquitous and punitive piece of social legislation.

---

*When the Stamp Act was repealed, in 1766, the Treasury was left with a bill for £630 in printing costs for stamps that had either never landed or had been burned or hidden away, never to be used, by angry Americans.

* * *

In January 1765, the preliminary work on the Stamp Act was completed. Just as Grenville was about to introduce the act, King George III was stricken with the first major attack of what is now known to have been the disease porphyria. The king, still a young man of only twenty-six, was very sick indeed, with nausea, fever, pulmonary difficulties, chest pains, weakness, and a feverish agitation. His bewildered and virtually helpless doctors reported on January 13 "a violent cold, a restless night, complained of stitches [pain] in his breast. His Majesty was blooded 14 ounces."

During this first attack, though the king was at times incoherent or distraught, at no time did he show signs of "madness" or mental derangement. The fever came and went. When he had a little strength, he would sign papers and dictate brief instructions. He even managed to receive George Grenville at least half a dozen times during the attack's three months' duration. They did not discuss the Stamp Act; it was simply a routine tax measure that was making its orderly progress through Parliament.

By March 22, the porphyria attack was beginning to recede. The king signed a royal decree of assent to the Stamp Act, along with several other pieces of legislation. He returned to full duties in mid-April.

A myth originated then that persisted for almost two centuries, that the Stamp Act was a by-product of the king's "madness." The Stamp Act may have been madness, but not the king's.

All the American colonies had agents in London at the time, but none of them appears to have lobbied very hard or effectively. Omniscient Jackson, although he had experience, personality, and plenty of excellent contacts, was, after all, Grenville's private secretary and a member of the House of Commons—in addition to being agent for Massachusetts, Connecticut, and Pennsylvania. His loyalties were . . . divided. Benjamin Franklin was still at home in Philadelphia and could do nothing. The London-based agents were largely lacking in experience, contacts, and credibility.

Grenville, having heard nothing untoward from the royal governors, had paid no attention to formal protests from the colonial assemblies. He did realize, however, that it made sense to give the colonial agents a polite hearing, so he invited four of the most influential to a meeting on February 2, 1765, four days before he would present the act to Parliament. Franklin, who had recently returned to London, attended. Omniscient Jackson sat in for Massachusetts; Charles Garth, who, like Jackson, was an MP, represented Maryland and South Carolina. The fourth man was Jared Ingersoll, a distinguished and influential conservative who was often in London representing Connecticut on important political and trade matters. Jared Ingersoll left the only known record of the meeting, in a letter to Thomas Fitch, governor of Connecticut:

> Mr. Grenville gave us a full hearing and told us he took no pleasure in giving Americans so much uneasiness as he found he did—that it was the Duty of his Office to manage the revenue—that he really was made to believe that considering the whole of the Circumstances of the Mother Country and the Colonies, the latter could and ought to pay something, & that he knew of no better way than that now pursuing to lay such Tax, but if we could tell him of a better way he would adopt it.
>
> We then urged that the method the people had been used to—that it would at least seem to be their own Act & prevent that uneasiness & jealousy which otherwise we feared would take place—that they could raise the money best by their own Officers &c &c. . . . Mr. Grenville asked if we could agree upon the several proportions Each colony should raise. We told him No. He said he did not think any body here [in London] was furnished with Materials for that purpose; and that there would be no Certainty that every Colony would raise the Sum enjoined & to be obliged to compel some to do their duty, and that for perhaps one year only, would be very inconvenient. . . .
>
> Upon the whole he said he had pledged his word for offering the Stamp Act to the House, and that the House would hear all our objections and would do as they thought Best; that their Ears will always be open to any remonstrations from the Americans with respect to this bill both before it takes effect & after, if it shall take effect, which shall be exprest in a becoming manner, that is, as becomes subjects of the same common Prince.

With only two Americans at this meeting, matters were heavily weighted in Grenville's favor. Face to face with Grenville, the Americans did not attempt to protest the constitutionality of this "taxation without representation." In any case, with two MPs representing three of the colonies, there would be no consensus. They could do no more than resign themselves to the prime minister's will.

The only debate on the bill took place in the House of Commons on February 6. A handful of members—Jackson and Garth included—spoke up on behalf of the colonies, mildly remonstrating against the bill. Then Charles Townshend, speaking on behalf of the government, interjected this typically pompous rhetoric:

> Now, will these Americans, children planted by our care, nourished by our indulgence until grown to a degree of strength and opulence, protected by our arms, will they grudge to contribute a mite to relieve us from the heavy weight of that burden which we lie under for their defense?

Up rose Colonel Isaac Barré, a tall, fierce, rough-talking one-eyed veteran who had fought with Wolfe at the Plains of Abraham. Unlike virtually every other MP, Barré knew America firsthand and was devoted to the American cause. Barré turned on Townshend and replied in passionate oratory:

> They, planted by *your* care? No! Your oppression planted 'Em in America, They fled your tyranny to an uncultivated and unhospitable country where they exposed themselves to almost all the hardships to which human nature is liable, and among others to the cruelty of a Savage foe. And yet, actuated by the Principles of English Liberty, they met all these hardships with pleasure, compared with those they suffered in their own Country, from the hands of those who should have been their friends.
>
> They, nourished by *your* Indulgence? They grew up by your neglect of 'Em; as soon as you began to care about 'Em, that care was exercised in sending persons to rule over 'Em—sent to spy out their Liberty, to misrepresent their Actions, to prey on 'Em.
>
> They, protected by *your* Arms? They have nobly taken up Arms in your defense, have exerted a valour against their consent and Laborious industry for the defense of a Country whose frontiers, while drenched in blood, its interior Parts have yielded all its little Savings to your Emolument. And believe me, and remember I this day told you so, that some spirit of Freedom which actuated that people at first will accompany them still—but Prudence forbids me to explain myself further.
>
> God Knows I do not act at this Time to speak from motives of

party Heat, what I deliver are the Genuine Sentiments of my heart. I
claim to know more of America than most of you, having seen and
been conversant in that Country. The People I believe are as truly
Loyal as any Subjects the King has, but a people Jealous of their
Liberties who will vindicate them, if ever they should be violated—
but the subject is too delicate and I will say no more.

Isaac Barré was warning Commons that revolution could be in
the making, but this was something that George Grenville could
neither see nor comprehend. Jared Ingersoll, listening in the gal-
lery and taking notes on the speech, called it "very handsome and
moving." Nevertheless, Grenville kept the votes. The House of
Commons, by a vote of 245 to 49, agreed to go ahead with the
legislation. Final passage came by voice vote in Commons on February 27; it was nodded through the House of Lords on March 8.
The Stamp Act would take effect in the colonies on November 1,
1765.

The Treasury estimated that the Stamp Act would produce only
about sixty thousand pounds in its first year. Why, then, did George
Grenville stir up so much trouble for so little revenue? Partly because he was incapable of foresight, partly because the prevailing
attitude of the English, heavily taxed themselves, was that the Americans were making a big fuss over a paltry sum. The crucial point of
"taxation without representation" was ignored. One typical letter
to the London *Daily Advertiser* asserted, somewhat ungrammati-
cally, that Americans "must be the veriest beggars in the world if
such an inconsiderable duties appears to be an intolerable burthens
to their eyes."

But by the end of 1765, the rebellious colonies had embargoed
English goods, English factories were laying off workers, unemployment was on the rise. Politicians and letter writers now asked why
Grenville had risked so much to collect so little and in doing so had
plunged England into an economic depression. William Pitt called
Grenville "a wretched financier who sought to bring the Treasury a
peppercorn to the risque of millions to the nation."

A year after the passage of the Stamp Act, its repeal was under way
in Parliament. But it was too late to undo the damages on both

sides: Even as it voted for repeal, in March 1766, Parliament also voted an unnecessary, unwise declaration reasserting its sovereign right to impose taxes on its colonies. To this declaration, Parliament would cling blindly—all the way to war.

Chapter 5

THE CRISIS

By April 1765, King George III had recovered enough from his bout with porphyria to return to his duties. Domestic matters, not the American colonies, were uppermost in his mind. First, he wished to see quick enactment of a bill to provide a regent to assume his duties if he were again seriously incapacitated. Next, he would rid himself of George Grenville.

A bill to establish a Regency Council was introduced in Parliament by Grenville. At the king's request, legislation would establish a council, but it did not specify which of the council members would be regent. If he became ill again, the king wished to make that choice himself. Grenville's legislation appointed Queen Charlotte; the king's elderly uncle, the duke of Cumberland; and the king's four younger brothers as members of the council. But Grenville deliberately excluded the king's mother, the dowager Princess Augusta. Why? The princess was a friend of the earl of Bute, and Grenville was afraid that if she were on the Regency Council and then were named as regent by the king, she might immediately send for Lord Bute to form a government.

The king was furious at the omission. Horace Walpole wrote that it was "a heinous insult to the Princess and treachery to the King." The King's Friends in Parliament joined with Grenville's enemies, and together they maneuvered behind the scenes to amend the bill to include the princess's name. The king was now determined that Grenville had to go.

Once again, he made secret overtures to William Pitt, sending the ill and obese duke of Cumberland to the country to sound out Pitt on his terms for a return to power. The meeting only served to heighten Pitt's sense of indispensability and increase his terms for bailing out the king.

A period of icy hostility set in between the king and Grenville over the next six weeks. Government business came to a virtual standstill. The king snubbed Grenville—but where was he going to find a new prime minister? At this point, he wrote in some anguish to his "dearest friend" Bute:

> I have been for near a week as it were in a feaver my very sleep is not free from thinking of the men I daily see; paitence cannot last I en-cline much to putting everything to a quick upshot; that I may know who are my friends, and who secret foes; excuse the incoherency of my letter; but a mind ulcer'd by the treatment it meets from all around is the true cause of it.

While the king tossed in mental fever over Grenville, the American colonies were far from his thoughts, but not for much longer. News of the Stamp Act's passage had reached America about the same time as the king had returned from his illness. Even though the law was not to take effect for another six months, the Americans were not going to sit and wait to make their reactions known. The Stamp Act served as a torch to very dry political tinder: the growing list of grievances against the government in London. But it was not until the end of the summer of 1765 that London began to realize the full extent of the crisis that was brewing.

Even Benjamin Franklin, now settled back in his familiar London surroundings, failed to comprehend what was happening. He wrote in July to a Philadelphia friend, Charles Thompson, that "I took every step in my power to prevent the passing, but the tide was too strong against us." In a tone of resignation, he concluded:

> The nation was provoked by American claims of independence, and all parties joined in resolving by this act to settle the point. We might

as well have hindered the sun's setting. That we could not do. But since 'tis down, my friend, and it might take a long time before it riases again, let us make a good night of it as we can. We may still light candles. Frugality and industry will go a great way toward indemnifying us. Idleness and pride tax with a heavier hand than Kings and Parliament; if we can get rid of the former, we may easily hear from the latter.

These sentiments, coming from the comfort of Craven Street, were far from reflecting the mood on High Street (today's Market Street) in Philadelphia. Further, Franklin had made a questionable move in cooperating with the English on the Stamp Act. This would cost him dearly before the year was out. In his papers, Franklin recorded this miscalculation:

Some days before the Stamp Act was passed, to which I had given all the opposition I could with Mr. Grenville, I received a note from Mr. Whately desiring to see me the next morning. I waited upon him accordingly, and found several other colonial agents with him. He acquainted us that Mr. Grenville was desirous to make the execution of the act as little inconvenient and disagreeable to the Americans as possible; and therefore did not think of sending stamp officers from hence, but wished to have discreet and reputable persons appointed in each province from among the inhabitants as would be acceptable to them; for as they were to pay the tax, he thought strangers should not have the emoluments. Mr. Whately therefore wished us to name for our respective colonies, informing us that Mr. Grenville would be obliged to us for pointing out to him honest and responsible men, and would pay great regard to our nominations.

Since such patronage went hand in hand with power, this was an ingratiating offer from Grenville. It carried with it the certainty of good remuneration for those who became stamp agents. So, while Franklin had opposed the Stamp Act, it was now law, and he neither resisted nor remonstrated but instead cooperated, taking Grenville's bait.

Franklin passed Pennsylvania's appointment to a Philadelphia friend, John Hughes. In Massachusetts, Chief Justice Thomas Hutchinson lobbied on behalf of his brother-in-law. Franklin then urged Jared Ingersoll to offer his services, and Ingersoll was appointed for Connecticut.

In the fury that broke out during the summer and autumn of 1765, Hughes and Ingersoll were both hounded out of office before they had dispensed even a single stamp. Ingersoll's home was attacked, and he himself was later tried in absentia and burned in effigy. On the outskirts of Boston, the homes of both Hutchinson and his brother-in-law were burned. In Philadelphia, demonstrators surrounded Hughes's house but did not set it on fire. Then they headed for Franklin's house. Had Franklin not been in London, he might well have shared the fate of Ingersoll. The demonstrators came close to torching his home and were prevented only by a posse of Franklin's friends and supporters.

Meanwhile, in Williamsburg, Virginia, a newly elected twenty-nine-year-old lawyer had taken his seat in the House of Burgesses. Nine days later, on May 29, 1765, he delivered a speech that would make him an American immortal. He was Patrick Henry.

Virginia of the 1760s was by far the most populous of the colonies, larger than either Massachusetts or Pennsylvania by more than 100,000 (but this figure included some 140,000 black slaves). Virginia's gentlemen farmers were among the largest private landholders in the colonies, and the wealthiest. They lived a life of luxury in grand houses, attended by their many black servants. In their own eyes, they were both the aristocracy and the intelligentsia of America.

In the colonial government at Williamsburg, the older aristocrats held much the same oligarchic power as the Whigs in London. But when Patrick Henry was elected to the House of Burgesses, the younger political generation was already becoming restive.

The new member of the house was a lively blade with dash and charm who loved music and dancing. He had already made a name for himself as a lawyer more gifted in courtroom eloquence and drama than in depth or intellect. He arrived full of self-confidence and a determination to make an immediate impact on the Virginia legislature and politics—and he succeeded at once, and far beyond his expectations.

When Patrick Henry rose to address the House of Burgesses on that May morning, it was the end of the spring session. Most of the older legislators, as was their habit, had already departed for their country estates. Only 39 out of 116 members were still present in the chamber, and most of these were younger men.*

The Stamp Act was, of course, the hot topic in the colonies. An earlier session in the House of Burgesses had adopted and dispatched to London a carefully worded petition to the king and a memorandum to the House of Commons remonstrating against the new tax. The tidewater conservatives were content to leave it that way, but this was not good enough for Patrick Henry. He took the floor with a rousing denunciation of taxation without representation. Then, according to a Frenchman's account, Henry blazed out at King George and declared that "in former times, Tarquin and Julius had their Brutus, Charles had his Cromwell, and he Did not Doubt that some Good American would stand up, in favor of his country."

At this point, the Frenchman recorded, Henry was stopped by the speaker of the house, who called him to order for speaking "utter treason" and rebuked other members for not having interrupted. Henry replied to the speaker that "what he said must be attributed to the interests of his country's dying liberty which he had at heart, and the heat of passion might have led him to say something more than he intended, but if he said anything wrong he begged the Speaker's and the House's pardon." He was then allowed to continue.

Henry was well prepared. He pulled from his pocket a series of seven resolutions that he had drafted condemning the Stamp Act and asked for their immediate consideration. The house then adjourned, to return the next day for the final day of its session. The fascinated Frenchman also returned "and heard very hot debates still about the stamp duties."

Although most of the thirty-nine members still present were young hawks, there were among them three distinguished older men of the aristocracy: the colony's attorney general, Peyton Ran-

---

*It is a historic curiosity that the most detailed account of the proceedings was left by an anonymous Frenchman who happened to be visiting Williamsburg at the time. He listened, fascinated, from the visitors' lobby, and his account was subsequently published in a *Journal of a French Traveller in the Colonies*. He is believed to have been a French government agent, the chevalier d'Annemours.

dolph; former speaker of the house John Randolph; and George Wythe, a leading lawyer in the colony. They all argued that before they passed any more resolutions, they should await a response on earlier ones on the Stamp Act that had already been sent to London. But the younger men were defiant, and the seven resolves were submitted for approval.

The most important was the fifth, which read:

> *Resolved,* That the General Assembly of this colony *have the only and sole exclusive right and power to lay Taxes and Impositions upon the Inhabitants of this Colony* and that every Attempt to vest such Power in any Person or Persons whatsoever other than the General Assembly aforesaid has a manifest Tendency to destroy British as well as American Freedom. [Emphasis added.]

The sixth and seventh resolves were even more inflammatory and seditious. One declared that Virginians were "not bound to yield obedience to any law or ordinance whatever . . . other than laws or ordinances of the General Assembly." The other stipulated that "any person who shall by speaking or writing assert or maintain that any person or persons other than the General Assembly of this Colony have any right or power to impose or lay any taxation on the people shall be deemed an enemy to His Majesty's Colony." In effect, Patrick Henry was trying to suppress freedom of speech in Virginia in the name of American liberty!

In the ensuing debate, the older conservatives succeeded in having the sixth and seventh resolves withdrawn. (When news of the resolves spread to the other colonies, all seven were reported and printed as if they had all been adopted.) The first five were put to individual votes and passed. The largest majority for any one was 22 to 17. Virginia had spoken, and it did not matter that out of its total of 116 assembly members, only 39 were present, and only 22 had carried the resolves.

The effect was immediate. Instead of making another protest to London, the Virginia assembly had rejected the Stamp Act outright—in effect declared it illegal in the colony—and sanctified open resistance if the English tried to enforce it. Virginia had acted, and the other colonies would not lag far behind.

Violence and demonstrations against the Stamp Act flared up

along the Atlantic seaboard during the summer of 1765. The assemblies of eight other colonies passed resolutions similar to Virginia's, and at the end of the summer, on Massachusetts's initiative, nine colonies agreed to meet in New York in a Stamp Act Congress to take a stand on the taxation issue. New Hampshire, North Carolina, and Georgia stayed away. Virginia did not attend because its lieutenant governor, Francis Fauquier, had dissolved its rebellious legislature. Representatives of the nine met in New York in October. They agreed upon a declaration that was more moderate in tone than Patrick Henry's work but was just as unyielding in its attitude.

After declaring its affection for King George III and acknowledging "all due subordination" to Parliament, the Stamp Act Congress repeated the stand that the colonies could not be taxed except by their own assemblies. They asserted that England's monopoly on colonial trade was a sufficient contribution for America to make toward the expenses of the empire, and they expressed willingness to accept "external taxes" for regulation of trade but not an "internal tax" like the Stamp Act.

This rang a loud alarm bell in London. For the first time, the American colonies were uniting in an embryo federation to adopt a common policy against an act of the English Parliament. Along with its newfound political unity, the colonies were engaging in civil violence that was beginning to take on the force of a revolution.

By the time the news of all this reached London, the king had found a replacement for Grenville. More specifically, the duke of Cumberland, consulting with the most influential of old Whigs, the duke of Newcastle, had found one for him. In the four years since Pitt had been ousted, a bloc of younger Whigs had formed around the marquess of Rockingham in the House of Lords and a brilliant newcomer in Commons, Edmund Burke. The duke of Newcastle would have been unacceptable to the king as prime minister, but Newcastle was prepared to support Rockingham. Thus it was that the young Whigs took power in mid-July, with Rockingham as prime minister.

George Grenville had a final, frosty interview with the king on July 10. By now aware of the havoc the Stamp Act was causing, Grenville was nevertheless unyielding on how to deal with it. Solemnly, he intoned to the king that "as you value your own safety, allow no one to draw the line between your British and American dominions." The colonies were, he said, "the richest jewel in His Majesty's crown," and if anyone were to try to subvert or defeat "by a slackness of execution" the laws that governed the colonies, then that person should be considered "a criminal and a betrayer of his country." On that note, Grenville and the king parted.

The marquess of Rockingham, then thirty-five, was an honorable gentleman, amiable and well liked, but with little government experience. His greater interests lay in horse racing. An English historian wrote of him that he was "a shy young man, a tongue-tied politician, capable of winning a measure of support but not of esteem; a well-meaning but indolent leader whose good intentions, if they did not pave the streets of hell, too often trod the road to Newmarket [race track]." One of Rockingham's few contributions to political thought came in a remark to the duke of Cumberland: "I must say, Sir, that to hesitate is laudable."

In the House of Lords, Rockingham sat so attentive and silent— one of the most silent prime ministers in English history—that on one occasion when he did finally speak, the king wrote to him, "I am much pleased that opposition has forced you to hear your own voice, which I hope will encourage you to stand forth in other debates." The king was, however, relieved not to be constantly lectured, as he had been by Grenville. This was, nevertheless, a weak and insecure government under a prime minister notably lacking in leadership qualities.

Parliament had begun its long (six-month) recess when Rockingham became prime minister, so he found it politic to do nothing about the growing crisis in America. Both he in Lords and Henry Seymour Conway in Commons had viewed the Stamp Act as a mistake, but three members of his cabinet were strongly for it and adamantly opposed to any "retreat" before American demands. This group was led by the imperious attorney general Charles Yorke. So Rockingham hesitated till Christmas.

But in the colonies there was no such hesitation. In August, a Sons of Liberty mob in Boston sacked and burned the home of Chief Justice Thomas Hutchinson. When the news reached London

that the Americans were so out of control that they had threatened
a royal judge, it succeeded in driving home the gravity of the crisis.
On October 18, *Lloyd's Evening Post* gave the news a four-column
report, culled from newly arrived American newspapers. The paper's
London printer remarked on the seriousness of the disorders and
how they reflected on the spirits of the colonists. The printer declared it his paper's duty to provide "every information in our power
relative to the excesses," and he begged his readers "to excuse the
length of the following articles on account of the subject."

In August, when Franklin first read about the Virginia resolves in
the London press, he wrote to John Hughes, his nominee to be
Pennsylvania's stamp agent, saying that "the rashness of the Assembly in Virginia is amazing." He advised Hughes that efforts to get
the act repealed were under way, "but success is uncertain." He
counseled

> a firm loyalty to the Crown and faithful adherence to the government
> of this nation, which is the safety as well as the honour of the colonies
> to be connected with, will always be the wisest course for you and I to
> take, whatever may be the madness of the populace or their blind
> leaders, who can only bring themselves and country into trouble and
> draw on greater burthens by acts of rebellious tendency.

Philadelphians thought otherwise. By the time Franklin's letter
reached Hughes, the city had been engulfed. In September, a mob
formed and demonstrators demanded that Hughes resign. There
were motions to march on the homes of Franklin and Hughes.

William Franklin, now governor of New Jersey, hurried across the
Delaware River to persuade Deborah Franklin to return with him to
safety at his residence in Burlington. But Deborah stoutly refused to
be driven from her home. After it was all over, she wrote her husband a letter that probably reached him around the end of October.
She began, as each did when writing the other, by addressing him
as "My Dear child" (Deborah's spelling shows her to be bravely
semiliterate):

> You will se by the papers what worke has hapened in other plases and
> sumthing has bin sed relaiteing to raising a mob in this plase. I was for
> 9 day keep in one Contineued hurrey by pepel to removef and Salley
> [Franklin's daughter] was perswaided to go to Burlington for saiftey

but on sunday laste we had verey graite rejoysing on a Count of the Change of the Ministrey [Rockingham replacing Grenville] and a preyperation for binfiers att night and several houses threatened to be puled down. Cusin Davenporte Come and told me that more than twenty pepel had told him it was his Duty to be with me. I sed I was plesed to reseve Civility from aney boday so he staid with me sum time to wards night I sed he shold fech a gun or two as we had none. I sente to ask my Brother [John Read] to Cume and bring his gun all so so we a mid one room into a Magazin. I ordored sum sort of defens up Stairs such as I cold manaig my self. I sed when I was advised to remove that I was verey shuer you had dun nothing to hurte aney bodey nor I had not given aney ofense to aney person att all nor wold I be maid unesey by aney bodey nor wold I stir or show the leste uneaseynis but if aney one Came to disturbe me I wold show a proper resentment and I shold be very much afrunted with aney bodey. I was told that thair was 8 hundred men readey to asiste aney one that shold be molisted.

Deborah Franklin stood her ground and supported her husband's actions, there in their home not five minutes' walk from the State House. Faced with the protective body of tradesmen, the mob's anger subsided, and the mob dispersed without doing any damage. But the crisis mounted.

In London, it was not so much the news of demonstrations and house burnings that finally persuaded the government to deal with Grenville's blunder. It was the economic consequences, the swift drying up of trade and commerce with America. Merchants and shipowners from Boston to Charleston suddenly canceled orders and stopped buying English goods—not merely to protest the tax, but because they were afraid of the rioting and looting of imports from England. And there was a genuine upsurge of patriotism that had never been felt before, a unity in opposition to England and its laws, a new and growing force in colonial politics.

The colonies were doing more than just cutting off imports. As November approached, and with it the date on which the Stamp Act would go into effect, English authorities were finding it impossible even to land the hated stamps. Virginia had already declared that the stamps were null and void, illegal, never to be used within its borders. When the stamps arrived in South Carolina, the governor ordered them to be locked up at Fort Johnson in Charleston, guarded by a fourteen-man platoon. A Sons of Liberty band of 150 stormed the fort, found the stamps, and burned them. In New Jersey, the Loyalist governor, William Franklin, persuaded the captain of a Royal Navy frigate to store the stamps in safety aboard his ship off Staten Island.

Paradoxically, the Stamp Act made the colonial embargo on English goods doubly effective. When the act took effect on November 1, there were neither stamps nor agents to administer it and enforce the law. Law-abiding London merchants were left high and dry on goods shipped to the colonies, since payment could not be made without the proper stamps. Glasgow merchants calculated at the end of 1765 that they held £1.5 million in unpaid debts in Virginia and Maryland.

In January 1766, Lord Dartmouth declared to the House of Lords that "not less than 50,000 men in this Kingdom are at this time ripe for rebellion for want of work from the uneasy situation in the colonies."

Major General Thomas Gage had succeeded Amherst in 1763 as commander in chief in the colonies. Gage was a workmanlike, careful, unimaginative soldier who did not like to take chances or make mistakes. He was well suited to his colonial tasks. He had married an American, Margaret Kembal, the daughter of a wealthy New Jersey family, and he enjoyed living in America. On the whole, he managed his job without arousing any personal enmity.

When the Stamp Act furor started, Gage had the ultimate responsibility for securing the colonies against insurrection. However, he did not have nearly enough troops in the right places at the right time to take any military action. After Pontiac's War, he had wished to reduce English forces in the west and concentrate them on the Atlantic seaboard. This would have made much more political and strategic sense for the British—but Gage had not been able to get clear instructions from London for carrying out this redeployment.

As the insurrection escalated, General Gage vented his frustrations in a dispatch, written to London on November 4, 1765:

> The general agreement not to take stamps has put a stop to Business, the people idle and exasperated, the whole wou'd immediately fly to

Arms and a Rebellion began without any preparation against it or any means to withstand it. This insurrection is composed of great numbers of Sailors headed by Captains of Privateers, and other Ships; Inhabitants of the Town joined by many who come in from the Neighboring Country and provinces; the Whole may amount to some thousands and will be likely to increase as the only opposition has been made here [in New York] and the people from the Country are said to be flocking in. . . .

Nothing effectual has been proposed to prevent or quell the tumult. I have sent Expresses to endeavour, if the season will admit of it, by draining the nearest posts to assemble what force I can at Albany, and they may from thence be brought down here as occasion shall require; but the force to be got from thence can 't be considerable. The rest of the provinces are in the same situation, as to a positive refusal to take the Stamps and threatening those who shall take them to plunder and murder them.

Gage concluded his dispatch with a clear and careful warning to his superiors that "as this affair stands in all the provinces, unless the Act will from its own nature at length enforce itself, *nothing but a very considerable Military force can do it*" [emphasis added]. In Gage's opinion, chances for enforcement of the act had disappeared altogether.

In any case, the careful Gage could not and would not have taken military action on his own initiative. There was no state of war. Strict and correct British procedure dictated that in peacetime, the army could not be called out to deal with civil disobedience unless the civil authorities (the colonial governors) made a formal request to the military commander. During the Stamp Act riots, no governor anywhere in the colonies would have dared to call out the troops— even if Gage had had enough troops with which to respond.

Moreover, no matter how loud some of the London politicians were in their demands to restore order and enforce the Stamp Act, the Rockingham government took a realistic view of the use of force. Henry Seymour Conway, in his position as the secretary of state who dealt with the Americans, had sent these instructions to Gage on October 24:

Events will probably create Applications to You, in which the utmost Exertion of your Prudence may be necessary, so as justly to temper your Conduct between Caution and Coolness, which the Delicacy of such a Situation may demand, on the one hand, and the Vigour necessary to suppress Outrage and Violence, on the other.

Conway told Gage that "positive instructions" were not possible and that the situation had to be left largely to the commander's own judgment. This cautious approach by London fitted with Gage's way of dealing with this (or any) situation.

London was fully informed about the deteriorating situation in America. In mid-January 1766, the *London Chronicle* reported that in New York, "a ship from Charleston docked but could not unload for lack of stamps"; in Boston, "the Courts are unanimous to proceed without stamps"; in Providence, "people throughout the government have solemnly declared that they will never use any Stamped paper"; in Annapolis, "the full court is resolved to transact business as usual without Stamps."

In December, with Parliament due to return from its long recess, Rockingham began to stir. He took the unusual step of forming a lobby of English merchants to challenge an act of Parliament. There were about fifty merchants sitting in Commons, at least ten of whom had American connections. Members representing large urban constituencies whose manufacturing enterprises were hurt by the loss of American trade might also be lined up to vote for revision or repeal of the Stamp Act.

Rockingham, not much of a speaker himself, had brought with him into his private office as his secretary and assistant Edmund Burke, whose name would make parliamentary history. It was he who took on the task of rallying the merchants into a lobby. And Burke was soon in contact with Benjamin Franklin, with whom he formed a friendship that lasted until Franklin's departure on the eve of the Revolution.

Rockingham also called in an American merchant, Barlow Trecothick of Massachusetts, who was living in London. Trecothick was asked to organize merchants outside Parliament; with the government's blessing, he formed a committee of twenty-eight London merchants who drafted an appeal to others throughout England:

The present State of British Trade to North America and the prospect of encreasing Embarrassments which threaten the Loss of our depending prosperity there as well as to annihilate the Trade itself have occasioned a general meeting to be called of the Merchants of this City concerned in that Branch of Business. We ask your Concurrence and Assistance in Support of a regular application to Parliament, or otherwise by a petition from your Body and all the Interest you can make with your Members of Parliament in your Neighborhood. . . . We desire to unite with you in a measure so essential to the best Interests of Great Britain.

Rockingham and Trecothick worked together on the petition to see that it was worded so as to make it clear that repeal of the Stamp Act was demanded in *British* interests, not as a concession to the Americans.

The response to the merchants' lobby was rapid and was beginning to take on force when Parliament returned from recess. But Rockingham was still not sure of what further action he needed to take.

When the king opened the new session of Parliament, indecision was reflected in his traditional speech from the throne. "Matters of importance in the colonies," he said, would demand serious attention. This was not good enough for Grenville, who immediately rose to object to such a mild reference to what he called "outrages." He offered a motion to declare the colonies in a state of rebellion. Two cabinet ministers spoke up in support of Grenville but persuaded him not to force his motion to a vote. When Parliament recessed for Christmas, it still had no idea what the government would do.

On the twenty-seventh of December, Rockingham finally called together his inner circle of Whig leaders. For five months, they had done nothing but watch and wait on events. Now they met at an informal dinner party to discuss the crisis—and the discussion that Rockingham had been avoiding proved to be inconclusive. The conversation was quickly taken over by Charles Yorke, whose father, the earl of Hardwicke, had held the office of attorney general during the reign of George II. The son, who had inherited both the office and the family traits of pride and hauteur, was adamantly against any "concessions" to the Americans. Instead, he proposed to the dinner guests that the government put before Parliament a "declaratory" act, which would bluntly reaffirm to the nation and to the Americans the supreme and unbounded power of Parliament to enact whatever laws it pleased. The dinner party turned into a wrangle between Yorke and Conway; Rockingham sat by in silence. When the dinner party was over, he still had neither a policy nor an idea of where he wanted to go or what he wanted to do. What he urgently needed was some heavyweight support to counter the factional cliques in Commons. He got it, quite unexpectedly, from William Pitt.

When the Commons reconvened after Christmas, it was not at all certain that Pitt would be able to attend the debate scheduled for January 14. All his life, he had been in up-and-down health; gout, his most serious affliction, was constant, painful, and debilitating. Nevertheless, his carriage brought him from his home at Hayes (near the site of London's present-day Heathrow Airport). He arrived at Westminster late, after the session was well under way. He hobbled to his seat and was recognized at once by the speaker. He wasted no time getting down to cases and gave the House one of the most historic, electrifying speeches of his long career.

He began by regretting that he had been ill and unable to attend the House when the Stamp Act was first introduced. He warmed up his audience by saying that "so great was the agitation of my mind for the consequences, I would have solicited some kind hand to have laid me down on this floor, to have borne testimony against it." He then stunned the Parliament by vehemently declaring:

> It is my opinion that this Kingdom has no right to lay a tax upon the colonies, to be sovereign and supreme in every circumstance of government and legislation whatsoever. They are the subjects of this kingdom, equally entitled with yourselves to all the natural rights of mankind and the peculiar privileges of Englishmen.

The Americans' plea of "no taxation without representation" was at last heard in London, voiced by one of the strongest, most eloquent members of Parliament. Relentlessly, Pitt continued:

> When in this House we give and grant, we give and grant what is our own. But in an American tax, what do we do? We give and grant our own property? No—we give and grant to Your Majesty the property of Your Majesty's commons of America. It is an absurdity in terms. The distinction between legislation and taxation is an essential necessary to liberty. . . .

The Commons of America, represented in their several assemblies, have ever been in possession of the exercise of this, their constitutional right of giving and granting their own money. They would be slaves if they had not enjoyed it. At the same time, this kingdom, as the supreme governing and legislative power, has always bound the colonies by her laws, by her regulations, and restrictions in trade, in navigation, in manufactures—in everything except that of taking their money out of their pockets without their consent.

Pitt was declaring on a grand scale what almost no other member of Parliament had dared say. Pitt was not merely questioning the wisdom of George Grenville's Stamp Act; he was denouncing the constitutional premise of the taxation powers of Parliament over the colonies.

When he sat down, there was a perceptible pause. There were murmurs and the shuffling of papers. Then Conway stood up and thanked Pitt for his speech. Grenville, sitting opposite Pitt, was incensed. He rose to be recognized by the speaker, charging back at Pitt, saying:

That this kingdom has the sovereign, the supreme legislative power over America is granted. It cannot be denied; and taxation is part of that sovereign power. It is one branch of legislation. It is, it has been exercised over those who are now, and never were, here represented. . . . When I proposed to tax America, I asked this House if any gentleman would object to the right. I repeatedly asked it, and no man would attempt to deny it.

Protection and obedience are reciprocal. Great Britain protects America; America is bound to yield obedience. If not, tell me when the Americans were emancipated? The seditious spirit of the colonies owes its birth to factions in this House, Gentlemen who are careless of the consequences of what they say, provided it answers the purpose of opposition.

As soon as Grenville finished speaking, Pitt was on his feet. Under House rules, he was out of order in seeking to speak a second time on the same parliamentary matter, but the members cheered him on, and nobody was about to raise a point of order against him. He launched into a flight of impassioned oratory:

Gentlemen, I have been charged with giving birth to sedition in America. Sorry I am to hear the liberty of speech in this House imputed as a crime. But the imputation shall not discourage me. It is a liberty I mean to exercise.

The gentleman tells us that America is obstinate; America is almost in open rebellion. I rejoice that America has resisted. Three millions of people, so dead to all feelings of liberty as voluntarily to submit to be slaves, would have been fit instruments to make slaves of the rest. I come not here armed at all points, with law cases and acts of Parliament, with the statute book doubled down in dogs'-ears, to defend the cause of liberty. . . . I would not debate a particular point of law with the gentleman; I know his abilities; I have been obliged by his diligent researches. But for the defense of liberty upon a general principle, upon a constitutional principle, it is a ground on which I stand firm, on which I may meet any man.

I am no courtier of America, I stand up for this kingdom. I maintain that the Parliament has a right to bind, to restrain America. . . . The greater must rule the less, but so rule as not to contradict the fundamental principles that are common to both. If the gentleman does not understand the difference between external and internal taxes, I cannot help it. . . .

The gentleman asks, when were the colonies emancipated? But I desire to know, when were they made slaves? . . . A great deal has been said of the strength of America. It is a topic that ought to be cautiously meddled with. In a good cause, on a sound bottom, the force of this country can crush America to atoms. But on this ground, on the Stamp Act, which so many here will think a crying injustice, I am one who will lift up my hand against it. In such a cause, your success would be hazardous. America, if she fell, would fall like a strong man; she would embrace the pillars of state, and pull down the constitution along with her.

William Pitt's oratory rolled on. The Americans "have not acted in all things with prudence and temper; they have been wronged; they have been driven to madness by injustice," he declared. But then he continued:

Will you punish them for the madness you have occasioned? Rather let prudence and temper come from this side. . . . Upon the whole, I beg leave to tell the House what is really my opinion. It is, that the Stamp Act be repealed absolutely, totally and immediately. That the reason for the repeal be assigned that it was founded on an erroneous principle. At the same time, let the sovereign authority of this country over the colonies be asserted in as strong terms as can be devised, and be made to extend to every point of legislation and the exercise of every power whatsoever—except that of taking money out of their pockets without their consent.

Pitt had elevated and transformed the Stamp Act debate into an issue on the constitutional rights of Americans rather than the right of Parliament to make laws. He was not preaching American independence, but neither did he want the government in London to tear the empire apart on a matter of petty finance.

At last, there was a clear lead for the government, . . . but would it follow Pitt?

Chapter 6

FRANKLIN TESTIFIES, ROCKINGHAM REPEALS

Pitt had spoken, and Rockingham could delay no longer. The Stamp Act crisis was not going to go away to resolve itself. He would have to act, no matter what the political risks—and they were considerable.

Although the laws prohibited the publication of Pitt's speech, in London's tightly knit business and political circles, in the coffee-houses and taverns and clubs, what he said and how he said it were common knowledge. And there was plenty in the news about the demonstrations in America, the burning and looting of English goods, the sabotage of the Stamp Act by the extraordinary, spontaneous, and complete refusal to comply with it. No one who bought a London newspaper could fail to know that the Americans, by negating the Stamp Act, were plunging England into a trade recession and unemployment. In the letters columns, there was much support for the Americans and for repealing the act. But there was also plenty of righteous indignation against American behavior. On January 13, 1766, a letter signed by Anti-Sejanus appeared in *Lloyd's Evening Post:*

> If our timid and ill-judging Ministers intend to give way to the tu-
> multuous Americans, can it be supposed that the Colonies will ever

submit to bear any share in those grievous burdens and taxes with which we are loaded. And if they succeed this time, soon they will suffer no limitation on their trade and shake off all dependence. The Stamp Act should be kept, because of the riotous and illegal behaviour of the Americans in dealing with the right of taxation.

These sentiments were widely shared in the House of Commons. The Stamp Act had been passed by a 245-to-49 vote, and no matter how eloquent Pitt was, repeal would not be easy for Rockingham to obtain.

Further, most people assumed that King George would be firmly against repeal, or indeed any retreat before his American subjects. Since Rockingham had not formed a policy on the question of repeal, there had been no need for the king to disclose his position. It was known that three members of Rockingham's government would oppose repeal: Attorney General Charles Yorke, Paymaster General Charles Townshend, and Lord George Sackville, who held a minor (but lucrative) post as treasurer for Ireland.*

Until it was clear which way the king would want the debate to go, factionalism in the Commons would make it difficult to predict the outcome of a vote. Grenville would be able to assemble a bloc of seventy or more members against repeal. Bute was prepared to side with Grenville despite their mutual hatred, and this would add another forty-five votes. The King's Friends were opposed to retreat and waiting for a royal signal. Tory country gentlemen, who paid large land taxes, were very much in favor of taxing the Americans. On the other hand, Rockingham himself commanded only a small band of supporters, perhaps forty of the Young Whigs. The duke of Newcastle could deliver perhaps seventy-five Old Whigs. It would take heavy persuasion to line up or bribe votes for a repeal. And if the king said no, repeal would be impossible.

On January 20, after mulling over Pitt's speech, Rockingham decided on a first move. To hold his government together, he agreed to Charles Yorke's earlier proposal to frame a strong declaratory act that would assert Parliament's authority over the colonies in all leg-

---

*Ten years later, Sackville would change his name to Lord George Germain and would figure prominently in the government that fought the Revolutionary War.

islative matters, including taxation. This measure would both as-
suage and reassure the hard-liners, who were all for punishing the
Americans. After this act was on the statute books, put there by the
large majority in Commons that it would surely receive, Rockingham could then proceed to the task of maneuvering a repeal of the
Stamp Act. He would first sound the bugles to rally Parliament to
advance and then order a retreat.

While the Declaratory Act was in draft, there was an eruption in
the Commons. George Cooke, a friend of Pitt's, moved on January
27 to have the House receive the petition adopted by the colonies at
the Stamp Act Congress held in New York the previous October.
Cooke was acting against the wishes of Henry Seymour Conway,
who feared that such a move would only inflame the situation—
which it did. Grenville was on his feet at once to denounce the idea
of receiving a petition from "a dangerous federal union" in America. Pitt took the floor to retort that the Stamp Act had broken the
government's pact with the colonies, that the Americans had every
right to resist and to petition the government, and that the petition
should be received. With the Commons in an uproar, Sir Fletcher
Norton, a Bute supporter, called Pitt "a trumpet of rebellion."
Tempers were running high everywhere: Later, in the House of
Lords, Lord Hardwicke declared that Pitt "deserved to be sent to
the Tower for treason."

A week after this upheaval, on February 3, Conway introduced
the Declaratory Act. Once again, Pitt spoke for the American cause,
vigorously opposing the resolution on the grounds that the wording
of the act left it open for Parliament to continue to enact "internal
taxes" (such as stamp duties) on America. Colonel Isaac Barré
stoutly supported Pitt in efforts to get Parliament to see the uncon-
stitutionality of taxing the Americans—but theirs were voices in the
wind.

Edmund Burke made his first speech in the Commons on this
occasion. As a supporter of and private secretary to Rockingham, he
spoke in favor of the Declaratory Act, but he was also in favor of
repealing the Stamp Act. Burke felt that the act was unwise, irratio-
nal, unworkable, foolish. But he disagreed with Pitt that the act was
unconstitutional. He did not want to see Parliament voting a constitutional limit on itself; neither did he want to see that constitutional
right exercised with such poor judgment. Burke was for American

liberty—but not for American independence. This was a dichotomy that would be reflected in his speeches for the next fifteen years.

Once the Declaratory Act had passed its first parliamentary hurdle, George Grenville committed one of his familiar (but in this case helpful) blunders. At the opening of the parliamentary session in December, he had tried to have the American colonies declared in a state of rebellion. Now he returned to the attack. Without any forewarning, Grenville moved an address to the king, asking for "unqualified reinforcement" of the Stamp Act. This would, of course, undercut all efforts at repeal. He took his usual obstinate stance, refusing to countenance any revision of the act.

The vote was crucial. When the House divided, it looked as if the government might fall. But to the amazement of both the government and the opposition, Grenville's motion was defeated by an overwhelming vote of 274 to 134.

Rockingham could begin to breathe more easily about repeal, . . . but he still had to have help from the king.

During these crucial months, Benjamin Franklin's attitude toward the Stamp Act had swung from apathy to feverish lobbying activity. His good friend William Strahan, the publisher, wrote to a mutual friend:

The assiduity of our Friend Dr. Franklin is really astonishing. He is forever with one member of Parliament or another (most of whom, by the by, seem to have been deplorably ignorant with regard to the Nature and Consequences of the Colonies) endeavouring to impress them; first with the Importance of the present Dispute; then to state the Case clearly and fully; and lastly, to answer Objections arising either from a total ignorance, a partial Knowledge, or a wrong Conception of the matter. To enforce this repeatedly, and with Propriety, in the manner he has done in these last two months, I assure you, is no easy Task. By this means, however, when Parliament reassembles, many members will go into the House properly instructed, and be able to speak in the Debates with Precision and Propriety, which the Well-wishers of the Colonies have hitherto been unable to do. This is the most necessary and essential Service he could perform on this Occasion. All this while too, he hath been throwing out Hints in the Public Papers, and giving answers to such Letters as have appeared in them, that required or deserved an answer. In this manner he is now employed, with very little Intermission, Night and Day.

Franklin himself wrote to his wife that "I am excessively hurried, being every hour that I am awake, either abroad to speak with Members of Parliament, or taken up with People coming at home concerning our American Affairs."

All of this turned out to be preparation for Franklin's finest hour of all his years in London: four hours of wide-ranging, lucid, oral testimony under intensive questioning before the Commons on the case for repeal of the Stamp Act.

After the surprising defeat of Grenville's motion, leaders of the Commons took the unusual step of scheduling three full sessions to hear outside witnesses testify to the problems caused by the act and the effects of the colonial opposition. This would remove the debate, temporarily at least, from the constitutional issue and focus instead on the practical problems. The sessions were to take place on February 11, 12, and 13. The Commons would sit as a "committee of the whole" to permit outside witnesses to be called to the floor of the chamber.

On the first two days, several Americans then living in London testified. Among them were Barlow Trecothick, the Boston merchant; William Kelley of New York, who had testified that the Sugar Act would ruin the rum trade; and James Balfour of Virginia, who dealt with the problems of tobacco growers. Franklin was called to appear on the final day.

Like all other parliamentary proceedings, Franklin's testimony was to remain secret; publication in the press or public journals was forbidden by a 1738 resolution. This prohibition was regularly avoided by newspapers' imaginative reporting of debates in "political clubs" and other such subterfuges. In fact, editors and politicians alike were attacking the prohibition, and one of those who was determined to undermine it was William Strahan. Strahan set out to obtain a transcript of Franklin's testimony for his paper, the *London Chronicle*.

A House of Commons clerk had been assigned to record the proceedings. On May 10, three months after the events, Strahan was able to procure a manuscript copy "with great difficulty and with some expense" and send it to the Philadelphia printer David Hall.

Reluctant to rush it into print in London, Strahan urged Hall to publish it without delay, asserting that "to this very Examination, more than to anything else, you are indebted to a *speedy* and *total* repeal of this odious Law." Once Hall published, Strahan would follow.

Hall, however, delayed for several months, merely reading portions of the testimony to friends and discussion groups. It wasn't until September 1766 that it was finally published in Philadelphia. To circumvent the parliamentary prohibition, in effect even in America, the document appeared without a title page or a publisher's imprint—it was simply headed "Testimony before an August Body." Other reprints appeared in Boston and Williamsburg later in 1766; even a German translation was produced in Philadelphia. But the testimony wasn't published in England until the summer of 1767, when Strahan's *London Chronicle* published not the full text but just excerpts. The July issue of *Gentleman's Magazine* did the same.

At some point early on, when Franklin saw a copy of the record of his testimony, he tried to identify from memory as accurately as possible who each of his questioners had been. He numbered each of the 174 questions in the record, noting that others had been asked but not recorded. Then he noted either a name or a general identification, such as "adversary" or "by Friends" or "by one of the late Ministry (Grenville's)," and added comments of his own.

To a certain extent, the testimony was prearranged. Franklin had consulted with friends in the Commons to devise a series of sympathetic questions to elicit points that he wished to make. The order of questioning was spontaneous, however, with plenty of opposition voices. In the end, Franklin listed eighty-nine of the questions as having come from hostile members who were opposed to repeal.

Benjamin Franklin was a prolific writer of elegant and lively prose, and he was a stimulating conversationalist on an endless variety of topics. But he was not a public speaker, let alone an orator. Thomas Jefferson once said of both Franklin and Washington that he "never heard either of them speak ten minutes at a time, nor to any but the main point that was to decide the question. They laid their shoulders to great points, knowing that the little ones would follow of themselves." This was a mental discipline and personal style that was well suited to the give-and-take of questions and answers that

Franklin was about to undergo before the House of Commons. In the most courteous and restrained manner, with lucidity, clarity and an economy of words, with a wealth of facts and figures and precision of ideas, with skill at rejecting without giving offense, Franklin put on a bravura performance before supporters and critics of America.

Dressed in a plain suit of brown cloth, unadorned by any finery, he stood between the rows of opposing benches. At the speaker's request, he identified himself, simply as Franklin of Philadelphia. Questions began at once. It was four hours before the Commons finished and Franklin could sit down.

The first questioner was James Hewitt, member for Coventry, son of a textile manufacturer hard hit by the American resolve to embargo English goods. He had been briefed by Franklin with a question intended "to remove a common Prejudice that the Colonies paid no Taxes, and that their governments were supported by burdening the people here."

Q: Do Americans pay any considerable taxes among themselves?
A: Certainly many, and very heavy taxes.

Q: What are the present taxes in Pennsylvania, laid by laws of the colony?
A: There are taxes on all estates real and personal, a poll tax, a tax on all offices, professions, trades and businesses, according to their profits; an excise tax on all wine, rum and other spirits; and a duty of Ten Pounds per head on all Negroes imported, with some other duties.

Q: For what purposes are those taxes laid?
A: For the support of the civil and military establishments of the country, and to discharge the heavy debt contracted in the last war.

Q: How long are those taxes to continue?
A: Those for discharging the debt are to continue until 1772, and longer, if the debt should not be then all discharged. The others must always continue.

Q: Was it not expected that the debt would have been sooner discharged?
A: It was, when the peace was made with France and Spain. But a fresh war breaking out with the Indians, a fresh load of debt was incurred, and the taxes, of course, continued longer by a new law.

Q: Are not all the people very able to pay those taxes?

A: No. The frontier counties, all along the continent, having been frequently ravaged by the enemy, and greatly impoverished, are able to pay very little tax. And therefore, in consideration of their distresses, our late tax laws do expressly favor those counties, excusing the sufferers; and I suppose the same is done in other governments.

At this point, another of Franklin's well-briefed supporters took over. John Huske, an American member for Maldon, stood up with a question "to show the impracticability of distributing the Stamps in America."

Q: Are you not concerned in the management of the Post Office in America?

A: I am Deputy Post-Master General of North America.

Q: Don't you think the distribution of stamps, by post, to all the inhabitants, very practicable, if there were no opposition?

A: The posts only go along the sea coasts; they do not, except in a few instances, go back into the country; and if they did, sending for stamps by post would occasion an expense of postage, amounting, in many cases, to much more than the stamps themselves.

Q: Can you disperse stamps by post in Canada?

A: There is only a post between Montreal and Quebec. The inhabitants live so scattered and remote from each other, in that vast country, that posts cannot be supported among them, and therefore they cannot get stamps per post. The English Colonies too, along the frontiers, are very thinly settled.

Q: From the thinness of the back settlements, would not the stamp-act be extremely inconvenient to the inhabitants, if executed?

A: To be sure it would; as many of the inhabitants could not get stamps when they had occasion for them, without taking long journeys, and spending perhaps Three or Four Pounds, that the Crown might get Sixpence.

Q: Are not the Colonies, from their circumstances, very able to pay the stamp duty?

A: In my opinion, there is not gold and silver enough in the Colonies to pay the stamp duty for one year.

Questions then shifted to matters of population and trade, with Franklin estimating that Pennsylvania imported about £500,000 worth of English goods annually but exported barely £40,000 to Britain. At this point, George Grenville, who wished to return the questions to America's obligations to the mother country, was recognized.

Q: Do you think it is right that America should be protected by this country, and pay no part of the expense?

A: That is not the case. The Colonies raised, cloathed, and paid during the war nearly 25,000 men, and spent many millions.

Q: Were you not reimbursed by Parliament?

A: We were only reimbursed what, in your opinion, we had advanced beyond our proportion, or beyond what might reasonably be expected from us; and it was a very small part of what we spent. Pennsylvania, in particular, disbursed about £500,000 and the reimbursements, on the whole, did not exceed £60,000.

After more back-and-forth about how heavy the tax burden was in America and where it fell, another of Franklin's friends got the floor. This was Grey Cooper, a Rockingham supporter. In Franklin's notations, Cooper's questions "were intended to bring out such answers as they expected from me."

Q: What was the temper of America towards Great Britain before the year 1763?

A: The best in the world. They submitted willingly to the government of the Crown, and paid, in all their courts, obedience to acts of Parliament. Numerous as the people are in the several old provinces, they cost you nothing in forts, citadels, garrisons or armies to keep them in subjection. They were governed by this country at the expense of only a little pen, ink and paper. They were lead by a thread. They had not only a respect, but an affection for Great Britain, for its laws, its customs and manners, and even a fondness for its fashions that greatly increased the commerce. Natives of Britain were always treated with particular regard; to be an Old England-Man was, of itself, a character of some respect and gave a kind of rank among us.

Q: And what is their temper now?

A: Oh, Very much altered.

Q: Did you ever hear the authority of Parliament to make laws for America questioned till lately?

A: The authority of Parliament was allowed to be valid in all laws, except such as should lay internal taxes. It was never disputed in laying duties to regulate commerce.

Q: In what light did the people of America use to consider the Parliament of Great Britain?

A: They considered the Parliament as the great bulwark and security of their liberties and privileges, and always spoke of it with the utmost respect and veneration. Arbitrary ministers, they thought, might probably at times attempt to oppress them; but they relied on it that the Parliament, on application, would always give redress. They remembered, with gratitude, a strong insistence of this when a bill was brought into Parliament with a clause to make royal instructions laws in the Colonies, which the House of Commons would not pass, and it was thrown out.

Q: And they have not still the same respect for Parliament?
A: No, it is greatly lessened.

Q: Don't you think they would submit to the Stamp Act if it was modified, the obnoxious parts taken out, and the duty reduced to some particulars, of small moment?
A: No, they will never submit to it.

After various exchanges about why America's population was growing faster than England's ("Because people marry younger, more generally") and what American opinion would be on the Declaratory Act just passed ("They will think [it] unconstitutional and unjust"), a questioner from the Grenville faction brought Franklin to the key matter of internal versus external taxes.

Q: You say the Colonies have always submitted to external taxes, and object to the right of Parliament only in laying internal taxes; now can you shew that there is any kind of difference between the two taxes?
A: I think the difference is very great. An external tax is a duty laid on commodities imported; that duty is added to the first cost, and other charges on the commodity, and when it is offered to sale, makes a part of the price. If the people do not like it at that price, they refuse it; they are not obliged to pay it. But an internal tax is forced from people without their consent, if it is not laid by their own representatives. The Stamp Act says, we shall have no commerce, make no exchange of property with each other, neither purchase nor grant, nor recover debts; we shall neither marry nor make our wills, unless we pay such and such sums, and

thus it is intended to extort money from us, or ruin us by the consequences of refusing to pay it.

Q: But supposing the external tax or duty to be laid on the necessities of life imported into your Colony, will not that be the same thing in its effects as an internal tax?
A: I do not know a single article imported for the Northern Colonies but what they can either do without, or make themselves.

Q: Don't you think cloth from England absolutely necessary to them?
A: No, by No means absolutely necessary with industry and good management, they may very well supply themselves with all they want.

Q: Will it not take a long time to establish that manufacturing among them? and must they not in the mean while suffer greatly?
A: I think not. They have made a surprising progress already. And I am of the opinion that before their old clothes are worn out, they will have new ones of their own making.

Another Grenville supporter returned to the question of the effect of the new Declaratory Act in the colonies.

Q: Considering the resolutions of Parliament, as to the right, do you think, if the Stamp Act is repealed that the North Americans will be satisfied?
A: I think the resolutions of right will give them very little concern, if they are never attempted to be carried into practice. The Colonies will probably consider themselves in the same situation, in that respect, with Ireland; they know you claim the same right with regard to Ireland, but you have never exercised it. And they may believe you never will exercise it in the Colonies, any more than in Ireland, unless on some very extraordinary occasion.

Q: But who are to be the judges of that extraordinary occasion? Is it not the Parliament?
A: Though Parliament may judge of the occasion, the people will think it can never exercise such a right, till representatives from the Colonies are admitted into Parliament, and that whenever the occasion arises, representatives will be ordered.

Q: Did the Americans ever dispute the controlling power of Parliament to regulate commerce?
A: No.

Q: Can anything less than a military force carry the Stamp Act into execution?

A: I do not see how a military force can be applied to that purpose.

Q: Why may it not?

A: Suppose a military force were sent into America, they will find nobody in arms; what are they then to do? They cannot force a man to take stamps who chooses to do without them. They will not find a rebellion; they may indeed make one.

Q: If the act is not repealed, what do you think will be the consequences?

A: A total loss of respect and affection the people of America bear to this country, and of all commerce that depends on that respect and affection.

After a series of questions relating to the ability of the Americans to get along without English goods and to manufacture for themselves, George Grenville returned to the fray with a rather silly question that Franklin quickly flattened.

Q: Is it not the post-office, which they have long received, a tax as well as a regulation?

A: No; the money paid for postage of a letter is not of the nature of a tax; it is merely a *quantum meruit* for a service done; no person is compellable to pay the money; if he does not choose to receive the service. A man may still, as before the act, send his letter by a servant, a special messenger, or a friend, if he thinks it cheaper or safer.

Q: But do they not consider the regulation of the post-office, by the act of last year, as a tax?

A: By the regulations of last year the rate of postage was generally abated near thirty percent, through all of America; they certainly cannot consider such an abatement as a tax.

Another Grenvillite took over to return the questioning to the issue of enforcing the Stamp Act.

Q: Supposing the Stamp Act continued, and enforced, do you imagine that ill humour will induce the Americans to give as much for worse manufacture of their own, and use them, preferable to better of ours?

A: Yes, I think so. People will pay as freely to gratify one passion as another, their resentment as their pride.

Q: Would they suffer the produce of their lands to rot?

A: No, but they would not raise so much. They would manufacture more, and plough less.

Q: Would they live without the administration of justice in civil matters, and suffer all the inconveniences of such a situation for a considerable time, rather than take the stamps, supposing the stamps were protected by a sufficient force, where everyone might have them?

A: I think the supposition impracticable, that the stamps should be so protected as that everyone might have them. The act requires sub-distributors to be appointed in every county town, district and village, and they would be necessary. But the principal distributors, who were to have had a considerable profit on the whole, have not thought it worth while to continue in the office, and I think it impossible to find sub-distributors for to be trusted who would incur the odium and run the hazard that would attend it.

Q: But in places that could be protected, would not the people rather use them than remain in such a situation, unable to obtain any right, or recover, by law, any debt?

A: It is hard to say what they would do. I can only judge what other people will think, and how they will act, by what I feel within myself. I have a great many debts due to me in America, and I had rather they should remain unrecoverable by any law than submit to the Stamp Act. They will be debts of honor. It is my opinion the people will either continue in that situation, or find some way to extricate themselves, perhaps by generally agreeing to proceed in the courts without stamps.

Q: What do you think a sufficient military force to protect the distribution of the stamps in every part of America?

A: A very great force; I can't say what, if the disposition of America is for a general resistance.

This line of questioning brought the discussion very close to the idea of armed rebellion in the colonies. When a questioner then asked Franklin how many men in America were able to bear arms, he began to answer, "I suppose there are at least—" when the speaker ruled the question out of order and the answer halted. The questions then returned to politics:

Q: If the Stamp Act should be repealed, would not the Americans think they could oblige the Parliament to repeal every external tax law now in force?

A: It is hard to answer questions of what people at such a distance might think.

Q: *But what do you imagine they will think were the motives of repealing the act?*

A: I suppose they will think that it was repealed from a conviction of its inexpediency, and they will rely upon it, that while the same inexpediency subsists, you will never attempt to make such another.

A "friendly questioner" now posed a question that enabled Franklin to make what amounted to a brief speech on the situation as the Americans saw it: If Parliament should exercise its right to tax the Americans by "laying a small tax contrary to their opinion," would the Americans submit to paying it? Franklin replied:

A: The proceedings of the people in America have been considered too much together. The proceedings of the assemblies have been very different from those of the mobs, and should be distinguished as having no connexion with each other. The assemblies have only peacefully resolved what they take to be their rights; they have taken no measures for opposition by force; they have not built a fort, raised a man, or provided a grain of ammunition, in order to such opposition. The ringleaders of riots they think ought to be punished; they would punish them themselves if they could. Every sober sensible man would wish to see rioters punished; as otherwise peaceable people have no security of person or estate.

But as to any internal tax, how small soever, laid by the legislature here on the people there, while they have no representatives in this legislature, I think it will never be submitted to. They will oppose it to the last. They do not consider it as at all necessary for you to raise money on them, by your taxes, because they are, and always have been, ready to raise money by taxes among themselves and to grant large sums, equal to their abilities, upon requisition from the Crown. They have not only granted equal to their abilities, but during the last war they granted far beyond their abilities, and beyond their proportion with this country, you yourselves being judges, to the amount of many hundred thousand pounds, and this they did freely, only on a sort of promise from the secretary of state that it should be recommended to Parliament to make them compensation.

America has been greatly misrepresented and abused here, in papers and pamphlets and speeches, as ungrateful and unreasonable and unjust, in having put this nation to immense expense for their defense and refusing to bear any part of that expense. The Colonies raised, paid and clothed near 25,000 men during the last war, a number equal to those sent from Britain, and far beyond their proportion. They went deeply into debt in doing this, and all their taxes and estates are mortgaged for many years to come for discharging that debt. Far from being unwilling to bear a share of the burden, the Colonies did exceed their proportion, for if they had done less or had only equaled their proportion there would have been no room or reason for compensation.

George Grenville returned to the attack, endeavoring to get Franklin to agree that England had come to America's rescue in Pontiac's War.

Q: Was not the late war with the Indians, since the peace with France, a war for America only?

A: Yes; it was more particularly for America than the former, but it was rather a consequence or remains of the former war, the Indians not having been thoroughly pacified, and the Americans bore by much the greater share of the expense.

Q: Is it not necessary to send troops to America to defend the Americans against the Indians?

A: No, by no means. It never was necessary. They defended themselves when they were but an handful, and the Indians much more numerous. They continually gained ground, and have driven the Indians over the mountains, without any troops sent to their assistance from this country. And it can be thought necessary now to send troops for their defense from those diminished Indian tribes when the Colonies are become so populous, and so strong? There is not the least occasion for it; they are very able to defend themselves.

Another "friendly questioner" brought Franklin back to the question of raising money for the Crown. If the Stamp Act should be repealed, he asked, and the Crown should make a requisition to the colonies for a sum of money, would they grant it?

A: I believe they would. I can speak for the Colony I live in. I had it in instruction from the Assembly to assure the ministry that as they always had done, so they should always think it their duty to grant such aids to the Crown as were suitable in their circumstances and abilities, whenever called upon for the purpose, in the usual constitutional manner;

and I had the honour of communicating this instruction to that honourable gentleman then minister [Grenville].

The lengthy hearing now began to wind down, with repetitive questions being asked about the Declaratory Act and how to draw the line between an internal and an external tax, and then another Franklin friend brought it to a final exchange:

Q: *What used to be the pride of the Americans?*
A: To indulge in the fashions and manufactures of Great Britain.

Q: *What is now their pride?*
A: To wear their old clothes over again, till they can make new ones.

There is no way of assessing the direct effect of Franklin's lengthy testimony on the final vote by the Commons. There was, of course, no record of attendance at the hearing, but given the charged atmosphere, Franklin probably had an audience of two hundred or three hundred MPs coming and going during his testimony; many of these members may have been hearing an American for the very first time. Furthermore, he had given a devastating appraisal of the Americans' rejection of the Stamp Act, its unworkability, and the political and economic consequences if it were not repealed. Of course, when it came time for the final vote, there were many other domestic factors that figured in the minds of parliamentarians. But there was no doubt in the mind of William Strahan about the decisive effect of Franklin's appearance.

Strahan was a close friend and admirer of Franklin's, but he was also a man of wide social and political contacts, and as a publisher he was bound to stay tuned to public opinion. He wrote to David Hall, the Philadelphia publisher who eventually printed the testimony:

The Marquess of Rockingham told a friend of mine a few days after that he never knew Truth to make so great a Progress in so very short a time. From that Day, the repeal was generally and absolutely determined, all that passed afterwards being merely form, which even in Business the most urgent must always be regarded. Happy Man! In Truth, I almost envy him (Franklin) the inward Pleasure as well as the outward Fame, he must derive from having it in his Power to do his Country such eminent and seasonable Service.

Meanwhile, Rockingham finally braced King George directly on the question of repeal and the need for the monarch to make his position clear. Since Lord Bute and his followers were against repeal, it was generally assumed in the House of Commons that the king would be opposed. Such hints as the king had given out were generally in favor of simply amending the Stamp Act in some fashion.

But Rockingham now had the king in a political bind. He, Conway, Newcastle, and a majority of the cabinet were for repeal, and Pitt had thrown his weight on the scale. If the king would not support the government on repeal, then Rockingham would resign, leaving the king with no alternative but to send for Grenville and reinstall him as prime minister. This was about the last thing the king was prepared to contemplate. Thus, after seeing Rockingham on February 10, the king recorded this: "I told Lord Rockingham I had given him permission to say that I preferred repealing to enforcing the Stamp Act; but that modification I had ever thought both more consistent with the honour of this country, and all the Americans would with any degree of justice hope for." The king said that if the different parties were "too wild" to come to an agreement on modifying the act, then he would be for repeal rather than enforcement. This was enough to see Rockingham and his government past the last obstacle.

On February 22, Conway moved to introduce a bill repealing the Stamp Act. He drew a harrowing picture of the chaos the act was creating in English exports and manufacturing, in unemployment and bad debts, in American riots and lawlessness. But he was at pains to assert that repeal was in England's best interests, not to appease the Americans.

Grenville fought vigorously to defend his handiwork, contending that if the government gave way to the Americans just because the tax was unpopular, then the Navigation Act would go, and there would be no end to the unraveling.

Pitt appeared on crutches, cheered into the chamber by the crowd outside. He had enough fire to speak for an hour and a quarter. Declaring that he "would be an Englishman first and then an American," he said he came to the House of Commons because of "the miserable state of the country, the distresses of the manufacturers, the unhappy wife, the starving child, the universal bankruptcies" the act was causing. He pleaded for "absolute, total and unconditional repeal."

It was 2:00 A.M. when the vote was finally taken. The motion for repeal carried by a strong majority of 275 to 167. In Horace Walpole's account, when members left the chamber, Conway was "cheered heartily." Grenville "met with scorn and hisses" that so angered him he seized a man in the crowd, held him by the collar, and shook him. Finally, Pitt appeared, gaunt and tired, hobbling on his crutches, and "the whole crowd pulled off their hats, huzza'd, and many followed his chair home with shouts and benedictions."

Repeal of the Stamp Act and approval of the Declaratory Act were given royal assent by George III on March 18, 1766.

Chapter 7

THE CHATHAM FIASCO

Six weeks after King George III assented to the repeal of the Stamp Act, the news reached the American colonies. With each newly arriving ship, the news spread rapidly up and down the Atlantic seaboard—and so did jubilation. Americans drank to the repeal and ignored the accompanying Declaratory Act.

The *Virginia Gazette* was the first to publish. On May 2, 1766, the *Gazette* triumphantly printed the text of the repeal legislation and the Declaratory Act, in which the English Parliament reasserted its powers over the colonies "in all cases whatsoever." The Virginia tidewater gentlemen celebrated, characteristically, with "a ball and elegant entertainment at the Capitol" in Williamsburg.

In Boston, the Sons of Liberty turned out not for a riot but for a frolic. John Hancock, the wealthiest man in Massachusetts, gave a "grand and elegant entertainment in the genteel part of town" and rolled out a cask of his Madeira for the people.

In New York, the Sons of Liberty got together with the "Friendly Brothers of St. Patrick" for some serious drinking. The city voted to erect a statue of King George III.*

---

*They did so. A decade later, they melted it down for ammunition.

In Philadelphia, the waterfront taverns gave free drinks to every man on the ship that had brought the news from England. Three hundred Pennsylvania gentlemen attended a celebration that was conducted, on Benjamin Franklin's advice, "with great prudence." They resolved each to buy a new suit of English cloth.

In South Carolina, the Commons House voted to erect a statue, not of the king, but of William Pitt.

Euphoria lasted about as long as the party hangovers.

In London, Franklin, closer to the political reality and Parliament's mood, allowed himself only a small celebration. He wrote his wife on April 6, while news was still crossing the Atlantic:

> As the Stamp Act is at length repealed, I am willing you should have a new gown, which, you may suppose, I did not send you sooner as I knew you would not like to be finer than your neighbors unless in a gown of your own spinning. Had the trade between our two countries totally ceased, it was a comfort to me to recollect that I had once been clothed from head to foot in woolen and linen of my wife's manufacture, that I was never prouder of any dress in my life, and that she and her daughter might do it again if necessary. . . . I have sent you a fine piece of Pompadour satin, fourteen yards, costing eleven shillings a yard; a silk negligee and petticoat of broaded lutestring for my dear Sally, with two dozen gloves, four bottles of lavendar water.

In London, despite the political and economic realities that had made the repeal necessary, there was deep resentment that Parliament had been forced to retreat before colonial "subjects." The makeshift Rockingham government began to totter; many members of the House perceived the government as weak-kneed and too lenient. The king refused to allow any political retaliation against the 167 MPs who had voted against repeal, which left little doubt about royal unhappiness over the whole affair.

Meanwhile, repeal had left the government finances worse off. With the loss of an anticipated sixty thousand pounds in Stamp Act revenue, where would the government turn next? Whatever Franklin's forcefulness in his testimony before Parliament, he had scarcely dented the conviction of many members that the colonies could and should help pay for the troops in America.

In the colonies, behind the celebrations over repeal, the toasts of gratitude, and the expressions of loyalty, the Americans had shown that England's authority could be directly and effectively defied once there was unity of purpose. Moreover, the sources of conflict were far from having been removed. England could, under the Declaratory Act, still choose to force taxes on the colonies. Both sides were still very much on a collision course.

In the spring of 1766, Rockingham engaged in an uncharacteristic burst of activity. He pushed through three measures that had the contradictory effect of seeming to placate the Americans while causing more trouble and making the difference between "internal" and "external" taxes even murkier.

First, he decided to revise Grenville's Sugar Act. He reduced the duty on molasses from threepence per gallon to only a penny. The rum distillers in New England protested, saying it was time to abolish this tax along with the Stamp Act.

Next, he established a free port on the island of Dominica in the West Indies. This had long been sought by American merchants trading in the Caribbean as a place where they could unload and transfer cargoes for French, Spanish, and Dutch goods and bullion. But, while this move was welcomed by the Americans, it backfired on Rockingham in London. English sugar planters and plantation owners in the West Indies had a small but very strong and very vocal lobby in Parliament, and they cried "Unfair!" Rockingham quickly offered some trade concessions to them, but the damage was done, and support for his government further unraveled.

Finally, he decided to revise the Mutiny Act of 1765. This had been passed at the behest of Major General Thomas Gage, ostensibly to enforce controls over the colonials. Modeled on the English Mutiny Act, it gave broad powers for calling out the army and using troops to quell any riots or uprisings. Rockingham's revision would eliminate the authority of the English to billet troops in private American homes, but it would require Americans to make available on order quarters in empty houses, barns, or barracks. Americans must also supply troops on march with kitchen utensils; salt; vinegar; small beer, cider, or rum; and candles and firewood.

The Mutiny Act had been used very sparingly in America, but its mere existence exacerbated the choleric colonial mood. News of the revisions were therefore not seen as conciliation but as preparation for freer use of the act. Proof of this was not long in coming. In June of 1766, not long after the act's amendment, General Gage requested billets and supplies for a movement of troops from the western frontiers to Albany and New York. The New York Assembly refused. The clash with the royal governor would sputter on for two years.

In May of 1766, the secretary at war, Viscount Barrington, produced a recommendation for the cabinet that had long been urged by General Gage: evacuation of all British troops from the western frontiers of America. Declaring it unlikely that England would ever again find itself engaged in hostilities with the Indians, Barrington proposed that all British forts, garrisons, and settlements be abandoned. If, he said, the colonies should become embroiled in Indian troubles by their own misconduct, then "let them get themselves out of it, or let them beg for military assistance, acknowledge their want of it and pay its expenses." He recommended that English forces be concentrated in garrisons located in eastern Florida, Canada, and Nova Scotia. This would save money; at the same time, troops could be readily moved by sea to wherever they might be needed along the Atlantic coast.

Barrington argued perceptively that troops around the American port cities were only an irritant and not likely to be used. Civil authorities would always be reluctant to call on them, as the Stamp Act troubles had shown. But General Gage disagreed. He was all for concentrating the British forces, but he argued that if more troops were stationed in the populous areas on the coast, then the civil authorities would be ready to act more vigorously.

Unfortunately, Barrington was not a major figure in that era. He was, however, a sensible man with a certain integrity and staying power in the midst of much hypocrisy. As administrative head of the army, he was not a cabinet member, but he did enjoy ready and constant access to the king. Although he persisted in his recommendation, it was not acted on until 1768.

In the meantime, the Rockingham government was running out of steam. The end was hastened by another of those petty arguments, so frequent in the governments of that time, between the king and whoever was his prime minister. The king's uncle, the duke of Cumberland, had died, and the duke's annual allowance of twenty-five thousand pounds was now available to be spent else-where. The king decided to divide the money among his three younger brothers (the fourth brother had also died in the past year), a decision that would need the consent of Parliament.

But Parliament was about to begin its long summer-and-autumn recess. Rockingham took advantage of this to confront the king with an unwise and incomprehensible demand: Before he would introduce the allowance bill, he told the king, he wanted assurances that there would be no change of government during the long re-cess. He was saying, in effect, no assurances, no money bill. The king was incensed by what seemed like political blackmail on Rock-ingham's part. He wrote an angry letter to Lord Egmont, leader in the House of Lords and a royal confidant, that "my prudence is now exhausted and I am enclin'd to take any step that will preserve my honour" to be rid of a government of "a few weak boys."

In July, he turned to William Pitt and asked him to form another government, the fifth in the six years of his reign.

This time, the king did not send any intermediaries to Pitt; he sent him a direct invitation to come in person. The invitation reached Pitt at a country estate he had acquired in Somerset, one of the western counties. Pitt replied on July 18, "I shall hasten to Lon-don as fast as I possibly can; happy could I change infirmity into wings of expedition." The prospect of returning to power seems to have overcome, temporarily at least, the incapacitating pain of his gout. He left in a carriage that swayed over the potholed roads on the long trip to London.

Six years before, a younger George III had called William Pitt "a true snake in the grass" and vowed that "I can never bear to see him in a future ministry." The king's sudden resolve to recall Pitt did not signal any great act of political wisdom or even any deep change of heart. (He would resume his vendetta after this experiment in bring-ing him back to power was over.) This was a last-ditch effort to be rid of another government he had come to hate and avoid being thrown back into the arms of George Grenville.

If Pitt had ever been aware of the king's derogatory remarks, it would not have mattered. Pitt was an ultraroyalist, almost reli-giously devout about the monarchy, regardless of the king's abilities or personality. It was power that interested Pitt, . . . and the king could confer power. Once installed, Pitt could pursue his own agenda, his own politics and policies. But when it came to proclaiming humble, slavish devotion to the king, nobody could outdo William Pitt.

Even making allowances for the conventional exaggerations of eighteenth-century letter writing, Pitt was extravagantly fulsome and verbose in his expressions of gratitude and humility to the king. It was to be said of Disraeli that he laid it on for Queen Victoria with a trowel. Pitt laid it on for George III with a shovel. In his letters, he begged to be permitted to lay himself, with all duty and humble submission, at the king's feet, . . . he entreated the king's pleasure with deepest veneration, . . . he most humbly renewed the tender of his devoted services, . . . he lacked words to offer his ardent acknowledgment of the king's boundless goodness, . . . he would prostrate himself before His Majesty's gracious wishes, . . . he entreated the king's understanding of the misfortunes of his devoted servant. And so on and so on.

Beneath this puffery, Pitt had his hidden agenda: He wanted a peerage, and one way to get it was by returning to the king's service. As the Great Commoner, he had dominated the political scene—but he was still a lowborn outsider as far as Whig society, with its inner circle of the wealthy, titled aristocracy of the House of Lords, was concerned. Pitt wanted in.

When the king and Pitt met on July 12 to discuss forming a new government, each had something to give to the other, and each had something the other wanted. Both had a dream of a government blessed with pristine competence, one that would obliterate all the tedious factionalism of the houses of Parliament. The king longed for a government that would be popular, stable, loyal, an ornament to his crown. Pitt, at fifty-eight, was certain that he was the man who could provide the leadership behind which the factions would unite for king and country. For both men, this was political romanticism, not reality.

Initially, their talks went well. Pitt assured the king that "he wished as far as possible to dissolve all factions and see the best of all parties in employment." He smoothly assured the king that as far as the hated Lord Bute was concerned, he had no reason to see why His Majesty "should not frequently have the comfort of his conversation" if he so wished: It was not for ministers to meddle with the king's private acquaintances.

But when Pitt got down to cases and began to select members of the cabinet, difficulties began. First, he wanted another of his brothers-in-law, Lord Temple, to become his chancellor of the Exchequer. Temple refused. He was an archconservative, a supporter of his brother, George Grenville, who had opposed repeal of the Stamp Act. Moreover, he firmly believed that he, not Pitt, should have been called by the king to form a new government. So he refused to join any dream "ministry of all talents."

Irritated and agitated but undeterred, Pitt pushed ahead. Uncertain of his own health, he decided not to become prime minister but to direct and control the cabinet from a less demanding, nonadministrative post from which he could fix the agenda and leave it to others to carry out.

To become prime minister and first lord of the Treasury, he summoned a devoted follower, the duke of Grafton. Grafton was a young man of thirty-one when he became head of the government. His qualifications for the office were hardly outstanding—devotion to Pitt, a friendship with the king (Grafton was descended from one of the many mistresses of King Charles II), a love of social pleasure, and an adequate but not particularly forceful sense of responsibility. In other words, Grafton was a lightweight. But this would not matter as long as Pitt was actively commanding from the background.

Most of the new Pitt government was built on the old Rockingham government. Henry Seymour Conway was retained as leader in the Commons. But another of Pitt's younger supporters, the earl of Shelburne, became secretary of state for the Southern Department in charge of the American colonies.

The most important—and unfortunate—appointment was the new chancellor of the Exchequer. At Grafton's urging, Pitt entrusted this position to the brilliant, erratic, unpredictable Charles Townshend, paymaster general in Rockingham's cabinet. An effective orator, he could charm and amuse the House of Commons—and take all sides of any question in the same speech. Elevated to the Exchequer, he wrote to a friend that he would be going "from a lazy to laborious employment, from cheerfulness to anxiety, and from indifference to some degree of responsibility." Charles Townshend was not exactly a man for all seasons.

Pitt was able to keep his biggest surprise till last: He would run the government from the office of lord privy seal, which carried with it a peerage and a seat in the House of Lords. Henceforth, William Pitt would be known as the earl of Chatham.

At a stroke, William Pitt undermined everything he was trying to achieve. Before the first cabinet meeting was called, the confidence and credibility in Pitt's leadership and power were diminished. He had put together a government in which he would be *roi-soleil*, a sun king around whom ministers would orbit like well-ordered satellites. The essential character and strength of the government were supposed to be vested in the political leadership of William Pitt— but when he moved away from the Commons and into Lords, this strong center went into eclipse. He had abandoned the arena where his strength as the Great Commoner had been built. As Horace Walpole observed, "The silence of the House of Lords and the decency of debate there was not suited to that inflammatory eloquence by which Lord Chatham had been accustomed to raise huzzas from a more numerous auditory." The *Whitehall Evening Post* of August 7, 1766, summed up the change more succinctly: "Pitt was adored—but Chatham is quite unknown."

The Americans, who knew of Pitt's pivotal role in the Seven Years' War and the repeal of the Stamp Act, greeted the news of his return with rejoicing. All the other English politicians who clustered and cluttered and came and went around George III were faceless names in the news. And Pitt, having been out of office for five years, was clear of any responsibility for the irritations suffered by the Americans. Thus it seemed that the colonies could breathe more easily, that liberties would be protected and common sense prevail.

When the earl of Chatham got down to work in August 1766, there were a few brief weeks during which the vision and leadership qualities of William Pitt still showed. Charles Townshend remarked after a cabinet meeting, "Lord Chatham has just shown us what inferior animals we were." Chatham had objectives that were clear-cut, quite a contrast to Bute's fumbling, Grenville's obstinacy, and Rockingham's diffidence. As he had intended, Chatham was initially able to dominate the government from his sideline seat as lord privy seal. He wished to calm the Americans, construct a new continental alliance against the French, and bring the rapacious East India Company under imperial control. These objectives were briskly set in motion—after which Chatham retired to Bath to nurse his gout for the remainder of the long recess. By the time he returned, all three of his policy objectives had bogged down in the quicksand of politics and diplomacy.

As far as American policy was concerned, Pitt was an empire builder through and through, and he did not want to see that edifice undermined by foolish, provocative measures such as the Stamp Act. He wanted conciliation—but not appeasement. And he was being challenged: The New York legislature had already refused to comply with General Gage's request for barracks and supplies. Soon Chatham was muttering about the Americans, calling them "an irritable and umbrageous people quite out of their senses." He gave instructions to Lord Shelburne that "measures for the proper subordination of America must be taken, but he hoped that it was not understood to intend any violent measures unless absolutely necessary." He was not going to make the situation worse by ordering a confrontation.

At the same time, Chatham worried obsessively over the threat of England's old enemy, France. He realized, as neither Bute nor Grenville could, that England must avoid exacerbating troubles with America because difficulties anywhere in the empire would inevitably be exploited by the French. He knew the French were brooding over revenge after the Seven Years' War; ever since the peace treaty of 1763, he had been warning of the possibility of French resurgence and another war. Further, when he had taken office, he had been handed intelligence that showed that the combined fleets of France and Spain were now far stronger than England's—more than one hundred flag. The Royal Navy, thanks to Grenville's budget cuts, could put to sea only sixty-two men-of-war. England, in Chatham's view, urgently needed more ships and more allies.

First, he installed Admiral Sir Charles Saunders as head of the Admiralty and gave him orders to restore the Royal Navy to equal the Franco-Spanish fleet. Next, he sent a personal envoy to St. Petersburg, but his approaches to Catherine the Great were fruitless. In return for supporting England, the Russians wished to have English support against the Turkish Ottoman Empire—and that was that. Chatham also drew a blank with Frederick the Great of Prussia. This ally of the Seven Years' War told the British ambassador that renewal of continental war seemed unlikely, and entering into a new alliance with England just now might create more friction than peace. Beyond that, Prussian interest and diplomacy were focused on Russia and the east; Frederick was seeking an agreement with Catherine to carve up Poland and add East Prussia to his realm.

Chatham also wanted to impose government control on the East India Company, which was ruthlessly exploiting the Indian subcontinent for its own expansion and profit while remitting no revenues to the Crown. Chatham intended to see sovereignty over India transferred to King George III and the East India Company required to pay revenues to the Crown, not just profit to its stockholders. But as soon as his intention became known, friends of the company swarmed to the defense of vested interests—and the East India Company had plenty of money to feed the flames of opposition to Chatham's ideas of reform.

After two months of feverish activity, Chatham headed wearily back to Bath. Whatever the wisdom of his vision, his leadership was not working any magic on the problems. In October, with Parliament still on the long recess, the government was left to fend for itself under the duke of Grafton.

While the captain lay ill in his cabin, Charles Townshend, chancellor of the Exchequer, became a loose cannon on the deck of the ship of state. Ten years older than Grafton and twelve years older than Shelburne, ready to abuse all and sundry, Townshend was so fickle that he changed sides and ideas as frequently and as easily as he changed his flashy waistcoats. As soon as Chatham departed for Bath, Townshend was rolling.

From his position, Townshend set out to scuttle the policy to curb the East India Company. He himself had invested in it and certainly didn't want to see it sustain any losses. With the company's help, he had little trouble lining up enough factional support in Commons to sabotage Chatham's plans. Henry Seymour Conway, leader of the Commons, deserted Chatham and joined Townshend. The Rockingham and Grenville-Temple factions rallied to the defense of the company. Thus Townshend was able to move quickly to cut a deal while Chatham was still absent. In the end, instead of stripping the East India Company of its concession, he offered an agreement to renew the company's exclusive rights for another two years. In return, the company agreed to make a contribution of £400,000 to the Treasury, a sum it could easily afford without in the least disturbing the investments of its shareholders.

Grafton, aware of what Townshend was up to but unable to stop him, appealed to Chatham for help. The great man was too ill even to think about it, let alone respond or act. So, by December of 1766, Chatham's objectives for India had been sidetracked and the company could continue with business as usual.

Then, when Parliament returned to work in January, Townshend began to derail Chatham's American policy as well. A parliamentary debate had been arranged for January 26, 1767. Grenville, still smarting over the repeal of the Stamp Act and determined that the Americans must be made to pay, offered a now familiar motion calling upon the government to require that the colonies bear the expense of troops stationed there. Townshend airily declared that he already knew of a way to draw revenue from the Americans without arousing their ire—but he chose not to elaborate. Echoing the Declaratory Act, he asserted that Parliament had the absolute right to impose both internal and external taxes and "laughed unmercifully" at the idea that there was any distinction between the two. (This was his third flip-flop on the subject: He had vigorously supported the Stamp Act when he was in the Grenville government, belatedly backed its repeal when he served with the Rockingham government, and now was shamelessly deserting Chatham on this most provocative of all American issues.)

As soon as Townshend had finished speaking, Grenville leaped up to ask if the chancellor would now pledge himself to the Commons to raise colonial revenues. Townshend could not have withdrawn at this point even had he wished to do so. He promised that in due course, he would raise revenue in America. Immediately after the session, a bewildered Lord Shelburne wrote to Chatham, "What he means, I do not conceive."

A month later, Townshend presented his budget for the year. The national debt would be reduced by the East India Company's contribution. He would continue the land tax of four shillings to the pound on Tory gentlemen and other landholders. He said nothing about taxing America.

The opposition immediately moved to reduce the land tax to three shillings. Such a motion would normally have been waved away, but the Tory squires, Grenville supporters, and Rockingham faction combined, by prearrangement, to trap the evasive chancellor. They applauded his news of the revenues from the East India Company. And they reminded him forcefully of his pledge, made only a month before, to tax the Americans. They demanded to know why he was not making good on the promise. It was time, they argued, that English property owners got a tax break. Townshend pleaded that new taxes on the Americans "would be done by degrees and on mature consideration." This had no effect on the vote. The motion to reduce the land tax was swiftly carried, thereby wiping out the revenue gain from the East India Company and leaving government finances worse off than ever. Townshend's promise to levy taxes on the colonies had come due.

Three days later, the earl of Chatham arrived in London, having made a painful journey from Bath with a recuperative halt along the way. He found his India policy sabotaged and his American policy about to be reversed by Townshend. His first act was to write an instruction to Grafton to get rid of Townshend: "The writer hereof and the Chancellor of the Exchequer aforesaid cannot remain in office together; or Mr. C. Townshend must amend his proceeding. Duty to the King and zeal for salvation of the whole will not allow of any departure from this resolution." He instructed Grafton to offer the post of chancellor to Lord North. North, however, well aware of the state of Chatham's health and the growing disarray of the government, quickly declined the offer. He doubted the ministry would last much longer anyway.

When news of North's refusal reached Chatham, it proved to be a last straw for both his health and his nerves. Barely two weeks after returning to London, he collapsed almost completely. This time, it was not only the terrible pain of gout but the start of a nervous breakdown as well. The great man was moved to a house in Hampstead lent to him by a friend. Here he was devotedly cared for by his wife, Hester, and here he languished in nervous collapse for nearly two years, too distraught even to resign his office of lord privy seal.

So it was that after only eight months, the new government had lost its leader and was now the sole responsibility of the duke of Grafton. Chatham was gone, but contrary to Lord North's expectations the government remained. Despite the fiasco of the Chatham interlude, the king was determined not to go looking for another prime minister. He also felt that it was politically stabilizing to continue Chatham in office. Perhaps he would recover and return.

The king's sympathy for Chatham was genuine, and his feelings of loss considerable. He sent regular letters of sympathy and concern to Chatham during those first weeks, even proposing to visit his sickbed "to have the world know that I attended Lord Chatham." Chatham pleaded off. Finally, after the breakdown began, the king wrote, insisting that Chatham at least see Grafton. Chatham had not yet descended into complete breakdown; his reply, agreeing reluctantly to the king's request, was typically effusive:

> Penetrated and overwhelmed by your Majesty's letter and the boundless extent of your royal goodness, totally incapable as illness renders me, I obey your Majesty's commands, and beg to see the Duke of Grafton tomorrow morning, though hopeless that I can add weight to your Majesty's gracious wishes. Illness and affliction deprive me of the power of adding more, than to implore your Majesty to look with indulgence on this imperfect tribute of duty and devotion.

On June 1, Grafton's carriage arrived at the Hampstead house. He found Chatham in nervous prostration and near hysteria. His frame shook; at intervals, he would burst into tears at the smallest excuse. He collected himself only enough to tell Grafton that he would remain in office as long as nothing—*nothing*—would be expected of him. He did not resign his office until October 1768.

Meanwhile, there was now nothing to stop Charles Townshend from plunging England into yet another crisis with its American colonies.

Chapter 8

THE TOWNSHEND CRISIS

If the British Empire was acquired in a fit of absentmindedness, as the English have said in deprecation of their success, then the loss of the American colonies was certainly accelerated by a fit of absentmindedness when Charles Townshend made his brief flight across the pages of history in May of 1767.

After seeing America stirred to near rebellion over the Stamp Act, it would have been common sense for England's leaders to pause and reflect, to allow things to cool down in the colonies, to think through carefully what was essential and what was not in the ties that bound England and America together. Instead, with the newly ennobled earl of Chatham eclipsed by a nervous breakdown, the House of Commons allowed Charles Townshend to pass another tax bill and launch another crisis.

Even with the repeal of the Stamp Act, various issues still simmered in America, but in general the mood was quiescent. There was the new penny-per-gallon tax on molasses imports, there was the new Mutiny Act, and there were supposed restrictions on the westward migration of settlers. But none of these irritants was enough to inspire rebellion.

As the Chatham cabinet was forming in July of 1766, the New York Assembly was refusing for a second year to vote money for the support of English troops. The Grenville faction and others who had fought against repeal of the Stamp Act only months before were crying, "We told you so!" But New York had a particular gripe in that the preponderance of English troops was within its boundaries. General Gage was headquartered at the Battery in Manhattan; his main supply base was on Governors Island. There were additional troops at Albany and at Fort Ticonderoga, securing the Hudson and the inland route to Canada via Lake George, Lake Champlain, and the Richelieu River. In most of the other colonies and in the territories beyond, there were few—if any—troops: a handful in Massachusetts, New Jersey, and South Carolina; companies on remote garrison duties in Detroit and the west; and some in Pensacola and St. Augustine, Florida. Thus the New York Assembly judged that it was an unfair burden and another form of English taxation that New York citizens be required, under the Mutiny Act, to pay for the expense of supplies and billets.

The earl of Shelburne, in his position as secretary of state for the Southern Department and thus responsible for the colonies, had tried, at Chatham's instructions, to use a combination of firmness and moderation to move the New York Assembly. The assembly would not budge. In the last months of 1766, he dithered over what to do. Finally, in pathetic frustration, he wrote to Chatham at Bath, "After a great deal of painful consideration on so disagreeable a subject, I have nothing to submit to your lordship, except what I took the Liberty to say to the King this morning, that I hop'd both He and Parliament would distinguish between *New York* and *America*." Any action from London, in other words, should be directed only toward New York, not toward the colonies in general. This scarcely constituted a policy recommendation for dealing with the problem.

In February, Shelburne again wrote to Chatham, proposing that the royal governor of New York, Sir Henry Moore, be recalled and replaced by a military man. The name of Colonel John Burgoyne was suggested. But by this time, Chatham was so ill that he could only reply that he "could not enter into the details of things" and suggested that Shelburne and the duke of Grafton lay the American problem before Parliament and invite it to decide what to do.

Charles Townshend, knowing that Parliament craved to teach the Americans a lesson, leaped into the situation with great zest and no heed of the consequences.

* * *

In his vainglorious speech in January, Townshend had promised the House of Commons that he knew of a way of raising revenue in the colonies to which the Americans could not object. He repeated this promise when he presented his budget in February. Now, with Chatham incapacitated, Grafton bewildered, and Shelburne hesitant, Townshend was ready to make good on that promise.

On April 24, he presented a major package of American measures to a full cabinet meeting. Beginning with New York, his remedy was quite simple: Suspend the assembly until it was ready to comply with General Gage's request for funds. Next, to save money on the scattered deployment of English troops in America, withdraw them from the frontier country and concentrate them in the more volatile regions on the Atlantic coast. Two years before, the then secretary at war, Barrington, had recommended to the Rockingham government that troops be withdrawn from the colonies *entirely* and concentrated in Canada, Nova Scotia, and Florida. Townshend, however, grandly declared that he would never leave America open to another French invasion. Therefore, he said, "an army in America, and consequently American revenue, is essentially necessary."

He next turned to new taxes. Not surprisingly, he chose to expand the list of "external taxes"—new duties to be levied on American imports of tea, glass, lead, paint, and paper. After all, hadn't the Americans said that they would pay customs duties levied by England to control trade? But there was one important difference in the new duties: Townshend was proposing that these duties were not merely to control trade. His purpose, openly declared, was to *raise revenue* from the Americans.

Nor did Townshend stop with increasing the duties. He announced that the Treasury would soon send a new Board of Commissioners of Customs to America to improve the administrative machinery and revenue collection for the Crown. The new commissioners would set up headquarters in Boston. To tighten the screws further, he announced the expansion of the hated Admiralty Court. New branches would open in Boston, Philadelphia, and Charleston. To the Americans, more courts simply meant more prosecutions.

And he proposed that the powers of royal judges in America be extended to allow them to grant "writs of assistance." These writs would allow English customs officers to enter and search without warning any private homes or shops or warehouses where they thought they might find prohibited imports or smuggled goods.

Finally, in the most surprising and in some ways the most provocative move of all, Townshend announced that he was taking away from the colonial governments their responsibility for paying the salaries of royal governors, lieutenant governors, judges, and other high officials appointed by the Crown. In the future, Townshend decreed, these officials would be placed on a "civil list," just like civil servants in England. Their pay would be controlled from London, not by the colonies, and he proposed that these salaries be paid out of the revenue collected under the new customs duties. This removed any pretense that the duties were merely for the regulation of trade.

Thus Townshend headed into a new crisis with the Americans. Clearly, his objective was to insulate and protect the English authorities from having their pay withheld by angry colonial assemblies. But he had figured out nearly every way he could to incite trouble with the Americans. This hastily bundled package, which was intended to raise a mere forty thousand pounds, defied common sense. Townshend had made no effort to gauge the probable reaction. And there was no one to hold him back.

When he outlined his proposals to the cabinet, he was of course aware that there would be opposition. With Chatham so very ill, all Townshend had to do to quash the opposition was threaten to resign if he didn't get full backing. The cabinet hastily knuckled under.

And so Townshend went before Parliament on May 8, 1767, and one year after the repeal of the Stamp Act he effectively killed any chances of accommodation with America. Townshend brought to bear all his talent for humor, invective, and sarcasm. The Stamp Act, he assured the Commons, had not been the end of the British Empire; now the Americans would indeed be made to pay: "If once we lose the superintendency of the colonies, this nation is undone." His performance was later dubbed a "champagne speech" for its bubbly, heady effect on the listeners. His audience gave hardly a moment's thought to the hangover that might follow.

In the debate that ensued, Edmund Burke opposed the new taxes on the sensible grounds that it no longer mattered to the Americans whether taxes levied by London were external or internal—they would oppose either. Burke was right. Even George Grenville opposed Townshend's plan, telling him that "the Americans will laugh at you." Now a wiser man, Grenville predicted that the new levies would raise more harm for British merchants and manufacturers than they would revenues for the Exchequer. Instead, Grenville said, assess the colonies £400,000 for imperial costs, and require them to raise that money themselves. But on May 15, Townshend's package was approved by a vote of 180 to 98. It would take effect six months later.

It was Benjamin Franklin's subsequent judgment that the anti-American mood in Parliament was such that any measures would have been passed, with or without Townshend. Horace Walpole wrote that Parliament "acted to exercise its right to tax the colonies lest Americans give free reign to their high and imperious ambition of being themselves a nation of independent states." This was probably how many MPs felt when they voted.

Four months after his triumph, Charles Townshend died suddenly during an influenza epidemic. He never had to face the consequences of his measures. The House of Commons was a public stage, one well suited to the histrionic talents of Charles Townshend. When his curtain came down, his audience was still applauding, . . . but not for much longer.

In mid-April, while Townshend was preparing his American tax package, Benjamin Franklin wrote a *cri de cœur* to his friend Lord Kames, the Scottish High Court justice in Edinburgh. In the letter, Franklin warned of the breach between America and England that he saw coming:

America may suffer at present under the arbitrary power of this country; she may suffer awhile in a separation from it; but these are temporary evils that she will outgrow. America, an immense territory, favored by nature with all advantages of climate, soil, great navigable rivers and lakes, must become a great country, populous and mighty; and will, in a less time than is generally conceived, be able to shake off shackles that may be imposed on her and perhaps place them on the imposers. In the meantime, every act of oppression will sour their tempers, lessen greatly—if not annihilate—the profits of your commerce with them, and hasten their final revolt; *for the seeds of liberty are universally found there, and nothing can eradicate them.* And yet there remains among that people so much respect, veneration and affection for Britain that, if cultivated prudently, with kind usage and tenderness for their privileges, they might easily be governed for all ages, without force or considerable expense. But I do not see here a sufficient quantity of the wisdom that is necessary to produce such a conduct, and I lament the want of it. [Emphasis added.]

During his years in London, Franklin had continuously espoused the creation of a "consolidating union" between America and Britain in which the colonies would have a "fair and equal representation" in Parliament. But in writing to Kames, he acknowledged that the two countries were slipping farther and farther apart and that his idea of an imperial union was fading:

The time has been when the colonies might have been pleased with it; but they are now indifferent about it; and if it is much longer delayed they will refuse it. But the pride of this people [the English] cannot bear the thought of it; and therefore it will be delayed. Every man in England seems to consider himself as a piece of a sovereign over America; seems to jostle himself into the throne with the King, and talks of "our subjects in the colonies."

For all his love of London and his life there, Franklin was increasingly frustrated and losing patience with the blinkered mentality that had resulted in the Stamp Act and, now, the Townshend measures. After writing to Kames, Franklin took himself off on an extended visit to Paris and the French countryside.

In the colonies, initial reaction to Townshend's taxes was cautious and slow to form. The new taxes were of course limited in scope, not as inflammatory as the Stamp Act had been. Merchants, traders, and shopkeepers were enjoying a period of economic plenty and did not want to get into another trade war with England so soon after the repeal of the Stamp Act. But obviously, the issue of taxation without representation had not been resolved. Resentment was slower to rise this time, but as it did, it became stronger and deeper, more basic and widespread.

In the colonies, the man who gave voice to this stage in the long march to independence was a singularly undramatic, little-known lawyer in the Pennsylvania Assembly. His name was John Dickinson. Using straightforward, persuasive prose, Dickinson caught the minds and heart of his countrymen just as convincingly as had the flamboyant Patrick Henry two years before.

Dickinson, the son of a Maryland planter, was born in 1732. He received a classical education in America and then went to London to study law at the Middle Temple. After two years, he returned to the colonies and established a successful law practice in Philadelphia. By 1762, he had earned a modest fortune, entered politics, and won a seat in the assembly. Five years later, as the Townshend taxes were taking effect and the new Board of Commissioners of Customs was setting up shop in Boston, the first of Dickinson's *Letters from a Farmer in Pennsylvania to the Inhabitants of the British Colonies* appeared in Philadelphia's *Pennsylvania Chronicle*. In the simplicity of its opening passages ("With a good deal of surprise, I have observed that little notice has been taken of an Act of Parliament as injurious in principle to the liberties of these colonies as the Stamp Act"), Dickinson provided a voice that his fellow citizens wanted to hear. Over the next several months, he produced a series of twelve *Letters from a Farmer,* each attacking with legal and intellectual force a different aspect of the Townshend measures. The *Letters* were immediately picked up and reprinted in almost every colonial newspaper then published. The series was collected in pamphlet form, with three editions in Philadelphia, two in Boston, one in New York, and in June of 1768, one in London that included a brief preface by Benjamin Franklin. Other printings followed in Paris and Dublin.

Using the tone and style of a friendly family lawyer patiently leading a client through a discussion of legal interpretation, constitutional wisdom, and historic precedent, Dickinson dealt in turn with the implication of the suspension of the New York Assembly for American liberty, the establishment of the new Board of Customs Commissioners in Boston, the right of English judges to send English customs officers into American shops and homes, and the decision to remove royal governors and Crown officials from the pay of colonial governments in which they were employed.

Finally, Dickinson declared a new constitutional premise when he rejected entirely the Townshend "external taxes," the duties of tea, paint, glass, lead, and paper. The true issue, Dickinson declared, was

not whether a tax was internal or external but whether the intent of
the Parliament was to *raise revenue* rather than to regulate trade.
This was clearly the case with the new Townshend levies. Dickinson
acknowledged that Parliament could tax to regulate trade but asserted that it had no right to impose taxes simply to raise revenue.
This, he said, was the right of the colonial legislatures. Dickinson
called upon his countrymen to oppose Townshend's taxes just as
they had opposed the Stamp Act:*

> Here then, my dear countrymen, ROUSE yourselves and behold the
> ruin that hangs over your heads. If you ONCE admit that Great Brit-
> ain can lay duties upon her exports to us *for the purpose of raising
> money from us only,* she will then proceed to lay duties on articles
> which she prohibits us to manufacture—and the tragedy of American
> liberty is finished. If Great Britain can order us to come to her for
> necessaries we want, and can order us to pay what taxes she pleases
> before we take them away, or when we land them here, we are as
> abject slaves as France and Poland can show in wooden shoes and
> with uncombed hair.

But Dickinson was no rabble-rouser. He was a lawyer pleading a
case, and like Franklin, he was seeking an understanding, not revolution, and British respect for American liberties within the British
Empire.

He found some understanding in London when his *Letters* appeared there. The *London Magazine* gave him warm support in its
August 1768 issue:

> There is such just and cogent reasoning, such a spirit of liberty
> breathes through the whole of the American productions, at this
> time, as would not have disgraced ancient Greece or Rome, when
> struggling against oppression; at the same time that the authors and
> abettors of the present impolitick measures in England are as to argu-

---

*In building the second British Empire in the nineteenth and twentieth centuries,
the British followed Dickinson's constitutional reasoning. They left taxation for
revenue purposes entirely to the discretion of the local colonial and Commonwealth governments, but they created an effective trading system based on impe-
rial-preference tariffs. These were finally dismantled after World War II under heavy
U.S. pressure for worldwide free trade.

ment and language even below contempt. They are absolutely taking steps against the colonies that might have been expected from our princes and their wretched ministers in the 17th century, but rather disgrace the present reign, so distinguished for its blessings and its protecting the subject in enjoyment of liberty and prosperity. From our own observations we will venture to say that *nine persons in ten, even in this country, are friends to the Americans, and convinced that they have right on their side*. [Emphasis added.]

The rulers of England evidently did not agree.

On Townshend's sudden death, the duke of Grafton immediately offered the post of chancellor of the Exchequer to Lord North. Then thirty-five, North was conservative and noncontroversial, a man of no very strong political convictions except a desire to avoid dissent. He was perceived as a man on his way to the top, and it would not be long before he got there.

Grafton undertook other actions to shore up his unstable ministry. He turned to one of the most hard-nosed, nonliberal factions, that of the duke of Bedford. The Bedfordites, tired of being ignored, were willing to support Grafton, but their price was that the earl of Shelburne, whom they regarded as "weak" on America, be ousted. Grafton disliked Shelburne and would have been glad to be rid of him, but he was loathe to act directly or to dismiss a protégé of Chatham's, no matter how incapacitated Chatham might be. There was always the chance that the great man would rise up suddenly from his sickbed and take vengeance. Grafton therefore devised a strategy that he hoped would force Shelburne to resign: He invented the Colonial Department.

Over the years, the Board of Trade had administered England's growing collection of colonies. The board had been headed for nearly fifteen years by Lord Halifax, whose name is remembered in the leading port city of Nova Scotia. But in the cabinet, responsibility for directing policy was entrusted to the secretaries of state for the Southern Department, who dealt with the Americas and the Caribbean. This two-tier system was clumsy. With the king's approval, Grafton proposed to take policy away from Shelburne in the Southern Department, remove the administrative functions from the Board of Trade, and combine the two in a new, single office. This would be known interchangeably as the Colonial or American Department, and it would have its own secretary of state.

Grafton expected Shelburne to resign when he learned that his job had been axed—but Shelburne seldom made a decision without consulting Chatham, and Chatham was too ill to give advice to anybody. So Shelburne clung to his truncated office, isolated, even humiliated. The anti-American Bedfordites now entered the reorganized cabinet.

In January 1768, Viscount Hillsborough became Britain's first colonial secretary and head of the new American Department. He belonged to the faction known as the King's Friends, although this never meant the king's friendship. In fact, in later years, King George remarked that he did not know "a man of less judgment than Lord Hillsborough." Hillsborough, like Shelburne, was an Irish peer, but where Shelburne was difficult with people, secretive and insecure, Hillsborough was the opposite. He was loud and pompous, determined to play the strongman, but his personality could not long conceal his lack of talent, tact, or political wisdom. Almost as soon as he took office, the winds of trouble and unrest began to rise in the colonies, now often due to his own provocation. Once again, England had the wrong man in the wrong place at the wrong time.

In November of 1767, the new Board of Customs Commissioners had arrived in Boston and been given a distinctly chilly welcome.* Boston, the closest port of call to England, had a good harbor and an experienced (albeit unpopular) royal governor in Sir Francis Bernard. The new commissioners held their first meeting on November 18, 1767. They got right down to business, ordering effective measures for collecting taxes.

---

*Had the government in London been shrewd enough to have sent these commissioners to Philadelphia instead, history might have taken a different turn. The City of Brotherly Love, throughout this period and even during the Revolution itself, was far from being a cradle of liberty. Its politics was largely dominated by Quakers, whose tenet was to avoid violence and who wished to remain at peace with King George.

The Massachusetts Assembly, which had so effectively initiated the Stamp Act Congress two years earlier, responded quickly, drafting and voting a new Massachusetts Circular Letter to the other colonies, calling them once again to unite in opposition to the new taxes.

Samuel Adams was chief drafter of this circular, yet despite his crusty, combative patriotism, the document was no call to revolution: Its tone was moderate—had the English been able to regard it that way. Adams followed the reasoning and arguments of Dickinson on the tax question and did not seek to throw off English sovereignty, only to limit it. The circular was perhaps one of the clearest, most coherent statements made by the Americans on preserving colonial liberties within the framework of the British Empire. But it rejected unequivocally England's right to tax the colonies for revenue, and in English eyes this was tantamount to revolution.

The response of the other colonies to the circular was uncertainty. Pennsylvania opposed it: Joseph Galloway, speaker of the assembly, was a Quaker Tory who did not want Pennsylvania to get mixed up in the quarrels of her sister colonies. Galloway had deplored Dickinson's *Letters* as "fit only for the selectmen of Boston and mob meetings of Rhode Island." When the Pennsylvania Assembly received the Adams circular, he tabled it, intending to let it die. But the circular did not die of indifference in Pennsylvania or anywhere else in the colonies. Nor, most especially, in London.

The cabinet had decided that "a kind and lenient response" was the best way to deal with the circular, but it provided Viscount Hillsborough with his first major challenge, and he was not going to miss this opportunity to show the contumacious colonials who was in charge. He drafted his own circular letter of reply, which he sent to each of the colonial governors. In it, he said bluntly that the Massachusetts Circular was calculated "to promote an unwarrantable combination and to excite open opposition to the authority of Parliament." It was to be treated "with the contempt that it deserves." Hillsborough instructed the Massachusetts governor to order the assembly to rescind the circular immediately or face dismissal and not allow it to conduct other business until it had declared "disapprobation of this rash and hasty proceedings." Finally, he told all the governors that *any* colonial legislature that voted approval of the circular was to be dissolved immediately. Hillsborough's reply thus

attained high ranking as another English contribution to American
unity.

The duke of Grafton, who still retained something of Chatham's
sense of moderation, rebuked Hillsborough for ignoring the cabinet's original instructions to make a lenient response. But the letter
had already been shown to the king and was on its way across the
Atlantic. Grafton was no more able to control Hillsborough than he
had Townshend.

In Boston, the Sons of Liberty began to take things into their
own hands. Street demonstrations broke out. The homes of the
customs commissioners were threatened and in some instances
damaged. Customs-office "hirelings" were roughed up. The commissioners appealed to Governor Bernard for protection, but the
governor was powerless. He pleaded that his council (the equivalent
of a cabinet) would never approve requesting General Gage to order
out troops to patrol the city. Since the governor could not or would
not act, the commissioners, who could not carry out their revenue
collections without a show of strength, appealed directly to the
Royal Navy at Halifax for help. Commodore Samuel Hood, commandant at Halifax, was more than ready to oblige. The fifty-gun
warship *Romney* sailed into Boston Harbor.

Emboldened by this reinforcement, the commissioners decided
to strike back. They singled out Boston's leading shipowner and
merchant, John Hancock, who even if he hadn't actually taken to
the streets to demonstrate, was certainly in the forefront of the cause
of liberty. On June 10, 1768, customs officers boarded and seized a
small sloop owned by Hancock. The *Liberty,* as she was so provocatively named, had just arrived from Madeira with a mixed cargo of
wine and other dutiable goods. When the townspeople heard what
was going on, they descended on the wharf where the *Liberty* was
tied up and started a scuffle with the customs men. But a Royal Navy
contingent rowed over from the *Romney,* boarded the *Liberty,* and
quickly gained control. They took her out into the harbor and tied
her up alongside the *Romney,* a sight that was hardly cooling to
Boston tempers.

Just at this volatile time, Hillsborough's circular letter reached
Boston and the other colonial capitals. The Massachusetts Assembly
immediately rejected, by a vote of ninety-two to seventeen, the governor's demand to rescind its circular. Bernard promptly suspended

the legislature as ordered, but as an act of intimidation it failed utterly. The defiant assemblymen were hailed as the Glorious Ninety-two. The other seventeen were pilloried as traitors and British tools.

Colonial support for Massachusetts began to pour in. New Jersey, Connecticut, and Rhode Island would line up alongside Massachusetts by the autumn.

In the meantime, at the end of June, Maryland's governor, Horatio Sharpe, sent the Hillsborough letter to the Maryland Assembly. The delegates replied to the governor that "[they] would not be intimidated from doing what we think is Right." Next day, they voted to petition the king, echoing Massachusetts by saying that "a fixed and unalterable principle in the nature of things, and a part of the very idea of property, is that whatever a man hath honestly acquired cannot be taken from him without his consent." Governor Sharpe immediately dissolved the assembly.

Virginia passed its own circular letter, which followed along the same lines as that of Massachusetts. The governor promptly dismissed the House of Burgesses.

Delaware formally accepted the Virginia Circular and voted its own petition to the king. Its assembly was dismissed.

North Carolina copied Delaware, but Governor William Tryon judged that the mood of the colony was so volatile that he did not dare dismiss the legislature.

South Carolina acted in November, Georgia in December. Their assemblies were dismissed.

Pennsylvania's previously peaceable attitude changed with the arrival of the Hillsborough letter. Governor John Penn wrote to his uncle Thomas in London that "those persons who were the most moderate were now set in a flame and have joined the General Cry for Liberty." The *Pennsylvania Chronicle* called the letter "a daring insult to a free legislature" and declared that if Americans were to be prevented from protesting British oppression, "they were in a worse situation than their Negroes, who have the privilege of Petitioning their Masters whenever they please."

Joseph Galloway bowed to this change. When the assembly met in September to debate solidarity with Massachusetts, Galloway tried to salvage something of his Loyalist position by limiting the assembly's action to a petition to Parliament. The petition claimed for Americans "the rights of Englishmen" on taxes but did not endorse the Massachusetts Circular. Thus it saved itself from being dissolved.

By the end of 1768, every colonial legislature had voted for liberty and most had been dismissed. In the face of such treatment of their elected representatives, colonial merchants, shippers, and shopkeepers united once again in a "nonimportation policy" against English goods. So, as the year turned, the bonding of the American colonies was stronger than ever.

Chapter 9

ANOTHER REPEAL

In June 1768, Massachusetts governor Sir Francis Bernard had dissolved the assembly, and the Royal Navy's *Romney* was moored in Boston Harbor. In London, Hillsborough now took a step that the governor had avoided. He issued secret orders to General Gage to move at least one—and if possible, two—regiments from New York to Boston. He also ordered two more regiments, then on garrison duty in Ireland, to sail promptly for Boston.

On October 1, the British army took over Boston Common. The results were predictable. Merchants, shipowners, and shopkeepers embargoed British goods, and again economic sanctions took their toll. British exports to America fell by some 40 percent over the next months.

In May, while this new crisis was building in America, elections were being held in England for a new House of Commons. Out of a total of 558 seats, there would be 164 new members, including two of the most flamboyant political characters of eighteenth-century England, John Wilkes and Charles James Fox.

Wilkes and Fox were from vastly different backgrounds. Never either friends or allies, separated in age by a full generation, each

lived for the political spotlight. Neither had the personality or inclination to join the ranks of the tame and predictable politicians who
worked their way up the ladder to power; both enjoyed the freedom of opposition more than the discipline of office. Each in his different way would leave his mark as England stumbled into war with
America.

Charles James Fox, not yet twenty, was elected to the Commons
from a controlled, "safe" seat in Midhurst, Sussex. He was not even
in England at the time of the election, but on a leisurely grand tour
of Europe.

Fox was born with a silver spoon (and as it later turned out, a
silver tongue, too) in his mouth. He was the third son of Lord Holland, who as Henry Fox and member of the Commons, had helped
purge the Old Whigs for King George III in 1762. Holland had
passed on to his son a love of gambling, high living—and politics.
Charles James Fox was schooled at Eton and spent two indolent
years at Oxford. He wrote in 1766 to a friend, Richard Fitzpatrick:

> I am totally ignorant in every part of useful knowledge. I am more
> convinced every day how little advantage there is in being what at
> school and university is called a good scholar. One receives a good
> deal of amusement from it, but that is all. Indeed, I am afraid that my
> own natural idleness will in the end get the better of what little ambi-
> tion I have, and that I shall never be anything but a lounging fellow.

Lord Holland's solution for his idle but talented son was to get
him elected to the House of Commons. From Nice, where he was
laid up during the election, Fox wrote to Fitzpatrick that

> I have had one pox and one clap this tour. I believe I am the most
> unlucky rascal in the universe. We live a mile distant from the town of
> Nice which is perhaps the dullest town in the world, and what is a
> terrible thing there are no whores. I am now quite well; my poxes and
> claps have weakened me a great deal, and by means of the cold bath
> I recover again. *Je travaille toujours le matin,* and in the evening read,
> lounge, play at cards and talk.

It was often hard to know when to take Charles James Fox seriously. Horace Walpole, writing in his journal in 1774, recounted:

> Fox did not shine in the debate [in Commons], nor could it be won-
> dered. He had sat up playing hazard at Almack's from Tuesday eve-

ning, the 4th, till 5 in the afternoon of Wednesday, the 5th. An hour before, he had recovered £12,000 that he had lost, and by dinner, which was at 5 o'clock, he had ended losing £11,000. On Thursday he spoke in the debate; went to dinner at past 11 at night; from thence to White's where he drank until seven the next morning; thence to Almack's where he won £6,000 and between three and four in the afternoon he set off to Newmarket. . . . There being a report that Charles was going to be married, it was told to his father who replied: "I am glad of it, for then he will go to bed at least one night."

Nevertheless, Fox had a quick intelligence and the perceptive mind of the born politician; he was an amusing speaker and a great debater rather than a disciplined thinker. Neither was he as indolent as he pretended. If he had been indifferent to most of his studies at Oxford, he was nevertheless a voracious reader and loved languages. He read both Greek and Latin and polished his fluent French and Italian on his frequent trips to the Continent. These natural talents and his exaggerated self-assurance were well suited to the theater of Parliament, where he performed a major role as an irrepressible and lively figure for nearly four decades. One contemporary remarked, "Fox does not leave his hearers to follow; he drives them to follow him."

John Wilkes was of an altogether different social background and had a more provocative temperament than Fox. Wilkes was an outsider who made his mark by challenging the established order— from the king to government ministers to clergy to judiciary. He took on just about anyone he could find and held him up to ridicule. By doing so, he made himself a champion of the people at a time when the people had no political voice.

Born in 1725, Wilkes was elected to the House of Commons in 1757. He was a popular and witty gadfly who aligned himself wholeheartedly with Pitt. He also joined the circle led by Sir Francis Dashwood, who liked to conduct Rabelaisian "masses" and weird orgies at a private "black monastery" on his country estate. Wilkes worked at being notorious, but this was the accepted routine of ambitious young MPs in those times. When the earl of Sandwich told Wilkes that he would "either die of the pox or die on the gallows," Wilkes laughingly replied in what is still quoted as a classic English riposte: "That depends, my lord, on whether I embrace your principles or your mistress."

Seeking a wider audience than the Commons, Wilkes founded his own newspaper, the *North Briton,* which he used to launch a scurrilous campaign against the earl of Bute over the ousting of Pitt in 1762. Bute was so enraged that he resorted to an ill-judged tactic of issuing a general warrant to close down the paper. Wilkes went to court. A legal battle over the freedom of the press ensued; Wilkes won, which boosted his image as folk hero. Emboldened, he went on to attack the king. This time, he landed himself in a libel action. When it became clear that he would lose and go to jail, he decamped for France. In Paris, he was supported for four years by various friends at home, including the marquess of Rockingham.

He was declared an outlaw and stripped of his seat in the Commons. But by 1768, as the time for a new general election neared, he judged that things had cooled down enough for him to return and run for a seat. He got on the ballot to represent a radical constituency in Middlesex, a few miles outside London, and was elected at the head of the poll.

The king, still smoldering over Wilkes's libel four years before, wrote to Lord North, then leader of the Commons, "I think it highly proper to apprise you that the expulsion of Mr. Wilkes appears to be very essential and must be effected." For the king to order the expulsion of an elected member of the House of Commons was, to say the least, a very dubious, if not totally unconstitutional, action to take. Nevertheless, Lord North, ever dutiful, complied with the king's wishes.

Now began one of the most bizarre charades in English parliamentary history. One month after the election, Wilkes was arrested on the 1764 libel conviction, but he was freed by a mob of his supporters as he was being escorted to court. Then, on June 8, a court ruled that since he had again been elected to Parliament, his conviction was null and void. Ten days later, he was seized again and brought in front of another court, which sentenced him to prison on the four-year-old libel conviction. This time, the sentence stuck, and Wilkes went to jail. There, however, he was treated with uncommon kindness and given special food, wine, tobacco, linen, and reading matter.

In January 1769, when the new House of Commons met, Lord North maneuvered a series of procedural votes to deny Wilkes his seat. From prison, Wilkes announced that he would run again in Middlesex. In February, not only was he reelected without opposition, but the voters of Middlesex even raised a subscription to pay his legal fees.* But the king refused to bow to the voters of Middlesex.

For a second time, Lord North managed to swing enough votes to declare Wilkes "incapable of being elected to serve in the present Parliament." Wilkes promptly declared from his jail cell that he would, for the third time, be a candidate in the Middlesex by-election. By now, "Wilkes and liberty" was a cause célèbre not only in England but in America as well. Virginia patriots shipped a supply of tobacco to Wilkes in jail, and the South Carolina Assembly voted a grant of fifteen hundred pounds for an organization, the Middlesex Society for Supporting the Bill of Rights, to back Wilkes. The appropriation was promptly vetoed by South Carolina's royal governor.

In April 1769, as Middlesex voters prepared to go to the polls yet again, Lord North persuaded a Loyalist in the Commons, one Henry Luttrell, to resign his seat and run against Wilkes. No one else was prepared to take on such an assignment, and with good reason. When the campaign got under way, mob support for Wilkes was so volatile that wagers were offered that Luttrell's candidacy might cost him his life. In the end, Wilkes polled 1,143 to Luttrell's 246. But on May 8, Lord North collected sufficient votes in the House of Commons to declare Luttrell the winner.

The Wilkes affair dominated news and debates for more than a year. Wilkes's eventual loss was far from the end for him and turned out to be a Pyrrhic victory for the king. When Wilkes was released from prison in April 1770, he was elected an alderman of the City of London, where the king could not interfere. He finally won a seat in the Commons, unchallenged by the king, in 1774. As a member of Parliament, he supported the American cause throughout the Revolution. His name and that of Colonel Isaac Barré are remembered in the Pennsylvania city of Wilkes-Barre.

---

*About this time, Benjamin Franklin wrote to his son William, "I went last week to Winchester, and observed that, for fifteen miles out of town there was scarce a door or window-shutter next the road unmarked with 'Wilkes and Liberty.' "

* * *

In denying John Wilkes his elected place in Parliament, the king had created a folk hero. If the king could order Parliament to deny seating to Wilkes, could he not do the same to other members? Civil liberties and the growing power of the king became a rallying point for a new radicalism in English politics.

The Wilkes affair, the beginnings of this new radicalism, Lord Hillsborough's moves to "discipline" the Americans, and the spring elections of 1768 coincided with a downturn in the economy. A new American embargo on English goods was taking effect. Unemployment and lawlessness were on the rise, due in part also to the stresses of the early stirrings of the Industrial Revolution. The great landowners were displacing tenants and enclosing their acreage to consolidate fields, improve irrigation and drainage, and produce larger crops. The result was poverty in the rural areas and an increase in the cost of living as the population migrated to the cities, where unemployment was also rising.

With the first wave of industrialization, workers were crowding into factories that were little better than work prisons. Without trade unions, without the right to vote, without any voice in how England was governed, it was inevitable that rioting, demonstrations, and lawlessness became the way that people made themselves heard. Moreover, the American embargo on English imports added to the problem of joblessness and economic recession.

In May of 1768, Benjamin Franklin wrote to his Philadelphia friend John Ross this chilling description of life in London at the time:

Even this capital, the residence of the King, is now a daily scene of lawless riot and confusion. Mobs patrolling the streets at noonday, some knocking down all that will not roar for Wilkes and Liberty; courts of justice afraid to give judgments against him; coal heavers and porters pulling down the houses of coal merchants that refuse to give them more wages; sawyers destroying sawmills; sailors unrigging all the outward bound ships and suffering none at all to sail until merchants agree to raise their pay; watermen destroying private boats and threatening bridges [across the Thames]; soldiers firing among the mobs and killing men, women and children, which seems only to have produced a universal sullenness, that looks like a great black cloud coming on, ready to burst in a general tempest . . . while the ministry, divided in their counsels, with little regard for each other, worried by perpetual oppositions, in emotional apprehension of changes, intent on securing popularity in case they should lose favor, have for some years past had little time or inclination to attend to our small affairs, whose remoteness makes them appear still smaller.

At this chaotic juncture, further complicating matters for the duke of Grafton and his government, the earl of Chatham rose from his sickbed in October of 1768 and informed the king that he wished to resign as lord privy seal, the office he had continued to hold but never filled. As usual, Chatham laid it on thick in his letter of resignation:

Sir, Penetrated with the high honour of your Majesty's gracious commands, my affliction is infinite to be constrained to lay myself again at your Majesty's feet for compassion. My health is so broken that I feel all chance of recovery will be entirely procluded by continuing to hold the Privy Seal. . . . Under this load of unhappiness, I will not despair of your Majesty's pardon, while I again supplicate on my knees to your Majesty's mercy. . . . Shou'd it please God to restore me to health, every moment of my life will be at your Majesty's devotion. . . . I am, Sir, with all submission and profound veneration your Majesty's most dutiful and devoted servant.

Chatham's resignation was not welcome news for Grafton. He now had to find a replacement not only for the lord privy seal but also for the earl of Shelburne, who resigned when Chatham did. He managed to plug these vacancies with men who would keep his ship of state afloat for a while longer. It would not be long before Chatham would show that he was still a political force in the land.

When the House of Commons reconvened in November, George III stoutly declared the government's intention of "defeating the mischievous designs of those turbulent and seditious persons, who, under false pretenses, have but too successfully deluded numbers of my subjects in America." Behind these words, however, the government was faced with the same dilemma that had confronted Rockingham's government over the Stamp Act. Once again, the government was sounding the bugles of advance to prepare for a retreat.

In December, both houses of Parliament held special debates on the American situation. Not surprisingly, these debates ended with large majorities endorsing Hillsborough's measures "to secure royal government and parliamentary supremacy of the colonies." Both houses also voted an additional resolution, in which, invoking a treason law from the reign of Henry VIII, they called for the American "traitors" to be transported to England for trial. Lord Hillsborough and the Bedfordite faction of ultra-Loyalist hard-liners thus gained a clear upper hand to act virtually as they wished in order to bring the American colonies to heel.

Nevertheless, after the parliamentary debates were concluded and the votes counted, Hillsborough held an unusual meeting with the colonial agents in London. He disclosed to them some important second thoughts about the wisdom and usefulness of the Townshend measures. Hillsborough told the agents that he personally did not like the Townshend duties. He believed, quite rightly, that these were the root of the current colonial troubles, and he wished, he said, that they had never been proposed. But as to getting rid of them, he said, Americans would simply have to understand that Parliament would not yield on the right to levy taxes on the colonies. Townshend's taxes would not be repealed on any constitutional grounds (such as Pitt had declared against the Stamp Act), and if these laws were to be repealed, it would be only for the sake of "expediency." Hillsborough made it clear that what was at stake was not the rights of the Americans but the amour propre of the king and Parliament. At least Hillsborough had acknowledged a mistake.

It is not clear whether Benjamin Franklin was present at this meeting. If he was, he left no record. In any case, he had formed a mistrust and dislike of Hillsborough early on. Hillsborough's pompous, arrogant attitude toward all, and Americans in particular, fully justified Franklin's feelings.

Franklin wrote to Joseph Galloway, speaker of the assembly in Philadelphia, that "our friends are evidently increasing, but such is the ministerial influence in the House of Lords that one can scarce expect determination against the resolves [approved during the debates on America]." Franklin added that "the clamours of the manufacturers here are the most likely thing to bring the American minister [Hillsborough] to his senses."

Franklin was right in reporting that "our friends are . . . increasing," for on April 19, 1769, Thomas Pownall, a former deputy governor of New Jersey and royal governor of Massachusetts, now a member of the House of Commons, rose to deliver a remarkably bold speech in which he moved that Parliament repeal the Townshend duties entirely. If Pownall did not have the eloquence of Pitt, his speech nevertheless represented a turning point.

Thomas Pownall was one of the few men of politics in England who made a consistent, sympathetic, and informed effort to analyze and understand the problems confronting Britain in the social, economic, and political changes and pressures evolving in the colonies. Unlike so many of his peers, Pownall knew what he was talking about. He had spent six years in America during the French and Indian Wars; he had many American friends, including Franklin; and he had been successful as governor of Massachusetts. John Adams, who did not readily bestow compliments on Englishmen, wrote that Pownall was "a friend of liberty, the most constitutional governor, in my opinion, who ever represented the crown in this province."

Pownall's biographers have praised his character and intelligence, asserting that "his ideas show more originality than those of almost any of his contemporaries," that he "showed a broader understanding of the colonial point of view than almost any other British public man could display," and that "if any British politician saw the way to prevent an imperial revolution, it would have been Thomas Pownall." Unfortunately, Pownall spent his career at the fringes, never at the center of power.

Pownall entered the House of Commons in 1767. He carefully and deliberately maintained his independence and avoided any factional alignment. He was not much of a speaker, but he commanded respect and attention. He was a prodigious writer on a variety of subjects, such as linguistics, archaeology, economics, geography, and politics. His basic work on America, *Administration of the Colonies,* was first published in 1764. A second edition came out in 1765, at the time of the Stamp Act; a third, after the Stamp Act's repeal; a fourth, in 1768, when the Townshend taxes were approved. A fifth and final edition appeared in 1774.

Pownall's vision coincided with Franklin's—that is, a union in which Americans would sit in Parliament with the same rights, privileges, and responsibilities as their English counterparts. He examined thoroughly every conceivable aspect of the American problem, from geography to Indians to taxation and trade. Pownall's writings were consistently intelligent and sympathetic to Americans. He disparaged the mistakes he saw committed in London. Thomas Pownall became one of the first in the House of Commons, when the Revolutionary War began, to come out for prompt and unequivocal British recognition of American independence.

Pownall's basic premise was that the British government and the colonies were assuming mutually exclusive positions and that compromise was therefore necessary. He attacked the Townshend measures as unjust because the intent was to raise revenue to pay for royal governors and civil servants. He did not, however, challenge the constitutional right of Parliament to impose customs duties on the colonies. Pownall provided a sensible way for the government to back off from the confrontation without giving up Parliament's sacred rights. Though there was not the slightest possibility that Pownall could either force or win a vote against the government, his voice seems nevertheless to have been heard.

In May of 1769, three weeks after Pownall's motion for repeal, Grafton's government finally got down to cases on the Townshend measures. While Hillsborough had concluded that the duties had been a mistake, both he and Lord North, chancellor of the Exchequer, insisted that full repeal was impossible, that at least one tax must be retained. North repeated his argument that "if we are to run after America in search of reconciliation this way, I do not know a single act of Parliament that will remain." North then devised an ingenious rationale for retaining the tax on tea while rescinding the duties on paint and paper, lead, and glass. The latter four commodities, he reasoned, were manufactured in England; tea, however, came from India. It was not in Britain's interest to collect customs on its own products, so these duties should be repealed. The cabinet split, five to four, to retain the tax on tea and kill the other duties. Lord Clare, a distinguished lawyer of moderate views, told the

House of Lords that the government was keeping "a peppercorn of acknowledgment of the right to tax, of more value than millions in trade without it."

The cabinet authorized Hillsborough to notify the colonies that rescinding the Townshend taxes would be taken up at the start of the next parliamentary session. Meanwhile, troops in Boston would be reduced by half. The troops departed for Halifax, and the royal governor, Sir Francis Bernard, was instructed to return to London on permanent leave. Boston celebrated his departure in August with street parties.

The cabinet again instructed Hillsborough to adopt a "kind and lenient" tone in his message to the colonies. Hillsborough once again ignored this instruction and wrote angrily that "no measure should be taken [by the colonial governments] which can in any way derogate from the legislative authority of Great Britain" and that London expected "full execution of the laws" by colonial authorities. Grafton wrote in his autobiography that Hillsborough's tone "was calculated to do all mischief, when our real [intent] might have paved the way to some good."

Lord Hillsborough congratulated himself in the House of Lords, declaring that he now had "no apprehension of everything going well in the colonies, if they be let alone by Parliament and their affairs were not intertwined with opposition points."

This was an exaggerated hope. For the present, however, a sense of moderation did return.

In November 1769, William Strahan wrote to Benjamin Franklin, asking if he would outline his considered views on the colonial situation. In anticipation of the upcoming new session of Parliament, at which the Townshend duties were expected to be the first order of business, he submitted a list of basic questions for Franklin to deal with. Strahan's intention was to pass along Franklin's reply to the duke of Grafton in the hope, as he put it, that "Every Well Wisher to the peace and Prosperity of the British Empire must be desirous of seeing even the most Trivial Causes of Dissention amongst our Fellow-Subjects removed."

Franklin's reply was one of his major statements on colonial affairs. It did indeed reach the duke of Grafton, although without any discernible results, for the duke left office soon afterward. But it was a strong warning of things to come.

A partial repeal of the Townshend duties, Franklin said, was not likely to satisfy the colonies. It was not the tax, Franklin wrote, "but the principle of the Act express'd in the preamble, viz. that these Duties were laid for the Better Support of Government and Administration of Justice in the Colonies—This the Colonists think *unnecessary, unjust, and dangerous* to their Most Important Rights." Americans, he continued, objected to the whole of the Townshend duties "and will continue if the whole is not repealed."

After dealing in detail with each of Strahan's questions, Franklin concluded that

> I will go a little farther, and tell you what I fear is more likely to come to pass in Reality:
>
> I apprehend that the Ministry, at least the American part of it, being fully persuaded of the Right of Parliament, think it ought to be enforc'd whatever may be the Consequences. . . . I think it likely that no thorough redress of Grievances will be afforded to America this session. This may inflame Matters still more in that Country; further rash Measures there may create more Resentment here, that may Produce not merely ill-advis'd and useless Dissolutions of their Assemblies, as last Year, but Attempts to Dissolve their Constitutions; more Troops may be sent over, which will create more Uneasiness; to justify the Measures of Government your Ministerial Writers will revile the Americans in Newspapers, as they have already began to do, treating them as Miscreants, Rogues, Dastards, Rebels, &c, which will tend farther to alienate the Minds of the People here from them, and diminish their Affections to this Country.
>
> Possibly too, some of their warm Patriots may be distract'd enough to expose themselves by some mad action to be sent for Hither, and Government here be indiscreet enough to Hang them on the Act of Henry VIII. Mutual Provocation will thus go on to complete the Separation; and instead of that cordial Affection that once and so long existed, and that Harmony so suitable and so Necessary to the Happiness, Safety and Welfare of both Countries, and Implacable Malice and Mutual Hatred will take place. . . .
>
> I hope, therefore, that this may all prove False Prophecy; and that you and I may live to see as sincere and Perfect a Friendship estab-

lish'd between our respective Countries as has subsisted between Mr.
Strahan and his truly affectionate friend. . . . B. Franklin

Six years before the Revolution, Franklin could see clearly how
fixed attitudes and repeated misjudgments were bringing open conflict far closer than anyone in the king's high councils was prepared
to see.

Parliament reconvened on January 9, 1770. First, of course,
would come the king's speech, which always opened a new session.
As the Parliament awaited His Majesty in the House of Lords, in
tottered that frail ghost from the past, the earl of Chatham.

Since his resignation in 1768, he had recovered from his nervous breakdown and resumed many of his social and political activities. Now here he was, for the first time in three years, back in
Westminster.

The king arrived and delivered a cliché speech in which he
pledged to give serious attention to North America. When the king
finished, he and members of the House of Commons departed,
. . . and Chatham rose painfully to his feet to address the Lords.

He dealt with America only briefly, albeit provocatively. It was his
hope, he said, that the colonies would not return to tranquillity until
the invasion of their liberties had been redressed. He added his voice
to those in favor of rescinding the Townshend duties.

Then he continued, saying, "I need not look abroad for grievances—the grand capital mischief is fixed at home." To the uneasy
surprise of the peers, Chatham launched into the case of John
Wilkes, still in jail. The root of discontent in England—its "notorious dissatisfaction," Chatham called it—lay in the fact that the
House of Commons had illegally deprived an elected member of his
seat. And since John Wilkes had been deprived of his seat, Chatham
declared, the whole Parliament was sitting illegally, should be dissolved, and new elections held. With all of his old eloquence and
fervor, Chatham told the House of Lords that

The character and circumstances of Mr. Wilkes have been very im-
properly introduced into this question. With one party he was a patriot of the first magnitude; with the other the vilest incendiary. For
my own part I consider him merely and indifferently as an English

subject, possessed of certain rights which the laws have given him, and which the laws alone can take away from him. I am neither moved by his private vices nor by his public merits. In his person, though he were the worst of men, I contend for the safety and security of the best; and God forbid, my lords, that there should be a power in this country of measuring the civil rights of a subject by his moral character, or by any other rule but the fixed laws of the land.

When Chatham concluded, Lord Camden, the lord chancellor and a key member of the government, rose to admit that he also now regarded the expulsion of Wilkes as an illegal act and regretted that in his position as the highest legal officer of the government, he had not opposed the action. A few days later, at the prodding of the king, Camden was removed from office. The king quickly renewed his enmity toward Chatham. The government had begun to unravel.

Nine days after Chatham's speech, the lord mayor of London, William Beckford, member of the House of Commons and a Chatham supporter, led a large crowd of Wilkes supporters to Whitehall. They bore a petition declaring that Parliament no longer represented the people, that its acts were unconstitutional, and that it was controlled by the king's ministers, who should be dismissed. The citizens of Westminster drew up a similar protest. Still more protests came from a freeholders organization that claimed to represent sixty thousand voters in Bristol, Leeds, Yorkshire, Worcestershire, Herefordshire, Somerset, Cornwall, Northumberland, Devonshire, Derbyshire, Gloucestershire, Wiltshire, Newcastle, and Morpeth. "Wilkes and liberty!" remained a battle cry in English politics for many years.

Chatham had renewed himself as a standard-bearer emeritus opposing the king, his government, and the encroachment of royal power. But the strength of this opposition, even with Chatham once again on board, was only in voices, not in votes. Nevertheless, Chatham's speech did succeed in bringing down the duke of Grafton, whom he had placed in power in 1766. Three weeks after Chatham's speech, on January 28, 1770, Grafton resigned his wearisome and unsuccessful tenure.

Lord North was waiting in the wings to succeed him.

Chapter 10

THE KING FINDS A PRIME MINISTER

After five prime ministers in ten years, King George III had at last found his man. From 1770 to 1782, Lord North made the phrase "the king's government" mean exactly that. He never made any pretense that it was *his* government, as others had done. Seldom did he challenge the king or question his judgments or decisions. Nor did he attempt to assert himself, particularly in matters concerning the American colonies; he did not press his opinions on a king who had more than enough opinions of his own. The king fixed policies; Lord North carried them out. Thus, without exercising much will or influence of his own, he became the prime minister who lost the American colonies.

Lord North would probably have been an outstandingly successful peacetime prime minister—but the war engulfed him. He was an amiable, good-humored, equitable man, one of the most skillful and effective parliamentarians ever to run a government. He wielded power—in the name of the king—with a light touch, but there was never any doubt who was in charge. Earlier, the earl of Bute had served the king with total personal loyalty, but Bute made enemies and failed politically. Lord North made friends and succeeded. Grenville wrote, with some admiration, of Lord North, "He betrayed no ostentation or vainglory in his position, never offended by an undue exhibition of the powers he wielded, and restricted himself to the discharge of his duties as an adviser to the Crown."

North had entered the House of Commons in 1754; his father, the earl of Guilford, sat in Lords. From the outset of his political career, he avoided taking on a specific identity or aligning himself with any particular clique or faction. He was easygoing and popular; he had few enemies and no powerful backers. He displayed no notable ambition, did not intrigue for power. His amiable personality gave him advantages the more contentious politicians did not enjoy. He managed with deftness, humor, and efficiency.

One of his diverting ways of dealing with long, windy debates in the Commons was to tilt his large, jowly head back on his seat and doze off while the speakers droned on. (This was often justified by the sessions that went on till 3:00 A.M. or even later.) On one occasion, George Grenville embarked on a lengthy speech on his favorite subject, government finance. North tilted himself back and said to a neighbor, "Wake me up when he gets to modern times." When his neighbor eventually nudged him, North opened his eyes, listened for a minute or two, and then said loudly, "Zounds! You have waked me a hundred years too soon!" On another occasion, when a member complained that while he spoke, the prime minister was sleeping, North murmured audibly, "Would to God I were."

Soon after North became prime minister, Horace Walpole wrote this vivid description:

> Nothing could be more coarse or clumsy or ungracious than his outside. Two large prominent eyes that rolled about to no purpose, for he was utterly shortsighted, a wide mouth, thick lips, and inflated visage that gives him the air of a blind trumpeter. A deep untunable voice which, instead of modulating, he enforced with unnecessary pomp, a total neglect of his person, an ignorance of every civil attention, disgusted all who judged by appearance, or withheld their approbation till it was courted.
>
> But within that rude casket were also encoused* many useful talents. He had much with, good humour, strong natural senses, assurances and promptness both of concept and elocution. He had

---

Encoused is a word used in the eighteenth century but now obscure.

knowledge and though fond of his amusement, seemed to have all the necessary activity until he reached the summit.

But in later years, when Walpole wrote his *Memoirs of the Reign of King George III,* he had stiffened his opinion and sharpened his critical judgment: "As a minister, he had no foresight, no consistence, no firmness, no spirit. He miscarried in all he undertook in America, and was more improvident than unfortunate, less fortunate than he deserved to be. He stooped to be but a nominal prime minister." Walpole heaped more blame than North deserved. North's strength was his total loyalty to the king—but this was also his weakness. It was out of unswerving loyalty that he carried out the policies that led to disaster. He was no war leader, and he knew it, and yet despite his numerous attempts to resign, the king would not let him go. His potential for success was blown away by the eight years of the American Revolution. And yet, remarkably, he kept his equitable temper to the end.

A month after becoming prime minister, North was ready to deal with rescinding the Townshend taxes. On March 5, 1770, he moved in the House of Commons to repeal all but the duty on tea. Thomas Pownall moved yet again that *all* the offending duties should be repealed. But Lord North had received a written instruction from the king, informing him bluntly that while "there is no inclination for the present to lay fresh taxes upon them . . . I am clear that there must always be one tax to keep up the right, and as such I approve of the tea duty." Lord North, doing the king's bidding, simply brushed Pownall's motion aside. He reminded the Commons that the government was repealing those duties that were hurting English exports—paper, paint, lead, and glass—and retaining the one tax that would not hurt British industry. After minimal debate, Pownall's motion was put to the vote and defeated by 204 to 142. The tea tax would remain.*

Benjamin Franklin, who still held a certain sentimental belief in

---

*For the next decade, in most votes in the House of Commons that concerned the American colonies, the pro-American opposition numbered about 140.

the benign wisdom of King George III, was unaware that it was the king who was insisting on retaining the tax on tea. He wrote of the matter to a friend in Philadelphia:

> I think the full repeal could have been carried, but that the ministry were persuaded by Governor Bernard [recently returned from Boston] and some lying letters said to be from Boston, that the associations not to import [English goods] were all breaking to pieces, that America was in the greatest distress for want of goods, that we could not possibly subsist any longer without them, and must of course submit to any terms Parliament should think fit to impose on us. This, with the idle notion of the dignity and sovereignty of Parliament, which they are so fond of, and imagine will be endangered by further concessions, prevailed, I know, with many to vote for the ministry. . . .
>
> Though Lord North and the Duke of Grafton were and are, in my opinion, rather inclined to satisfy us, yet the Bedford party are so violently against us that the more moderate measures could not take place. This party never speaks of us but with evident malice; "rebels" are the best name they can afford us, and I believe they only wish for a colorable pretense and occasion of ordering soldiers to make a massacre among us.

By chance, a "colorable pretense and occasion . . . to make a massacre among us" took place on the very same day—March 5, 1770—that the Commons voted partial repeal of the Townshend taxes: the Boston Massacre.

By March 1770, English troops in Boston had been reduced by half. The civilian population's awe at the sight of redcoats had also diminished, replaced by open resentment and contempt. Fights and brawls broke out regularly between civilians and off-duty soldiers.

British Army soldiers of that day were often press-ganged into uniform, subjected to the harshest of discipline, paid pennies. They were, however, permitted to look for off-duty work from the Boston merchants or farmers.

On March 2, an off-duty soldier turned up at a ropewalk on the Boston waterfront. When he asked for work, he was told by the rope maker, "You want work—clean my shithouse." The soldier replied by swinging his fists at the rope maker, took a beating in return, retreated from the scene—and then returned shortly with some of his fellows. A brawl ensued between the redcoats and the factory hands and continued till the brawlers finally wore themselves out.

Next day, more fighting broke out between soldiers and civilians. More and more men were drawn in, and clubs and cutlasses replaced fists. March 4 was, fortunately, a Sunday. Boston braced itself for a riotous Monday.

March 5: freezing weather and snow-covered streets. Bostonians, looking for trouble, headed for the Customs House on King Street, the focal point of demonstrations since the Stamp Act.

On his way down King Street (at the corner where modern-day State and Congress Streets intersect) a young Boston apprentice, Edward Gerrish, encountered a British soldier and yelled at him, saying there were no gentlemen among the officers of his regiment. A soldier in the uniform of the same regiment who was on sentry duty at the Customs House stepped into the street and clouted the apprentice from behind. Other soldiers in the vicinity jumped Gerrish. Within minutes, civilian reinforcements joined in the melee, and the outnumbered soldiers retreated—all but the lone sentry at the Customs House, who had struck the first blow. He stood his post, facing a growing and angry mob yelling, "You damned rascally Scoundrel Lobster son of a bitch!"

The soldier, Private Hugh White, lowered his bayonet and threatened to run through anyone who came for him. The colonials pelted him with snowballs and chunks of ice. Bells began ringing in the nearby churches. The mob swelled.

From the main guard post a short distance away, Captain Thomas Preston, an experienced officer, watched the mounting uproar. He had to act. He ordered out a full guard of six privates and a corporal to the assistance of Private White. Marching through the crowd in good military order, their bayonets fixed, Preston's reinforcements reached the Customs House. But instead of immediately returning to the guardhouse with Private White, Preston ordered them to form a line in front of the Customs House.

An ugly standoff built up. Richard Palmes, a Boston merchant, pushed to the head of the mob and warned Preston not to order his troops to fire. Preston acknowledged the warning, but by now the crowd was pressing almost against the bayonets.

Then someone hurled a piece of ice. It almost struck a soldier, but not quite. Even so, the soldier slipped and fell, and as he regained his footing, he fired—certainly without orders, but whether by accident or design was never clear. Now the other soldiers aimed into the mob and fired. Eleven civilians were hit. Three were killed instantly, one died a few hours later, and another lingered on for several days. Six were only wounded. Throughout the city, there was a total breakdown of order.

Lieutenant Governor Hutchinson immediately ordered Preston and his soldiers off to jail. Twenty-four hours later, he ordered the rest of the army to withdraw to Castle William, a fortified island in Boston Harbor.

A trial had to take place, but a superior-court justice ruled that in the volatile atmosphere, Captain Preston and his soldiers could not get a fair hearing. Judicial action was postponed for six months.

Hutchinson's report on the Boston Massacre reached London in late April, by which time calm had been restored. There was nothing to be done from London. However, the belligerent Viscount Hillsborough, who had been retained in Lord North's government as head of the American Department, set up a special committee of the Privy Council to undertake a full secret examination of colonial affairs and to make recommendations for future action.

News that the Townshend duties had been repealed reached the colonies in mid-April. Nevertheless, patriot activists tried to persuade merchants and shopkeepers to protest the tax on tea by continuing to refuse to handle English imports. But the Boston Massacre had a cooling effect on patriotic passions. When things got out of hand, merchants and shopkeepers were always more vulnerable to damages and financial losses than were the leaders of demonstrations, no matter what or how good the cause. The *New York Gazette* commented, "It's high time a stop was put to mobbing, without which property will soon be very precarious, and God knows where it will end."

Thus tempers calmed and the atmosphere returned to normal. New legislatures were being elected to replace those that had been dissolved or dismissed on Hillsborough's orders two years before.

Pennsylvania, despite Franklin's exhortations from London, re-opened its warehouses and resumed trading in English goods—except for tea*—in May. New York followed.

Lord North certainly preferred calm to confrontation. Hillsborough's measures—withdrawing English troops from the frontier posts and moving them to the seaboard, thus reinforcing General Gage—appeared to ease confrontation. By withdrawing the troops, England no longer pretended to control the westward expansion of white settlers prohibited by the 1763 edict. Regardless of the risks of moving into Indian territory, settlers were pushing west.

In December, Benjamin Franklin, who had served as the London agent for Pennsylvania, Georgia, and New Jersey, was now voted by Massachusetts to become its representative as well. Accordingly, Franklin sought a meeting with Lord Hillsborough for what he expected would be a routine presentation of his new credentials.

Franklin, who had been dealing with Hillsborough off and on for two years, had an infinite capacity for getting on with difficult men—as long as the intellectual qualities were there and the civilities were maintained. But he had found scarcely anything pleasant or redeeming in Hillsborough, who was, he wrote, characterized by "conceit, wrong-headedness, obstinacy and passion," who constantly made American affairs worse by "perverse and senseless management." Franklin expected the worst from Hillsborough and was prepared to deal with it, but on January 17, 1771, he was pushed nearly to the breaking point.

For Hillsborough, Massachusetts was the most troublesome colony in America, at the root of the American problem. He was determined to show Franklin who was in charge, who was laying down the law. Franklin, always the good journalist, left an account of the conversation between them. While it was not of great historical importance, it reveals much about the attitude of King George III's ministers: "I went this morning to wait on Lord Hillsborough," he

---

*Instead of tea from England, the colonies were consuming large quantities of tea smuggled in from Holland. Some East India Company tea was coming in legally, but the smuggled tea was cheaper.

began. "The porter at first denied his lordship. I left my name and drove off." But as he drove away, his coachman heard a call and turned back to Hillsborough's door. An agitated porter came to the carriage and said, "His lordship will see you, sir."

Franklin was ushered into a waiting room, where he found, among others, ex-governor Bernard, home from Boston. A secretary soon appeared and said that Hillsborough would see him immediately. His account continues:

> His lordship came towards me and said: "I was dressing in order to go to court; but hearing that you were at the door, who are a man of business, I determined to see you immediately." I thanked his lordship and said that at present my business was not much; it was simply to pay my respects and to acquaint him with my appointment by the House of Representatives of Massachusetts Bay to be their agent here, in which station if I could be of any service—I was going to say, to the public, I should be happy; but his lordship, whose countenance changed at my naming that province, cut me short by saying something between a smile and a sneer.

A vigorous exchange ensued. Hillsborough suddenly inflated a simple matter of protocol into an issue of relations between the king's government and the colonies:*

LH: I must set you right there, Mr. Franklin. You are *not* agent.

BF: Why, my lord?

LH: You are not appointed.

BF: I do not understand your lordship. I have the appointment in my pocket.

LH: You are mistaken. I have later and better advices. I have a letter from Governor Hutchinson; he would not give his assent to the bill.

BF: There was no bill, my lord. It was a vote of the House.

LH: There was a bill presented to the governor for the purpose of appointing you and another, one Dr. Lee, I think he is called, to which the governor refused his assent.

---

*The following exchange is Franklin's verbatim account. Punctuation, italics, and parenthetical matter are his.

BF: I cannot understand this, my lord; I think there must be some mistake in it. Is your lordship quite sure that you have such a letter?

LH: I will convince you of it directly. (Rings the bell.) Mr. Pownall (a Board of Trade secretary) will come in and satisfy you.

BF: It is not necessary that I should now detain your lordship from dressing. You are going to court. I will wait on your lordship another time.

LH: No, stay; he will come immediately. (Pownall comes in.) Have you not at hand Governor Hutchinson's letter, mentioning his refusing assent to the bill appointing Dr. Franklin agent?

Pownall: My Lord?

LH: Is there not such a letter?

P: No, my lord. There is a letter relating to some bill for the payment of a salary to Mr. De Berndt (former agent) and I think to some other agent, to which the governor has refused his assent.

LH: And there is nothing in the letter to the purpose I mention?

P: No, my lord.

BF: I thought it could not well be, my lord; as my letters are by the last ships, and they mention no such thing. Here is the authentic copy of the vote of the House appointing me, in which there is no mention of any act intended. Will your lordship please take a look at it? (With seeming unwillingness he takes it but does not look into it.)

LH: An information of this kind is not properly brought to me as secretary of state. The Board of Trade is the proper place.

BF: I will leave the paper then with Mr. Pownall to be . . .

LH: To what end would you leave it with him?

BF: To be entered on the minutes of the board, as usual.

LH: (Angrily) It shall not be entered there. No such paper shall be entered there while I have anything to do with the business of that board. The House of Representatives has no right to appoint an agent. We shall take no notice of any agents but such as are appointed by acts of Assembly to which the governor gives his assent. We have had confusion enough already. Here is one agent appointed by the

Council, another by the House of Representatives. Which of these is agent for the province? An agent appointed by an act of Assembly we can understand. No other will be attended to for the future, I can assure you.

BF: I cannot conceive, my lord, why the consent of the governor should be thought necessary to the appointment of an agent for the people. It seems to me that . . .

LH: (With a mixed look of anger and contempt) I shall not enter into a dispute with *you,* sir, upon this subject.

BF: I beg your lordship's pardon; I do not presume to dispute with your lordship; I would only say that it seems to me that every body of men who cannot appear in person where business relating to them may be transacted should have the right to appear by an agent. The concurrence of the governor does not seem to me to be necessary. It is the business of the people that is to be done; he is not one of them; he is himself an agent.

LH: (Hastily) Whose agent is he?

BF: The King's, my lord.

LH: No such matter. He is one of the corporation by the province charter. No agent can be appointed but by an act, nor any act pass without his assent. Besides, this proceeding is directly contrary to express instructions.

BF: I did not know there had been such instructions. I am not concerned with any offence against them, and . . .

LH: Yes, your offering such a paper to be entered is an offence against them. (Folding it up again without having read a word of it.) No such appointment shall be entered. When I came into the administration of American affairs I found them in great disorder. By my firmness they are now something mended; and while I have the honor to hold the seals I shall continue the same conduct, the same firmness. I think my duty to the master I serve, and to the government of this nation, requires it of me. If that conduct is not approved, they may take my office from me when they please. I shall make them a bow and thank them. But while I continue in it I shall resolutely persevere in the same firmness. (Spoken with great warmth and turning pale in his discourse, as if he was angry at something or somebody besides the agent, and of more consequence against himself.)

BF: (Reaching out his hand for the paper which his lordship returned to him.) I beg your lordship's pardon for taking up much of your time. It is, I believe, of no great importance whether the appointment is acknowledged or not, for I have not the least conception that an agent can *at present* be of any use to any of the colonies. I shall therefore give your lordship no further trouble.

On that note, Franklin withdrew, and his account ends. A few days later, he wrote to his friend Samuel Cooper in Boston:

I have since heard that his lordship took great offense at some of my last words, which he calls extremely rude and abusive. He assured a friend of mine that they were equivalent to telling him to his face that the colonies could expect neither favor nor justice during his administration. I find he did not mistake me.

From then on, Franklin avoided transacting any business with Hillsborough directly. He acted as agent for Massachusetts, requiring no blessing from Hillsborough to pursue his lobbying activities, his social life, or his correspondence (which by now was being read by the English espionage services, as Franklin well knew).

News of Hillsborough's snubbing of Franklin spread quickly through parliamentary circles. Edmund Burke, who had been appointed agent for New York the previous year, responded vigorously, leaping on the constitutional point that giving royal governors veto power over the appointment of agents would tighten the king's grip over colonial governments and people. Burke wrote:

This I consider in Effect as destructive of one of the most necessary mediums of communication between the Colonies and the parent Country. The provinces ought in my opinion to have a direct intercourse with the Ministry and Parliament here, by some person who might be truly confidential with them, and this would totally frustrate this end, and the agent would become a mere officer of the crown.

Hillsborough was well on his way toward creating another crisis when he suddenly left office in August of 1772. Ironically and quite by accident, Franklin played a significant role in Hillsborough's downfall.

                                *   *   *

Franklin may well have been the only man in London who tried
to think through a clear course that might have avoided the Revolutionary War had his advice and wisdom been listened to and followed by the men in power. But neither Lord North, nor
Hillsborough, nor anyone else at that level in the government had
any interest in his American views. Franklin wrote home at one
point that "[a]s to my own sentiments, I am weary of suggesting
them to so many different inattentive heads, though I must continue to do so while I stay among them."

Franklin had by now given up on his idea of seating Americans in
the House of Commons, and he had finally concluded that Parliament had no right whatsoever to legislate for the colonies. He
wrote:

> The more I have thought and read on the subject, the more I find
> myself confirmed in my opinion that no middle doctrine can be
> maintained. Something might be made of either of the extremes—
> that Parliament has the right to make all laws for us, or that it has the
> power to make no laws for us; and I think the arguments for the latter
> more numerous and weighty than those for the former. Supposing
> this doctrine was established, the colonies would then be so many
> separate states, only subject to the same King, as England and Scot-
> land were before the union.

In Franklin's evolving concept, the colonies were bound to England not by the powers of Parliament but by an abstract sovereignty of the king. In a pamphlet, *The Causes of the Present
Distractions in America Explained,* Franklin wrote in 1769:

> There is in America scarce a man, there is not a single native of our
> country who is not firmly attached to his King by principle and by
> affection. But a new kind of loyalty seems to be required of us, a
> loyalty to Parliament; a loyalty that is to extend, it seems, to a surren-
> der of all our properties, whenever a House of Commons, in which
> there is not a single member of our choosing, shall think fit to grant
> them away without our consent, and to a patient suffering loss of our
> privileges as Englishmen, if we cannot submit to make such surren-
> der. We were separated too far from Britain by the same ocean, but
> we were united strongly to it by respect and love, so that we could at

any time freely have spent our lives and our little fortunes in its cause. But this unhappy new system of politics tends to dissolve these bands of union and to sever us for ever.

On another occasion, he said this:

The sovereignty of the Crown I understand. The sovereignty of the British legislature outside of Britain I do not understand. The British state is only the island of Great Britain. The British legislature are undoubtedly the only proper judges of what concerns the Irish state, and the American legislature of what concerns the American states respectively. Parliament has the power only within the realm.

Where he had once lagged behind, Franklin was now ahead of even the New England patriots in his position. His concept was too farsighted for King George III and his government.

There was one more "might have been" period before the Revolution for working out a genuine understanding of a fundamental relationship between England and America as defined by Franklin. This was the brief period of calm between 1771 and 1772, after the partial repeal of the Townshend duties and before the Boston Tea Party. Not for ten years had a prime minister been so secure with both king and Parliament. All that was needed was strength of vision, political courage, statesmanship, and a readiness to change. But these qualities were not to be found in Lord North or in Lord Hillsborough and certainly not in the king.

From Boston that spring of 1771, Samuel Cooper wrote to Franklin of "a pause in politics," which, he said, would give the government in London "a fair opportunity of adopting the mildest and most prudent measure respecting the colonies without the appearance of being threatened or drove."

Behind the scenes, General Gage was taking a particularly hard line in his secret dispatches to London. Gage had managed to achieve a degree of acceptance, if not popularity, in the colonies, having married an American socialite from New Jersey and enjoying as he did Loyalist social circles and hospitality in New York. But in his dispatches, he wore a different face. A period of calm, he wrote, was a time for England "to assert, but also support that supremacy which she claims over members of the Empire, or she will soon be supreme only in words and we shall become a vast empire of many different parts, disjointed and independent of each other without any head." He warned that "democracy is too prevalent in America, and claims the greatest attention to prevent its increase with fatal effects." He urged that London cramp American commerce and industry "as far as it can be done prudently."

This kind of advice was expected by the king and Lords North and Hillsborough, not the philosophizing of Benjamin Franklin. Hillsborough, fixated on preparing for a crisis, set his own pot to boiling.

In the spring of 1772, Hillsborough notified the Massachusetts authorities that payment of the salaries of all of the superior-court justices would now be removed from colonial administration, in accordance with a provision of the Townshend Act that had not been rescinded, and handled by the British from funds to be collected in the form of duties on tea. Already the salaries of Thomas Hutchinson, now governor, and Andrew Oliver, lieutenant governor, were being paid by the British. Clearly, the reason for this new action was to tighten London's control over Massachusetts.

The move roused Samuel Adams to action. When Governor Hutchinson refused Adams's request to convene the legislature to discuss the proposal, Adams mobilized the local town meetings, which were immune to the governor's authority. He formed a Committee of Correspondence, whose purpose was "to state the rights of the Colonists of this Province in particular, as Men, as Christians and as Subjects . . . with the Enfringements and Violations thereof that may have from time to time been made."

Hillsborough's expectations of an incendiary crisis were fulfilled. In June, a zealous, arrogant Royal Navy lieutenant, William Dudington, who commanded a small patrol vessel, the *Gaspée,* assisting the English customs service, ran his ship aground not far from Providence, Rhode Island. At the time, he was pursuing an American packet that he suspected was attempting to smuggle in tea from Holland. When the Providence merchants learned that Dudington's little boat was aground, they wasted no time in forming an expedition to end its career. Late on the evening of June 9, a citizens' party rowed out to the stranded ship in eight longboats, swarmed aboard, and woke Dudington, fast asleep in his cabin. He rushed on deck, where he was greeted with New England profanity and a shot in his belly. His crew gave up the unequal fight, and all were transported to shore, where Dudington's wound was tended. The *Gaspée* was burned to the waterline.

The Royal Navy commander in America, Admiral John Montagu, sent an angry report, which reached Hillsborough late in July. So also did a letter from Governor Hutchinson, who urged that "if the affair is passed over without full inquiry and due resentment, our liberty people will think that they may with impunity commit any acts of violence." Hutchinson, from one of the colony's founding families, was rapidly becoming a Loyalist and losing the respect of Massachusetts patriots.

Meanwhile, Hillsborough acted with the firmness he so enjoyed exercising. With the authority of the cabinet, he instructed the governor and royal officials of Rhode Island "to exert themselves most actively for the discovery of the offenders." The authorities in London ruled that the burning of the *Gaspée* was a crime of high treason and that those who were apprehended were to be returned to England for trial.

In demanding this, Hillsborough again set up a major confrontation. To seize and transport an American to England to be hanged for treason would have been an act of unbelievable folly, no matter what the excuse. But suddenly, Lord Hillsborough resigned from office, the result of a surprising and almost irrelevant cause—a land-grant request by Americans Samuel Wharton and Benjamin Franklin and the English backers of the Grand Ohio Company.

The Grand Ohio Company speculators had requested a grant of twenty million acres of prime land in what is now the state of Ohio. For almost a year, Hillsborough backed the request but delayed taking any action. In March 1772, the English backers grew impatient and managed to persuade the king himself to prod Hillsborough into action on the application, which had been referred to the Privy Council.

Hillsborough reversed himself and recommended that the application be turned down. But the Privy Council still had the last word. A committee was arranged to review the request; Samuel Wharton presented a lengthy prospectus that had been prepared by Franklin. Wharton performed effectively under cross-examination. He was followed by Thomas Walpole, whose name and business acumen held great influence with the Privy Council. The council overruled Hillsborough's recommendation. Hillsborough's pride was deeply wounded, and he promptly resigned as head of the American Department—blaming Benjamin Franklin for everything and declaring Franklin to be "one of the most mischievous men in England."

Franklin received the news of Hillsborough's resignation with equanimity. Hillsborough was, he wrote, "the most unequal in his treatment of people, the most insincere, and the most wrong-headed." Franklin continued:

> Witness, besides his various behavior to us, his duplicity in encouraging us to ask for more land: "Ask for enough to make a province" were his words, pretending to befriend our application, then doing everything to defeat it. Thus his mortification becomes double. He has served us by the very means he meant to destroy us, and tripped up on his own heels into the bargain.

The Grand Ohio Company speculators never got their land. Before the grant could be formally enacted, it was overtaken by the onrush of events leading to the Revolution. Hillsborough's ego was salved by the king, who elevated him to an earldom.

To Franklin's pleasure and relief, Hillsborough's successor at the American Department was the earl of Dartmouth, stepbrother of Lord North and a tactful, moderate man who believed in accommodation rather than confrontation.

However, the *Gaspée* affair still had to be dealt with, and hard-liners in Parliament were ready to pounce on any sign of weakness or retreat.

Chapter 11

LORD NORTH'S TEA PARTY

The arrival in the American Department of the conciliatory earl of Dartmouth seemed to augur well for easing tensions and pursuing understanding between England and the colonies. Or so thought Benjamin Franklin.

"He received me very obligingly," Franklin wrote his son William, "and I fully expect to obtain more favor in our colonies upon occasion than I could for some time past." To his friend Joseph Galloway in Philadelphia, he said that Dartmouth "has much more favorable dispositions toward the colonies, and has hitherto expressed some personal regard for me." Gone, it seemed, were the hostility and arrogance of Hillsborough.

But it would take more than "favorable dispositions" to change the pattern of events. In the colonies, the cumulative effect of London's tightened controls was to turn even minor matters, such as the molasses tax, into a constant and growing litany of causes for action. In London, news of each defiant act in the colonies seemed to require chastisement.

Initially, Lord Dartmouth made a sincere effort to pull back from confrontation—but events kept overtaking him. The climax came with Lord North's misjudgment and mishandling of a threepence-per-pound tax on tea, the last remaining of the Townshend duties.

*   *   *

The earl of Dartmouth and Lord North were stepbrothers. North's mother had died in 1734, when he was only two years old. Four years later, his father remarried an attractive young widow of high social standing. She brought to her new marriage her five-year-old son, William. He and Frederick North grew up together, went to Eton and Oxford together, spent two years traveling and studying in Germany, Italy, and France together. William became the second earl of Dartmouth at the death of his grandfather, in 1750; Frederick became Lord North when his father moved up the peerage ladder to become the earl of Guilford.

Dartmouth had all the best qualities of a cultured English gentleman. He was intelligent, high principled, and pious, a Methodist who was deeply religious but not at all bigoted. Devoted to his family, he went into public office out of a sense of duty rather than ambition.

He had served in the Rockingham government as head of the Board of Trade and had strongly supported repeal of the Stamp Act. Imbued with the Whig principles of conciliation and accommodation, he was nevertheless too gentlemanly, too lacking in political drive to carry off his convictions. He was also too loyal to his stepbrother to force his views on big issues with any impact. In the cabinet, he was surrounded by much more vocal, ambitious, and prejudiced colleagues, who had applauded Hillsborough's aggressive handling of the American problem. So, whatever the degree of Dartmouth's courtesy and goodwill, the progress of events toward revolution continued unchanged.

Initially, Dartmouth avoided any major confrontation over the *Gaspée* affair. As soon as he took office, he passed the word that he would not order the suspects to be transported to England and tried for treason. In his view, a person "should take his trial in the country where the offence was committed."

In Rhode Island, meanwhile, the royal governor offered the not insignificant sum of one hundred pounds for information leading to the conviction of the perpetrators, but a widespread amnesia overtook the citizens. Nobody would talk. The only suspect ever detained was a black house servant named Aaron, whose information was so vague that he was finally dismissed from custody.

Dartmouth, under pressure for more vigorous action, dispatched a special Commission of Inquiry to Providence in January 1773. One of the commissioners, Chief Justice Smyth, reported to Dartmouth that "hundreds of inhabitants" must have known one or more of the participants in the burning of the *Gaspée* but that hatred of Lieutenant Dudington "was so universal" that no one would give information. In May, a full year after the incident, the Commission of Inquiry gave up. The affair had petered out, but not without consequences.

In March, after the commission had completed its first frustrating round of inquiries, the Virginia House of Burgesses held a debate on the intrusion of the English into a matter of colonial justice. Thomas Jefferson and the other Virginians voted to follow Sam Adams's lead in Massachusetts and establish a Committee of Correspondence to propagandize against English encroachments on colonial rule. Virginia then proposed that each of the other colonies should do the same and establish a network of such committees from New Hampshire to Georgia to exchange information about grievances and decide on common actions in response.

By the end of the year, Committees of Correspondence had been formed in all the colonies except Pennsylvania, where Joseph Galloway, still speaker of the Pennsylvania Assembly, tried to block action on the Virginia proposal. But eventually, Pennsylvania would fall into line. Thus, although the *Gaspée* affair cooled, it had provided the impetus for organizing the thirteen Committees of Correspondence. These, in turn, would produce the first Continental Congress, which would meet in Philadelphia in September 1774.

Dartmouth kept himself better informed than had Hillsborough, using independent channels along with the stereotyped official reports Hillsborough had relied on. An English merchant, Charles Smith, traveling on business in the colonies, wrote to Dartmouth in March of 1773 that America was "full of rebellious sentiment [and increasingly ready] to throw off their dependence . . . there is a great need to cool and quiet the present tumults in New England and to chose the wisest men for governors of the different provinces." Another correspondent wrote, "Affairs are altering visibly and the people are almost universally determined to support an independent government unless Great Britain will confirm their liberties." A New England clergyman, the Reverend William Gordon, wrote that it was fortunate the *Gaspée* incident had ended without arrests, "for a trial would have set the continent into flame."

In England, Lord North's main concern at this juncture was not the colonies but the tangled affairs of the East India Company. Through poor management, greed, and corruption on the part of its directors, shareholders, and English employees, the company had drifted into virtual bankruptcy. It still had a powerful lobby, however, in Parliament and the City of London bankers and investors. These backers wanted a government bailout. Chatham had tried to deal with this problem in 1766, but Townshend had frustrated his efforts. Now, however, North had the king's backing to take a stronger stand.

After six months of behind-the-scenes bargaining as well as debating in the House of Commons, it was finally agreed that the government would provide a massive transfusion of £1.4 million. In return, the government would have a major voice in the direction of the company and would require a transfer of the company's "sovereignty" in India, gradually shifting control and power to the king and England's government.

There remained the question of what to do about an enormous stock of Indian tea that the company had stored in its London warehouses. Eighteen million pounds of tea, valued at some two million pounds, represented a three-year supply for the English market. The storage costs were considerable. How to get rid of it?

The stock of tea had accumulated largely because of the shutdown of the American market. The company paid two duties on its tea, the first when it was landed in England, the second, the Townshend tax, when it was landed in America. If one or the other of these taxes was abolished, then the price of East India Company tea would be equal to or less than that of tea being smuggled into America from Holland, and the American market would—at least in theory—be restored. In February 1773, the East India Company asked the North government "that leave be given to export tea duty free to America." (The company did not say *which* duty, but obviously it would have preferred that both be rescinded.)

Here, then, was a unique opportunity for Lord North to improve relations with the Americans, mend the fortunes of the East India Company, and get rid of its mountain of tea. All North had to do was eliminate the last of the Townshend taxes by a vote in the Commons.

Benjamin Franklin did not need to ponder the situation. He sought a meeting with Dartmouth to urge that relations with America would improve if the Townshend tax were abolished; the price of tea would come down, and a major irritant would disappear.

North, however, determined otherwise. King George had firmly stated that one tax on the Americans must be kept and that he approved of the tea duty. North would not challenge the king. He would abolish the duty in England but continue the threepence tax in America.

When Franklin got word of North's decision, he wrote bitterly to Thomas Cushing, speaker of the Massachusetts Assembly:

> It was thought at the beginning of the session that the American duty would be taken off tea. But now the wise scheme is to take off so much duty here, as will make the tea cheaper in America than foreigners can supply us, and to confine the duty there to keep up the exercise of the right. They have no idea that any people can act from any other principle but that of interest; and they believe that 3-pence on a pound of tea is sufficient to overcome all the patriotism of an American.

In April, Lord North introduced his East India Company relief measure in Parliament. William Dowdeswell, a pro-American oppositionist, rose immediately to ask why the prime minister "had no proposition to make with regard to the duty upon tea imported into America." He pointed out the damage already being done by the Americans refusing to buy East India Company tea and told Lord North bluntly that "if you don't take the duty off, they won't take the tea."

But Lord North told Parliament that the purpose of the duty was to raise money so England could pay the salaries of the royal governors and other English officials serving in the colonies. He replied to Dowdeswell:

> I am unwilling to give up that duty upon America, upon which the costs of government are charged. If the East India Company will

export tea to America, they will very much increase [revenue from] that duty, and consequently very much facilitate the carrying of government in that part. I see no reason to taking it off. I must see a very substantial reason before I part with a fund so applicable to the support of the Civil List salaries.

Dowdeswell didn't leave it at that. He noted that the tea imported into America had netted only about four hundred pounds in revenue the previous year. Again he said that Americans would not buy the tea until the duty was lifted, "and for this you risk the export of two million pounds of tea."

Barlow Trecothick, the Bostonian who sat in the Commons at the time, joined in urging that the duty be retained in England and repealed in America. William Pultenney warned North that he was risking an opportunity to increase the East India Company's sales by two million pounds of tea each year if he would only lift both duties and thus discover how great was the market for cheap tea. George Johnstone, a former governor of East Florida and a supporter of North, told North that no one was proposing that England give up the right to tax the colonies, only that the tax on tea was inhibiting the market. North, cornered again, this time took his stand on political rather than economic grounds, saying to Johnstone:

> No doubt there are political reasons, of such weight and strength that unless I find it absolutely necessary to take off the duty I shall be unwilling to touch that string. I know the temper of the [American] people. There is little deserving favor from thence, unless the reasons are very great.

The duty on tea landed in America was retained; the bill to eliminate the English tax passed without even a recorded vote on May 10, 1773. It would take effect in November. Why should there be trouble in America over a cheaper cup of East India tea?

In January 1773, Governor Thomas Hutchinson of Massachusetts decided to give his troublesome legislature a lecture on the basic truths of the relationship, as he saw it, between England and its colonies. The result was another step toward revolution.

Hutchinson, wealthy scion of one of Massachusetts's oldest families, was not exactly a man of the people. His public offices had all been by appointment rather than by election. One historian of the period tartly noted that "he lacked common sense." A dedicated Loyalist, Hutchinson was increasingly alarmed and dismayed by the growing movement toward independence—and illustrating his lack of common sense, he decided to say so to the legislature.

At the opening of the 1773 session, Hutchinson told the elected representatives that "the colonies were settled parts of the British dominions, and consequently as subject to the supreme legislative authority thereof . . . I know of no line that can be drawn between the supreme authority of Parliament and the total independence of the colonies."

This was a red flag, a serious challenge to the patriots. The legislators were prompt in striking back. Their response, in a resolution drafted by John Adams, was blunt and forceful. It asserted that England's Parliament had neither possessed sovereignty over the colony when it was founded nor acquired sovereignty since. If, as the governor contended, there was no line between the authority of Parliament and total independence, then the colonies "are vassals of Parliament or they are independent." The resolution stopped short of claiming independence, however. Instead, it stated that "the free and full exercise of the liberties and immunities granted by the charter of the Massachusetts Bay Company [would not endanger] that just sense of allegiance to the Crown." Thus the Massachusetts Assembly came to the same conclusion as Benjamin Franklin, that it was perfectly possible for the colonies to have independence without either renouncing or rejecting loyalty to the Crown.

News of Hutchinson's speech and the assembly's response reached London in April, just as Lord North was making his fateful move on the tea tax. In a letter to Thomas Cushing, Franklin said that initial criticism (presumably from Lord Dartmouth) was against Hutchinson, an "apprehension of some ill consequences from his forcing the Assembly into that dispute." A month later, Franklin reported that Dartmouth had said of Hutchinson, "What difficulties that gentleman has brought us by his imprudence." But Dartmouth added that "it [is] not possible for Parliament to ignore the Assembly's assertion of their independent authority."

Dartmouth then wrote a very firm instruction to Governor Hutchinson:

After so public an avowal in the representative body of the people of doctrines subversive of every principle of the constitutional dependence of the colonies upon this kingdom, it is vain to hope that they will be induced by argument and persuasion to yield due obedience to the laws of Parliament and to acquiesce in those arrangements which the King, consulting the welfare and happiness of his subjects, has thought fit to adopt. *I urge that you avoid any further discussion whatever upon these questions.* [Emphasis added.]

Dartmouth went even further. He took the unusual step of writing directly to Cushing—one of the very rare instances when a minister of the Crown sidestepped the usual channels and corresponded directly with an American on a serious policy question. He said to Cushing that he wrote "not in the discharge of my duties as a minister of the Crown, but only as a simple individual according to the dictates of my own private judgment and opinion." He then characterized the Massachusetts Assembly's resolution as "wild and extravagant doctrines . . . which appear to me so utterly inconsistent with any pretensions to a share in the privileges and advantages of British subjects that I could never subscribe to them." He declared firmly that it was not only his own belief but also the overwhelming belief of the majority of English people that the powers of Parliament over the empire were "inherent and inseparable from the supreme authority of the State [the Crown]." Having said that, he then offered Cushing his own particular olive branch:

> If my wishes and sentiments could have any weight with a British Parliament, the exercise of that right . . . should be suspended and lie dormant till some occasion should arise . . . in which the expediency and necessity of such exercise should be obvious to every considerate man in every part of the Dominions.

He concluded by urging Cushing to arrange for the assembly to withdraw its resolution. In return, he promised his aid and support in working for a general settlement of colonial complaints.

Dartmouth's sincerity is undoubted. He was taking a political risk, for his letter might have been leaked to the public. If such a letter had been sent to Massachusetts—or Virginia or New York or Pennsylvania—two years earlier, it might have opened the way to evolving an eighteenth-century commonwealth. But by the summer of 1773, time was running out. Cushing replied cordially (but carefully) that Massachusetts was not denying the supremacy of Parliament, only its right to legislate for the colonies. He pointed out that Americans were still subject to an imperial revenue tax and that only its repeal would bring about a settlement of differences.

In other words, each man demanded a prior concession by the other. Dartmouth's letter to Cushing was dated June 19; Cushing's reply, August 22. By the time it reached London, the East India Company had chartered its first ships to carry tea to America.

While Dartmouth sought to dampen the rumpus in Massachusetts, Benjamin Franklin dispatched to Boston a political time bomb that would blow the situation wide open.

Earlier that year, Franklin had come into possession of a set of thirteen private letters, some written by Hutchinson, then the colony's chief justice, and others written by the lieutenant governor, Andrew Oliver, to Thomas Whately, drafter of the Stamp Act, who had died in 1772. The letters were old, dating from 1767 to 1769. That did not diminish their political importance, however. Franklin sent them to Cushing, accompanied by a covering letter saying that "I am not at liberty to make them public; I can only allow them to be seen by yourself and by other gentlemen of the Committee of Correspondence, and a few other such gentlemen as you may think fit." This "few other such gentlemen" made a fairly large distribution list, even in an age of great discretion.

Hutchinson's evolution from respected citizen to all-out Loyalist was no secret, but the letters revealed the true depth of his duplicity. In one of the most damaging passages, Hutchinson offered this advice to Whately and the government in London:

I never think of the measures necessary for the peace and good order of the colonies without pain. *There must be an abridgement of what are called English liberties.* I relieve myself by considering what in a remove from the state of nature to the most perfect state of government there must be a great restraint of natural liberty. I doubt whether it is possible to project a system of government in which a colony 3,000 miles distant from the parent state shall enjoy all of the liberty of the parent state. I wish for the good of the colony when I wish to see some further restraint of liberty rather than the connection with the parent state should be broken, for I am sure such a breach must prove the ruin of the colony. [Emphasis added.]

In his covering letter to Cushing, Franklin gave this interpretation:

The correspondence I have reason to believe laid the foundation of most if not all our present grievances. My resentment against [England] for its arbitrary measures in governing us, conducted by the late minister [Hillsborough] has, since my conviction by these letters that those measures were projected, advised and called for by men of character among ourselves, and whose advice must therefore be attended with all the weight that was proper to mislead and could scarce fail of misleading: My own resentment, I say, has by this means been exceedingly abated.

Under the circumstances, it was quite impossible that Franklin's injunction to keep the letters private would be observed.

Tempers in regard to Hutchinson were already high in the assembly. When Sam Adams saw the letters, he immediately circulated copies through his Committee of Correspondence to all town meetings of the colony. In June, the letters were made public to all citizens. By the end of June, the assembly had adopted a resolution requesting King George to remove Hutchinson and Oliver, declaring Hutchinson to be "in a conspiracy" to overthrow the free government established in Massachusetts in its charter of 1691, and branding him as "an enemy of the constitution."

It fell to Franklin, as agent for the colony, to deliver the resolution to Lord Dartmouth, who would lay it before the king. Dartmouth, however, was away at his country home in Staffordshire. Franklin sent the petition to him under a covering letter.

In London, the immediate question was how old, private correspondence to a British government official had been intercepted and how it had fallen into the hands of the Massachusetts Assembly. Reading other people's mail was frowned upon then as it is today. But Franklin remained silent on the subject. His own mail had been regularly tampered with by English officials, a fact he had noted as far back as 1771 in a letter to Thomas Cushing:

The letters I have received from my friends in Boston have come to hand badly sealed . . . appearing as if they had been opened and in a very bungling way closed again. . . . I suggest they might be sent under cover to some merchant of character who could forward them to me more safely.

And to his son William: "When a packet arrives [from America] a special messenger goes directly from the office with the [official] letters before the sorting is finished. Mine have been sometimes sent by the same messenger who called on me on his way to Lord H[illsborough], sometimes on his return." Opening mail, Franklin said, "is seldom used but in times of war, rebellion, or on some great public occasion." The practice against him apparently stopped when Hillsborough left office.

But who was the source of the leak? Coffeehouse gossip that September focused on William Whately, brother of the deceased Thomas and executor of his estate. When Whately learned of the gossip, he declared publicly that the letters had not been among his brother's papers. He charged that they had been purloined by a man named John Temple, a distant relative of George Grenville's. Temple had indeed been given access to the Whately papers, but it was to examine letters he himself had written. He swore the Hutchinson-Oliver letters were not among the papers when he examined them and that the only letters he took were his own.

Charges and countercharges moved from coffeehouse to print. Finally, John Temple challenged William Whately to a duel. On December 11, they fought with swords and pistols in Hyde Park. Whately was wounded; both came away angrier and more dissatisfied than ever. Franklin recounted what happened next:

Imagining all now was over between them, I still kept silence until I heard that the duel was understood to be unfinished, as having been interrupted by persons accidentally near, and that it would be repeated as soon as Mr. Whately, who was mending daily, recovered his strength. As the quarrel was for public opinion, I took what I thought was the shortest way to settle that opinion.

On Christmas Day, Franklin went public. He issued a personal statement in the *Public Advertiser,* where he frequently planted anonymous letters. He declared both William Whately and John Temple "totally ignorant and innocent of the whole affair." He concluded: "I alone am the person who obtained and transmitted to

Boston the letters in question. Mr. W. could not communicate them, because they were never in his possession; and for the same reason, they could not have been taken from him by Mr. T." Franklin never did disclose how or by whose hand the letters had come into his possession, and it remains a mystery to this day. But Franklin had handed his enemies a golden opportunity for revenge. Their glee was compounded by the fact that Franklin still held a royal appointment as assistant postmaster general for the American colonies. A postmaster holding in his hands other people's private correspondence did not present a very good picture, no matter what the circumstances.

But Franklin's disclosure of his role was soon engulfed by events in Boston that same December.

The East India Company, Lords North and Dartmouth, and merchants on both sides of the Atlantic had blandly assumed that Americans would accept the good East India tea at its reduced price and would hardly care about a hidden duty of threepence. They were completely blind to the mood that lay beneath the superficial calm.

Samuel Cooper of Boston wrote to his friend Thomas Pownall in London: "Though a high Ferment cannot be expected to continue long among the People, and the Irritation into which they were thrown has been abated, yet their inward sentiments are not altered, but by far the greater part have a settled Persuasion that we are in a State of Oppression."

News of Lord North's decision on the tea tax began to circulate in the colonial press in August. In September, Philadelphia's *Pennsylvania Journal* wrote:

Being a great schemer, Lord North struck out the plan of the East India Company's sending this Article to America, hoping thereby to outwit us, and to establish that act [the Townshend duty] effectually which will for ever be pleaded as precedent for every imposition the Parliament of Great Britain shall think proper to saddle us with. It is much to be wished that the Americans will convince Lord North that they are not yet ready to have the yoke of slavery riveted about their necks, and send back the tea whence it came.

The *Journal*'s interpretation was rapidly picked up by other newspapers. John Dickinson took up his pen again, this time writing under the pen name of Rusticus. He attacked the East India Company for barbarities allegedly happening on their tea plantations:

The Company has given ample Proof how little they regard the Laws of Nations, the Rights, Liberties or Lives of Men. Fifteen Hundred Thousand, it is said, perished by Famine in one year, not because the Earth denied its Fruits, but this Company and its servants engrossed all the Necessaries of Life, and set them at so high a Rate that the Poor could not purchase them. And now they cast their eyes on *America,* as a new Theater, whereupon to exercise their Talents of Rapine, Oppression and Cruelty.

Dickinson concluded by calling on the merchants of Philadelphia to deny the company use of their wharves and warehouses, the longshoremen to refuse to unload their tea, and the shopkeepers to refuse it in their stores. Finally, he wrote, "Let the Watchmen be instructed as they go their Rounds to call out every Night, *Past Twelve O'Clock, beware of the East India Company.*"

Alert readers had no trouble identifying Rusticus as the ci-devant Old Farmer, Dickinson. Soon Dickinson's call for resistance was echoing in journals up and down the coast.

By November, mutterings had turned into direct threats of violence against the merchants who were planning to handle the tea. Delaware River pilots and ship captains were handed a printed broadsheet warning "What think you, Captain, of a Halter around your Neck, then Gallons of liquid tar decanted on your Pate—with Feathers of a dozen live Geese laid over that to enliven your appearance."

The New York firm of Pigout and Booth received, from a group calling itself the Mohawks, warning of "an unwelcome visit in which they shall be treated as they deserve" if they handled any of the tea. Pigout and Booth threw in the towel, writing to the East India Company in late November that they would not handle the tea, which they said, could not be landed without the repeal of the duty.

On October 21, the Boston Committee of Correspondence prepared a circular on the dangers of the tea tax, calling for measures to prevent its taking effect. In early November, the Sons of Liberty began preparing for demonstrations. There were short-lived riots in front of Clarke's Store on King Street, the place where the first shipments of tea were supposed to be stored.

In mid-November, ships arriving from England reported that a ship with a tea cargo was on its way. Hutchinson, who had previously been confident of the general calm, was feeling the heat. He wrote to his fellow governor Tryon of New York that "I am in a helpless state." He talked of retiring to the safety of Castle William in the harbor, where English troops were billeted.

On Sunday, November 28, the ship *Dartmouth* (fortuitously named) sailed into Boston. She had aboard 114 chests of East India Company tea. Her captain, ignorant of the temper of the Bostonians, made his way peacefully through the outer harbor and dropped anchor inside the legal limits of the inner harbor. Here the law took over the fate of his cargo.

First, the captain was required to register his arrival and his cargo with the customs officer of the port (an Englishman, not a colonial official). Then the consignee of the cargo was required to make payment within twenty days on any dutiable goods. Failing that, the cargo would be seized.

The Bostonians were utterly determined that the tea must not be landed under any circumstances. A crowd of some five thousand had rallied at Faneuil Hall just before the *Dartmouth*'s arrival to underscore vociferously that determination. To allow the tea to land and pay the duty were unacceptable; so was allowing it to land and be stored pending instructions from London. It might still leak onto the market. So when the *Dartmouth*'s captain had filed his papers, the Americans insisted he dock his ship at Griffin's Wharf. There they posted their own guard to make sure the tea was not surreptitiously landed.

The owner, Francis Rotch, was prepared to go along with this in order to unload at least part of his general cargo and perhaps prepare the vessel for an early return voyage to England. The deadline for completing the unloading and paying the duties was not, after all, till December 17.

Two weeks of talk among the governor, his officials, the patriots, and the customs officials resulted in deeper deadlock. The ship could not sail without customs clearance, and that would not be granted until the status of the tea was cleared up. The ship could not slip away since it would have to pass beneath the guns of Castle

George III, 1738–1820; king of England, 1760–1820. His stubborn refusal of compromise or conciliation cost him his American colonies. (Library of Congress)

Benjamin Franklin, 1706–1790. A statesman, diplomat, writer, and philosopher, he represented American interests in London and Paris, 1757–1785. (Library of Congress)

William Pitt, 1708–1778. (New York Public Library)

Edmund Burke, 1729–1797, opposition orator and writer. (New York Public Library)

Charles James Fox, 1749–1806, opposition politician. (New York Public Library)

Lord North, 1732–1792. He served as the king's prime minister, 1770–1782. (New York Public Library)

William Pitt, the earl of Chatham, 1708–1778, war leader of the Seven Years' War, opponent of the American war. (Library of Congress)

General Sir Henry Clinton,
1738–1795, commander in chief
in North America, 1778–1782.
(New York Public Library)

Lord George Germain,
1716–1785, the secretary of
state who directed and
misdirected British forces in
the American war from
London, 1775–1782.
(Library of Congress)

General Washington crossing the Delaware, Christmas Day, 1776. The Battle of Trenton, which followed, changed the fortunes of the American Revolution. (Library of Congress)

Major John André, 1751–1780. (New York Public Library)

The hanging of Major John André, British spy, in New York, October 2, 1780. He was 29. (Library of Congress)

Colonel Daniel Morgan, 1736–1802, rough and resourceful Continental Army commander. His marksmen were instrumental in the victory at Saratoga, October 1777. (Library of Congress)

William and several Royal Navy ships on its way out. Apart from the legalities, Governor Hutchinson appeared to be maneuvering to have the cargo seized by the Royal Navy and customs and locked away for nonpayment of duty.

On Thursday, December 16, another crowd of five thousand gathered, this time at Old South Meeting House at 10:00 A.M. Everyone was aware that if customs seized the tea and unloaded it, then the consignee would pay the duty, and the tea would go on the market. After two hours, the rally was suspended to allow Rotch to visit Hutchinson and plead for permission to sail out with the tea aboard. Hutchinson refused. The rally resumed at 5:00 P.M.

When Rotch announced the governor's refusal, cries of "A mob! A mob!" broke out. Rotch told the crowd that he would unload his tea only if he were ordered to do so by the authorities and if he were protected. Samuel Adams rose up and declared with finality that he did not see what more the citizens could do. This worked like a signal, for all at once shouts filled the meetinghouse. "Boston Harbor a teapot tonight!" and "Hurrah for Griffin's Wharf!" and "The Mohawks are come!" There were indeed already men costumed as Indians clustered around the entrance to Old South. The meeting broke up around six-thirty, and the crowd surged down to Griffin's Wharf.

Who organized it, how it all came about is not clear. What happened is history.

Two other tea ships, the brig *Beaver* and the *Eleanor,* had arrived after the *Dartmouth* and were tied up at Griffin's Wharf. All three were boarded by "Indians." The customs officers were dumped ashore. Blocks and tackle were rigged to haul the heavy tea chests up from the hold. On deck, they were broken open with axes and their contents dumped over the side. Soon, loose tea was floating all around the three vessels. A crowd watched in silence. Admiral John Montagu, the Royal Navy commander in Boston, watched from a house only a hundred yards away, at the foot of Griffin's Wharf; his nearest warship was only a few hundred yards distant. In a report written to London the next day, Montagu said, "I could easily have prevented the Execution of this Plan, but must have endangered the Lives of many innocent People by firing upon the town."

After it was all over, another strange case of collective amnesia, very similar to that which had overtaken the people involved in the

Gaspée incident, overcame the citizens of Boston. One man waited until he was ninety-three years old before giving names he remembered from that night. There were hints that the Grand Lodge of Masons had had a hand in the planning and also other groups, such as the Long Room Club and the North End Caucus.

By 9:00 P.M., less than three hours after it had begun, the Tea Party was over. It had been bloodless and quiet. Not a shot had been fired.

News of the Tea Party reached Philadelphia eight days later, on Christmas Eve. It was greeted with the ringing of bells and coffee-house celebrations all over the city. A special edition of the *Pennsylvania Journal* spread the news.

On Christmas Day, the tea ship *Polly* entered Delaware Bay. River pilots refused to assist the captain. He navigated carefully up the Delaware until he was stopped by a citizens' patrol south of Philadelphia Harbor. He was "persuaded" to head back to England. The tea ship *Renown*, bound for New York, ran into a terrible storm and changed course for Antigua. When it finally reached Sandy Hook, New Jersey, the following April, it provisioned for a return voyage to London without crossing New York's harbor line. In Charleston, the tea ship *London* arrived on December 2. For the statutory twenty days, it was unable to unload. The tea was finally seized, peacefully, by customs and locked up in a warehouse. It was eventually sold to raise money for the Revolution.

John Adams, using rare hyperbole, recorded in his diary the day after the Tea Party:

> This is the most magnificent Movement of all. There is a dignity, a Majesty, a Sublimity in this last Effort of the Patriots that I greatly admire. . . . This Destruction of the Tea is so bold, so daring, so firm, intrepid and inflexible, and it must have so important Consequences and so lasting, that I cannot but Consider it as an Epocha in History.

Chapter 12

"BLOWS MUST DECIDE"

News of the Boston Tea Party reached London in late January of 1774. The January 20 issue of the London *Evening Post* reprinted an account from the *Boston Gazette*, which arrived by the ship *Hayley* (owned by John Hancock) after a particularly fast crossing of only twenty-eight days. A week later, an official account from Governor Hutchinson reached Lord Dartmouth.

The political temperature began rising rapidly. Shock became anger; indignation turned to outrage. The moderates who had looked for conciliation were silenced, and it would be many months before they attempted to be heard again. Among politicians and the public, there was nearly unanimous agreement that this time the Americans had gone too far. They must be made to pay.

Edmund Burke, as agent for New York, summed up the hostile mood in a bluntly worded report to the New York Assembly:

The popular current both within doors and without at present sets sharply against America. That you may not be deceived by any Idle or Flattering report, be assured that the Determination to enforce Obedience from the Colonies to Laws of Revenue by the most powerful means seems as firm as possible, and that the Ministry appears stronger than I have ever known it.

Retribution was the order of the day, as King George promptly made clear to Lord North. The newly promoted Lieutenant General Thomas Gage, then in London on leave from the colonies, hastened to an audience with the king. The king recorded their conversation in a memo to North written on February 4, dated at precisely 6:46 P.M.:

> I have seen General Gage, who came to express his readiness, though so lately come from America, to return on a day's notice, if the conduct of the colonies should induce the directing of coercive measures. His language was very consonant to his character of an honest determined man. He says they will be lyons, whilst we are lambs; but if we take the resolute part they will undoubtedly prove very meek. He thinks four regiments intended to relieve so many regiments in America, if sent to Boston, are sufficient to prevent any disturbances. I wish you could see him, and hear his ideas as to the mode of compelling Boston to submit to whatever may be thought necessary; indeed all men now seems to feel that the fatal compliance in 1766 [repeal of the Stamp Act] has encouraged the Americans annually to increase their pretensions to that thorough independency which one state has of another, but which is quite subversive to the obedience which a colony owes to its mother country.

This was neither the first nor the last time General Gage misjudged the temperament of the Americans. Gage was telling the king what he wanted to hear.

Gage delayed his return until May, waiting for various measures against Boston to be pushed through Parliament. But when he got back to Boston, now in his new, dual capacity as captain general and governor of Massachusetts, his dispatches began to sound more cautious, less confident, even pessimistic. The king and his ministers noted this change with increasing irritation: For England, the Tea Party represented an overt, militant American assault on England's ships, her officials, her commerce, her flag. It was a violent act against a mercantile empire, a challenge to England's status as a world power. The economic and social forces, the whole patriotic ethos of England victorious had been assailed.

The actions that Lord North's government took in retaliation precluded any compromise. North began to prepare what were called in England the Coercive Acts against Boston and the Massachusetts Bay Colony.

For the earl of Dartmouth, his sincere if largely ineffectual efforts to steer away from open conflict were now ended. The hard-liners had taken over completely. Dartmouth did what he could behind the scenes, arguing that the American reaction to the Coercive Acts would make such extreme measures counterproductive and create even greater difficulties for England. He got nowhere.

Meanwhile, England's wrath over the Tea Party fell upon Benjamin Franklin.

Early in January, Franklin received a summons to appear before the Privy Council to testify on the petition of the Massachusetts Assembly for removal of Governor Hutchinson and Lieutenant Governor Oliver. The petition had reached the king, who had sent it on to the Privy Council for a hearing and recommendation. Franklin was told to appear on January 11.

Privy Council hearings took place in a committee room in Westminster known then, as it is still known today, as the Cockpit.* Franklin's first appearance in the Cockpit was brief. He thought the hearing would be on the merits of the petition, but Alexander Wedderburn, the government's solicitor general, informed Franklin that "we are reserving to ourselves the right of inquiring" how he had obtained the Hutchinson and Oliver letters to Whately. Sensing difficulties ahead, Franklin told the Privy Council that he would need the assistance of a lawyer and three weeks to prepare. The hearing date was fixed for January 29. By this time, news of the Tea Party had reached London. When the Privy Council gathered in full array, the atmosphere was supercharged in opposition to both Massachusetts and its agent, Benjamin Franklin.

Alexander Wedderburn, who would conduct the hearing, had a quick mind and was known as one of the most intelligent, formidable debaters in Parliament, possessed of an ability to use language

---

*In the days of King Henry VIII, when Westminster was being used as a royal palace, the king built a pit for cockfighting on this spot. A tennis court adjoined. Eventually, the "playground" was built over. The cockpit became a committee room of Parliament.

like a rapier. At the same time, he was one of the nastiest, most unscrupulous, most ambitious politicians of the period.

He grew up in Edinburgh and began his career in the Scottish law. Handling a case in court at age twenty-four, he became so abusive of the court president, aged seventy-two, that an apology was demanded by the entire bench. Instead, Wedderburn withdrew from the Scots bar and decamped for London. Aware of the English contempt for the Scots, he worked assiduously to rid himself of his Scottish brogue. He won a seat in the House of Commons through Robert Clive, conqueror of India, and aligned himself with Lord Bute.

Lord North decided politically that it would be better if Wedderburn, who had supported John Wilkes during that long fight, were inside the government rather than in opposition. For his part, Wedderburn was not inhibited by principles and could readily lend his debating talents to any side of any question. He was appointed solicitor general.*

An exceptional audience crowded the Cockpit chamber on the twenty-ninth. Not only did Lord North attend but also Lieutenant General Thomas Gage, General Sir Jeffrey Amherst, and the earl of Hillsborough, who relished the thought of Franklin under fire. Edmund Burke was there; so was Dr. Joseph Priestley, physicist, Presbyterian minister, political radical—and Franklin's good friend of many years. The audience was ready for theater, and it got it.

The Privy Council, all thirty-six of its members, sat at a long table. Wedderburn was seated at the center, at the side of the president of the council, Lord Gower. Everyone else stood, including Franklin, who took a position at the corner of the fireplace, opposite the council and Wedderburn. Franklin, who had just passed his sixty-eighth birthday, had dressed for the occasion in a suit of figured Manchester velvet and an old-fashioned full-bottomed wig.

The proceedings began in a routine fashion. Franklin read the text of the petition from the Massachusetts Assembly. He was followed by the two counselors he had chosen to assist him, John Dun-

---

*Later he became attorney general and, eventually, the lord chancellor of England.

ning and John Lee. They elaborated on the reasons for the petition and the letters that had in part prompted it. They concluded by saying that the colony was appealing to the king's "Wisdom and goodness" to remove the governors "to quiet the present unrest and restore the ancient peace and unity."

Wedderburn leaped to his feet. Moving swiftly for the kill, he declared that there had been no misconduct on the part of either Hutchinson or Oliver. Rather, this affair was due entirely to Franklin's having intercepted their letters and sent them to Boston. He continued:

> Nothing will acquit Dr. Franklin of obtaining them by fraudulent or corrupt means, for the most malignant of purposes; unless he stole them from the person who stole them. This argument is irrefragable. I hope, my lords, you will mark and brand this man, for the honour of this country, of Europe, and of mankind. He has forfeited all the respect of societies and of men. Into what companies will he hereafter go with an unembarrassed face or the honest intrepidity of virtue? Men will watch him with a jealous eye; they will hide their papers from him and lock up their escritories. He will henceforth esteem it a libel to be called a man of letters.

According to others present, Franklin froze as Wedderburn's attack progressed. For nearly an hour, he simply watched his accuser, emotionless, unblinking, no change of expression, scarcely a muscle moving. Wedderburn's diatribe continued:

> With a whole province set in flame, with all this weight of suspicion and with all this train of mischiefs before his eyes, Dr. Franklin's apathy sets him quite at ease, and he would have us think that he has done nothing more than what any other colonial agent would have done. My lords, others have received the proposal with horror. One of them said it was profaining the word duty to apply it to such a purpose; another that if it had been their agent he would sooner have cut off his right hand than have done such a thing.

> My lords, Dr. Franklin's mind may have been so possessed with the idea of a Great American Republic that he may easily slide into the language of the minister of a foreign independent state. A foreign ambassador might bribe a villain to steal or betray any state papers; he is under the command of another state and is not amenable to the laws of the country where he resides; and the secure exemption from

punishment may induce a laxer morality. But Dr. Franklin, whatever he may teach the people at Boston, while he is here, at least, is a subject, and if a subject injure a subject he is answerable to the law.*

As Wedderburn poured on the invective, the Privy Council and members of the audience began to grin, to laugh, to nudge one another and enjoy the show at the expense of the immobile, expressionless Franklin. One who was clearly not amused, however, was Lord North. He was beginning to show some annoyance at the performance being staged by his solicitor general.

Wedderburn went on, charging Franklin with designs to become governor of the province himself:

Nothing surely but a too eager attention to an ambition of this sort could have betrayed a wise man into such conduct as we have now seen. . . . I hope that Mr. Hutchinson will not meet with the less countenance from your lordships from his rival's being his accuser. Nor will your lordships, I trust, advise the having Mr. Hutchinson displaced in order to make room for Dr. Franklin as a successor.

And he seized the opportunity to mention the Tea Party:

Was it to confute or prevent the pernicious effect of the letters that the good men of Boston have lately held their meetings, appointed their committees, and with their usual moderation have destroyed the cargo of three British ships? If an English consul in any part of France or Spain, or rather Algiers or Tripoli, had not called this an outrage on his country, he would have deserved punishment. But if a governor at Boston should presume to whisper to a friend that he thinks it somewhat more than a moderate exertion of English liberty to destroy the ships of England, to plunder their goods, to pull down their houses, or even to burn the King's ships of war, then ought he to be removed?

Finally, he wound down by saying that "the governors are convinced that the people, though misled, are innocent, . . . [that] for

---

*After the government's publication of the proceedings, Franklin wrote to Cushing that "grosser parts of the abuse are omitted, appearing, I suppose, in their own eyes too foul to be seen on paper." He did not give any details.

the sake of the people they wish some faults corrected, anarchy abolished and government reestablished."

When the solicitor general finished, the Privy Council voted at once to dismiss the petition and retain Hutchinson and Oliver in their posts. Wedderburn moved to an anteroom, where he bathed in the glow of congratulations and cheers for his triumphant performance.

But was it a triumph? Franklin had more loyal, firm friends than Wedderburn. Further, Franklin's imperturbable demeanor had served as a silent refutation of an attack that far exceeded either the importance or the substance of the issue at hand. Dr. Priestley later wrote:

> No person belonging to the Council behaved with a decent gravity except Lord North, who, coming late, took his stand behind a chair opposite me. When the business was over, Dr. Franklin, in going out, took me by the hand in a manner which indicated some feeling. I soon followed him, and going through the anteroom saw Mr. Wedderburn, who stepped forward as if to speak to me, but I turned aside and made what haste I could out of the place.

It was, in the end, a hollow victory for Wedderburn. Burke called Wedderburn's attack "beyond all bounds and measure." Lord Shelburne wrote to the earl of Chatham that "it is agreed on all hands to have been a scurrilous invective." Nor did Franklin lack support in the press. The *London Packet* of February 2 reported Wedderburn's performance as "a most severe Philippic on the celebrated American philosopher, in which he loaded him with all the licensed scurrility of the bar, and decked his harrangue with the choicest flowers of Billingsgate."

The following day, a letter was delivered to Craven Street, informing Franklin that he had been stripped of his royal appointment as deputy postmaster-general for the American colonies—and of its annual three hundred-pound stipend from King George. When Priestley came to have breakfast that morning, Franklin told him, "I have never before been so sensible of the power of a good conscience."

However much Franklin might have burned over the affair, he remained outwardly philosophical. To Cushing, he wrote that "censures I have generally passed over in silence, conceiving that when they were just I ought rather to amend than defend; and when they were undeserved that a little time would justify me."

To Jan Ingenhousz, a Dutch friend living in Vienna, he said:

> I do not find that I have lost a single friend on the occasion. All have visited me repeatedly with affectionate assurances of their unaltered respect and affection, and many of distinction with whom I had before but slight acquaintance. On this occasion it suited the ministry to have me abused, as it often suits the purpose of their opposers to abuse them. And having myself been long engaged in public business, this treatment is not new to me. I am almost as much used to it as they are themselves, and can perhaps bear it better.

In Philadelphia, the physician Benjamin Rush got word of the Cockpit affair and his friend Franklin's dismissal from the colonial post office. Rush wrote:

> As a result of this humiliation, Franklin is a very popular character in every part of America. He will be received and carried in triumph to his house when he arrives amongst us. It is to be hoped that he will not consent to hold any more crown offices under government. No step but this can prevent his being handed down to posterity among the first and greatest characters in the world.

Benjamin Rush need not have worried. Franklin would not have accepted any favors from the king, even if they had been offered.

On March 14, Lord North introduced in the House of Commons the first of the four Coercive Acts he had been constructing. The first bill was intended to close down completely the port of Boston until the East India Company was paid for the tea that had been dumped into the harbor and the imperial revenue compensated for its loss on dutiable goods. The prime minister told a receptive, even enthusiastic House, "The good of this act is that four or five frigates will do the business without any military force. . . . Now is the time to proceed with firmness and without fear. They will never reform until we take a measure of this kind."

North then went on to repeat another one of the basic misjudgments that dogged England. He assured the Commons that "the rest of the colonies will not take fire at the proper punishment inflicted on those who have disobeyed your authority . . . whatever the consequences we must risk something; if we do not all is over."

At this juncture, Lord North must have known that East India Company tea had been turned back at Philadelphia, landed and impounded without payment of duty at Charleston, and warned off in New York. Only Boston had destroyed the tea. Nevertheless, the government continued to base its policy on the belief that the other colonies would turn from lions into lambs at the sight of Boston taking its punishment.

The bill breezed through Parliament. William Dowdeswell objected that the Commons was rushing things. Rose Fuller, a prominent Whig merchant with strong views, proposed that Boston be fined to pay for the tea, not closed down. Colonel Isaac Barré, who on so many occasions had been such a vigorous supporter of the Americans, this time deserted them, telling the Commons, "I like the bill, adopt it and embrace it cheerfully for its moderation."

The legislation needed only a voice vote to pass. King George gave his royal assent before the end of March. From June 1 on, the Royal Navy would close down the port of Boston to all oceangoing trade, a crippling punishment for the city, until the king ordered otherwise.

With the Boston Port Bill on the books, North moved quickly to enact the three remaining measures—the Massachusetts Government Act, the Administration of Justice Act, and a new Quartering Act for the British Army. On March 28, the prime minister presented the first of these to Parliament. He made no bones about its intent:

> I propose in this bill to take the executive power from the hands of the democratic part of the government. I would propose that the governor should act as a justice of the peace, and that he should have the power to appoint the officers throughout the whole civil authority.

The bill completely overturned the sacred Massachusetts charter of 1691. It decreed that members of the Massachusetts Council would be appointed by the governor, not elected by the assembly, and that the cherished town meetings could take place only with the governor's permission. It gave the governor full power to appoint local officials and the judiciary and decreed that in the future, juries would be appointed by sheriffs, not elected by freeholders. This was strong medicine, which Massachusetts would certainly not swallow. Moreover, the act broke the constitutional rules of England itself. In the past, royal charters had been altered only by legal proceedings in the courts, never by legislation. Taxation without representation paled compared with legislation to change a charter without consultation.

The Administration of Justice Act provided that any British official serving in the colonies who was accused of a capital offense could be removed from the colony and sent to another colony or to England for a fair trial. This meant that if another event like the Boston Massacre were to occur, the British soldiers involved would be whisked away to stand trial far from the scene.

Lord North introduced the Quartering Act requested by General Gage just before Gage set sail for Boston. He would be given additional powers to quarter British officers and troops in the private homes of colonial citizens.

Little wonder that the Coercive Acts passed by the English Parliament became known as the Intolerable Acts when they were published in America.

By June of 1774, all four acts had been passed by Parliament and approved by King George III. Although the votes had been overwhelming (239 to 64 on the Massachusetts Government Act), they did not pass without a few strong voices in Parliament warning of the consequences.* Two great orators, Edmund Burke and the earl of Chatham, spoke up.

Burke took the floor in the House of Commons on April 19, during the debate over the Massachusetts Government Act. In one of the outstanding speeches of his career, he focused on the root

---

*A new recruit to the pro-American opposition emerged during the debate over the Coercive Acts. This was none other than Charles James Fox, who in February had been dismissed by Lord North from a secondary post in the Treasury for one of his periodic acts of undisciplined voting. Freed of the burden of supporting the government, Fox aligned (more or less) with the Rockingham faction and Burke on the American question and would become a thorn in the side of North and the king for the next seven years.

problem, the history of taxation of the American colonies as it had evolved from their earliest days. Never—until the Stamp Act—had England tried to raise revenue for its own imperial purposes in America. Parliament, Burke said, was now trying "meanly to sneak out of difficulties into which [it] had proudly strutted." He did not argue that Parliament had no right to tax but declared:

> Again and again, revert to your old principles—seek peace and ensue it—leave America, if she has taxable matter in her, to tax herself. I am not going into the distinctions of rights, nor attempting to mark their boundaries. I do not enter into these metaphysical distinctions; I hate the very sound of them. Leave the Americans as they anciently stood, and these distinctions, born of our unhappy contest, will die along with it. They and we, and their and our ancestors, have been happy under that system. Let the memory of all actions, in contradiction to that good old mode, on both sides, be extinguished forever. Be content to bind America by laws of trade; you have always done it. Do not burthen them by taxes; you were not used to doing it from the beginning. . . . Reflect how you are to govern a people, who think they ought to be free, and think they are not. Your scheme yields no revenue; it yields nothing but discontent, disorder, disobedience; and such is the state of America, that after wading up to your eyes in blood, you could only end just where you begun; that is, to tax where no revenue is to be found.

Chatham hobbled into the House of Lords on May 26 and said, with all his old fire and eloquence:

> [I must first] condemn in the severest manner the late turbulent and unwarrantable conduct of the Americans, particularly of the riots of Boston. . . . But, my Lords, the mode which has been pursued to bring them back to a sense of their duty to their parent state has been so diametrically opposite to the fundamental principle of sound policy that individuals, possessed of common understanding, must be astonished at such proceedings. By blocking the harbor at Boston, you have involved the innocent trader in the same punishment with the guilty profligates who destroyed your merchandise. You clap a naval and military extinguisher over their harbor and punish a crime of a few lawless depredators and their abettors upon the whole body of the inhabitants. . . . The moment they perceived your intention was renewed to tax them, under a pretence of serving the East India

Company, their resentment got the ascendant of their moderation, for I sincerely believe the destroying of the tea was the effect of their despair.

This has always been my received and unalterable opinion, that I will carry it to my grave, that this country has no right under heaven to tax America. It is contrary to all principles of justice and civil policy, which neither the exigencies of the state, nor even the acquiescence in the taxes would justify upon any occasion whatever. . . . Instead of adding to their miseries, as the bill before you most undoubtedly does, adopt some lenient measures which may lure them to their duty. . . . Instead of these harsh and severe proceedings, pass an amnesty on all their youthful errors. . . . Adopt a more gentle mode of governing America; for the day is not far distant when America may vie with these kingdoms, not only in arms, but in arts also.

Neither the logic of the young Burke nor the eloquence and vision of the aging Chatham could alter the mind-set of king, government, or country. In the final stages of this debate, Lord North's response was to tell Parliament:

The Americans have tarred and feathered your subjects, burnt your ships, denied obedience to your laws and authority; yet so clement and so forbearing has our conduct been that it is encumbent on us now to take a different course. . . . They deny our legislative authority, not in all places but there are those who hold and defend that doctrine. If they deny our authority in one instance, it goes to all. We must control them or submit to them.

Rose Fuller, the Whig merchant, had opposed the Coercive Acts, and it was he who pronounced an epitaph on the legislation, saying sadly, "It is not an error of the ministry, it is an error of the nation. I see it everywhere I go."

Parliament was scheduled to end this session on June 22. But before it recessed, it passed another piece of legislation that soon became bracketed with the four Intolerable Acts. This was the Quebec Act.

In its time, this act was considered quite liberal, an effort by the English to make social and political peace with the French Canadian Catholics who were now subjects of George III. It combined English criminal law and French civil law in a more humane legal system. Most notably, it gave Canada's Catholics civil equality and guaranteed religious tolerance.

For Americans, the provocative feature of this act was a provision annexing to Quebec vast areas of the American midwest, including land that today comprises Wisconsin, Michigan, Illinois, Indiana, and Ohio. Americans cried out against what they perceived as a mandate for Roman Catholic popery to march down from the north and invade Protestant America. And since the bill was apparently giving away a vast territory west of the Appalachians, the colonists condemned it as an insidious attempt by the English to create a new French Canadian and Indian threat.

Having completed the Quebec Act, Parliament adjourned, optimistic that the Boston Tea Party's bluff had been called and the fractious American children would soon come to order. On May 6, the king sent his congratulations to Lord North:

> Passage of the Massachusetts Act by a great majority gives me infinite satisfaction. Perseverance and the meeting difficulties as they arise with firmness seem the only means of either credit with success or terminating public affairs. Your conduct on the American disturbance is a very clear proof of the justness of that proposition.

Thomas Hutchinson returned to London at the end of June and was promptly received by King George, who informed Lord North on July 1:

> I was desirous of hearing his account how matters were when he left his government, and am now well convinced they will soon submit; he owns that the Boston Port Bill was the only wise and effectual suggestion for bringing them to a speedy submission, and that the change in the legislature will be a means of establishing some government in that province, which till now has been one of anarchy.

News of the Port Bill reached Boston on May 11, 1774. General Gage arrived a week later to take charge; Hutchinson departed, unmourned, a few days after. Sam Adams and friends had already convened a first Boston town meeting to decide at once on what action to take. A few conservative citizens and merchants talked of paying for the tea. They were brushed aside by others, who cried that they preferred "to abandon the city to flames" rather than pay so much as a farthing to help the East India Company. Paul Revere, already Boston's favorite dispatch rider, was sent off to New York and Philadelphia to appeal for solidarity through the Committees of Correspondence.

On June 1, the day the port of Boston was to be closed, all up and down the colonies, from one hamlet and town and city to the next, shops were closed, flags were lowered to half-mast, church bells tolled while special services were held. Effigies of Lord North were burned. Demonstrators marched through the streets, remembering the Stamp Act, the Townshend duties, and the Boston Massacre.

By now, Sam Adams's radicals had drawn up, and sent off through the Committees of Correspondence, a proposal calling for all the colonies to join in a "Solemn League and Covenant" to cut off all trade with England, both imports and exports, until the Port Bill was rescinded. This was too strong a measure for the merchants of New York and Philadelphia, who rightly perceived that such an abrupt, complete suspension of trade would probably harm America more than it would England.

Instead, the New York Committee of Correspondence hastily drew up a counterproposal to convene a Continental Congress to adopt a unified response to King George and Parliament, similar to the special Stamp Act Congress that had been convened in New York in October of 1765.

Boston was not pleased with the New York proposal. Boston preferred a full trade embargo first and a Continental Congress to follow. The leaders in both New York and Pennsylvania were moderates, however, and while they were ready to make a show of unity, they were nevertheless determined to impose moderation on the New England radicals.

Sensing what was afoot, Boston objected that it would take time to assemble a Continental Congress and that action might come too late to save their city. New York responded with a promise of food for Boston sufficient to withstand a ten-year siege. Donations began to pour in: rice, wheat, sugar, flour, even hundreds of sheep, driven from Connecticut and New York to Massachusetts.

By July, twelve of the colonies had agreed to send delegates to a first Continental Congress, at which the Boston proposal for a total trade embargo would be debated. (The lone holdout was Georgia, which was fighting an uprising of the Creek Indians and worried that if it joined in, the English might cut off the supply of arms and gunpowder.) The Congress was set to convene the first week of September in Philadelphia, largest city and geographic midpoint of the colonies.

However, the citizens of Boston were not prepared to sit and wait. General Gage had been instructed by Lord Dartmouth that "every care is to be taken to quiet the people by gentle means. . . . Troops are not to be called out unless it is absolutely necessary."

"Gentle means," Gage quickly realized, were neither practical nor possible if he were to enforce the Coercive Acts. He did manage, during the first weeks of his impossible mission, to move the seat of Massachusetts government from Boston to Salem, and the hated Customs Office to Plymouth, but to no avail.

The Boston Citizens' Committee decided that Massachusetts would go ahead and proclaim its own new "covenant" to embargo English goods, even if the other colonies were not prepared to join. General Gage reacted to this with a proclamation denouncing the proposed covenant as "a traiterous combination" and threatened to arrest anyone who signed it or encouraged its circulation. Predictably, the response was an upsurge of signatures and rapid adoption of the covenant by one town meeting after another. The support spread even to New Hampshire and Connecticut. Thus Gage quickly learned how limited his power was: He could scarcely arrest all of New England's citizens or close down all the towns.

In this explosive atmosphere, Gage moved next, as ordered, to dissolve the elected Massachusetts Council, appoint a council in its place, suppress the town meetings, and appoint a flock of Loyalist officials.

Gage chose twenty-four new councillors of reliable Loyalist sentiments. When these new appointees stepped outside their homes, they were jeered and cursed by crowds of citizens. Some were even fired upon. Threats greeted new judges, magistrates, and sheriffs. Gage couldn't send out troops to protect them, so the new officials soon were streaking for the protection of the city.

By the end of August, most of the new councillors had been so terrorized that they resigned, and the courts had virtually ceased to function. General Gage was virtually besieged in Boston, the only place his rule held sway. On September 2, he wrote a piteous report to Lord Dartmouth: "Civil government is near its end. . . . Conciliation, Moderation, Reasoning is over. Nothing can be done but by forceable means." He told Dartmouth that he had too few troops to control the situation, even with the four additional regiments that had arrived and the extra frigates and Royal Navy ships needed to enforce the port's closure. He said that he intended to "avoid a bloody crisis as long as possible" and that he would leave it up to London "to judge what is best to be done"—scarcely what the government expected of its commander in America.

This, then, was how things stood when delegates began convening in Philadelphia in September 1774.

Benjamin Franklin had adopted a low profile in London after the Cockpit hearing. In early February, a week after the hearing, he wrote to Thomas Cushing: "It is not possible for me to act as your agent, apprehending I could as such be of no further use to the province." He added that he would continue "to give what assistance I can as a private man," and he did continue to correspond with Cushing and others—on a much reduced basis, however. He was by now certain that his mail was again being intercepted and read by the English secret service.

On April 16, he wrote to Cushing, in a letter probably sent by private courier, that he "suspected letters of mine [may] be returned to London, their contents [deemed] treasonable for which I should be prosecuted." He added that he had written nothing that he would consider treasonable, but clearly he was concerned. He probably felt that in light of Wedderburn's attack, anything was possible with the English. He suggested to Cushing that he write back "by different conveyances." In July, he commented to Cushing that he hadn't heard from him for quite some time, and that "I have written several times and hope the correspondence has not been intercepted."

Meanwhile, he was able to continue as agent for Pennsylvania and New Jersey since neither province had been involved in the affair of the Hutchinson and Oliver letters. But during his final months in London, he avoided transacting any official business with the Privy Council.

When Parliament recessed, Franklin joined the summer exodus, spending most of August visiting friends. Toward the end of the month, returning to London from Brighton, on the south coast, he paused to have dinner with his friend Lord Stanhope. Quite unexpectedly, Stanhope told Franklin that the earl of Chatham, whose country home at Hayes was not far away, would like Franklin to call.* Next morning, Franklin took Stanhope's carriage to Hayes:

> That truly great man received me with an abundance of civility [and he] inquired particularly into the situation of affairs in America, spoke feelingly of the severity of the late laws against Massachusetts, and expressed great regard and esteem for the people of that country, who he hoped would continue firm and united in defending by all peaceable and legal means their constitutional rights.

The two settled down for a long discussion. Franklin noted that "in former cases great empires crumbled first from their extremities" too remote to be understood by central governments and too often left in the hands of bad governors. Chatham talked of "restoring the ancient harmony of the two countries which he most earnestly desired" but told Franklin that a coalition against the North ministry could not be expected; many Englishmen doubted the value of further concessions to America. He then asked Franklin whether "America aimed at setting up for itself an independent state." Franklin later wrote:

> I assured him that, having more than once travelled almost from one end of the continent to the other and kept a great variety of company, eating, drinking and conversing with them freely, I never had heard in any conversation with any person drunk or sober the least expression of a wish for a separation or a hint that such a thing would be advantageous to America.

This statement in 1774 was still basically valid, and Franklin recorded that Chatham "expressed much satisfaction in my having called upon him, and particularly in the assurances I had given him that America did not aim at independence." Chatham asked that they meet again. Franklin wrote of his reply, "I should not fail to

---

*As far as the records show, this was the first meeting between the two men. During Franklin's first tour as agent, 1757–62, Pitt had been preoccupied with other affairs. When Franklin returned in 1764, Pitt was out of office and frequently ill thereafter.

avail myself of the permission he was pleased to give me, being very sensible of the honor and advantage I should reap of his instructive conversation, which indeed was not a mere compliment."

The House of Commons that had been elected in 1768 would not come to the end of its mandate until the spring of 1775, but King George was determined on an early election. Lord North was hesitant, feeling that the situation in America and the potential disruption of trade might play into the hands of the opposition and reduce the government's substantial majority. But the king insisted. In a memorandum to North written at the end of August, he said:

> I add a few lines on the calling of a new Parliament: The general Congress now assembling in America; the Peace of Russia with the Turks and the unsettled state of the French Ministry are very additional reasons to shew the propriety of the measure; besides I trust that it will fill the House with more Gentlemen of landed property, as the Nabobs, Planters and other Volunteers are not ready for the [election] battle. As soon as You can fix a proper day for the dissolution I desire you will Write to the Chancellor and the Lord President, but not above a week before the mandate is to be executed.

The king wanted a surprise election. When the king commanded, North obeyed. He dissolved Parliament in September for polling in late October. When the ballots were counted, the king's instincts—helped by liberal spending from public funds—proved correct. On November 14, North was able to report to the king that "with as much caution as possible, and every member left out of the list of Pros whose sentiments are not perfectly known," he could count on the votes of 321 in a total House of Commons membership of 558. The majority ensured that the king's American policies could not be successfully challenged or changed.

The king never wavered in demanding firmness in dealing with the Americans. In mid-September, North had sent the king a private, conciliatory appeal that had been drafted by a Quaker group in Pennsylvania. It had been sent in the form of a letter to Quakers in London, who passed it on to the prime minister. The king's response was that

The letters from the Quakers of Pennsylvania to some of the chiefs of that persuasion in London shews that they retain that coolness which is a very strong characteristick of that body of peoples; but I was in hopes it would have contained some declaration of their submission to the Mother Country; whilst by the whole tenour they seem to wish for England giving some degree of way to the opinions of North America. The die is now cast, the colonies must either submit or triumph. I do not wish to come to severer measures but we must not retreat; by coolness and an unremitting pursuit of the measures that have been adopted I trust they will come to submit.

For the king, there would be no retreat, no compromise. So it would be also for the government.

Franklin certainly felt the rising tension. In mid-October, he wrote to Joseph Galloway in Philadelphia:

My situation here is thought by many to be a little hazardous; for that by some accident the troops and people of New England should come to blows I should probably be taken up; the ministerial people affecting everywhere to represent me as the cause of all the misunderstanding; and I have been frequently cautioned to secure my papers and by some advised to withdraw. But I venture to stay, in compliance with the wishes of others. I might be of some use when the American Congress is heard from. I confide in my innocence, that the worst which can happen to me will be an imprisonment on suspicion, though that is a thing I should much desire to avoid, as it may be expensive and vexatious as well as dangerous to my health.

On September 5, 1774, in Philadelphia began that remarkable first gathering of the Continental Congress. Fifty-six men, the most distinguished, thoughtful, intellectually endowed Americans of their time met in Carpenters' Hall, a modest little structure barely as large as the nearby City Tavern. John Adams wrote to his wife, Abigail, in Braintree, Massachusetts, "The magnanimity and public spirit which I see here makes me blush for the sordid, venal herd which I have seen in my own province."

The Congress met for seven weeks. It produced a Declaration of Rights, forerunner of the Declaration of Independence, a sweeping rejection of the right of Parliament to legislate for the colonies in any respect whatsoever. It also included a detailed list of bills enacted by Parliament since 1763 that infringed on colonial rights. "Repeal of them is essentially necessary," the declaration said, "in order to restore harmony between Great Britain and the American colonies."

At no time in the proceedings had there been a proposal to declare independence, or war, to achieve colonial aims. The declaration's premise was simple: If England accepted the document and Parliament repealed all of the legislation that controlled American affairs, there would be peace and harmony between the two countries.

After framing the Declaration of Rights, the Congress turned to the Boston Port Bill. All agreed to ban imports from England, beginning December 1, 1774, and continuing until the siege of Boston ended. But when it came to banning exports to England, Virginia insisted—and refused to budge—on waiting till the summer of 1775, after the next crop of tobacco had been harvested, dried, and shipped. South Carolina refused to embargo its exports of rice and indigo. In the end, Congress agreed to delay the export ban until September 1775 and exempt South Carolina's rice from the ban altogether. Meanwhile, a "nonconsumption ban" against English goods would go into effect. To ensure compliance with the trade embargoes, an "association agreement" was drawn up, outlining common measures to be taken throughout the colonies.

As its final act, the Congress adopted a direct appeal to King George, outlining the colonies' grievances and rights and asking for understanding. Drafted by John Dickinson, its language was firm and its hope and intent fervently clear:

As your Majesty enjoys the signal distinction of reigning over free men, we apprehend the language of free men cannot be displeasing. Your royal indignation, we hope, will rather fall on those designing and dangerous men, who daringly interposing themselves . . . have at length compelled us, by the force of accumulated injuries, too severe to be any longer tolerable, to disturb your Majesty's repose by our complaints. . . . We ask but for peace, liberty and safety. *Your royal authority over us, and our connexion with Great Britain, we shall al-*

ways carefully and zealously endeavor to support and maintain. [Emphasis added.]

While it was hardly realistic for the Americans to address an appeal to the king against his appointed government, there was still a certain belief in the ultimate fairness of George III and in his concern for the interests and welfare of all his subjects.*

The king made no response to the Congress. A response would have been tantamount to recognizing the Congress as a legitimate legal body; this neither the king nor his government was about to do. Instead, the king commented, in a long memorandum sent to Lord North:

> There is no denying the serious crisis to which the dispute between the Mother Country and its North American colonies are growing, and that the greatest temper and firmness are necessary to bring matters to a good issue. . . . Had the Americans in prosecuting their ill-grounded claims put on an appearance of mildness it might have been very difficult to chalk out the right path to be pursued; but they have boldly thrown off the mask and avowed that nothing less than a total independence of the British legislature will satisfy them.
>
> This indeed decides the proper plan to be followed, which is to stop the trade of all those colonies who obey the mandate of the Congress for non-importation, non-exportation and non-consumption, to assist them no further with presents to the Indians, and give every kind of assistance to those who conduct themselves otherways; which will make them quarrel among themselves. Their separate interests must soon effect this, and experience will then show them that the interference of the Mother Country is essentially necessary to prevent their becoming rivals.

If the king read all the various declarations adopted by the Continental Congress (and he was indeed very thorough and methodical in his conduct of business), he showed little understanding, and less interest in the significance, of what had happened in Philadelphia.

---

*The extent to which the king was actively directing the repressive policies on the colonies only became clear many decades later, when the archives at Windsor Castle were opened.

In November, while the news of the Congress's decisions was still crossing the Atlantic, General Gage had written North a candid but improvident dispatch in which he declared that the Massachusetts Government Act had been rendered unworkable, not by a mob but by men of property and influence. Gage recommended a political retreat, the temporary suspension of the Coercive Acts until the situation could be brought under control. The king wrote angrily to Lord North:

> I return the letters received from General Gage; his idea of Suspending the Acts appears to me the most absurd that can be suggested. . . . We must either master them or totally leave them to themselves and treat them as Aliens; I do not by this mean to insinuate that I am for new measures; but I am for supporting those already taken.

Instead of taking warning from Gage's proposal, the king, who was not hearing what he wanted to hear, began to look for a replacement for the general. This, however, would be neither a quick nor an easy matter for Lord North and his increasingly agitated cabinet.

In the meantime, the king's messages exhorting firmness flowed with even greater urgency. In mid-December, he wrote to Lord Dartmouth:

> Nothing can be more provoking than the conduct of the inhabitants of Massachusetts Bay. Some measures must undoubtedly be adopted after Christmas to curb them, and by degrees bring them to a due obedience to the Mother Country; but reason not passion must point out the proper measures.

Reason, however, was not a strong point in the king's character. In another message to Lord North, the king threw reason to the winds: "I am not sorry that the line of conduct now seems chalked out, which the enclosed dispatches [from America] thoroughly justify. The New England governments are in a State of Rebellion. *Blows must decide* whether they are to be subject to this country or independent."

Chapter 13

FRANKLIN'S LAST TRY

By Christmas of 1774, all England knew that there was a full-fledged rebellion in America. The king was ready for war. For him, it was easy. Not so for Lord North, who had neither the conviction nor the ruthlessness to fight a war. On the ship of state, North was like a pilot who suddenly comes out of the fog and sees rocks dead ahead.

King George, in opening the first session of the newly elected Parliament, spoke of "a most daring spirit of resistance and disobedience to the law" in Massachusetts. He continued, "These proceedings have been countenanced and encouraged in other of my colonies and unwarrantable attempts have been made to obstruct the commerce of this Kingdom by unlawful combinations." He did not say what the government intended to do, and nowhere did the speech mention war.

On December 12, Lord North showed his hesitancy when he presented the army and naval estimates for the coming year. Instead of summoning troops to prepare for war, he announced that there would be a reduction in recruiting. He proposed enlisting only 16,000 seamen (down 4,000 from the year before) and 17,500 troops (also a reduction). The East India fleet was being recalled to home waters, and North seemed to believe that this force, plus the new recruits, would be sufficient for any contingency. He disclosed that seven army battalions and five artillery companies had already been sent to America and that three more battalions were being ordered to Boston. (Gage already had about one soldier for every five inhabitants.) North told Parliament that the troops in America "were sufficient, unless from the conduct of the other colonies it should be judged necessary to extend the line with respect to them."

Torn by indecision, the prime minister hoped that his skill would make it possible to maneuver a way out of war. He had already proposed to the king the idea of sending a special commission to America to discuss grievances and perhaps resolve disputes. But the king, in a memo dated December 15, firmly rejected negotiating: "I am not so fond of sending Commissioners to examine into the disputes. . . . I do not want to drive [the colonies] to despair, but to submission, which nothing but feeling the inconvenience of their situation can bring their pride to submit to."

Since the king had ruled out any open approach, Lords Dartmouth and North were, in the meantime, secretly sounding out Franklin on possible terms for a settlement. The first intermediary for these secret talks was a rich Quaker banker, brewer, and merchant in the American trade, David Barclay, who dabbled in politics and was a good friend of the moderate Lord Hyde, who was chancellor of the duchy of Lancaster. The second was Dr. John Fothergill, also a Quaker and a medical man of high repute whose patients included both Lord Dartmouth and Benjamin Franklin.

In early December, Barclay called on Franklin, telling him there was a need "for some person who could contrive some means of preventing a terrible calamity and bring about a reconciliation." He urged Franklin to take the role. Franklin was skeptical and replied that he would be happy if he thought he could do so good a work but that he saw "no prospect of it." The government, he told Barclay, was not interested in settlement but "wished to provoke the North American people into open rebellion." Barclay replied that he was certain that "some ministers would be glad to get out of their embarrassment on any terms, only saving the honor and dignity of the government." He urged Franklin to draw up his own thoughts on terms of a settlement. Franklin demurred but agreed to think it over.

Two days later, Franklin received an invitation from Dr. Fothergill to come to his home at five o'clock on Sunday, December 5, for a further discussion with Barclay. At this meeting, both Fothergill and Barclay insisted that there were those in the government who were disposed to accommodation, and they urged Franklin to "draw up a plan." Franklin recounted:

> If I would draw up a plan, which we three upon considering should judge reasonable, it might be made use of, and answer some good purpose, since he believed that either himself or David Barclay could get it communicated to some of the most moderate among the ministers, who would consider it with attention. They both urged this with great earnestness, and when I mentioned the impropriety of my doing any thing of the kind at the time we were in daily expectation of hearing from the Congress who undoubtedly would be explicit on the means of restoring a good understanding, they seemed impatient, alleging that it was uncertain when we should receive the results of the Congress and what it would be; and that the least delay might be dangerous; that additional punishments for New England were in contemplation, accidents might widen the breach and make it irreparable.

Franklin reluctantly agreed to put his thoughts down. Thus he began his last try to avert a war for independence.* At the outset, Franklin did not know, nor did the Quaker intermediaries make it clear, whether they were taking this initiative on their own or whether they were acting directly for Lords Dartmouth and Hyde. Franklin acted on the assumption that they were communicating with these ministers. So he took up his pen and wrote a paper called "hints for Conversation upon the Subject of Terms that might probably produce a durable Union between Britain and the Colonies." Franklin's memorandum listed seventeen points:

1. The tea destroyed to be paid for.
2. The tea-duty act to be repealed, and all the duties that have been received upon it to be repaid into the treasuries of the several provinces from which they have been collected.

---

*His fruitless effort was not recorded on the English side and therefore became nothing more than a footnote to history. Fortunately, during his voyage home three months later, Franklin spent most of his time in his cabin writing a detailed account of his efforts.

3. The acts of navigation to be re-enacted in the colonies.

4. A naval officer appointed by the Crown to reside in each colony to see that those acts are observed.

5. All acts restraining manufactures in the colonies to be repealed.

6. All duties arising on the acts for regulating trade with the colonies, to be for the public use of the respective colonies, and paid into their treasuries. The collectors and customs-house officers to be appointed by each governor, and not sent from England.

7. In consideration of the Americans maintaining their own peace establishment, and the monopoly Britain is to have of their commerce, no requisition [for revenue] to be paid from them in time of peace.

8. No troops to enter and quarter in any colony but with the consent of its legislature.

9. In time of war, on requisition made by the King, with the consent of Parliament, every colony shall raise money by the following rules or proportions [which were then detailed].

10. Castle William to be restored to the province of Massachusetts Bay, and no fortress built by the Crown in any province, but with the consent of its legislature.

11. The late Massachusetts and Quebec Acts to be repealed, and a free government granted to Canada.

12. All judges to be appointed during good behavior, with equally permanent salaries, to be paid out of the province revenues by appointment of the assemblies. Or, if the judges are to be appointed during the pleasure of the Crown, let the salaries be during the pleasure of the assemblies, as heretofore.

13. Governors to be appointed by the assemblies of each province.

14. If Britain will give up the monopoly of the American commerce, then the aid above-mentioned to be given by America in time of peace as well as in time of war.

15. The extension of the act of Henry VIII concerning treason to the colonies, to be formally disowned by Parliament.

16. The American admiralty courts to be reduced to the same powers they have in England, and the acts establishing them to be re-enacted in America.

17. All powers of internal legislation in the colonies to be disclaimed by Parliament.

This represented more of a negotiating document than did the Declaration of Rights by the Continental Congress, which arrived in London in mid-December. But while Franklin's "Hints" implicitly recognized a continuing linkage between America and England, Franklin was quite firm on what England must give up. Thus his "Hints" differed little from the Continental Congress's demands.

Franklin, Fothergill, and Barclay had a long discussion on the "Hints." In the end, Franklin made some minor changes but no revision of any substance. When they were finished, Fothergill asked Franklin if he might communicate the paper to Lord Dartmouth, whom he saw regularly as his doctor. Barclay wondered "if there would be anything amiss if I showed [it] to Lord Hyde." Franklin recorded:

> I had drawn up the paper at their request, and it was now theirs to do with as they pleased. Another question then arose, whether I had any objection to their mentioning that I had been consulted? I said, none that related to myself; but it was my opinion, if they wished any attention to be paid to the propositions, it would be better not to mention me; the ministry having, as I conceived, a prejudice against me and everything that came from me. For my part, I kept this whole proceeding a profound secret, but I soon after discovered that it had taken air by some means or another.

The American embargo on English imports took effect on December 1. Meanwhile, the congressional Declaration of Rights arrived, together with the petition to the king, and Franklin and the other colonial agents presented these to Lord Dartmouth on December 21. Dartmouth commented that the direct petition to the king seemed to him to be "decent and respectful"—but then he was the most anxious of all the cabinet ministers to avoid war. Other ministers were incensed. Lord Rochford declared that "absurd as you are inclined to believe the Americans to be, the Congress has exceeded all ideas of rebellion, and even inconsistency." Lord North grasped at the straw that the declaration "did not deny the right of Parliament" even though it demanded repeal of all controls passed since 1763.

The king, who still believed that the colonies would split under pressure, instructed Lord North to prepare more punitive legislation. He was to impose a counterblockade along the American coast to prevent any foreign ships from entering and to stop the New England fishing boats from sailing to the abundant waters of the

Grand Banks. But North hesitated, well aware of the unease among London merchants and traders over the loss of the American market. The king put more pressure on his reluctant prime minister. He sent a new instruction to North concerning the American embargo of English goods: "The proper plan to be followed is to stop the trade of all those colonies who obey the mandate of the Congress for the non-importation, non-exportation and non-consumption, and give every kind of assistance to those who conduct themselves otherwise."

On December 18, the king proposed General Sir Jeffrey Amherst as a replacement for Gage:

> A general plan is necessary to be formed for America, the whole to be digested before any step is taken. Should it be thought right to give Command of the Forces in America to Sir Jeffrey Amherst, it would be right he should be consulted as to the Generals to Serve with him.

But Amherst, who hated America and Americans, politely declined the appointment.

Meanwhile, news reached London that Americans had made secret purchases of gunpowder, lead, flints, and muskets from Holland. Customs officials in Rhode Island had reported purchases by the colony of three hundred barrels of gunpowder and forty thousand flints, which were transshipped through the Dutch West Indian island of St. Eustatius in early December. When ordered by Gage to tighten up on suspicious cargoes, customs could only reply that "no Check can possibly be put . . . but by Armed Vessels placed in each of the channels."

The British ambassador to The Hague was instructed to seek an explanation.

Franklin's Christmas was not a quiet one that year. On Christmas Day, the secret peace exploration took an unexpected turn.

In recent weeks, Franklin had called two or three times on a genteel and engaging widow of fifty-three. She was Caroline Howe, daughter of a distinguished military family and sister of Admiral Viscount Howe and Major General William Howe. Mrs. Howe (as she was called in widowhood) had extended invitations to Franklin to play chess. He found her an intelligent companion and opponent. On Christmas Day, he called on her again, but on this occasion soon after his arrival, Mrs. Howe told him, he later recorded, that Admiral Viscount Howe "wished to be acquainted with me; that he was a good man, and she was sure we would like each other." A servant was sent to the admiral, who lived close by. Lord Howe arrived shortly, and after a minimum of polite greetings, he got down to cases.

His reason for seeking a meeting, he told Franklin, was "the alarming situation of our affairs with America." In a roundabout way, Howe came to much the same point that Fothergill and Barclay had made nearly three weeks before. Franklin recorded:

> He gave it to me as his sincere opinion that some of the ministry were extremely well disposed to any reasonable accommodation, preserving only the dignity of the government; and he wished me to draw up in writing, some propositions containing the terms on which I conceived a good understanding might be obtained and established, and the mode of proceeding.

Somewhat surprised by this new approach, Franklin nevertheless agreed to "draw up something of the kind," and they planned to meet the Wednesday following.

Next day, Franklin journeyed out to Hayes. He had taken advantage of his recent acquaintance with Lord Chatham to send him copies of the Declaration of Rights and the petition to the king and had proposed a meeting to discuss them. The meeting was both stimulating and encouraging:

> He received me with an affectionate kind of respect, from so great a man extremely engaging, but the opinion he expressed of the Congress was still more so. They had acted, he said, with much moderation and wisdom. There were not in their whole proceedings above one or two things he could have wished otherwise. The rest he admired and honored. He thought the petition [to the King] decent, manly and properly expressed.

Chatham told Franklin that he hoped the government "might soon come to see its mistakes." If his health permitted, he said, he might "prepare something for its consideration" when Parliament met after the holidays. Franklin responded by emphasizing

> the very hazardous state I conceived we were in by the continuance of the army in Boston, that it could not possibly answer any good purpose there, and might be infinitely mischievous; that no accommoda-

tion could properly be proposed and entered into by the Americans, while the bayonet was at their breasts; that to have any agreement binding, all forces should be withdrawn.

Franklin recorded that Chatham "seemed to think these sentiments reasonable." Chatham acted on Franklin's advice when he next addressed the House of Lords.

Two days after his meeting with Chatham, Franklin had a less satisfactory meeting with Admiral Howe. He had not had time to draw up the promised memorandum, but Howe nevertheless assured him that both Dartmouth and North "had a sincere disposition to listen favorably" to any propositions he might put forward. Then Howe asked Franklin what he thought of sending a commission to America to look into the grievances. The admiral thought that he himself might be suitable for such a mission. Franklin gave his guarded approval. Next, Howe pulled from his pocket a copy, in David Barclay's hand, of Franklin's "Hints." Franklin, concealing his surprise, acknowledged he had drawn up the paper. Howe expressed his disappointment and said he saw no likelihood of settlement on that basis.

Howe then dangled before Franklin a not very oblique offer of a bribe if he could come up with more acceptable terms. In Franklin's account:

> He expatiated on the infinite service it would be to [England] and the great merit in being instrumental in so good a work; that he should not think of influencing me by any selfish motive, but certainly I might with reason expect any reward in the power of the government to bestow. This, to me, was what the French vulgarly call "spitting in the soup." However, I promised to draw up some sketch of a plan at his request, though I much doubted, I said, whether it would be thought preferable to that he had in his hand.

Franklin was clearly disgusted by this "offer," so typical of English politics of that era. But he was not going to close any doors. Instead, he wrote out a new set of proposals, which followed the lines of the original "Hints" but was more elaborate in content and presentation. This he sent through Mrs. Howe to the admiral at his country home.

When Howe returned to London in mid-January, he and Franklin met again. Howe chided Franklin; he seemed to think, Franklin wrote, that "I had powers or instructions from the Congress to make concessions that would be more satisfactory." Franklin's response was to ask for "some propositions from the ministers themselves." Howe promised that Franklin "should learn more in a few days," but this didn't happen.

Why had Howe intervened in the process started by Fothergill and Barclay? Since there is no British record of the talks, there is no clear answer, nor is there any evidence about the origins of the Quaker initiative. Barclay and Fothergill were private citizens, Howe a distinguished admiral and member of Parliament. Perhaps Howe acted at the behest of Lord Hyde, his friend and neighbor, who was genuine in his friendship with America and truly wished to avoid a calamity. Perhaps the government ministers decided to enlist Howe in the hopes that he could add weight to the secret talks and convince Franklin to frame softer terms. The offer Howe made to Franklin of a suitable reward had to have come from the government—it was not an offer that could or would have been made to Franklin by the Quakers—and it was a great mistake. Franklin was contemptuous of it, and it may have stiffened his disdain and mistrust for those with whom he was dealing.

On January 19, 1775, Franklin received an invitation from Lord Chatham to attend the House of Lords the next day. At two o'clock, Franklin arrived; Chatham was waiting. Franklin wrote:

> Taking me by the arm and leading me along the passage, [Chatham] delivered me to the door-keeper, saying loudly, "This is Dr. Franklin, whom I would have admitted into the House," when they readily opened the door for me accordingly. As it had not been publicly known that there was any communication between his lordship and me, this I found occasioned some speculation. His appearance in the House, I observed, caused a kind of bustle among the officers who were hurried in sending messages for other members.

In a direct reflection of Franklin's earlier urging, Chatham further surprised the Lords by presenting a brief motion that troops be completely withdrawn from Boston "in order to open the way towards an happy settlement of the dangerous troubles in America." With fire and vigor, Chatham thundered that the British troops were "an army of impotence and contempt, penned up in the town and unable to act." The Americans could never be defeated, he said, and further, "it was our own violent proceedings that have roused their resistance." His peroration was devastating:

> If the ministers thus persevere in misadvising and misleading the King, I will not say that they can alienate the affections of his subjects from his crown, but I will affirm that they will make his crown not worth wearing. I will not say that the King is betrayed, but I will announce that the Kingdom is undone.

The debate that followed was brief. The motion to withdraw the troops was, Franklin said, "no more than whistling in the wind." It was defeated seventy-seven to eighteen.

Next day, Chatham sent Franklin a copy of the motion, Franklin noted, "that I might be possessed of it in the most authentic manner."

In mid-January, after Parliament's recess, Lord North began to act on the king's earlier commands. A motion was prepared to declare Massachusetts to be in a state of rebellion, the equivalent of declaring war. Accompanying this was an act empowering the Royal Navy to "stop all foreign trade of New England, particularly to their fishery on the banks of Newfoundland, until they return to their duty." Initially, this act would apply to Massachusetts, Rhode Island, and Connecticut. North hoped it would cause a split among the colonies.

After this was adopted, Lord North intended to offer a conciliation, a resolution that might rescind the tea tax. Meanwhile, more troops were ordered to America, and discussions about hiring mercenaries were initiated with the German principalities. The king also intended to approach Catherine the Great of Russia to see if Russian soldiers might be hired for service in America.

Next, the government had to sort out the question of who would command the military in America. The king had instructed that while he wanted to replace Gage, he did not want him disgraced. Thus three generals were sent to serve with Gage, who would be recalled to London later in the year for "consultations." The senior of the trio was Major General William Howe. Accompanying him were Major Generals Henry Clinton and John Burgoyne.

Finally, in January 1775, after much prodding, Dartmouth began drafting a lengthy letter to Gage, telling Gage in many, many words, to get moving against the rebellion. Since the people of Massachusetts were ready "to commit themselves at all events to open rebellion . . . force should be repelled by force." In fact, Dartmouth wrote, since all three of the New England colonies seemed resolved "to cast off their dependence upon the government of this Kingdom . . . the only consideration that remains is, in what manner the force under your command may be exerted." More troops would soon be on their way, he told Gage, but he questioned whether they would be needed before Gage took action:

> A smaller force now, if put to the test, would be able to encounter them with greater probability of success than might be expected from a greater army, if the people would be suffered to form themselves upon a more regular plan, to acquire confidence from discipline, and to prepare those resources without which every thing must be put to the issue of a single action.

In other words, stop waiting around while the Americans get ready to fight. Further, he instructed Gage to arrest "the principal actors and abettors" even though Gage had earlier warned that "such a proceeding should be a signal for hostilities."

There now occurred an unexplained and extraordinary delay in dispatching Dartmouth's letter to Boston: It was dated January 27, 1775, but it was not sent until six weeks later and did not reach Gage until April 14—just as he was preparing to march on Concord and Lexington. Perhaps North and Dartmouth were reluctant to take this last, decisive step. Perhaps they waited hoping for results from the talks with Franklin.

On January 27, as Dartmouth composed his letter to Gage, Franklin set out to visit Chatham at Hayes. There the two men held a long discussion of various points in a motion Chatham was drafting to attempt settlement of the American dispute. Franklin was invited to stay for dinner, "his [Chatham's] family only present." On the twenty-ninth, Chatham went to Craven Street to call on Franklin, who recorded with some satisfaction that

> He staid with me near two hours, his equipage waiting at the door; and being there while people were coming from church, it was much

taken notice of and talked of, as at that time was every little circumstance that men thought might possibly in any way affect American
affairs. Such a visit from so great a man, on so important a business,
flattered not a little my vanity; and the honor of it gave me the more
pleasure, as it happened on the very day twelve months that the
ministry had taken so much pains to disgrace me before the Privy
Council.

Chatham brought with him his "peace plan," which he intended
to unveil the following Wednesday, February 1. He asked Franklin
to give the plan detailed consideration, draft any comments he
might have, and then visit at Hayes for further discussion on Tuesday. This Franklin did. He spent four hours with Chatham but recorded that

> his lordship, in the manner of, I think, all eloquent persons, was so
> full and diffuse in supporting every particular I questioned, that there
> was not enough time to go through half my memorandums. He is
> not easily interrupted, and I had such pleasure in hearing him that I
> found little inclination to interrupt him.

In any case, "neither of us had much expectation that the plan
would be adopted as it stood," only that it might be the basis for
alterations.

On February 1, Franklin, escorted by Lord Stanhope, arrived at
the House of Lords. Chatham presented his plan, in which he called
for the Continental Congress "to be declared legal" so that it could
act for all the colonies and for the suspension of "all grievous Acts
whereof Americans had made complaints" (which the motion listed
in detail). He did insist on the "supremacy of Parliament" and the
king's right to station forces in the colonies.

When Chatham concluded, Lord Dartmouth moved that the
plan be accepted for discussion. Lord Sandwich, an anti-American
activist, demanded immediate rejection. Franklin recorded:

> Lord Sandwich rose, and in a petulant vehement speech gave his
> opinion . . . that he could never believe [this motion] to be the pro-
> duction of any British peer. That it appeared to him rather the work
> of some American; and turning his face towards me, who was leaning
> on the bar [of the visitors' box] said he fancied he had in his eye the
> person who drew it up, one of the bitterest and most mischievous

enemies [England] had ever known. This drew the eyes of many lords upon me; but as I had no inducement to take it to myself, I kept my countenance as immovable as if my features had been made of wood.

Franklin summed up Chatham's reply to Sandwich:

He took notice of the illiberal insinuation that the plan was not the person's who proposed it, declared it was entirely his own. That it had been heretofore reckoned his vice not to be apt to take advice; but he made no scruple to declare that if he were first minister of this country, and had the care of settling this momentous business, he should not be ashamed of publicly calling to his assistance a person so perfectly acquainted with the whole of American affairs as the gentleman so alluded to, and so injuriously reflected on; one, he was pleased to say, whom all Europe held in high estimation for his knowledge and wisdom, and ranked with our Boyles and Newtons; who was an honor not to the English nation only, but to human nature!

Franklin modestly concluded that "I found it harder to stand this extravagant compliment than the preceding equally extravagant abuse [referring to Sandwich's intervention]; but kept as well as I could an unconcerned countenance, as not conceiving it to relate to me."

Chatham's motion was defeated by a vote of sixty-one to thirty-two. Next day in the House of Commons, Lord North moved that the colony of Massachusetts be declared in a state of rebellion against the Crown.

On February 4, Franklin received a note from Dr. Fothergill, asking that they meet that evening with Barclay. After two months, the intermediaries had finally received a reply from Lord Dartmouth to Franklin's seventeen "Hints."

The discussion that evening was relatively brief and, according to Franklin, occasionally heated. Twelve of Franklin's points had either been agreed to or accepted in principle. But Franklin's demands for revocation of internal legislation, withdrawal of British troops, and most of the Coercive Acts and the Navigation Act were dismissed as "inadmissible." The Boston Port Bill would be rescinded only after payment for the tea destroyed in Boston Harbor, and there would be only limited changes on restraints of trade. Basically, the English revision of the Massachusetts charter would remain in effect.

Franklin declared flatly that "while Parliament . . . [can alter] our constitutions at pleasure there can be no agreement." Barclay injudiciously talked about how an agreement could restore to Franklin his "old place," presumably as deputy postmaster general for the colonies. Franklin was incensed at another so thinly veiled bribe and said to Barclay, "I need not tell you, who know me so well, how improper and disgusting this language is to me. I sincerely wish to be serviceable, and I need no other inducement than to be shown how I might be so."

At the end of the meeting, Fothergill said he would report all this to Lord Dartmouth the next day.

On February 16, the three met again to discuss a proposal by Barclay that the Continental Congress promise to pay for the Boston tea, which would mark "a commencement of conciliation measures." Franklin was impatient and dismissive of what he called "a method too dilatory" to deal with the problem. Payment for the tea was a matter for Massachusetts alone, not the Congress, not all of the colonies. Then he made the audacious promise that he would pay for the tea himself in order to get the settlement process moving. This, he later acknowledged, would have cost him a large part of his fortune—but he had made the offer, and he meant it.

Lord Howe now reentered the picture, sending word to Franklin via his sister that he would like to meet on February 19. They did, and Franklin found Howe "very cheerful, having, I imagine, heard from Lord Hyde that I had consented to engagement for payment of the tea." Howe brought up again the idea of sending a commissioner to America "for settling differences" and said that the government was considering him for the mission. Then, after much flowery discussion, he asked Franklin if he would "[go] with him in some shape or other, as a friend, an assistant or secretary." Franklin thanked Howe for the flattery but said that first he "wished to know what propositions were intended for America."

Howe resorted again to "spitting in the soup," offering Franklin a "proper consideration" for his services and a promise of "subsequent rewards." Howe even hinted that the government might arrange immediate payment of his salary as agent for New England. This time, Franklin's reply to yet another bribe was lofty. He told Lord Howe:

I shall deem it a great honor to be joined with your lordship in so good a work, but if you hope service from any influence I may be supposed to have, drop all thoughts of procuring me any previous favors from ministers. My accepting them would destroy the very influence you propose to make use of; they would be considered as so many bribes to betray the interest of my country. Let me see the *propositions,* and if I approve them I will not hesitate a moment to support your lordship.

By now, Franklin's secret talks had been going on for more than two and a half months, and were quite clearly running out of steam.

The House of Commons had declared Massachusetts to be in a state of rebellion and had passed the bill to halt trade and fishing. Then North, on February 20, introduced his "conciliation motion," taking the Commons by complete surprise. The motion, which would "offer grounds on which negotiation could take place," had been kept a tight secret, and North had, in public at least, preached and acted nothing but firmness. Now he seemed to be shifting course.

The conciliation motion infuriated his hard-line Tory supporters. North, faced with an uproar, waffled. He wasn't giving up Parliament's right to tax, he explained, only suspending that right in certain cases. He would not negotiate or compromise Britain's authority over the colonies; he would continue to enforce policies already approved. He was not abandoning British sovereignty, but he did not think all Americans were rebels. North's supporters were confused. His opposition, led by Charles James Fox, jeered. The bill was an utterly meaningless gesture, they said—and indeed, it was. But in the end, his meaningless motion was approved, 274 to 88. This was the best England would offer on the eve of war.

But two weeks later, the news reached England that each of the colonies had approved the acts proposed by the Continental Congress and would embargo totally the import and sale of English goods. On March 9, the Commons voted to extend the Restraining Act against American trade to New Jersey, Pennsylvania, Maryland, Virginia, and South Carolina. New York was still exempt, but would not be for long.

*   *   *

Late in February, Franklin received word that his wife, Deborah, had died of a stroke on December 19. The vagaries of winter weather in the North Atlantic had delayed the news, and in any case their correspondence had been intermittent at best. In September 1774, having not heard from her for six months, he wrote expressing concern for her health. Now word came that she had died peacefully just five days before his letter reached Philadelphia. Franklin's daughter, Sally, and her husband, Richard Bache, were with her. William rushed down from New Jersey, arriving only half an hour before her remains were taken to Christ Church for burial.

When Franklin next saw Lord Howe, he told him that his wife's death made it necessary for him "to return to Philadelphia as soon as conveniently might be." Under pressure from Howe, Franklin reluctantly agreed to have a face-to-face talk with Lord Hyde before leaving, and a meeting was arranged for March 1.

The meeting proved fruitless—and exasperating for Franklin, whose mind was clearly fixed on getting home. Hyde irritated Franklin by yet again offering a bribe if Franklin were

> to offer more acceptable constituents. . . . It was thought that if I would cooperate with them, the business would be easy. I was in high esteem among the Americans; if I would bring about a reconciliation on terms suitable to the dignity of the government, I might be as highly and generally esteemed here, and honored and *rewarded,* perhaps *beyond my expectations.* I replied that I thought I had given convincing proof of my sincere desire of promotion of peace when . . . I offered to engage for payment of the tea. . . . I was willing to do everything that was expected of me. But if any supposed I could prevail with my countrymen to take black for white and wrong for right, it was not knowing either them or me. They were not capable of being imposed on, nor was I capable of attempting it.

But disgusted as he was by the futility of his efforts and by the repeated hints at bribery, Franklin maintained civilities to the end. Only in a letter to Joseph Galloway, written shortly before his departure, did he show how fed up he was with the English:

> When I consider the extreme corruption prevalent among all orders of men in this old rotten state, and the glorious public virtue so pre-

dominant in our rising country, I cannot but apprehend more mischief than benefit from a closer union. I fear they will drag us after them in all plundering wars which their desperate circumstances, injustices and rapacity may prompt them to undertake; and their wide-wasting prodigality and profusion is a gulf that will swallow up every aid we may distress ourselves to afford them.

Here numberless and needless places, enormous salaries, pensions, perquisites, bribes, groundless quarrels, foolish expeditions, false accounts or no accounts, contracts and jobs, devour all revenue, and produce continual necessity in the midst of plenty. I apprehend, therefore, that to unite us intimately will only be to corrupt and poison us also. . . .

However, I would try anything and bear anything that can be borne with safety to our just liberties, rather than engage in a war with such relations, unless compelled to it by dire necessity in our own defense.

Franklin made good-bye calls on Fothergill and Barclay. He also had a brief, final meeting with Lord Howe, who was still trying to create a role for himself as peace commissioner in America.

A procession of friends began streaming continually through Craven Street to say good-bye. Edmund Burke came for a visit that lasted several hours. Joseph Priestley's visit lasted a whole day. Priestley recorded that "tears filled my eyes and ran down my cheeks" as they talked. On March 21, Franklin left by carriage to take a Philadelphia packet from Plymouth.

The very next day, Edmund Burke spoke to the House of Commons:

The temper and character which prevail in our colonies, are, I am afraid, unalterable by any human art. We cannot, I fear, falsify the pedigree of this fierce people, and persuade them that they are not sprung from a nation in whose veins the blood of freedom circulates. The language in which they would hear you tell them this tale would detect the imposition; your speech would betray you. An Englishman is the unfittest person on earth to argue another Englishman into slavery.

Remove the Americans' causes for complaint, Burke cried, for "unless you consent to remove the cause of difference it is impossible with decency to assert that the dispute is not upon what it is avowed to be." Then he added lines that ring in history: "Magnanimity in politics is not seldom the truest wisdom; and a great Empire and little minds go ill together."

Franklin's voyage home was a long one. He used the early part of the trip to write a lengthy journal of his last try for peace. After that, he recorded daily observations of the ocean waters, taking the water temperature two or even four times a day. Thus he was able to establish the easterly flow of the Gulf Stream's warm waters. He also noted the changing color of the water and even the weeds. Once home, he wrote to his friend Priestley that he had made "a valuable discovery which I shall communicate to you when I get a little time."

He arrived home on May 5 and was greeted with the news that Gage's troops had marched on Lexington and Concord on April 19. The day after his arrival, the Pennsylvania Assembly elected him as one of its delegates to the Second Continental Congress, which would convene in four days' time. He had come home none too soon.

Two months later, he wrote a caustic letter to William Strahan in London:

> Mr. Strahan,
>   You are a member of Parliament and one of that Majority which has doomed my Country to Destruction. You have begun to burn our Towns and murder our People. Look upon your Hands! They are stained with the Blood of your Relations! You and I were long Friends. You are now my Enemy and I am
>
> > Yours,
> >
> > B. Franklin.

But Franklin reconsidered his outburst against an old friend. The letter remained among his papers and was never sent.

Chapter 14

ENGLAND AT WAR

At the end of May 1775, Parliament had just begun its long summer recess, content that the American problem was being dealt with firmly. When news of Lexington and Concord reached London, it was greeted with surprise and disbelief. Surely the report was exaggerated? But no. Nevertheless, it took a while for the realization to sink in that war with America had begun.

In the May issue of the monthly *Gentleman's Magazine*, the most widely read of the London publications, a report dated May 28 read:

Captain Derby from New York arrived express from Southampton in the evening. By the ship in which he came were letters dated April 25, containing the particulars of an affair that happened on the 19th, between a detachment from General Gage's army and the provincial militia of Massachusetts Bay, in which about forty of the latter were said to have been killed and 29 wounded, although the loss of [Gage's troops] by American account exceeds 200. The following is the substance of the account as handed about, but of which the government disclaims all knowledge.

"General Gage, having heard that the insurgents were drawing up some cannon a few miles from Boston, he dispatched an officer with some troops to demand that the cannon be delivered up, which the insurgents refused to comply with. A second message was sent when the officer informed them that he must obey his orders, which were in case of refusal to surrender them he must fire upon those that surrounded them, but that he hoped they would prevent by immediately relinquishing them. This they absolutely refused to do, on which the troops opened fire on them which killed about sixty. On this the country arose and assisted the insurgents to load the cannon, and they directly fired upon General Gage's troops which did great execution, near 100 being killed and sixty wounded. The noise of the cannon alarmed General Gage, who immediately sent Lord Percy with a large party of troops to inquire into the matter. When his lordship came to the place, he heard the officer's account of that dispute and then returned back with the troops to General Gage's entrenchments, as he did not find any authority to proceed further.''*

The government "disclaimed all knowledge" because it had not heard directly from Gage. The patriot leaders in Massachusetts were determined to be first in getting their story of Lexington and Concord to London. They engaged a light, fast schooner owned by Richard Derby of Salem and commanded by Derby's son John. Dr. Joseph Warren prepared a set of depositions from witnesses to the action and an estimate of casualties and sent it in a package along with a published account from the *Salem Gazette*. Captain Derby's little schooner, *Quero,* slipped out of Salem on the night of April 28 and made Southampton in four weeks. General Gage's account went via a heavy cargo vessel and did not reach the government until two weeks later.

In London, Derby was questioned by government officials. The press report was sent at once to the king, who was spending the weekend at his country palace at Kew. The king set the tone of "official reaction" in his message to Lord Dartmouth, written on the evening of May 29:

By the newspaper you have transmitted, which undoubtedly was drawn up with the intention of painting a skirmish at Concord in as

---

*The account is substantially correct. Final casualties from the "shots heard round the world" for the English were 73 killed, 174 wounded, and 26 missing; for the Americans, 49 dead, 41 wounded, and 5 missing.

favorable a light as possible for the insurgents, I am far from thinking the General has reason to be displeased. The object of sending the detachment was to spike cannon and destroy military stores; this has been effected, but with the loss of an equal number of men on both sides. The die is cast. I therefore hope you will not see this in a stronger light than it deserves.

Dartmouth was agitated, as he showed in a hasty and rather pointless dispatch that he dashed off to Gage on June 1:

An account has been printed here, accompanied with depositions to verify it, of Skirmishes between a Detachment of your Command and different bodies of the provincial Militia. . . . It has been published by a Captain Derby who arrived Friday or Saturday at Southampton, and from every circumstance it is evident that he was employed by the Provincial Congress to bring this account which is plainly made up for the purpose of conveying everypossible Prejudice and Misrepresentation of the Truth. . . . It has had no other effect here than to raise that just Indignation which every honest Man must feel at the rebellious Conduct of the New England Colonies. . . . At the same time it is very much to be lamented that we have not some Account from you of this Transaction, for we know from Derby that a Vessel with Dispatches from you sailed four days before his. We expect the arrival of that Vessel with great Impatience, but till she arrives I can form no decisive Judgment of what has happened.

No matter who fired the first shot at Lexington (and this has never been clear), the Americans certainly succeeded in getting off the first volley of news in London—much to the irritation of the government.

General Gage's dispatch, dated April 22 and addressed to Viscount Barrington, secretary at war, finally arrived on the cargo ship *Sukey* on June 10. It is a curious document, laconic, seeking to minimize the whole affair. It doesn't even mention casualty figures, which followed later in a separate dispatch. Considering that a war had begun, it opened with one of what must surely be the most dismissive downplays of history: "I have now nothing to trouble your lordship with, but of an affair that happened here on the 19th instant."

With few details, Gage reported the march to Concord and back. He had special praise for Lord Percy, who had virtually rescued the

English raiding party that had been sent to destroy the secret American store of cannon and gunpowder: "Notwithstanding a continual skirmish for the space of fifteen miles, receiving fire from every hill, fence, house, barn &c., his lordship kept the enemy off and brought the troops to Charles Town, from whence they were ferried over to Boston."

It took a while for the king and his government to comprehend the enormity of the news. . . .

In Philadelphia on May 10, the Second Continental Congress gathered in the State House, which was more spacious than the cramped quarters of Carpenters' Hall, where the delegates had first met eight months before.

One of the first orders of business was a report from Dr. Joseph Warren, who wrote in his capacity as president of the Massachusetts Provincial Congress. He pleaded for "direction and assistance" from the Continental Congress and, above all, for the creation of a powerful colonial army to confront the English and defend liberty.

Next, the New York delegation asked Congress what its response should be to the arrival of large numbers of reinforcements of English troops, expected any day in New York Harbor.

On May 17, news arrived that Ethan Allen and his Green Mountain Boys of Vermont, along with Benedict Arnold of Connecticut, had marched into New York territory and seized the strategic forts at Ticonderoga, which straddles the narrow neck of land between Lake Champlain and Lake George, and Crown Point, several miles north, on the western edge of Champlain. The attack had been launched partly to revenge American deaths at Lexington and Concord.

The news was not entirely welcome in Philadelphia. The mood was still cautious; there was apprehension over how the English would react to American aggression. While the New Englanders demanded action, the rest of the colonies were cautious. Nevertheless, Congress was generally determined to act together. As John Adams put it, "Swiftest horses must be slackened and the slowest quickened, that all may keep an even pace."

So Congress mixed caution with action. It advised New York to respond peaceably to any arrival of English reinforcements, but if the troops invaded private property or attempted to cut communications between New York and the other colonies, then New York would be justified "to repel force with force."

Congress tempered its enthusiasm for the capture of Ticonderoga with a resolution (which was passed and subsequently ignored) directing that the cannons and stores seized by Ethan Allen and Benedict Arnold should be inventoried and held "in order that they may be safely returned when the restoration of the former harmony between Great Britain and these colonies, so ardently wished for by the latter, shall render it prudent and consistent with the overruling law of self-preservation."

The Congress formed a committee to make recommendations on the military situation and on ways and means of procuring supplies. On June 3, it voted to borrow six thousand pounds for the purchase of gunpowder. On June 14, it voted to raise a Continental Army. Recruits from Pennsylvania, Maryland, and Virginia were to be paid by Congress and sent to Boston to reinforce New England.

An army would require a commander in chief. The mantle fell almost automatically on the massive shoulders of George Washington. There were other contenders, distinguished mainly by their own ambitions, but Washington's military experience and prestige were paramount. Moreover, it was essential for the unity of the American effort that the command should go to a Virginian rather than a New Englander. Virginia was the largest and wealthiest of the colonies; the other colonies looked to Virginia, not to New England, for leadership. Washington could unify where other candidates could not.*

The Second Continental Congress thereupon voted on June 15 to place Washington in command "of all the Continental forces, raised or to be raised, for the defense of American liberty." And they voted a currency issue of two million pounds to finance the new army. Before Washington set off for New England, the Congress

---

*Washington had been a staunch Loyalist and believer in America's place in the British Empire. Like Franklin, he gradually lost faith. He had also served with the British Army. Had the English been shrewd enough to have given him a royal commission and made him a full-fledged officer in His Majesty's forces during the Seven Years' War, American history might have taken quite a different turn.

approved a list of names, ranks, and commissions for colonial officers who would serve as subordinates to the new commander in
chief.

Having taken these actions, Congress heeded the urging of its
moderates and adopted a final appeal for conciliation. John Dickinson, he of *Letters from a Farmer,* took the lead in proposing and
drafting what became known as the Olive Branch Petition, addressed directly once again to King George. The resolution expressed a desire for restoration of harmony with England and
beseeched the king to prevent further hostile action until a reconciliation could be worked out. But the king was not reading any
communications from the Continental Congress.

While the Congress was completing its work and preparing to
recess, George Washington set out on horseback for Massachusetts.
He arrived at Cambridge and assumed command of the Continental
Army on July 2—two weeks after the battle at Bunker Hill.

Three British major generals arrived in Boston on May 25 to reinforce the unhappy General Gage. William Howe, John Burgoyne,
and Henry Clinton were competent, experienced professional soldiers. Each would, in turn, use his own particular tactics to try to win
the war in America. Each would return home without winning any
laurels and retire to oblivion. They would be defeated by geography,
logistics, bad strategy, poor judgment—and the politics back home.
Most of all, the nature of America, and the cause that Americans
were fighting for, would defeat them.

None of them ever felt that he had the manpower or reinforcements he needed (few commanders ever do). They all won tactical
victories, but then, being at the end of long supply lines, they
hesitated. Replacements of men and supplies had to come from
three thousand miles away. Since scrounging food from the hostile
countryside was a very uncertain business, even basic food rations
had to be shipped from England. America was a vast country,
and they were never able to convert their victories into strategic
success.

When they arrived in Boston, each general brought with him a
payment voucher for five hundred pounds for uniforms. This represented a great deal of money out of Gage's war chest. He was partic-

ularly irked because in all his twenty years in America, he had never been given a special allowance for uniforms.

Of the three new arrivals, William Howe was the senior in service. He was forty-six, and came from a distinguished family of several generations' military and political service to England. As a lieutenant colonel under Major General James Wolfe, he had commanded a battalion of light infantry at the Battle of Quebec in September 1759. He was solid and careful rather than forceful and driving.

John Burgoyne, fifty-three, was very different from Howe. He was a socializer with a man-about-London lifestyle, flamboyant and ambitious, a political-activist supporter of the government. He was a better politician than military commander.

Henry Clinton, although only thirty-seven, considered himself the military and intellectual superior of the other two—and he was probably right. His father, Admiral George Clinton, had been royal governor of New York from 1741 to 1751, so Henry had spent part of his boyhood in America. He returned to England to be commissioned in the Coldstream Guards, saw active service in Germany during the Seven Years' War, then went home and obtained a seat in the House of Commons. The early death of his beloved wife deepened in him the personality of a loner. Of his voyage to America, he wrote that "at first I kept my distance, and seldom spoke until my two colleagues forced me out." Though Clinton became commander in chief in America after the battle at Saratoga, he was never able to translate his abilities as a soldier into effective leadership. He was better at giving advice than making decisions.

It was not a very chummy voyage for the three generals.

When they arrived, they plunged immediately into preparing for battle. Across the Charles River from Boston, the Americans were busy fortifying two modest little heights, Breed's Hill and Bunker Hill. Possession of these heights would enable the rebels to outflank the English forces in the city and threaten the Royal Navy in Boston Harbor. The four generals agreed that they would have to attack. Clinton, who had gone out to reconnoiter for himself, proposed that Gage bring in the Royal Navy to cover a British landing farther up the Charles, behind the American positions. He urged this strategy on Gage with more enthusiasm than tact. Gage, however, supported by Howe and Burgoyne, determined on a frontal assault and gave Howe the operational command.

So, on June 17, General Howe marched 2,200 British regulars into battle. The British were stoic in attack on well-fortified American positions until the American marksmen, running out of ammunition, broke off. By this time, Howe had lost about 40 percent of his troops: 232 were killed, including a high proportion of professional officers; 950 were wounded; many were missing. (The Americans had 140 killed and 441 wounded.) When news of this "victory" reached London at the end of July, William Eden, undersecretary of the Northern Department, remarked that "if we have eight more victories such as this there will be nobody left to bring news of them."

Any complacency that might have existed for the English prior to Bunker Hill now evaporated, as official dispatches and personal letters showed. Gage himself wrote with particular anguish in a personal letter attached to his formal report to Lord Dartmouth:

> The trials we have had show that the rebels are not the despicable rabble too many have supposed them to be, and I find it owing to a military spirit encouraged amongst them for a few years past, joined with an uncommon degree of zeal and enthusiasm, that they are otherwise. Wherever they find cover they make a good stand, and the country, naturally strong, affords it them and they are taught to assist its natural strength by art. . . . Your lordship will perceive that the conquest of this country is not easy and can be effected only with time and perseverance and strong armies attacking it in various quarters and dividing their forces. . . . In all their wars against the French, they never showed so much conduct, attention and perseverance as they do now.

Gage agonized to Lord Barrington on June 26:

> These people are now spirited up by a rage and enthusiasm as great as ever people were possessed of, and you must proceed in earnest or give the business up. A small body acting in one spot will not avail, you must have a large army's making diversions on different sides to divide their forces. The loss we have sustained is greater than we can bear, small army's can't afford such losses, especially when the advantage gained tends to little more than the gaining of a post. . . . I wish this cursed place was burned, the only use is its harbor, which may be

said to be material; but in all other respects it is the worst place either to act offensively or defensively.

Charles Stuart, the earl of Bute's son, served as a young officer in the battle. He wrote to his father:

The attack was made in the strongest place, the enemy, taking advantage of an imprudence, fought the ground inch by inch in a spot well calculated for defense by nature and assisted by all the artifice of a shrewd, artful and cunning people. The rebels fought with a resolution that dependence on their breastworks and palings almost heightened to a frenzy.

Burgoyne wrote, in a letter that eventually reached King George himself, that "the defense at Bunker Hill was well conceived and obstinately maintained; the retreat was no flight; it was even covered with bravery and military skill, and proceeded no further than to the west hill, where a new post was taken and new entrenchments instantly begun."

In a private letter to Lord Palmerston, a friend, Burgoyne wrote more expansively on the implications of the battle:

Our prospects are gloomy. Enthusiasm and a combination of artifice on one side, perhaps mismanagement on the other, and accident on both have produced a crisis that my little reading of history cannot parallel. The British Empire in America is overturned, without great exertions [response] on your side of the water. If the confederacy [unity] on this continent is general, as I am inclined now to believe, and you determine to subdue it by arms, you must have recourse to Russia or Germany; such a pittance of troops as Great Britain and Ireland can supply will only serve to prolong the war, to create fruitless expense and insure disappointment. . . . Our victory has been bought by an uncommon loss of officers, some of them irreparable, and I fear the consequences will not answer the expectations that will be raised in England.

After Bunker Hill, the four generals agreed on one strategic objective: They had to get the British Army out of Boston and conduct war from New York. Burgoyne wanted to seize Rhode Island. Clinton proposed marching on both Rhode Island and New York. Howe and Gage thought they should head for Halifax for the winter, there to prepare for a major offensive the following spring.

Normally, the summer and fall months were prime time for eigh-teenth-century warfare, but Gage and his generals were genuinely staggered by their losses at Bunker Hill. They had no disposition to throw themselves once again on the fortifications around Boston that General Washington was now supervising, and they knew that more forces would be joining them in the spring. Thus all further fighting ceased for the remainder of 1775.

Gage wrote to Lord Barrington on August 19:

I thought I saw the storm gathering many months ago, and it has happened pretty much as I guessed, when I took the liberty to tell your lordship that no expense should be spared to quash the rebellion in its infancy. And if you thought ten thousand men sufficient that you would vote twenty, and that blood and treasure would be saved in the end. The die is cast, and tho' the rebels have been better pre-pared than any body would believe, affairs are not desperate if [En-gland] will exert her force. You have too many amongst you of the same stamp as the American rebels who wish to overturn the consti-tution; the Americans have duped many others and made them their tools. . . . You have gone too far to retreat, therefore proceed with all the force you can collect, whether national or foreign force, and I think you will not fail to bring these rebellious provinces to your terms.

Then, in the last letter to Barrington before departing for En-gland, Gage wrote on September 28:

The want of men, at such a crisis as the present, is indeed to be la-mented, for you must have formidable corps in this country if you expect success. . . . It gives me pleasure to join in opinion with your lordship concerning the disposition of the forces; for New York is certainly a place where a very large corps of troops ought to be posted. People would not believe that the Americans would resist in earnest, tho' there was strong indication that they would rise in arms, and they then did actually rise. . . . If what I then wrote to your lordship had been attended to, affairs would now be in a far better situation.

Gage left for England in mid-October, ostensibly for consulta-tions. He turned over his command to General Howe and never returned.

*   *   *

Washington, meanwhile, was concerned during that summer of
'75 with creating an army that would take orders, march together,
maneuver and fight together. Bunker Hill had been successful because of the way Howe had attacked, but Washington's citizen army
was a long way from being anything more than raw marksmen-farm-
ers. Washington was content to see the summer slip away without
further fighting. In addition to training his recruits, he was busy
doing the impossible, dragging across New York and Massachusetts
the heavy cannons and stores captured by Ethan Allen and Benedict
Arnold at Ticonderoga so that he might reinforce his positions
around Boston.

In London, Lord North and Lord Dartmouth, shaken by the
news from America and at a loss as to what to do, waited in hopes
that the Second Continental Congress might produce some action,
some move to which they could respond. They did not yet want to
issue a general proclamation of rebellion, the equivalent of declaring
a state of war in all the colonies besides Massachusetts. Bad news
from the colonies continued unabated. In its July 1775 issue, *Gentleman's Magazine* ran seven full pages of news from America. The
issue contained fifty-two pages; the page size was a little smaller than
that of present-day newsmagazines, but the hand-set type was
smaller, and the columns were uninterrupted by any art. One of the
reports read:

> This unhappy affair has had amazing effect on every part of America.
> The city of New York which was looked upon as the most moderate
> is now become the most violent. The inhabitants have resorted to
> arms and surrounded the King's troops that were there for the pro-
> tection of the well-affected, in such a manner that they expected to be
> cut to pieces unless they delivered up their arms. The provincials
> seized their cannon and removed them to strong pits about eighteen
> miles off where a camp was then forming with tents and all military
> requirements.
>   It is moreover reported that Governor Tryon, who arrived from
> England during the violence and commotion, had been peremptorily

forbidden to come ashore as no royal government any longer subsisted in the country, the garrisons and fortifications of the town, the
arms and the ammunition belonging to the King's troops, the arsenal
with all the stores being now in the possession of the leaders of the
opposition. In the harbor there were two ships with stores for General Gage which they seized and unloaded.

In Virginia at a meeting of the delegates of the colony, it has been
unanimously resolved that a well-regulated militia composed of gentlemen and yeomen is the natural strength and only security of a free
government, that the establishment of such a militia is at this time
particularly necessary, and that a plan for arming, embodying and
disciplining such a number of men as may be sufficient for that purpose should be immediately carried into execution.

The English public was kept generally well apprised of what was
taking place in America. With the outbreak of fighting, the tone of
the letters columns, previously sympathetic, hardened against the
Americans. It was many months before opposition to the American
war began to appear.

In mid-August, the Olive Branch Petition was brought to London by Richard Penn, scion of the Penn family and a moderate Loyalist. Acting as envoy from the Continental Congress, he delivered
the petition to Lord Dartmouth's office on August 21, . . . but
Dartmouth had gone to his country home for a rest.

In Dartmouth's absence, the hawks in the government decided to
ignore the petition on the grounds that the Crown did not recognize the Continental Congress. Instead, the ministers issued the
general Proclamation of Rebellion, which put England and all the
colonies into an official state of war, on August 23, 1775. The war
would end formally almost exactly eight years later, on September 3,
1783.

Manpower, ships, and supplies—these were the sinews of war. In
the summer of 1775, England was short on all three. There was even
a shortage of seasoned lumber for shipbuilding, which had to be
stockpiled in the open air for at least six months before it could be
used. Further, the New England forests, previously a major supplier
of the tall, straight pines used for masts, were cut off after the Battle
of Bunker Hill.

The earl of Sandwich, vigorous if unpopular first lord of the Admiralty, was determined to see the American rebellion crushed—but he also had to be concerned about security at home and England's natural and ever restive enemy, France. Lord Barrington looked across the Channel with equal apprehension. He was against draining away manpower to fight three thousand miles away because he did not believe that America could be subdued by a large army. Barrington was, after a long time, proved right, but in the meantime he had no say in strategy or deployment. In the early stages of the war, Barrington had written to Gage, "I have never changed my original opinion, communicated to you some months ago, that the true way to reduce America is by sea only; but I wish I may be mistaken."

Sandwich joined Barrington in urging a sea-power strategy, but he did so primarily to argue for more money, men, and ships for the Royal Navy. Barrington wrote to General Gage on July 24:

> I understand the whole Cabinet is of the opinion to augment the land forces under your command to the utmost extent, and in this I think they are right, since the measure of land operations has been adopted. . . . The difficulty of raising and supporting a sufficient land force in America has always been foreseen and represented by me, and it has been one of the principal grounds of my unalterable opinion, that America should be subdued by sea and not by land. Notwithstanding all I have said, you may depend on the utmost support of troops which this country can give you.

Thus Barrington and Sandwich at the outset lost the argument about using sea power; a land campaign was decided on as the strategy to pursue.

Manpower was a problem for England that continued to the very end. In 1775, the British Army totaled approximately twenty-nine thousand troops; the Irish infantry provided another ten thousand. These troops were scattered, posted at Gibraltar, the Mediterranean, the Caribbean, Africa, and Canada, as well as in America. This left a very small pool of manpower of about eleven thousand infantry at home and only seven thousand in Ireland. Further, because they could find few men who would volunteer to fight the Americans, many of the regiments were behind in their recruiting targets. When the North government decided to increase the troops in America to twenty thousand by the spring of 1776, it was impossible to do this either through recruiting or by using the small home force. Inevitably, the government decided to hire mercenaries.

King George could still give orders in his German principality of Hanover. This he had done. On August 1, he wrote to Lord North:

> I received an answer to the orders I had wrote to Hanover, and have already given every necessary order that five battalions will be ready to embark at Stade early in September, provided money is sent from hence to put them in motion. The officers are poor, and are not able to prepare their equipage; many articles are wanting for the men to be able to go to this distant service. I suppose an advance of £10,000 will effect it. Though brave on shore, Continental forces fear the sea, and we must preach the little difficulties that will arise in their voyage.

The earl of Suffolk, who as secretary of state for the Northern Department, directed foreign policy with the courts of Europe, sent off an instruction from the king to the English ambassador to St. Petersburg. The king wished to open negotiations with the Empress Catherine the Great to obtain twenty thousand Russian soldiers to serve as mercenaries on English pay and help put down the rebellion in America. The Russians, Suffolk told political friends, "would be charming visitors at New York, and civilize that part of America wonderfully."

Catherine felt otherwise. She had other things for her soldiers to do. Eventually, King George received a reply from St. Petersburg. It left him spluttering with indignation, as he recorded in a memorandum to Lord North on November 3, 1775:

> The letter of the Empress is a clear refusal, and not in so genteel a manner as I should have thought might have been expected from Her; She has not had the Civility to answer in her own hand, and has thrown out some expressions that may be civil in a Russian Ear, but certainly not to more civilized ones.

During January and February 1776, the government completed a series of treaties with the German principalities for eighteen thousand additional troops commanded by tough, seasoned officers and trained in the school of Frederick the Great of Prussia and Ferdinand of Brunswick. However, the Germans did little for the English cause. They won no battles and roused bitter animosity among the colonials. So, when an English soldier was killed or wounded in America, there was no replacement for him until fresh units arrived from England.

Throughout the entire war, British commanders had to husband their food supplies almost as carefully as they had to husband their ammunition. A third of a ton of food per man per year was required to victual the army. Since they could not count on eating off the countryside, the men were dependent on the shipments of such staples as salt beef and pork, bread, flour, oatmeal, rice, butter, and salt that came across the Atlantic. Occasionally cheese, bacon, fish and molasses also got through.

Transporting horses (and their feed) across the Atlantic was a major problem.* In 1776, a Treasury report noted that out of 950 horses shipped across the Atlantic, 400 never reached New York. For a while, the British also shipped cattle to provide fresh meat for the army but had to give that up because of the demand for shipping space.

Eventually, a large purchasing and supply depot was established at the Irish port of Cork. Blessed with a good harbor and a plentiful agricultural hinterland, Cork was as much as a week closer to America in sailing time. Nevertheless, delays in supplies were constant and unpredictable. Often North Atlantic storms would blow ships so far off course that they would wind up limping into the West Indies for repairs.

Wastage was immense—from poor quality, poor packing and loading, theft, spoilage in hot weather, and damaged barrels and casks. Graft and rake-offs on supply contracts were the normal order of business.

In addition to all the other problems, there were the camp followers. It was at that time a standing regulation of the British Army that each battalion ordered overseas for extended service was permitted to take along forty women.† The officers could make additional arrangements on their own for female company.

---

*And the British certainly couldn't count on getting horses in America. Gage wrote, in a letter to Barrington dated May 13, "Captain Delancy went to New York to purchase horses, but the revolution has prevented all designs of that nature."
†For example, Burgoyne's Queen's Light Dragoons sailed with 490 officers and men plus 42 women, 54 servants, and twenty-six tons of officers' baggage.

The German mercenaries brought along large contingents of women—and larger baggage trains—all of which added greatly to the shipping problem. It was up to the English to provide ships to transport these troops, their women, and their equipment from Bremerhaven, Hamburg, Lübeck, and various other ports in Holland and along the North Sea.

These problems were so staggering that Admiral Sir Hugh Palliser, a senior officer in the Admiralty, recorded in December 1775 that

> The demands for the small army now in America are so great as to be thought impossible to furnish. The waggons and draft cattle [then being shipped for beef] is prodigious. If this is the case, what will it be when we have another army there above 20,000 men, if they can't make good their quarters and command carriages and cattle, and subsist and defend themselves without the aid of the fleet, and whilst so employed can perform no other service? I think some people begin to be astonished at the unexpected difficulties we are in.

Lord Barrington was not alone in foreseeing "the difficulty of raising and supporting a sufficient land force in America." The adjutant general of the army, General Edward Harvey, said openly that "taking America as it at present stands, it is impossible to conquest it with our British Army. . . . To attempt to conquer it by our land force is as wild an idea as ever controverted common sense."

General Amherst also had grave doubts and, like Barrington, would have preferred a naval strategy. But once the government had decided to fight it out on land, Amherst did not oppose the decision. Barrington, on the other hand, offered his resignation (although it was two years before the king would let him go).

Uncertain as it was, the supply system was nevertheless sufficient to fight the war, and it was not the shortages that decided the war. But there was, from the outset, a "caution of conscience" with which the British Army fought, and to this caution the supply problem, manpower shortage, and the difficulties of American geography all contributed. Of this underlying factor, British historian Piers Mackesy wrote in *The War for America:*

> Force was adopted with reluctance, and throughout the struggle the attempt to seek a solution by political means was never abandoned,

though at times it was temporarily shelved while the army attempted to crack the shell of American obstinacy. Thus a war of unlimited destruction was ruled out. There were limits to what conscience and policy would allow. . . . The systematic burning of towns was an expedient sometimes considered but never accepted. . . . The British Army's attitude to the struggle was ambivalent. They were professionals doing a duty, but they could not easily forget they were fighting against some of their own race. "Here pity interposes," wrote General William Phillips, "and we cannot forget that when we strike we wound a brother." Even the King, whose heart was hardened against the rebels, never forgot they were his subjects. Thus his reaction to Howe's successes in New York in 1776. "Notes of triumph would not have been proper when successes are against subjects and not a foreign foe." An officer wrote that Howe "was right to treat our enemies as if they might one day become our friends."

While these limits may not have been apparent at the time, and while they have not been evident in American history books, nevertheless, they should neither be dismissed nor ignored.

Lord North told the king at an early stage, "The war can hardly be well conducted unless there is a person in the Cabinet capable of leading, of discerning between opinions, of deciding quickly and confidently, and of connecting all the operations of the government that this nation might act uniformly and with force." The prime minister knew that he was not that man, nor did he pretend to be. The political finesse that made him such an amiable, good-humored, and effective leader of the House of Commons, one with whom even enemies remained friendly, was not an attribute for running a war. Further, North began to experience bouts of depression, and he would simply shut the door on his troubles. He made regular attempts at resigning, and the king just as regularly refused.

At the same time, North was reluctant to change his carefully constructed government, lest the whole political edifice come apart. Although his stepbrother, the earl of Dartmouth, was completely disheartened by the failure of his own lame attempts at conciliation and the subsequent events in America, North felt a greater than ever need to keep his closest confidant by his side. As he pondered how to reshuffle his cabinet, he got an unexpected break.

Grafton, North's predecessor, had stayed on in the government as lord privy seal. Though noted more for indolence than vigor, when Parliament reassembled after the battles at Lexington, Concord, and Bunker Hill, Grafton suddenly bestirred himself. He took the floor of the House of Lords and startled everyone with a speech criticizing the government for the outbreak of fighting and for refusing to receive the Olive Branch Petition. This unexpected (and lonely) act of rebellion produced a prompt request that Grafton surrender his seals of office and depart, thus clearing the way for North to reshuffle the cabinet and bring forward Lord George Germain.

Germain, who had been waiting impatiently for some months, was absolutely certain that he was going to be the man of the hour. He was sure of his abilities and sure that he would have the king's ear and his support. He was right.

Nevertheless, the changes were not entirely simple to make. Dartmouth would stay, but only if he became lord privy seal, a post that was also coveted by Lord Weymouth. North got around this problem with a strong assist from the king: The decrepit earl of Rochford was persuaded by an excessively generous royal pension to retire as secretary of state for the Southern Department; Weymouth was appointed in Rochford's stead. Dartmouth became lord privy seal, outside the cabinet but still very much at his stepbrother's service. Germain took over the American Department from Dartmouth and entered the cabinet on November 15. No one had the slightest doubt as to who was in charge, nor did anyone doubt Germain's determination to crush the rebellion.

Germain, then fifty-nine, was possessed of high energy, experience, and authentic ability. Like many others of the aristocracy, he had combined an active military career (rising to the rank of lieutenant general) with a seat in the House of Commons. He was a shrewd and aggressive operator with many admirers but few friends. He had a dark malevolence, unrestrained arrogance, a caustic tongue, and vindictive nature, . . . and he had a deep love of power.* He also had

---

*Piers Mackesy wrote that "this strange man is perhaps the most traduced of English statesmen." The American historian and biographer of Germain, Alan Valen-

an indelible stain on his military record that only a man of brazen self-confidence and ambition could have overcome.

The affair that ended his military career and blighted his political life took place in Germany at the Battle of Minden in 1759. This was one of those endless military actions of the Seven Years' War that might not have made the history books at all had it not been for one man's presence. Lord George Sackville (as Germain was then titled) was a lieutenant general in command of the cavalry, a rank he had earned through ability and hard service (in addition to the right family background, political admirers, and royal connections, of course). His commander in chief was Prince Ferdinand of Brunswick. At a crucial moment in the battle, Ferdinand dispatched an officer with orders for his English subordinate to launch an immediate attack on the flank of the opposing French. Sackville failed to respond promptly, and the French successfully withdrew. Sackville's failure was officially recorded in a general order issued by the prince immediately following the battle. Sackville was recalled to London, stripped of his rank, and dismissed from the army.

Sure of exoneration but risking being shot if he were wrong, Sackville insisted on a court-martial. This was finally granted in April 1760. The verdict hinged on whether he had merely lost valuable time because of confusing orders or whether he had indeed disobeyed orders. The proceedings lasted a month. In the end, he was found guilty, and since he had already been dismissed from the army, he was now declared "unfit to serve His Majesty in any military capacity whatsoever." It mattered not at all that he had demanded the court-martial himself. There is little doubt that politics played a part in the outcome: King George II and Prince Ferdinand were close compatriots. Sackville had also offended the king by being too friendly with the earl of Bute and the household of the young Prince of Wales. But it is equally probable that politics saved Sackville from the death penalty.

---

tine, wrote, "I have searched for every episode and interpretation that could be turned in his favor, but though I have found enough to temper my distaste for him I have not found enough to remove it." Germain inspired, both then as well as now, more venomous hostility than reason for praise. He himself cared little about either.

The day after the verdict, he made a casual, and startling, appearance in the House of Commons. His military career might have ended in a humiliating fashion, but he still had a seat in Parliament and a reputation as a forceful speaker of independent mind who commanded notice. He also came from one of the oldest, most aristocratic families in England.* Given his lineage and his confidence in his own abilities, he was not about to retreat into oblivion just because a military court had returned a verdict that he considered unjust.

Six months after the court-martial, King George III came to the throne and Lord Bute to power. Sackville embarrassed both by rushing too precipitously to one of the first levees at the Court of St. James's. He was wasting no time in taking to the road of political rehabilitation. Eventually, Rockingham gave him the minor but lucrative post of vice treasurer of Ireland.

When the Rockingham government fell, Sackville was turned out by the earl of Chatham, who disliked him intensely. He resumed waiting and lobbying. Along the way, he changed his name: A wealthy widowed Sackville aunt, Lady Betty Germain, died and left George, her favorite nephew, with a grand house, a country estate, and large quantities of money—on the condition that he take the Germain surname. He complied promptly.

For another ten years, he played the role of an active insider. His effectiveness appealed to Lord North, and so it came about that fifteen years after his court-martial, he took charge of His Majesty's forces, the forces in which he had been judged unfit to serve. Whether he ever said it himself, many others said it for him: He intended to revenge himself for the Battle of Minden by conquering America.

Lord North's government was clearly strengthened by the changes in the cabinet; the prime minister welcomed the assistance of a strong front-bench speaker in the House of Commons. The king was also pleased. Now it was a matter of getting on with the war.

Lord North and the king thought they had a government similar

---

*He was the third son of the first duke of Dorset. The first earl of Dorset, Thomas Sackville, was lord treasurer to Queen Elizabeth I.

to the Pitt-Newcastle arrangement that had been victorious in the Seven Years' War. But Pitt had had enormous popularity in the country and the power with which to dominate the Commons. Germain had neither. Pitt was fighting against England's long-time enemy, France. Germain was fighting England's compatriots, the Americans. Pitt was ruthless and a hard taskmaster, but he was also a statesman and strategist who inspired. Ruthless and petty, Germain inspired no one, least of all the generals he was directing. With Howe, Carleton, Burgoyne, and Clinton, he was contradictory and confusing in his orders, quarrelsome in his demands, and vindictive in his treatment of each general in turn. Whatever North's government had gained in efficiency, it was lost in duplicity. It remained, all the way to the end, in Burke's phrase, a "government of little minds."

Chapter 15

THE HOWE BROTHERS TRY WAR AND PEACE

For two crucial years in America, 1776 and 1777, the war on the English side was conducted, rather than waged, by Admiral Viscount Richard Howe and his brother, Major General Sir William Howe. When they were sent to America, they were generally considered to be the best, most experienced, most innovative commanders that the British Army and the Royal Navy had to offer.

General Howe had won a well-deserved reputation as the soldier who developed important light-infantry companies in the British Army for quick tactical movements, a vast improvement on the ponderous maneuvering and close order of the traditional heavy infantry of continental warfare. He was also an effective trainer of soldiers, administrator, and logistician.

Admiral Howe had a solid reputation in the Royal Navy as an aggressive commander with a sympathetic responsibility for the seamen under him—a quality that was not usually a distinguishing mark of English captains. At the same time, he had made his intellectual mark by revising and simplifying the navy signals system, giving greater freedom of action to captains of individual vessels.

When he arrived to take over command of the Royal Navy in American waters in July of 1776, his orders from the Admiralty called for a vigorous naval campaign to strangle America by blockade. But he also carried a separate set of instructions from His Majesty's government that named him as a peace commissioner to negotiate with the Americans, with his brother as his deputy. It soon became difficult to determine which had the brothers' priority and which conviction or objective was governing their conduct of the war.

The Howes were sincere in their sympathy for America—or at least in their idea of America. They displayed an inability—perhaps a refusal—to understand the political realities of the struggle going on around them, even after the Declaration of Independence. They undertook to wage war and seek peace at the same time, a contradictory mission that could only fail. But when they began their mission, both Howe brothers were confident that they could wave the olive branch and wield the sword in America.

The brothers came from a distinguished military family. They had a close, personal relationship with King George, and they carried appropriate political qualifications as members of the House of Commons. (Lord Howe sat in Commons because his peerage was Irish rather than English.)

Their mother was a formidable lady who was reputed to have been a mistress of King George I before her marriage (and she never seems to have denied the gossip). When she married, George I gave her a pension of £750 a year. In the reign of George II, she became a traveling companion of one of the new king's mistresses. Later she received a household appointment from George III, one of whose younger brothers had served with Lord Howe during the Seven Years' War. And George III's wife, Queen Charlotte, stood godmother to one of Howe's children. The Howes were, in short, a family well-known and favored by the Hanoverian court of England.

The Howes' particular feelings about America and the Americans came from a family tragedy. Their eldest brother, George, who had held the family title as the third Viscount Howe, was killed at the Battle of Ticonderoga in 1758, during the Seven Years' War, when General Amherst was advancing on Canada. George had made himself particularly popular in America, to the extent that on hearing of his death, the people of Massachusetts raised funds to place a monument to his memory in Westminster Abbey. The family never forgot, and always paid tribute to, the act of homage given the eldest son by the American colonists of Massachusetts.

The Howe brothers acknowledged their debt to the Americans in the House of Commons. On American questions, they leaned toward the Whigs and reconciliation. As military men who had served in the Seven Years' War, they were on good terms with William Pitt; they both opposed the Stamp Act and voted for its repeal.

Lord Howe (Richard succeeded his brother to the title) was more politically active than his brother William, who seldom if ever spoke in the Commons. In the general election of 1774, however, William Howe did speak up, telling his constituents in Nottingham that he was against the policy of coercion of the Americans. He declared that he would vote to repeal the Massachusetts Government Act, which was punishing the colony that had honored his brother, and that he would refuse military service against the Americans.

But less than a year later, William was on his way to America as the senior major general of the trio being sent to bolster, and eventually replace, General Gage. He dismissed his earlier electioneering by saying that as a soldier, he could not refuse an order from the king. He sailed for America in the summer of 1775 with the clear hope, shared by his brother, of showing that reconciliation with the colonies would be possible through leniency and negotiation.

Admiral Howe had already shown where he stood on American conciliation during the long discussions with Benjamin Franklin of January and February of 1775. Although the talks with Franklin had failed, this did not dampen Lord Howe's desire to head a peace commission to America, nor his firm belief that he could find a path of reconciliation. If he and his brother could confront the Americans with the military might of England, Howe's logic ran, then he could surely conjure, cajole, coddle, and convince the Americans to give up their aims of independence and return peacefully to the British Empire.

After William sailed for America, Lord Howe, with his rank of senior admiral and reputation for aggressive leadership, began importuning the king, Lord North, First Lord of the Admiralty Lord Sandwich, and Lord George Germain to recognize his talents and availability and send him to America.

*   *   *

In the autumn of 1775, with the military stalemate in Boston, both the Americans and the English attempted to strike into other parts of North America, seeking both political and military success. Both failed—the Americans in Canada, and the British in the Carolinas.

The American incursion into Canada was one of the most audacious ventures of the War of Independence, and it came very close to success before it unraveled. It was led by two exceptional soldiers, Major General Richard Montgomery and Colonel Benedict Arnold.

Aware that the British military governor and commander in Canada, Major General Sir Guy Carleton, had reduced his army to send reinforcements to Gage and Howe in Boston, the Americans hoped that if they gave the Canadian tree a good shaking, it would fall into the colonial camp of independence.

Montgomery, with a force of some twelve hundred men, advanced along the inland route, up the Hudson River and north on Lake Champlain to Montreal. Arnold, commanding a force of about the same size, made an extraordinary winter march through the wilderness of northern Maine to Quebec City. Montreal, lightly defended, fell to Montgomery in November. Carleton barely escaped capture, rowing away with muffled oars in the dark of night and heading for Quebec. Arnold emerged on the Plains of Abraham outside Quebec in late November. He was joined a few days later by Montgomery, who was in hot pursuit of Carleton.

It seemed as if a major victory were in their grasp. But Carleton had managed to scrape together a pick-up army with a small core of English soldiers and volunteers plus Canadian recruits. Altogether, Carleton had nearly three thousand men, double that of the American forces, now depleted by hard marching through winter forests. Nevertheless, Montgomery, as senior commander, launched a sudden assault on Quebec on December 31 during exceptionally bitter weather. The attack was repulsed on New Year's Day, and Montgomery was killed. This was a major loss for the fledgling army, for Montgomery was a capable, experienced soldier.

Arnold, hard driving and fearless in action, continued to besiege Quebec despite the miserable winter conditions. Carleton was content to wait it out in relative comfort behind the walls of Quebec. Although Washington sent reinforcements to Arnold, there were never enough men to attempt another assault.* In May of 1776, the siege came to an abrupt end when English reinforcements, headed up by Major General John Burgoyne, sailed up the St. Lawrence after winter ice broke. Arnold had to pack up and return home.

This was not quite the end of the story, however. Bolstered by Burgoyne's reinforcements, Carleton began a slow pursuit of the retreating Americans. Along the way, he restored his rule in Montreal. Arnold, on reaching Lake Champlain, threw his energies into hasty construction of a small flotilla of gunboats. These he intended to use to attack Carleton's transports when they sailed down from the north. In October, Arnold's "navy" launched a surprise attack, damaging the British transports sufficiently to halt Carleton's advance even though the American boats were completely wiped out in the process. At this point, Carleton made the unexpected decision to give up any further advance toward Fort Ticonderoga. Winter was coming, and he chose not to risk his army by fighting at the end of a long supply line.

For the Americans, Arnold's little naval action on Lake Champlain had a ripple effect on the war. Had Carleton pressed on and taken Ticonderoga in the fall of 1776, the war would probably have gone very differently in 1777. The strategic defeat of the British at the Battle of Saratoga might never have happened. Carleton did know that the Americans had rebuilt and strengthened Ticonderoga and that they had a sizable garrison waiting there under Major General Horatio Gates. But perhaps Carleton's fresh memory of the siege at Quebec stopped him. Whatever the case, his decision remains one of the imponderables of the war.

*   *   *

---

*In April 1776, an American delegation, headed by the venerable Benjamin Franklin, made the long trip to Montreal to attempt to persuade the Canadian leaders to join the colonies in shaking off English rule. The Americans thought the French Canadians in particular would be ready for revolution, but it turned out they didn't want to fight with, for, or against anybody or anything. General Carleton, it seems, was an adept and popular governor. Ironically, the Americans turned out to be as wrong in their expectations of the Canadians as the English had been in their beliefs about American Loyalists.

The English, meanwhile, attempted a quick descent on the southern colonies, hoping or expecting a welcome by American Loyalists.

In September of 1775, Governor Josiah Martin of North Carolina had literally been chased out of his capital by rebellious patriots. He took refuge on a Royal Navy warship cruising off the Carolina capes and promptly prepared a dispatch to London, in which he reported that he had received addresses signed by thousands of loyal backcountry settlers who wanted no part of the rebellion. He urged that a nucleus of English troops be sent and a supply of arms raised for a Loyalist force. If this could be done, then revolt in the Carolinas would be subdued and rebellion in Virginia quenched—or so Governor Martin believed. At the same time, other Loyalist evidence began arriving in London. Thus the Charleston expedition was born.

Lord Dartmouth, still in charge of the American Department when Martin's dispatch arrived, consulted with General Sir Jeffrey Amherst, newly elevated to commander in chief of the army. Since General Howe's main force was immobilized in Boston, a modest expedition to the Carolinas looked like an easy, economical way to restore some military momentum in the colonies. So Dartmouth issued orders to the Board of Ordnance to ship a stand of ten thousand arms to America to be turned over to the Loyalists, and he asked Howe if a battalion could be moved out of Boston and sent south.

In October, the cabinet reviewed this proposal and gave its approval to an enlarged plan. The five regiments being readied in Ireland to reinforce General Howe would be sent first to the Carolinas to seize Charleston. After that, they could join Howe in the summer. Howe sent his approval from Boston and proposed that his second in command, Major General Henry Clinton, be assigned command of the expedition.

So it was that sailing orders were issued in December for the Royal Navy to embark the Irish regiments at Cork and head across the Atlantic to rendezvous with a fleet in the American waters off Cape Fear, North Carolina. General Clinton would meet them at the end of February with additional reinforcements from Boston, and the combined armies would head for Charleston.

The orders had barely been written when the capricious weather of the British Isles took over and derailed the timetable. Heavy winds prevented the ships from sailing. It wasn't until December 29 that Commodore Sir Peter Parker could form the convoy and sail for Cork. There gale winds delayed the expedition for another five weeks. Finally, on February 12, the convoy got under way. Then western Atlantic gales scattered and delayed it even further. It reached its rendezvous point off Cape Fear at the end of April, more than two months behind schedule.

While the navy was coping with terrible weather, in Boston General Clinton was arguing with General Howe, expressing his increasing doubts about the expedition. He finally sailed in January. Clinton arrived promptly at the Carolina capes, and while he waited for the arrival of Commodore Parker, he met with the anxious governors of Virginia, North Carolina, and South Carolina to discuss the spreading revolution. These discussions only deepened his misgivings about the wisdom of the expedition. He became convinced that the Loyalists were not as strong as advertised, that they would need English protection, and that they would in the end prove more of a liability than an asset. However, when Commodore Parker at last arrived, he was all for pressing ahead and taking Charleston. An army commander could not overrule a navy commodore, so they headed for Charleston, arriving in late June.

They had neither sound intelligence nor even very good maps. Clinton decided to avoid a direct assault and put his troops ashore on Sullivans Island. He expected to be able to move to Charleston across shallow water to attack. Instead of shallows, he found seven-foot depths at high tide. He was stranded. It was too shallow for the navy to come to his aid and too deep for him to move.

The welcome they had anticipated from Loyalists failed to materialize, and gunfire from the city's fortifications was stronger than they had expected. Parker, who had been cruising around, firing ineffectively at the city, lost one of his frigates. Clinton finally called off the whole frustrating operation and left for New York at the end of July. The general was not in a very happy mood as he sailed north to rejoin General Howe.

Although Lord Dartmouth had given General Howe discretionary authority in September of 1775 to withdraw from Boston as he wished to do, Howe wound up spending a miserable winter there.

Blockaded on land by Washington's troops, who manned fortifications behind the city, Howe found the winter seas equally hostile. The Royal Navy was unable to provide sufficient ships for the evacuation of some six thousand troops and was unwilling to risk a stormy winter voyage to Halifax with heavily loaded transports. Howe finally managed to extricate himself and sail for Halifax in March, taking with him about a thousand Yankee Loyalists, who would settle in Canada.

In Halifax, Howe reorganized and waited for more reinforcements, stores, and transports. In June, he began a massive movement to New York, where he and Clinton planned a summer rendezvous.

Thus, by the middle of 1776, the British had called off their Carolinas expedition; the Americans were out of Canada but still fending off Carleton's advance toward Lake Champlain; Howe was gone from Boston; and General Washington moved the Continental Army to New York, which would clearly be the next testing ground. This is how things stood when Admiral Howe arrived in New York in July 1776 in his dual role as commander of the Royal Navy in America and peace commissioner.

In this latter role, Howe's instructions as to what he might offer the Americans were severely limited. When Lord North first proposed a peace commission in November 1774, King George had rejected it. Now the prime minister had been able to sell the idea to the king, since England was in a position of growing strength. A large buildup of forces under General Howe would soon be in place; further, North was about to introduce in Parliament a punitive measure under which a complete blockade would be imposed on the colonies. North decided that it would be both expedient and prudent to couple this measure with a peace gesture—on England's terms, of course. The king gave grudging approval to the peace commission, being somewhat mollified by the fact that North proposed to entrust this mission to Admiral Howe, whom King George looked upon with favor.

Howe had insisted that he would not go to America as peace commissioner unless he were also given command of the Royal Navy. This demand put him on a collision course with the earl of

Sandwich, first lord of the Admiralty. Sandwich, touchy and jealous of his prerogative to decide on all naval appointments that would be recommended to the king, balked. He disliked Howe for his influence and connections and his Whig views about America and peace. The dislike was mutual. Admiral Howe's bid to be given the American naval command progressed, in part because of the inadequacy of the commander who was already on site, Vice Admiral Samuel Graves. Nevertheless, the king himself had to intervene behind the scenes, providing a face-saving formula for Sandwich to make the command change.

Then Lord George Germain interposed himself on the instructions that the government would give to Howe to guide, or bind, his peace mission. Germain was against the whole idea. He had joined the government to make war, not peace. So he was determined to handcuff the peace commission with instructions that would ensure its failure. In this, he had the enthusiastic support of most of Lord North's ministers—except North himself and Lord Dartmouth.

The first draft of the instructions was drawn up by Alexander Wedderburn, enthusiastic detractor of Benjamin Franklin's two years earlier and now serving in the government as solicitor general. Howe was instructed to tell the colonies to dissolve the Continental Congress, the army, and all assemblies. They were to reinstate all royal governors, judges, and laws of England, and they were to declare acceptance of the supreme authority of Parliament. After these capitulations, the situation would be reviewed. All Howe could do with these instructions was keep them secret—which he did.

Howe, with little support from Lord North, attempted to gain some modification of these impossible demands. He threatened to resign—which only irritated the king, who had gone to great lengths to get the Royal Navy command assigned to him. Howe won on only two points, that his brother serve with him as a joint commissioner, rather than one of Germain's cronies, and that he could listen first to what the Americans might have to say before he presented the English demands.

North's bill to impose the American blockade went to the House of Commons on November 20, 1775. Although the bill included a clause appointing the peace commission to seek a settlement, the secret instructions to Howe reflected a mind-set unchanged since 1765.

Admiral Viscount Howe sailed from Portsmouth on May 11, 1776, aboard the sixty-four-gun H.M.S. *Eagle*. He intended to meet his brother in Halifax, but storms delayed his crossing. When he reached Halifax on June 23, General Howe had already departed for New York with the first contingents of his army. The admiral headed south on what should have been a voyage of only a week or ten days. But again, strong head winds from the south kept the *Eagle* pitching in heavy swells off Nantucket for three weeks. On July 12, he finally entered the Narrows, to a welcome salute fired from the guns of the fleet awaiting his command and his brother's army camped on Staten Island.

Eight days earlier in Philadelphia, the Continental Congress had proclaimed the Declaration of Independence.

In England, the Declaration of Independence was a non-event. When the news arrived in London in August, Parliament was in its long recess and the government in its vacation slumbers. Since the government had already declared the colonies to be in a "state of rebellion" the year before, no further response was possible.

In any case, the declaration was not addressed to England, nor did the signers expect any response from England. It was not even sent to London or to King George. The declaration was *proclaimed*. It was left to other governments and peoples to read, note, and respond as they might choose. The Continental Congress had ordered that copies of the declaration "be sent to the several assemblies, conventions and committees or councils of safety, and to the several commanding officers of the Continental troops; that it be proclaimed in each of the United States, and at the head of the army."

Congress had deliberately waited until after England had declared the colonies to be in a "state of rebellion." This removed them from the king's protection and suspended their rights under English law. It was the equivalent of declaring a state of war, and the Declaration of Independence was the logical and inevitable response. The vital question was how other nations would react. Clearly, if other sovereign states stepped forward to recognize the independence of a new American state, they might also find themselves at war with England.

While few ministers were in London to take official notice of it, the declaration was published promptly and in full in the August issue of *Gentleman's Magazine*. The text was buried in a fifty-two-page issue under the unadorned heading "Declaration by the American Colonies." (Ironically, on the facing page was a favorable review of the newly published first volume of Gibbon's *History of the Decline and Fall of the Roman Empire*.)

There was no political reaction and little public interest. In the next month's issue, the printer found only one letter to publish, a marked contrast to the nine and a half pages of comments published at the height of the Stamp Act crisis in 1766. The letter, signed simply Englishman, took a rather pompous exception to the American claim that "all men are created equal":

> In what way are they created equal? Is it in size, strength, understanding, figure, moral or civil accomplishment? Every ploughman knows they are not created equal in any of these. All men, it is true, are equally created, but what is this to the purpose? It is certainly not reason why the Americans should turn rebels because the people of Great Britain are fellow creatures, created as well as themselves.

The Englishman went on to say that the American assertion of an inalienable right to liberty "is not nonsense, but it is not true; there are slaves in America and where there are slaves, liberty is alienated." It is safe to assume that this Englishman found a nodding agreement among the readers of *Gentleman's Magazine*.

In the colonies, Admiral Howe's peace mission had been anticipated for some months. In Philadelphia, there was some apprehension that he might bring a generous offer that would end the dispute with sufficient appeal to call off the armed struggle. The Tory Loyalists would have welcomed this, but the patriots need not have worried.

Admiral Howe, taking no notice of the Declaration of Independence, launched his peace mission immediately on his arrival. He dispatched a letter to his friend Benjamin Franklin as soon as the *Eagle* dropped anchor, along with copies of proclamations announcing his peace mission and offering pardons to any and all who wished to declare loyalty to England. In his covering letter, he wrote:

I cannot, my worthy friend, permit the letters and parcels which I have sent to be landed without adding a word upon the subject of the injurious extremities in which our unhappy differences have engaged us.

You will learn the nature of my mission from the official dispatches forwarded by the same conveyance. Retaining all the earnestness I ever expressed to see our differences accommodated, I shall conceive, if I meet with the disposition in the colonies I was once taught to expect, the most flattering hopes of proving serviceable in the objects of the King's paternal solicitude, by promoting the establishment of lasting peace and union with the colonies. But if the deep-rooted prejudices of America must keep us still a divided people, I shall from every private as well as public motive, most heartily lament that this is not the moment wherein those great objects of my ambition are now to be attained; and that I am to be longer deprived of an opportunity to assure you personally of the regard with which I am your sincere and faithful humble servant.

Lord Howe disclosed nothing to Franklin or anyone else of the instructions that would make his mission impossible. Howe hoped for at least some direct dialogue with Franklin and the other colonial leaders. Thus he sent out his proclamations and announcements and appeals in unsealed envelopes and parcels, ensuring that someone would open and read them. He also began encouraging Loyalists to visit his flagship off Staten Island.

He was not put off by Franklin's frosty, vigorous reply from Philadelphia on July 20:

I received safe the letters your lordship so kindly forwarded to me, and beg you to accept my thanks.

The official dispatches to which you refer me contain nothing more than what we had seen in the act of parliament, viz., offers of pardon upon submission, which I am sorry to find, as it must give your lordship pain to be sent so far in so hopeless a business.

Directing pardons to be offered the colonies, who are the very parties injured, expresses indeed that opinion of our ignorance, baseness and insensibility which your uninformed and proud nation has long been pleased to entertain of us; but it can have no other effect than that of increasing our resentment. . . .

Long did I endeavor, with unfeigned and unwearied zeal, to preserve from breaking that fine and noble China vase, the British Empire; for I knew that being once broken, the separate parts could not retain even their share of the strength or value that existed in the whole, and that a perfect reunion of those parts could scarce ever to be hoped for. Your lordship may possibly remember the tears of joy that wet my cheek, when, at your good sister's in London, you once gave me the expectations that a reconciliation might soon take place. I had the misfortune to find these expectations disappointed, and to be treated as the cause of mischief I was laboring to prevent. My consolation under that groundless and malevolent treatment was, that I retained the friendship of many wise and good men of that country, and among the rest some share in the regard of Lord Howe. . . .

I consider this war against us, therefore, as both unjust and unwise. . . . I know your great motive in coming hither was the hope of being instrumental in a reconciliation; and I believe when you find that impossible on any terms given you to propose, you will relinquish so odious a command and return to a more honorable private station.

The Howe brothers were not so naive as to think that after everything that had happened, the Americans were going to welcome the peace mission. The rebellion was unlikely to end unless the Americans suffered militarily.

Supplies and reinforcements for General Howe had been pouring in to Staten Island. By mid-August, the general was ready to apply his sword against General Washington's Continental Army, now concentrated across the Narrows at Brooklyn Heights.

Before the general did so, Admiral Howe dispatched a reply to Benjamin Franklin. Despite Franklin's stinging rebuff, Howe, mixing his peace mission with his brother's military strategy, wrote on August 16:

I am sorry, my worthy friend, that it is only on the assurance you give me of my having still preserved a place in your esteem that I can now found a pretension to trouble you with a reply.

I can have no difficulty to acknowledge that the powers I am invested with were never calculated to negociate a reunion with America under any other description than as subject to the crown of Great Britain. But I do esteem these powers competent, not only to confer and negociate with any gentlemen of influence in the colonies upon the terms, but also to effect a lasting peace and reunion between the two countries, were the temper of the colonies such as professed in the last petition of the Congress to the King [the Olive Branch Petition]. . . . Nor did I think it necessary to say more in my public declaration; not conceiving it would be understood to refer to peace on any other conditions but those of mutual interest to both countries, which could alone render it permanent.

Thus Admiral Howe continued concealing how limited his negotiating really was. Now it was General Howe's turn.

General Howe was not the kind of commander who was prepared to take risks. He lacked both confidence and stature despite his high rank. With a three-thousand-mile-long supply line, he worried constantly about logistics and overcommitting his forces. After extricating himself from Boston, Howe showed his caution when he wrote to Germain from Halifax: "The apparent strength of the army for Spring does not flatter me with hope of bringing the rebels to decisive action." As he prepared to move the army to New York, he again wrote to Germain, on May 7, 1776: "I tremble when I think of our present state of provisions, having now meat for no more than thirteen days in store." He was also reluctant to surround himself with strong subordinates, and he did not have the confidence to handle critical advice, particularly from General Clinton.

But he did enjoy the perquisites and pleasures of high command. Although he was comfortably married, he did not make constancy a virtue during the long separation from his wife. Subordinate officers with attractive wives were frequently seen at Howe's table, and the general's pleasure often extended well beyond port and conversation. A popular ditty of the times ran

> Awake, Awake, Sir Billy
> There's forage on the plain,
> Oh leave your little Filly
> And open the campaign!

Howe reached Staten Island at the end of June with about six thousand troops. Then he waited for seven weeks for reinforcements and supplies from England. General Clinton returned from his fiasco in Charleston with about three thousand troops, including a regiment withdrawn from Jamaica. A convoy of twenty-two ships arrived in late July, bringing English, Scottish, and Hessian soldiers. Howe waited for tents, camp equipment, food stores, and cooking kettles, which finally arrived on August 12. He now had approximately twenty-four thousand soldiers supported by several hundred transports and small boats. Thirty Royal Navy warships were moored around Staten Island and New York. At last, Howe was ready to move.

The British held lower Manhattan and Governors Island with a garrison of several thousand. Washington moved part of his army, under Major General Israel Putnam, to upper Manhattan to hem in the British. He placed the bulk of his forces (about ten thousand men) on Brooklyn Heights, across the East River from Manhattan and Governors Island. Here he waited.

Before dawn on August 22, under the protection of the Royal Navy's guns, a transport flotilla began rowing the British Army across the Narrows to Long Island. Some six thousand soldiers, under the joint command of Generals Howe, Clinton, and Cornwallis, were landed on that eighteenth-century D day, a very considerable feat even though the landings were unopposed. Washington's army waited behind the fortifications on Brooklyn Heights, watching while Howe's army advanced slowly, bringing up artillery and supplies.

Cornwallis took the town of Flatbush. Then Clinton urged Howe to make a feint at the left side of Washington's fortifications and to send a major force around and through the countryside to hit the Americans on the right flank. These attacks went off as planned on August 27 and 28. Howe won a considerable victory. With only about 370 casualties themselves, the British killed, wounded, or captured more than a thousand of Washington's soldiers and trapped the rest on the Brooklyn shore of the East River. This seemed like ample compensation for the casualties Howe had suffered at Bunker Hill. But inexplicably, he lost the complete victory. He failed to press on with his attack. Perhaps he thought it was inadvisable to go for a major kill while his brother was trying to start peace talks. Perhaps, with his memory of Bunker Hill still so fresh, his innate caution in husbanding men and supplies took over. Whatever the reason, on the night of August 29, under the cover of a storm and summer fog, Washington successfully withdrew his entire remaining force. Boats evacuated the troops across to Manhattan.

For Washington, this escape from Brooklyn Heights was the first of a long series of tactical withdrawals by which he avoided defeat for his army for the next six years. Washington had written soon after assuming command of the Continental Army, "We should on all occasions avoid a general action, or put everything to risk, unless compelled by a necessity into which we ought never to be drawn." This was Washington's survival strategy. In a sense, Howe played right into it, allowing Washington to fight and get away to fight again.

While his brother was deciding what to do after Brooklyn Heights, Admiral Howe found a new opportunity to keep up his peace initiative. When he had first arrived in New York, he had attempted to open a correspondence with Washington himself. He had addressed his letter with deliberate condescension "To George Washington, Esq., etc., etc., etc." Colonel Joseph Reed, the Washington aide who had been sent to receive Howe's communication from a courier, looked at the envelope, handed it back to the courier, and said, "If Lord Howe wishes to communicate with General Washington, he must address him properly."

Washington was well aware of Howe's peace mission and very skeptical. He commented that giving the Howe brothers a military mission and a civil mandate for peace "must be conclusive to every thinking man that there is to be little negotiation of a civil kind."

But during the Battle of Brooklyn Heights, two of Washington's senior officers, Generals John Sullivan and Lord Sterling, were captured. They were promptly invited to dine with Admiral Howe aboard the *Eagle,* even as Washington was withdrawing to Manhattan. They found the admiral to be cordial and sympathetic, the soul of hospitality. He expanded on his peace mission in fulsome terms and described the American generosity to the brother killed at Ticonderoga. He assured the officers that he was not in America merely to offer pardons but had the power to make peace. He declared his own conviction that Parliament had no right to tax the colonies or interfere in their domestic affairs. He even said he doubted Britain could conquer America and that he considered the war pointless. General Sullivan was impressed and offered to convey the admiral's sentiments to the Continental Congress in Philadelphia. Howe thereupon ordered the officers released. When Washington heard Sullivan's account of the dinner, he gave him permission to travel to Philadelphia, where he arrived on September 2.

Sullivan's report led to a sharp debate among the leaders of Congress. Radicals felt it was either a hoax or a trap. Moderates said they couldn't dismiss it; they had to find out. Finally, it was decided to send a committee of three—two radicals and one moderate—to meet formally with Howe. They were Benjamin Franklin, John Adams, and Edward Rutledge. On September 11, they took carriages and headed north.

Howe proposed they meet on Staten Island. The Americans rode to Perth Amboy, New Jersey, which was in American hands. Lord Howe sent his admiral's barge to convey them across Raritan River to Staten Island, where a house had been requisitioned as the site of the meeting. One of Howe's officers was designated to stay in Perth Amboy as a hostage, but Franklin said this was not necessary. The hostage returned with the committee, much to Howe's surprise.

Admiral Howe began by telling the delegation that "he could not treat with [them] as a committee of Congress," thus setting the tone for failure. The Americans replied that "he might consider us in what light he pleased . . . but we could consider ourselves in no other character than that in which we were placed by order of Congress." Howe then got down to cases. Franklin, Adams, and Rutledge reported, when they returned to Philadelphia:

> His lordship entered into a discourse of considerable length, which contained no explicit proposition of peace except one, viz., that the colonies should return to their allegiance and obedience to the government of Great Britain. The rest consisted principally of assurances that there was an exceeding good disposition in the King and his ministers to make that government easy to us, with intimations that in the case of our submission, they would cause offensive acts to be revised.

The Americans' reply to Lord Howe was blunt:

> We gave it as our opinion to his lordship that a return to the domination of Great Britain was not now to be expected. We mentioned the repeated humble petitions of the colonies to the King and Parliament which had been treated with contempt and answered only by their tyrannical government; and that it was not till the last act of

Parliament [the proclamation of rebellion] which denounced war against us and put us out of the King's protection, that we declared our independence.

The delegation went on to express an American desire for peace, and a "willingness to enter into a treaty with Britain that might be advantageous to both countries." But of course Lord Howe was not empowered to discuss a treaty between England and an independent United States. "His lordship then saying that he was sorry to find that no accommodation was likely to take place, put an end to the conference."

The three Americans returned to Philadelphia that same afternoon. Soon thereafter, Franklin sailed secretly for France to begin his vital diplomatic mission at the court of Versailles.

Four days after Admiral Howe's meeting with the Americans, General Howe loaded a division of four thousand men onto flat-bottomed transports and moved them across the East River to Kips Bay in Manhattan (near the present-day site of the United Nations). General Clinton, who was in command of the troops, begged that he be allowed to march straight across Manhattan to the Hudson and cut off all of the Continental Army below. Howe refused and held the British on the modest heights of Murray Hill. The American forces, commanded by Major General Israel Putnam, were thus able to withdraw successfully from lower Manhattan and join Washington above the Harlem River. The British staged a short, sharp attack at Harlem Heights, which ended in a small success for the Americans. But Washington knew that he had been outflanked, and he was forced to pull back all the way to White Plains in Westchester County.

Howe paused after Harlem Heights until October 12, when he once more loaded his army onto transports on the East River and moved it to a landing on the Westchester County side of Long Island Sound. From here, after building up his forces to more than four thousand men, he began advancing on Washington in White Plains. He reached the area on October 28. His initial flank attack again turned the American lines; Washington withdrew to a stronger defense position on hilly terrain. Howe hesitated. His hesitation was reinforced by a heavy rain that dampened not only his enthusiasm but also his gunpowder stores. On November 1, the Americans heard the British supply wagons moving and braced themselves for an attack. They found instead that Howe was withdrawing, heading back to Manhattan. Howe had not pressed, and Washington's army was still intact.

Washington headed for Peekskill, in the Highlands of the Hudson forty miles north of Manhattan, to cross the Hudson and march down to New Jersey. He intended to cover Philadelphia against British attack. However, believing that his army would be able to hold a secure position above New York City, he left a considerable supply of artillery, arms, and ammunition, and three thousand troops, most of them concentrated at Fort Washington on the Hudson.

But on November 16, Howe's forces, returning from White Plains, struck the Americans at Fort Washington with determination and strength. They overwhelmed the Americans, killing or capturing the entire garrison and its supply of 146 cannons, 12,000 shot and shells, 2,800 muskets, and 40,000 musket balls. It was a terrible loss of men, equipment, and morale, one that Washington could ill afford.

Four days later, General Cornwallis crossed the Hudson from Manhattan to New Jersey with four thousand men to begin a harassing pursuit of Washington.

In the first week of December, General Howe, at the urging of both his brother and Lord George Germain in London, launched an assault on Rhode Island. A force of six thousand, commanded by General Clinton, sailed from New York to seize Newport and Narragansett and threaten Providence. Clinton had argued against dispersing the forces. He thought the whole army should instead concentrate to seize Philadelphia and trap Washington. But Admiral Howe declared that the Royal Navy needed the good harbor at Newport for winter action off the New England coast. Occupying Rhode Island was quick work and succeeded with little waste of lives or ammunition.

Thus, by December of 1776, the British were riding a wave of success. The Continental Army was in poor shape after spending the summer moving from Boston to New York and then fighting from New York to White Plains. Moreover, the one-year enlistments would expire in December. Nevertheless, General Howe had written Germain in September cautiously: "Though the enemy is much dispirited from the late successes of His Majesty's arms, yet I have not the smallest prospect of finishing this contest this [1776] campaign, nor until the rebels see preparations in the spring that may preclude thoughts of further resistance."

Meanwhile, General Washington, harried by Cornwallis, with his army down to about three thousand men, reached Newark and continued on to New Brunswick. While Cornwallis halted to await further orders, Washington moved on to Princeton and Trenton. By the time Cornwallis resumed his pursuit, Washington had crossed the Delaware and destroyed every boat he could find along the river. His ragtag army, such as it was, had survived.

Howe gave orders early in December to withdraw his main force to New Jersey for the winter, leaving only a detachment of a few thousand behind to occupy Manhattan. The fact was that although Howe had captured a grand prize by forcing Washington out of New York, possession of the city also had its drawbacks. It was easy to defend but not to supply. Local supplies had to come from foraging in the areas around New York, and the British were getting very little cooperation from the countryside. So Howe himself withdrew to Staten Island to await the spring and scattered his army through New Jersey to threaten Philadelphia and forage as best it could. Howe had explained this to Germain in a letter written on November 30:

> In consequence of my expectation that Lord Cornwallis will shortly be in possession of East Jersey, I propose to quarter a large body of troops in that district, without which we should be under much difficulty to find covering, forage and supplies of fresh provisions for the army. The plan of the enemy, by their public orders, is to destroy all species of forage and stock as they retire before His Majesty's troops, which I am hopeful they will not have time to accomplish. Their further design seems to be to retreat behind the Raritan River, or perhaps behind the Delaware to cover Philadelphia.

In this same letter, Howe detailed his strategy for the 1777 campaign, telling Germain that he intended "if possible to finish the war in one year by an extensive and vigorous exertion of His Majesty's arms" on three fronts. He proposed to secure Providence and then "penetrate from thence towards Boston and if possible reduce that town." Next he planned to deploy "an offensive army in New York to move up the North [Hudson] River to Albany." Finally, he would use "a defensive army to cover Jersey by giving up a jealousy [threat] to Philadelphia, which I would propose to attack in the autumn." He told Germain he would need reinforcements of twenty thousand to pursue these three campaign objectives.

However, in mid-December Howe received a dispatch from Germain, dated October 18, giving fulsome praise for the New York campaign and encouraging an advance on Philadelphia:

> I think it not improbable that if Mr. Washington's army should soon disperse, that you may pay a visit to Philadelphia before this campaign ends. The punishing of the seat of the Congress would be a proper example to the rest of the Colonies, but I confess if we are to have another campaign I trust that Boston and the Massachusetts Bay will feel the distress of that war which their detestable principles have occasioned, encouraged and supported.

General Howe also learned from Germain that King George had knighted him for his successful New York campaign and that he had been promoted to full general.

Admiral Howe, meanwhile, sought to cash in on his brother's success at New York by stepping up his peace campaign with an appeal directly to the colonists. On November 30, he issued a proclamation calling upon Congress to renounce the powers it had usurped from the king. He also requested that the Continental Army disperse and its soldiers and militias apply to the king's authorities for royal pardon and release "from all forfeitures, attainders and penalties." With Washington in hasty retreat, the proclamation drew a response that the English took to be encouraging, although it was not as great as Howe had hoped for and expected. Governor Tryon of New York reported that oaths of loyalty had been administered to sixteen hundred militiamen who had deserted Washington's army on Long Island. Another three hundred citizens had been given certificates of protection. From New Jersey came a report that said all but "an inconsiderable proportion" of rebels were asking for pardons. Admiral Howe was not entirely taken in by this, for he wrote to Germain on December 18 that the proclamation would "only be coextensive with the Power of the Sword." Howe's private secretary, Henry Strachey, wrote to the undersecretary in Germain's office with a warning that "no province would submit until occupied by British troops."

But General Howe was sufficiently impressed by this apparent upsurge in Loyalist support to change his original campaign plans for 1777. He outlined these important changes to Germain in a letter written on December 20:

> The opinions of people being much changed in Pennsylvania, and their minds in general, from the late progress of the army, disposed to peace, in which sentiment they would be confirmed by our getting possession of Philadelphia, I am from this consideration fully persuaded the principle army should act offensively on that side where the enemy's chief strength will certainly be collected.
>
> By this change the offensive plan towards Boston must be deferred until the proposed reinforcements arrive from Europe, that there may be a corps to act defensively upon the lower part of Hudson's river to cover Jersey on that side, as well as to facilitate in some degree the approach of the army from Canada.
>
> We must not look for the Northern army to reach Albany before the middle of September; of course the subsequent operation of that corps [in New York] will depend on the state of things at that time.

General Howe had changed the entire focus and strength of the British strategy for 1777. The historian Piers Mackesy summed it up thus: "With this dispatch, Howe broke from the design which ruled British strategy since Bunker Hill." Howe's dispatch took two months to reach London. When it arrived, on February 23, 1777, Germain was deeply involved in finalizing plans for General John Burgoyne's offensive from Canada to Albany. A disaster was in the making. The two commanders, instead of meeting, would be far apart.

Then late on Christmas night, 1776, in freezing wet weather, General Washington recrossed the Delaware River with a handful of troops and advanced on the town of Trenton. Seldom in history has such a small battle had such a profound effect on the outcome of a war.

Chapter 16

THE ROAD TO SARATOGA

When George Washington retreated across the Delaware in December of 1776, he was grimly aware that the war for American independence was on the verge not of defeat but of collapse. So far, survival had been his only victory. At the end of December, the one-year enlistments of his soldiers would expire, and this threatened to decimate the Continental Army as much as battle or smallpox.

"You may as well attempt to stop the winds from blowing or the sun in its diurnal as the regiments from going home when their terms expire," Washington wrote bitterly. Fearful of how many soldiers would head home, knowing that the fate of the Revolution was in his hands, Washington needed a victory, and he had to act promptly.*

He had loyal supporters in his officer corps, and his leadership did

---

*It was in December of 1776 that Thomas Paine published his pamphlet *The American Crisis*, with the famous words "These are times that try men's souls. The summer soldier and the sunshine patriot will, in this crisis, shrink from the service of their country; but he that stands it *now* deserves the love and thanks of man and woman. Tyranny, like hell, is not easily conquered."

not go unheeded. Another twenty-seven hundred soldiers who had escaped British capture in New York arrived in Philadelphia, along with Pennsylvania militiamen who turned out for short-term duty. By December 20, he had an army of about six thousand to defend Philadelphia. From this force, he picked a contingent of sixteen hundred men and prepared to cross the Delaware for his audacious strike at the British in Trenton.

General Howe was somewhat complacent after forcing Washington out of New York and his successful attack to seize Newport, Rhode Island. His lines were overextended from Staten Island across New Jersey to Princeton, Trenton, and Bordentown. Near the Delaware, at these last two outposts, he had placed Hessian mercenaries, who had pleaded with him for the "honor" of being at the most dangerous position. Colonel Johann Räll occupied Trenton with fifteen hundred troops, and Colonel Karl van Donop was farther south, at Bordentown, with another two thousand. Sharing Howe's complacency, they had not bothered to prepare entrenchments or fortifications. Who would attack them at Christmastime?

Late on Christmas Day, Washington's force of sixteen hundred, with horses and artillery, moved to the Delaware north of Philadelphia and crossed the river that night in freezing sleet and rain. In darkness, they marched to Trenton, encircling the town at opposite ends of its main road as the Hessians slept in their barracks. At first light, around eight o'clock, American artillery pieces opened fire, and the Hessians roused and came pouring out of their barracks. Colonel Räll was killed in action before he could issue any orders. In total confusion, the Hessians were unable to form any coordinated defense. Hemmed in by Washington's men at either end of the little town, they threw down their arms, and the battle was over in barely an hour. Washington marched off with about a thousand Hessian prisoners and was astounded to find that not a single American had been killed.

The Revolution was saved from collapse.

When the news of Trenton reached General Howe at his headquarters in New York, he wrote to Lord George Germain on December 31:

Räll's defeat has put us much out of our way. His misconduct is amazing. Had he remained to defend the village he could not have been forced, nor could the attack have been pushed to any length, as the enemy would have been too much exposed to his rear from Princeton and to Colonel Donop's corps of 2,000 men at Bordentown. Donop's conduct upon this occasion is by no means commendable. Retiring from his post without orders, leaving his sick behind, denotes panic. . . . The rebels have taken fresh courage upon this event and have returned over the Delaware in force, which will give us some trouble in our cantonments, and their success will probably produce another campaign. I hear French officers flock to them fast. Our most advanced post toward the Delaware is now Princeton, where we must endeavor to cover a strong corps to keep them *hors d'insulte*.

Even as Howe was writing this dispatch, Washington had recrossed the Delaware and headed back to Trenton on January 1, 1777, with five thousand men. Howe had ordered his most aggressive commander, Major General Lord Cornwallis, to rush south from New York and restore the situation.

Cornwallis got to Trenton in the late afternoon of January 2 and skirmished briefly with the Americans before darkness fell. During the night, Washington spirited his troops around the eastern side of Trenton on a back road and advanced toward Princeton in order to come up behind Cornwallis. He intercepted British reinforcements moving to join Cornwallis and routed them in a bayonet fight. Cornwallis retreated from Trenton to Princeton; Washington continued north to Morristown, where he found ideal terrain for winter quarters. From there, he could threaten British lines to the north or the south. Howe, meanwhile, abandoned attempts to hold Princeton, Trenton, and Bordentown and retreated to New Brunswick. He now had a very different war on his hands.

News of Howe's setbacks reached London in mid-February. On February 24, King George wrote a note of determined optimism to Lord North:

The surprise and want of spirit of the Hessian officers as well as soldiers at Trenton is not much to their credit, and will undoubtedly rather elate the rebels, who till then were in a state of the greatest despondency. I wish Sir W. Howe had placed none but British troops in the outposts; but I am certain by a letter I have seen from Lord Cornwallis that the rebels will soon have sufficient reason to fall into the former dejection.

* * *

The defeats at Trenton and Princeton soon became more than a mere setback for the Howe brothers. In London, the news reinforced a growing disenchantment with their conduct of the war. General Howe had not yet won a decisive victory, and yet he was asking Germain for another twenty thousand men to carry out the next campaigns. Admiral Howe's peace efforts had got nowhere. Hard-liners in London, led by Germain, were highly critical of Howe's offers of pardons for the rebels, and King George came to agree with them. Moreover, Admiral Howe wasn't having much success in blockading the American coast, and he appealed constantly for more ships. In London, the feeling was that the admiral had already tied up the Royal Navy supporting his brother's land operations and was spending too much time talking peace.

Germain, who had strongly opposed any peace initiatives from the very beginning, began to send dispatches to Admiral Howe that were decidedly cooler in their tone, and in January 1777 he wrote tartly to Lord North:

> I cannot approve the general pardon from the commissioners. It is poor encouragement for the friends of the government who have been suffering under the tyranny of the rebels to see their oppressors without distinction put upon the same footing as themselves. . . . This sentimental manner of making war will, I fear, not have the desired effect.

The British losses at Trenton and Princeton made it certain that there would be no early end to the rebellion. After this news reached London, Germain wrote to General Howe:

> I fear that you and Lord Howe will find it necessary to adopt such modes of carrying on the war that the rebels may be effectively distressed, so that through a lively experience of Losses and Sufferings they may be brought as soon as possible to a proper sense of duty.

The king was also irritated with the Howes. On March 5, he first impatiently dismissed as impractical the general's request for twenty thousand troops, then added:

> If he and his brother will act with a little less lenity, which I really think cruelty, as it keeps up the contest, the next campaign will bring

the Americans in a temper to accept such terms as may enable the Mother Country to keep them in order; for we must never come into such as may patch for a year or two, and then bring on new boils; the regaining of their affections is an idle idea; it must be the convincing of them that it is in their interest to submit, and then they will dread further boils.

The king would have no further peace overtures, but there was as yet no suggestion of any change of command in America.

On March 3, Germain wrote to Howe, specifically approving his revised plans to advance south to Philadelphia instead of taking the offense in New York north to Albany: "I am now commanded to tell you that the King entirely approves of your proposed deviation from the plan which you formally suggested, being of the opinion that the reasons which have induced you to recommend this change are solid and decisive."

When Howe received this dispatch, discussions had been going on in London for nearly three months between Germain and Burgoyne on campaign plans to descend on New York from Canada. Gentleman Johnny (as he was called) had returned on leave from Carleton's army in Canada in December 1776, partly because of his wife's death earlier that year, partly to advance his plans on how to win the war in America.

Burgoyne was nothing if not confident of his ability to win: On Christmas Day 1776 a bet was recorded in the wagers book at Brooks Club, one of London's fashionable gambling clubs: "General Burgoyne wagers Charles Fox one pony that he will be home victorious from America by Christmas Day, 1777."*

Burgoyne found ample opportunity to promote himself and his plans for winning the war. He sought an immediate audience with the king and reported dutifully to Germain that "[a]s the arrangements for the next campaign might possibly come under his royal

---

*A pony equaled fifty guineas, or fifty-five pounds, which represented about a year's wages for a common laborer of those days. But by the time the debt was due, Burgoyne was America's most distinguished prisoner of war. Whether Burgoyne ever paid Fox off is not recorded.

contemplation, I humbly laid myself at His Majesty's feet for such active employment as he might think me worthy of."

After meeting with the king, Burgoyne departed to take the waters at Bath and write a lengthy memorandum for Germain, "Thoughts for Conducting the War from the Side of Canada." He returned to London in February and sent his memo to Germain for consideration by the cabinet and submission to the king.

There was nothing original about Burgoyne's proposal. He simply set out to finish the job that Carleton had started the year before, after the siege of Quebec was lifted. He would advance south from Montreal, sail down Lake Champlain, take Fort Ticonderoga, and march down the Hudson River to Albany and cut off the New England colonies from the south:

> These ideas are formed upon the proposition that it be the sole purpose of the Canada army to effect a junction with General Howe, or after cooperation so far as to get possession of Albany and open communications to New York, to remain upon the Hudson's River, and thereby enable that general to act with his whole force to the southward.

He accurately predicted the difficulties that he expected: that Fort Ticonderoga would be heavily defended by the Americans, that he would find enemy gunboats a strong presence on Lake George, that the passage of his army and supply trains would be hampered by trees felled across roads and bridges taken out by the Americans, that his army should expect harassment and sniper fire.* He specified in his memo that in light of these conditions, the commander should be given *"latitude"* in determining the operations of the advance. But his final orders, drafted by Germain, read that he was *"to force [his] way to Albany"* [emphasis added].

His plan went into minute detail, even including the specific units of the army he wanted to use and timetables for their movements. He asked for an army of at least eight thousand British and German regular infantry, and he expected Carleton to recruit two thousand

---

*In his authoritative *History of the British Army,* Sir John Fortescue commented that "Burgoyne indicated the purely military difficulties of the advance so clearly that a wise man might well have hesitated to incur them."

Canadians. He also intended to enlist a thousand or more Indian "savages."

The government was looking for action, and Burgoyne promised to deliver it. At the end of February, Germain recommended, and the cabinet adopted, Burgoyne's plan.

Germain briefly considered naming Clinton as commander and sending Burgoyne as Howe's second in command. But Burgoyne had sold himself to the king, and the king confirmed his command. Clinton, in London on leave at this same time, was sent back to New York with a knighthood.

Thus, during the first week of March, Germain sent off approval of Howe's plans to head south to capture Philadelphia while drafting final orders for Burgoyne. He seems not to have given any thought to ironing out the discrepancies between the two plans. The historian Sir John Fortescue summed it up by saying, "Howe was left with directions to attack Philadelphia, and Burgoyne with positive and unconditional commands to advance on Albany and there place himself under Howe's orders. . . . Never was there a finer example of the art of organizing disaster."

Burgoyne departed London on March 27 and arrived in Quebec on May 8. He carried with him a set of dispatches addressed to General Sir Guy Carleton that contained his orders to force his way to Albany. In addressing the orders in this way, Germain acknowledged that Carleton was the senior officer in Canada but relegated him to a backseat, confining him to the defense of Canada. Carleton was incensed. He wrote immediately to Germain, requesting that he be relieved of his post entirely. To Burgoyne, Carleton offered cold and correct assurances of cooperation and support, but he pointed out that Germain's restrictions were such that his support for operations in New York would have to be very limited. Thus, by adhering to Germain's orders, Carleton washed his hands of Burgoyne's problems.

Burgoyne was to head for Albany—but what about General Howe? Burgoyne and Carleton had been told that Germain had sent a duplicate copy of their orders to Howe in New York, and they, knowing nothing yet of the Philadelphia plans, assumed that Howe would head for Albany. Howe, of course, had no such direct instructions and was left to decide on his own operational priorities.

Later, after the disaster at Saratoga, the earl of Shelburne spread the story that Germain had never sent a copy of Burgoyne's orders to Howe. Although this wasn't true, it did add to the confusion surrounding Saratoga. The truth was eventually brought out by William Knox, an undersecretary in Germain's department. On March 26, when Germain entered Knox's office to sign Burgoyne's orders, his carriage was waiting to take him to his country home. When Knox pointed out that no covering letter had been prepared to accompany the duplicate set of orders being sent to General Howe, Germain's temper flared: "So, my poor horses must stand in the street all the time and I shan't be to my time anywhere!" Knox said he would write the letter, "and with that his Lordship was satisfied, as he could never bear delay or disappointment."

Knox did write the letter and send it along with the duplicate set of orders, but an office clerk failed to enter this fact in the official log of all documents sent and received by the secretary's office. This appeared to confirm Shelburne's story. And the records kept for General Howe in New York did indeed register the receipt of the dispatch from Germain's office on July 5, 1777. Howe was fully informed, but he did not change his priorities. In fact, Howe, in outlining his plans in the first place, had calculated that an expedition from Canada could not reach Albany before September and that he could use the summer to take Philadelphia. Further, the reduced force he would leave in New York would be used "to facilitate in some degree the approach of the army from Canada." Germain had approved all of this on March 3. After receiving a copy of Burgoyne's orders, Howe wrote to Germain on July 16:

> By the movement of the enemy's army in Jersey toward King's Ferry upon the North River, he [Washington] seems to point at preventing a junction between this and the Northern Army, which will no farther affect my proceeding to Pennsylvania. . . .
>
> The Enemy's movement taking this turn, I apprehend G. Burgoyne will meet with little interruption otherwise than difficulties he must encounter in transporting stores and provisions for the supply of his Army. . . . If G. Washington should march with a determination to force G. Burgoyne, the strength of G. Burgoyne's army is such as to leave me no room to dread the event.

In other words, Howe chose to believe that Washington's movement north was making it easier to capture Philadelphia. He saw no reason to anticipate disaster or to change plans for which he already had Germain's approval.

As the events of the war in America unfolded in 1776 and news of Howe's successes in New York and Rhode Island circulated, the voices of opposition in Parliament had almost literally fallen silent. Rockingham, Shelburne, even Charles James Fox and Edmund Burke were quiet; the earl of Chatham, again ill, was shielded from any news of the American conflict by his wife.

Sir George Savile, a member of Rockingham's faction, summarized it by saying, "We have fully enough expressed ourselves in Parliament. To do it again and again would be, I think, cheapening ourselves only to disturb that good humour with which the good company is doing mischief."

Rockingham wrote to Burke saying that "I look to the determination of the operations of the campaign; men's minds in the country are hung up, in the suspense of expectation. The end of the campaign is the settling day."

But as Parliament began its work in 1777, news of Washington's successes at Trenton and Princeton changed the picture, making it clear to the opposition and government alike that the war was getting longer and costlier, that decisive victory was still only a distant mirage.

As the stalemate continued, the opposition began to find its voice. The Old Whigs wanted to end the war and preserve the empire, but their reaction to the Declaration of Independence was embarrassed silence. They hoped, along with Chatham, that England could prevail without recognizing American independence.

Edmund Burke's thinking on American liberty was beginning to change toward acceptance of independence. In his *Letter to the Sheriffs of Bristol,* widely circulated in April of 1777, Burke argued that it was wrong to go on fighting a war to impose the supremacy of Parliament. He wrote:

If there be one fact in the world perfectly clear, it is this: That the disposition of the people of America is wholly averse to any other than a free government; and this is indication enough to any honest statesman, how he ought to adapt whatever power he finds in his hands to their case. . . . The extreme of liberty (which is its abstract perfection, but its real fault) obtains no where, nor ought to obtain anywhere. Liberty must be limited to be possessed. The degree of restraint it is impossible in any case to settle precisely. But it ought to be the constant aim of every wise public counsel to find out by rational, cool endeavours with how little, not how much of this restraint the community can exist. For liberty is a good to be improved, not an evil to be lessened.

Burke reinforced his *Letter* by introducing in the House of Commons a motion calling for the repeal of all acts concerning America that had been passed since 1763. Lord North brushed the motion aside.

Then, at the end of May 1777, the earl of Chatham reappeared in the House of Lords for the first time since Franklin's departure two years earlier. The sense of drama he was always able to invoke was heightened by his appearance, tottering into the House on a crutch, swathed in flannels to ease the pain in his gouty legs. Speaking in a voice so weak and low that at times he could barely be heard, he warned of the approaching danger of war with France. American representatives were in Paris for reasons that were all too clear, he said. Time was short and the danger great, for there was only a moment before France would recognize American independence and enter into a treaty with them. What was to prevent the English from forestalling this peril by reconciling with the colonies? he asked.

We called them rebels, but they were only defending their unquestionable rights. Nor could we in any case conquer them—it was impossible. And in attempting it we were forgetting their importance to us—for trade in times of peace and for support in times of war. We had been the aggressors, and it became us to be the first in offering reparation. It is no use harping, as the government does, on unconditional submission. We should never obtain it, nor did we deserve it. Let us try instead unconditional redress.

Then, like Burke and Fox before him, Chatham called for "repeal of all the laws of which the colonies complained" as a first step. His motion was rejected.

Now that Chatham had resumed public opposition, King George's animosities were fully aroused. He sent an indignant memorandum to Lord North the next day, May 31:

Lord Chatham's highly unseasonable motion can have no other use than to convey some fresh fuel if attended to by the Rebels; like most of the other productions of that extraordinary brain it contains nothing but specious words and malevolence, for no one that reads it, if unacquainted with the conduct of the Mother Country and its Colonies, must but suppose the Americans poor mild persons who after unheard of and repeated grievances had no choice but slavery or the Sword; whilst the truth is that the great lenity of this country encreased their pride and encouraged them to rebel; but thank God the Nation does not see the unhappy Contest through [Chatham's] mirror. If his sentiments were adopted, I should not esteem the situation in this country a very dignified one, for the Islands would soon cast off all obedience.

In June, as Burgoyne began his march out of Canada toward Saratoga, Howe prepared to leave New York for Philadelphia. Howe had persuaded himself that Philadelphia was an important military objective; in truth, there was neither a strategic nor a political victory to be won by its capture. It was a convenient central meeting place for the Continental Congress but not the fulcrum of the Revolution. When Howe's army approached, the Congress took off, first to Lancaster and then to York, Pennsylvania. The occupying army's supply problems were more tenuous. Supplies now had to come via the Delaware River, since the risk to wagons crossing New Jersey through hostile country was so great. In Paris, when Benjamin Franklin was told that General Howe had captured Philadelphia, he responded, "Ah no. Philadelphia has captured General Howe."

Concerning his advance on Philadelphia, Howe, in May of 1777, informed Germain of an important change in plans. Instead of marching across New Jersey, he decided to transport his army by sea, thus avoiding the threat of flank attacks by Washington. Germain approved this plan and expressed the forlorn hope that Howe would capture Philadelphia "in time for you to cooperate with the army ordered to proceed from Canada, and put itself under your command."

Howe had also informed Carleton of his new plan to move his army by sea and had told Carleton that he would leave a corps in

New York, "on the lower part of Hudson's river, sufficient to open the communications for shipping through the Highlands."

In June, Clinton returned from his leave in London to his post as second in command to Howe. He immediately challenged Howe's decision to move the army by sea and urged that a force start up the Hudson instead. Clinton was aware that having the armies join up at Albany was a priority for Germain, even if this had not been spelled out precisely in orders. He pointed out the obvious to Howe, that the army at sea or south in Philadelphia could be of little help to Burgoyne if help were needed. But Howe would not listen. All he would do was authorize a transfer of some British troops from Rhode Island to New York, giving Clinton a total of eight thousand to help Burgoyne if needed.

By mid-June, Washington knew from spies and scouts that Burgoyne was on the move out of Canada, and he fully expected Howe to move up the Hudson to support Burgoyne. He therefore kept his forces concentrated in northern New Jersey, ready to move in either direction, toward Albany or Philadelphia. When Howe used skirmishes to attempt to engage Washington in battle, Washington was even more convinced that Howe planned to move north.

Admiral Howe began gathering transports in New York for the voyage. Meanwhile, General Howe, before moving so much as a mile toward Philadelphia, wrote to Germain that he could see no possibility of ending the war in 1777. After taking Philadelphia, he said, he intended to "strike deep" into the southern colonies and end the rebellion in 1778. This was not what Germain wanted to hear. The war was getting longer.

As General Howe dithered, weeks of good weather slipped by. Not until early July did he begin embarking a formidable force of nineteen thousand British and German troops and supplies of cannons, gunpowder, food, horses, and fodder. But the 250 transports and warships assembled by Admiral Howe lolled in New York, becalmed. Not until July 23 did the fleet get under way.

At this same time, the Americans holding Fort Ticonderoga were forced to abandon their stronghold to Burgoyne. Washington, watching closely, was convinced that Howe was going to join Burgoyne. He worried that the British might try to draw him away from the Hudson. He watched while the British fleet sailed out of New York. Where were they heading? Boston? Charleston? Philadelphia?

When word reached Washington that the fleet had been sighted off Delaware Bay, he first detached an elite corps of riflemen under Colonel Daniel Morgan. These men were to head north, joining General Gates and the Continental Army near Saratoga. Washington left a light force behind in New York to protect West Point and the Highlands against a move by Clinton and headed south to cover Philadelphia with about ten thousand men.

When Admiral Howe reached Delaware Bay, an English patrol frigate joined the fleet, informing the admiral (not entirely correctly) that the Americans had mounted shore batteries and water obstacles along the Delaware River approaches to Philadelphia. It would be risky to move the ships upriver. So the Howe brothers turned back out into the Atlantic and headed for Chesapeake Bay.

It was a truly horrible voyage for the nineteen thousand men and horses. Their destination now was the northern tip of the Chesapeake Bay, the head of the Elk River, north of Baltimore. Altogether, the army spent seven weeks from the time it began loading supplies, during which it endured sweltering weather and wallowed in swells as the heavy warships drifted in light breezes, until it landed. The fleet carried only four weeks' food and animal fodder. Starving animals had to be thrown overboard as they inched across Chesapeake Bay, always in sight of land.

The army finally came ashore on August 25. Guns and stores had to be unloaded, forage found for the remaining animals and fresh food and water for the men. But they were still nearly seventy miles from Philadelphia, almost as far away as they had been in New York; transport had to be organized. It was remarkable that Howe's army made it across the Delaware countryside to the Brandywine Creek, north of Wilmington, by September 11. Here, still twenty-five miles south of Philadelphia, Washington's army was entrenched.

The Battle of Brandywine was much the same as other encounters between Howe and Washington. The British avoided a frontal assault against heavy defenses but made a successful flank attack. Washington took heavy casualties, about one thousand killed and wounded. Nevertheless, he managed to fall back with his main force intact. Howe, although he outnumbered the Americans almost two to one, pressed forward slowly. He entered Philadelphia on September 25. Washington moved northwest of the city, eventually to spend the winter at Valley Forge, Pennsylvania.

*   *   *

Burgoyne had left Canada in mid-June. If he had any concerns about a lack of clear orders or coordination with General Howe, he didn't show it. His early progress south was rapid and easy, and he reached Ticonderoga on July 2.

Gentleman Johnny lived and traveled in style, and he loved the glamour of eighteenth-century soldiering. Twenty-six wagons were allocated for the baggage belonging to Burgoyne and his senior staff: tents, camp beds, blankets, cooking stoves, dinner china, silver and crystal, wines, personal supplies, and of course, uniforms. Gentleman Johnny was immaculately uniformed.

The German dragoons with Burgoyne brought along their regimental band. Their commander, General Friedrich von Riedesel, was accompanied by his beauteous wife and their three children—and of course, their baggage. Baroness von Riedesel's social notes on the campaign recorded a spirited dinner party on the way to Saratoga: "General Burgoyne was very merry and spent the whole night singing and drinking and amusing himself with the wife of a Commissary [supply officer] who was his mistress, and who, like him, was fond of champagne."

None of this luxurious living appeared to tarnish Burgoyne's image with his army. He was a popular commander. A Lieutenant Digby, serving in Canada with the Fifty-third Foot, wrote of Burgoyne and Carleton:

> General Carleton is one of the most distant, reserved men in the world, he had a rigid strictness in his manner which is very unpleasing and which he observes even to his most particular friends and acquaintances. . . . He was far from being the favorite of the army. General Burgoyne alone engrossed their warmest attachment. From having seen a great deal of polite life, he possesses a winning manner in his appearance and address, which causes him to be idolized by the army. On every occasion he was the soldier's friend, well knowing the most sanguine expectations a general can have of success must proceed from the spirit of the troops under his command.

An easy success at Fort Ticonderoga lifted Burgoyne's outlook on the whole campaign. Although the Americans had repaired and strengthened the fort since capturing it in May of 1775, they had

neglected to fortify Sugar Loaf Hill, which overlooked Ticonderoga. A Swiss engineer officer with Burgoyne spotted the height
and quickly devised a route by which cannon could be dragged to its
crest. When the American commander, Major General Arthur St.
Clair, realized what had happened, he averted surrendering his men
by withdrawing under cover of darkness. By July 5, the fort was in
Burgoyne's hands. Burgoyne seemed to be on his way to victory,
but after Ticonderoga, his luck began to run out.

Even as his supply lines from Canada lengthened, his predictions
of the difficulties he could encounter began to come true. His advance was slowed by trees felled by the Americans along the rough
trails he had to follow. He got so little support from the hostile
countryside that General von Riedesel suggested a foray to the town
of Bennington in Vermont. Here, reports went, the Americans
had stocked food, wagons, oxen, horses, and fodder for their own
operations. So Burgoyne selected a strong force, predominantly
German, some of his best professional troops, and sent them off
on August 11.

By the time they reached Bennington, a militia force of fifteen
hundred Americans had gathered under a particularly able commander, General John Stark. On August 16, a running battle began.
American riflemen took a heavy toll of the Germans. Burgoyne sent
reinforcements rushing to the rescue, but when the battle was over,
on August 20, the German commander had been killed, and Burgoyne's army had lost some nine hundred, killed or captured, more
than 10 percent of his irreplaceable professionals. Burgoyne's dispatches to Germain began to take on a defensive tone:

> Had I a latitude in my orders I should think it my duty to wait in this
> position, but my orders being positive "to force a junction with Sir
> William Howe" I apprehend I am not at liberty to remain inac-
> tive. . . . When I wrote more confidently I little foresaw that I was to
> be left to pursue my way through such a tract of country and hosts of
> foes without any cooperation from New York, nor did I think the
> garrison of Ticonderoga would fall to my share alone, a dangerous
> experiment would it be to leave that post in weakness, and too heavy
> a drain is it upon the life-blood of my force to give it true strength.

Even if his orders had been framed with the "latitude" he had
asked for when he was in London, it is unlikely that Burgoyne would

have halted his advance after Bennington to spend the winter in northern New York or return to Canada. He was too proud and too savvy a political soldier to repeat General Carleton's mistake of the previous year. Nevertheless, with his army now seriously weakened and his supply situation growing more precarious, he began messaging frantically to Clinton in New York.

News of Ticonderoga reached London on August 22 and was hailed as the first clear success for the British since the setback at Trenton. Horace Walpole recorded in his diary that "the King is said to have run into the Queen's room saying 'I have beat them—the Americans!' " But this was the last good news to reach London. In fact, it was the last news to reach London for two months. Not until October 22 did Germain hear again from either General Howe at sea, heading for Philadelphia, or General Burgoyne. Powerless to influence events, all he could do was hope against hope that Howe had sent Clinton north to meet Burgoyne.

In late August, Clinton received word of Burgoyne's defeat at Bennington. In early September, a reinforcement of seventeen hundred men arrived from England, and Clinton felt he could finally move north. On September 10, he dispatched a message to Burgoyne, telling him he would head up the Hudson in about ten days' time. But by September 14, Burgoyne was already nearing the American lines above Saratoga.

The American commander at Saratoga was Major General Horatio Gates. English born and bred, the son of a duke's housekeeper, Gates had served in the British Army for nearly twenty years before retiring in 1765 to settle in Virginia. He joined the American cause in 1775 and, more popular than able, had been appointed to replace Major General Philip Schuyler at Saratoga.

Gates was fortunate in having the assistance of a Polish officer, Tadeusz Kościuszko, a skilled engineer, to supervise the Americans' defense works and artillery placement on the heights above the little town of Saratoga.

By now amply informed of Burgoyne's every move, American reinforcements poured in. Gates had nine thousand troops under his command for the first stage of the battle, and an additional six thousand militiamen joined in for the second phase. The Americans now outnumbered Burgoyne by two to one.

Burgoyne fought the first Battle of Saratoga on September 19. It was a wild day of maneuvering and skirmishing. Brigadier General Benedict Arnold played a major role in turning back the British, who broke off action at the end of the day with some 560 casualties, double the American losses.*

As Burgoyne prepared to attack again, he got word that Clinton was moving north. He decided to pause, to wait and see what effect this might have on Gates and the Americans. This pause at Saratoga lasted for three weeks. Meanwhile, Clinton did not leave New York until October 3, when he loaded three thousand troops onto river transports and sailed north toward the Highlands below West Point. On October 5, he routed the small American garrison at Verplanck, then pressed on to Fort Montgomery, which he seized on October 7. On October 8, he scribbled to Burgoyne, *"Nous y voilà* ['We're here'], and nothing now between us but Gates. I sincerely hope this little success may facilitate your operations. I heartily wish you success."

But the message never reached Burgoyne. The Loyalist courier who was carrying it was intercepted by American militiamen, the message found, and the courier hanged.

Burgoyne, waiting desperately for news from Clinton, faced overwhelming odds, his army reduced to barely forty-five hundred men fit for duty. He called his senior officers to a council of war. Any idea of retreat was rejected. On October 7, the day Clinton took Fort Montgomery, Burgoyne hurled his men against the Americans in a last wild but futile fight. Daniel Morgan's sharpshooters took a particularly heavy toll of English officers. By the end of the day, Burgoyne had sustained another 600 casualties. (The Americans had lost only 150.) Burgoyne withdrew to his camp near the town of

---

*In the second phase of the Battle of Saratoga, Arnold was wounded and his leg broken badly when his horse fell on him. He refused amputation and survived, to turn to treason.

Saratoga, leaving his wounded on the field. He dispatched a message to General Gates: "I recommend them to the protection which, I feel, I should show to an enemy in the same manner." (There was gallantry and bravery aplenty on both sides.)

Another pause ensued while the Americans moved off the heights that they had so effectively defended and began an envelopment of Burgoyne's army. On October 13, after another council with his senior officers, Burgoyne asked for terms for "a cessation of arms."

Instead of surrender, Burgoyne insisted on a "convention," an agreement for the laying down of arms, so that some point of military honor would be preserved. General Gates was accommodating—too accommodating, as it turned out, to suit General Washington and the Continental Congress.

On October 17, after four days of negotiation, the terms of a convention were accepted by Burgoyne. The remnants of his army formed up in parade order, 4,991 men in all: 2,139 British, 2,022 Germans, 830 Canadians. Gates spared them the humiliation of being observed by the Americans. Only two American officers watched as the soldiers, to the beating of drums, stacked their arms, emptied their cartridge boxes, and marched off as prisoners of war to head for Boston.

Burgoyne, immaculately uniformed, presented his sword to General Gates. Lieutenant Digby of the Fifty-third Foot recorded the scene:

> "The fortunes of war, General," Burgoyne said, "have made me your prisoner."
>
> "I shall always be ready," Gates replied politely, "to bear testimony that it has not been through any fault of your Excellency."

Gates returned Burgoyne's sword and invited him to be his guest at dinner—a menu of plain field rations washed down with watered New England rum, served at a table made of two planks laid across beef barrels.

When General Howe reached Philadelphia on September 25, he received from Clinton a copy of a dispatch from Burgoyne already blaming Howe for his precarious predicament. On the eve of capturing Philadelphia, Howe had to face the fact that he had gone to an enormous effort to bring his army to the wrong place at the wrong time. The decision virtually to ignore Burgoyne's advance had been Howe's, regardless of Germain's and the king's approval.

On October 21, news of Burgoyne's surrender reached Howe. He at once wrote Germain a lengthy dispatch of recapitulation, justification, explanation—and finally, his resignation.

In London, the days of the early fall wore on without definitive news from Burgoyne or even much news from America at all. Tensions mounted; rumors flew. Germain sent a note to the king, saying that "Lt. General Burgoyne's situation is bad, but it is to be hoped not so very bad as reported by the rebels."

Parliament was due to reconvene on November 20. What would the king say in his opening speech from the throne? There was still no word of what was happening to Burgoyne. On the appointed day, all the king could say was that there were hopes "of an important success" in America.

Lord Chatham once again struggled into the House of Lords to speak. After listening to the king, he lashed the government for "proclaiming its unalterable determination to pursue measures which had already brought ruin to our door." He thundered warnings of the French preparations to enter the conflict. He predicted disaster ahead and called for an end to the war:

> In three campaigns we have done nothing and suffered much. Howe had been obliged to withdraw from New York. Burgoyne's army has met with reverses and might at this very moment be a total loss. What more is to come we could not know. But one thing could be known now: We could not conquer America. . . . We could not conciliate America by our present measures, nor subdue her by any measures. What then could we do?
>
> Parliament must interpose. We could recommend to the King an immediate cessation of hostilities, and the commencement of a treaty to restore peace and liberty in America, strength and happiness in England, security and prosperity to both countries.

Chatham's call for an end to the war, coming as it did before the news of Saratoga was known in London, gave a prophetic voice and vigor to the opposition.

Twelve days later, the stunning news of Burgoyne's surrender arrived. On the evening of Tuesday, December 2, at nine o'clock, a ship's officer rushed into the Admiralty with a dispatch for the first lord, the earl of Sandwich. It reported that Burgoyne's entire army had stacked its arms and gone as prisoners of war to Boston. At nine-fifteen, Sandwich wrote a hasty note to King George:

> It is with much concern that Ld. Sandwich sends to your Majesty the unpleasant account that has just been received by Captain Mountray of the *Warwick* from Tulbeck. Captain Mountray is now here, and if your Majesty chooses to be troubled tonight Lord Sandwich will come with him to Queen's House immediately.

Chatham's warnings had come true, and for England the whole character of the war had changed. Next day in the House of Commons, Charles James Fox and Colonel Isaac Barré began an attack on Germain, as the architect of the disaster, that would go on for months. A shaken Lord North declared his "sorrow at the unhappy news" and hinted obliquely that he was considering resigning.

At ten-thirty on the morning of December 4, the king penned a soothing note to North:

> I cannot help taking up your time for a few minutes to thank you in the most cordial manner for your speech; the manly, firm and dignified part you took brought the House to see the present misfortune in true light, as very serious but not without remedy. . . . I shall only add that I can never forget the friendship as well as the zeal you have shown me by your conduct yesterday.

Lord North immediately forgot about resigning. His reply, written at eleven that morning, was carried to Buckingham House by royal messenger:

> I trust that I am incapable of abandoning your Majesty's service in time of difficulty whilst my continuance of it can be of any use to your Majesty or the Public, but what I submitted, or meant to submit is, that if a storm should arise upon the late misfortunes, which may be appeased by a change of Ministers, no considerations of favor or predilection should make your Majesty persist in your resolution of keeping or excluding any set of men whatsoever.

On hearing the news of Saratoga, Rockingham, believing that peace would now have to come, wrote to Edmund Burke, "My dear Burke, My Heart is at Ease."

When General Sir William Howe's letter of explanation and resignation, sent on October 21, reached Lord George Germain, he forwarded it to the king with the comment that "Sir William Howe's complaint of want of support is very unjust, but his desire of being recalled does not come unexpected."

The commanders would change, and the war would go on.

Chapter 17

A NEW WAR FOR ENGLAND

Burgoyne's surrender at Saratoga changed the whole character of the war for England, except for one crucial aspect: King George III's implacable determination never to concede American independence, never to contemplate the loss of any part of his empire. The near certainty of an enlarged war with its traditional enemy, France, and perhaps Spain as well seemed only to strengthen the king's unyielding stance toward the Americans.

Lord North, increasingly pessimistic that the war could be won, turned to what seemed to be the only course open to him. On December 4, 1777, two days after the news of Saratoga reached London, he dispatched a secret agent to Paris to contact the American commissioners there, Benjamin Franklin and Silas Deane. The agent's instructions were to explore the possibilities for ending the war.

The man chosen by Lord North for this mission was Paul Wentworth, an American from New Hampshire who had once served as that colony's agent in London. He had settled in London and got himself elected to the House of Commons. He was a successful stockbroker and speculator, a businessman who moved regularly between Amsterdam and Paris. He appears to have been on the English secret service payroll (earning two hundred pounds a year) while he was still agent for New Hampshire.

In charge of the secret service at the time was William Eden, an able and influential undersecretary in the Southern Department. It was he who drew up the instructions for Wentworth's mission to Paris.

Lord North kept this mission secret from his entire cabinet, Lord George Germain in particular. The king was informed; he had no objection to the idea of making peace—as long as it was peace without independence. The king was very skeptical that any peace could be reached with Franklin and wrote to North that "[t]he many instances of the inimical conduct of Franklin towards this country makes me aware that hatred to this country is the constant object to his mind."

Wentworth arrived in Paris on December 10 and unwittingly gave Franklin a timely opportunity to use the British approach for his own diplomatic endgame.

Double-dealing was rife in Paris. Franklin assumed, correctly, that his movements and the comings and goings of visitors to his home in Passy were being observed by the French police and that his mail was probably being intercepted as well. This had happened to him in London and had troubled him hardly at all. He was careful in his activities and secretive when he needed to be. What he did not know was that his personal private secretary at the American Commission, Edward Bancroft of Massachusetts, had become an English agent, apparently recruited much earlier by Paul Wentworth. Bancroft was regularly passing on to London weekly reports of Franklin's activities and secret intelligence about ship departures for America and, in particular, what cargoes those ships carried.

For more than a year, Franklin had been urging the French toward recognition of American independence and an alliance, but until that December he had been more successful in winning social attention and the applause of the Paris salons than he had been at gaining the backing of the French court. With victory at Saratoga, this was about to change.

On December 6, 1777, King Louis XVI had written *"Approuvé"* on a cabinet paper submitted to him by his foreign minister, the comte de Vergennes. The paper proposed that France inform the Americans of a willingness "to entertain proposals" for an alliance. Conrad-Alexandre Gérard of the French Foreign Ministry visited

Franklin at Passy to inform him of this decisive turn of events. Franklin began a draft of proposals at once.

On December 12, Franklin took a carriage to an address in Versailles, where another carriage picked him up and took him to a rendezvous with Vergennes and Gérard. At this meeting, Vergennes assured Franklin of the sincerity of the proposal but told him that the king did not wish to act without a similar agreement by Spain. It would take a courier about three weeks to travel to Madrid and back.

Meanwhile, Wentworth had arrived in Paris and requested Bancroft to arrange a meeting with Franklin. Instead, he was told to take up whatever business he had with Silas Deane. Franklin, who knew Wentworth from his days in London, decided to keep his distance and not arouse the French.

Wentworth had been instructed by Eden to ask questions and take soundings but not to make any proposals. He was to tell the Americans that "the original pretensions of the war are certainly moderated" and that there would be good prospects for ending it if the Americans "were prepared to revert to their old connection on new grounds." He was also instructed to express London's hope that America would not wish to "rest its future in the hands of France," an alien country without the common bonds of blood, language, and constitution that existed between England and America.

On December 15, Wentworth arranged a dinner meeting with Silas Deane. There he presented the "talking points" provided by Eden. These covered much the same ground as had the seventeen "Hints for Conversation" prepared three years earlier by Franklin. They had been rejected by the English then and were no more successful now with the Americans as a basis for settlement.

Deane told Wentworth quite firmly that the Americans would never give up independence. He suggested that England declare a cessation of hostilities, withdraw the forces from the colonies, and appoint a commission to negotiate with the American Congress on a basis for future Anglo-American relations.

Wentworth returned for another meeting with Deane on December 17. This time, they discussed at length the commercial, financial, and other arrangements that might form part of a settlement. They left the question of independence aside.

On December 17, at the same time that Wentworth was talking with Deane, Gérard called on Franklin to confirm that France intended to recognize American independence—but they were still awaiting word from Madrid.

On December 27, Wentworth met with Bancroft, who told him, correctly and emphatically, that an acknowledgment of American independence was an absolute, the first requisite to any understanding with England. He added that London must be told that a speedy response was now urgent. Wentworth immediately informed London that France and Spain were preparing to recognize American independence within six weeks and begin war with Great Britain. Foolishly, he urged Eden that it would be wise to promise the American commissioners *anything*, whether the promises could be kept or not.

But Wentworth's reporting was wordy and imprecise. Lord North had already complained to Eden that he had to spend hours reading Wentworth's reports and couldn't make any sense of them. Further, the king was refusing to take seriously the intelligence from Wentworth and Bancroft. The king dismissed the pair as "stockjobbers" and even speculated that they might be planting intelligence to influence the stock exchange. Of Wentworth's warning concerning the Franco-American alliance in the making, the king wrote to North:

> I have read the very voluminous and undigested letters from Mr. Wentworth whose productions I confess it is hard labor to wade through; from which I collect that he has been too precipitate of war as immediate. . . . Though French ministers wish to avoid it, yet they will not leave off their dealing with the Rebels, by which they every day may be drawn into what they do not desire.

This was wishful thinking on the part of the king, to say the least.

In Paris, meanwhile, rumors were spread (probably by the English) that the Americans were coming to an agreement with England to end the war. Franklin waited, seemingly aloof from the whole affair.

On December 31, Vergennes received word from Madrid that Spain declined to act with France in granting recognition to the Americans. For Franklin, this posed a serious question. Would France act alone, or would recognition and the alliance be called off? Franklin believed in Vergennes's sincerity, but he knew that there were other influences in the French court with no great love for the idea of democracy and independence for the colonies. Yet if France ended discussions at this point, the Americans would be thrown back on their own resources. They might even be forced back into the arms of King George.

After pondering the situation for several days, Franklin decided to prod the French. Having avoided Wentworth for nearly a month, he sent word to the British agent that he would see him on January 6. Franklin knew the French would be aware of the meeting; he intended it. He would leave it up to Vergennes to debate the implications. . . . Was Franklin weakening? Were the Americans getting serious in their discussions with the English?

What actually happened, according to Wentworth's account, was that Franklin was totally unyielding. Franklin did most of the talking and went on in a lengthy, rambling, at times heated harangue about England's behavior toward the colonies. He dismissed Eden's suggestions and talking points as "interesting but too late," and he recalled that he had been through these discussions before, with Dr. Fothergill, Admiral Howe, and Lord Hyde. When Wentworth suggested that a safe-conduct could be arranged so that Franklin might go again to London for talks, Franklin's response was "to work himself up into passion and resentment." Once again, Wentworth was left with no doubt that there could be no agreement unless American independence was the starting point.

The meeting between Franklin and Wentworth posed questions for the French. How strong would the Americans be if France were to falter, to delay recognition because of Spain? The French did not wait and worry for long. The day after "observing" Franklin's meeting, King Louis's council of ministers voted to proceed with the treaty of alliance if satisfaction could be obtained from Franklin on several questions. On January 8, Gérard returned to Franklin's residence at Passy. He handed over the list of questions and then left for an hour to give Franklin and the commissioners time to compose their answers.

Most important was the French request for "satisfaction" that the Americans would not enter into any separate "new connection" with England. Franklin wrote this response:

The Commissioners have long since proposed a treaty of amity and commerce, which is not yet concluded. The immediate conclusion of that treaty will remove the uncertainty they are under with regard to it, and give them such a reliance on the friendship of France as to reject firmly all propositions made to them of peace from England which have not their basis for the entire freedom and independence of America, both in matters of government and commerce.

In his skillful diplomatic wording, Franklin did not act as a suppliant giving a guarantee to France. He spoke as an equal who was ready to assume an equal treaty obligation while retaining eventual freedom of action toward England for the new American state.

Gérard returned and did not conceal his pleasure at Franklin's answer. Grandly, he informed the Americans that in the light of Franklin's assurances, he was at liberty to state that King Louis had given his word that a treaty could now be concluded.

It took until early February to complete drafting the texts of the separate treaties of alliance and commerce between France and America. The treaties were signed on February 6, subject to ratification by the Continental Congress.

Meanwhile, Bancroft, making full use of his position as Franklin's private secretary, had been sending on the substance of the texts to London. It was not until March 13, however, that the French ambassador formally notified His Britannic Majesty that France, through a treaty of commerce, had recognized the independence of the United States of America. The ambassador left immediately for Paris; Lord Stormont, the English ambassador, was summoned home from Paris even though war had not yet been declared.

The treaties crossed the Atlantic, arriving on May 2. Congress ratified them on May 4. On June 14, 1778, England formally declared a state of war with France. Four days later, General Sir Henry Clinton began a massive withdrawal of more than ten thousand troops from Philadelphia and began moving them to New York.

Franklin had achieved a diplomatic success the equal of the military victory at Saratoga.

By late December 1777, it had become evident in London from Wentworth's reports that the secret talks with Franklin and Silas Deane were getting nowhere and that a Franco-American alliance was imminent. North's close adviser, William Eden, therefore proposed that North take a new tack when Parliament reconvened. He urged that the government make public its proposals for ending the war and send another peace commission to America. The commission would carry with it a Conciliatory Plan, approved by Parliament, offering to clean out of the statute books all the parliamentary acts made since 1763 to which the colonies had objected—but the colonies must then rescind or abandon the Declaration of Independence. North agreed with this idea, and under Eden's direction drafting began in secret on legislation for another peace mission to America.

Eden also urged North to reorganize his cabinet, bring in some moderates from the opposition, and find a way of easing out George Germain. North, anxious to end the American war before France entered it and desperate to be rid of his own office, readily adopted Eden's advice. But he still had to deal with the implacable King George III.

The king was far from blind to the need for change after Saratoga. He was active, as always, deeply involved in the details of the strategic decisions as the "new" war unfolded in 1778. He recognized that changes would have to be made in the overall strategy, in the military commands, and in the deployment of the Royal Navy and England's limited military manpower overseas. But he adamantly rejected any ideas that England should give up what many were calling "the unwinnable war" in America and concentrate on fighting the French. Instead, the king constantly bombarded his harassed and overworked Lord North, who was beginning to slip into bouts of melancholia, with endless imperious messages, rigorously exhorting him to stiffen the fight and not give in to either political opposition or military setbacks:

> It has ever been a certain position with Me that Firmness is the Characteristick of an Englishman, that consequently when a Minister will shew a resolution boldly to advance, he will meet with support. If on the opening of the Session [of Parliament] the Speech from the Throne is penned with firmness . . . and Ministers in their speeches shew that they will never consent to Independence of America, and that the assistance of every man will be accepted on that ground, I feel certain that the cry will be strong in their favour.

King George was nearly forty years old; he was in the seventeenth year of his reign and at the peak of his success in centering and exercising the power of rule from the throne. He could reject or refuse realities that Lord North had to live with: the growing opposition to the war, the military reality of Saratoga, the new enemies surfacing in Europe—and the burden of directing a war when he had no stomach for the fight.

The king was scornful of North's wish to strengthen his cabinet and the government's position in the House of Commons by bringing into office some of the opposition:

> No consideration in life shall make me stoop to [accepting] opposition; I am still ready to accept any part of them that will come to the assistance of my present efficient ministers; but whilst ten men in the Kingdom will stand by me, I will not give up myself into bondage; I will rather risk my Crown than do what I think personally disgraceful; whilst I have no wish but for the good and prosperity of my country, it is impossible that the nation shall not stand by me; if they will not, they shall have another King, for I will never put my hand to what will make me miserable in the last hours of my life.

When Lord North proposed to defuse the growing opposition by dispatching another peace commission to America, the king commented sourly that "experience has convinced me that this Country gains nothing by granting her Dependencys indulgences, for opening the Door encourages a desire for more, which if not complied with causes discontent that the former benefit is obliterated."

Over and over again, he assured North and other ministers that "firmness" and "chastisement" alone would bring the colonies "to return to duty," and that "I am resolved to shew the world that neither Zeal, Activity nor Resolutions are wanting in me, when times require it, to forward with the greatest expedition every measure that can be necessary for the Security or Honour of my Dominions."

The king's attitude kept the war going for another four years, and Lord North was virtually a prisoner to the king in all this. North had great ability, political skills, and a capacity for hard work, but he was not a war leader. He felt weighted down by a sense of incapacity and irresolution. With great honesty and much pain, he told this to the king—over and over again. His entreaties to be released became more and more pathetic.

* * *

During the Christmas recess, after receiving the news of Saratoga, opposition members of Parliament had been actively writing back and forth and dining with one another, hoping to form a unified, decisive front against continuing the American war. The factional oppositionists had thus far failed to throw any united, collective weight against a war they had all opposed in varying degrees ever since the days of the Stamp Act. They failed in part due to their personal and political disagreements and rivalries and in no small degree to the king's absolute refusal to either treat with any of the group directly or let Lord North resign.

Perhaps the biggest political change after Saratoga was the simple fact that backing independence for America was no longer taboo; independence was, in fact, considered increasingly inevitable. Rockingham and his lieutenant, Edmund Burke, had begun discussing a plan to call for Great Britain's immediate and unconditional recognition of independence of her American colonies. The duke of Richmond prepared a similar motion for the House of Lords.

There was, however, one towering figure in the Whig opposition who clung resolutely to his previous views, and that was Chatham. His position—simple but impossible—was to end the war, yes, but recognize American independence? Never! Paradoxically, Chatham was now closer in agreement with the king's inflexible stance than he was with that of his own party. Further, Chatham's position made it logical for North to approach him about joining the government.

Rockingham wrote to Chatham in late January, not proposing independence but simply that they join forces to demand parliamentary inquiry into the "causes, mismanagements, disasterous state and impending ruin of the country." Chatham's response was brusque. He could not possibly cooperate with the Rockingham faction, which was also supporting independence. Hopes of a united stance evaporated.

The House of Commons returned on January 20, 1778, from Christmas recess. Lord North had promised its unhappy members that he would lay before them "a plan for treating with the Americans," but the atmosphere of national crisis had worsened. Parliamentary opposition was gaining in vigor and votes; North's fractious cabinet was ready to come apart over the conduct of Lord George Germain before, during, and after Saratoga. Faced with this unrest, North became even more secretive.

The cabinet crisis came to a head in mid-February when Lord Bathurst, the lord chancellor, suddenly informed North that he was resigning. Bathurst protested Germain's rudely worded draft of an order to General Howe, relieving him of his command in Philadelphia. Bathurst was a friend of Howe's and detested Germain.

Lord North immediately wrote the king, warning that the government was about to fall. In a memorandum dated February 16, North informed the king that Bathurst intended to resign and that "this is expected from other quarters." He urged the king "to turn his thoughts to some plans for alterations in the administration . . . such measures will certainly become necessary in a short time." Then he opened up the question of calling in the earl of Chatham: "There is no doubt if a change of administration should become requisite, Lord Chatham is, of all the opposition, the person who would be of most service to His Majesty, and probably the least extravagant in his demands."

The king disagreed. At first, he merely urged Lord North to persuade Bathurst to withhold his resignation. Germain, he suggested, should write a more soothing letter to General Howe. For the moment, the king ignored the suggestion concerning Chatham.

On February 17, the prime minister introduced his hitherto secret peace-commission proposal and Conciliation Plan in the House of Commons. It was greeted with stunned amazement by the ranks of government supporters. The opposition welcomed it with taunts and jeers, for it amounted to an ignominious surrender of practically everything North had supported and the British Army had fought for since 1763. The commission would go to America, hat in hand, empowered to end hostilities, reduce British forces, and suspend any and all acts relating to the colonies that had been passed since 1763, even the tax on tea—provided the Americans give up independence. Whatever the jeers, it passed by a voice vote.

Then, on March 13, the French ambassador formally advised the British government that France had recognized American independence and had signed a treaty of commerce with America. North began to press the king hard to send for Chatham and reorganize the government. On March 15, after Lord Stormont had been recalled from Paris, North wrote to the king with unusual vehemence:

The present Ministry cannot continue a fortnight as it is, and there is nothing which seems so likely to stem the first violence of the storm as sending to Lord Chatham. If his Majesty cannot consent to that, Lord North is afraid the whole system will break up and his Majesty be in a short time more at the mercy of the opposition than he would be at that of Lord Chatham if he were now invited to take the lead of affairs. Lord Chatham would certainly be more reasonable than Lord Rockingham's party.

Lord North sent this message at noon. That same afternoon, a messenger returned from the king:

I declare in the strongest and most solemn manner that though I do not object to your addressing yourself to Lord Chatham, yet you must acquaint him that I shall never address myself to him. . . . I cannot consent to have any conversation with him until the Ministry is formed. . . . I will, as he supports you, receive him with open arms. . . .

Having said this I will only add . . . that no advantage to this ministry nor personal danger can ever make me address myself for assistance to Lord Chatham or any other branch of the Opposition; honestly I would rather lose the Crown I now wear than bear the ignominy of possession of it under their shackles.

But North was so desperate to force the king's hand that he continued to communicate with Chatham, using Eden as intermediary. Chatham insisted that he must confer with the king himself, "in order that plans not be misrepresented." He expected to be a minister with access to the king; he must have "the appearance of forming a Ministry," and he would name "efficient men" to fill the high offices. He refused to serve in a ministry with Lord George Germain. When Chatham's terms were conveyed to the king, he responded brusquely that they were "totally contrary to the only ground upon which I would have accepted the services of that perfidious man." North pleaded that "it has become next to impossible to carry on government." But carry on is what he was forced to do.

If pursuit of victory was the king's course, the question was, How? In reviewing strategy, the cabinet had been informed by senior military men that another thirty thousand troops would probably be needed to subdue the colonies. Facing a new war with France, the Royal Navy was undermanned and the crews undertrained, and too many of its vessels were too old for the rigors of continuous sea duty.

On March 25, 1778, Lord North summoned up his courage and wrote to the king with extraordinary bluntness on the outlook for England:

> The condition of this country as in its [naval and military] faculties is deplorable; it is totally unequal to a war with Spain, France and America, and will, Lord North Fears, be over-matched if it is the contention of only the House of Bourbon. Therefore He owns that he should be glad if an accommodation with America would prevent for the present moment a war with France, as he thinks that Great Britain will suffer more in war than her enemies. He does not mean by defeats, but by an enormous expense, which will ruin her and will not in any degree be repaid by the most brilliant victories. Great Britain will undo herself while she thinks of punishing France.

In this same memo, North went on to say—yet again—that change must take place in the government "in a short time" and that it must affect both the composition of the government and its policies:

> Lord North begs leave to trouble His Majesty on a subject in which he is bound to speak the truth, the bad situation of affairs will be attributed to the obstinate perseverance in the American war. Ld. North's diffidence of himself is grounded upon seven years' experience, and will for ever render it fatal to His Majesty to continue him at the head of affairs. In short, peace with America and a change in the Ministry are the only steps which can save this country. Lord North, having said this much, is silent, but this much he could not, with peace of mind, refrain from saying.

Lord North was only telling the king what Chatham, Fox, Burke, and many others were already saying in public. The king, however, ignored the prime minister's appeal and wrote North that "if you decline continuing, you cannot I suppose refuse presiding at the Treasury and finishing the business of this Parliament." North replied at once, meekly reiterating his wish to be released but assuring the king that he "would certainly obey his Majesty's commands by continuing in his present office to the end of the Session of Parliament."

Early in April, the duke of Richmond announced that he would introduce in the House of Lords a motion to recognize American independence. Hearing this, Chatham at once sent word that he wished to speak. The date was fixed for April 7.

The Chatham who arrived to speak that day was a gaunt, shattered remnant of a man. He shuffled in, supported by his second son, the younger William Pitt. Only his piercing eyes gave life to his appearance. In a voice that could scarcely be heard, he rose and said he rejoiced that the grave had not yet closed in upon him before he could come and declare that he would never consent to deprive the king of his "fairest inheritance." He did not know the condition of England's preparedness for war, he said, but if there could not be peace with honor, then war should begin against the French immediately: "If we must fall, let us fall like men." When he finished speaking, he sank back into his seat, exhausted.

Richmond rose to respond. Suddenly, Chatham slumped over in a deep faint and had to be borne hastily from the chamber. The Lords, stunned and silent, suspended further business and adjourned. A carriage took Chatham to his country home at Hayes, where he died on May 11, aged seventy.

The king remained vindictive to the end. When the House of Commons voted for a public funeral and a monument to Chatham in Westminster Abbey, the king wrote sourly to Lord North, "This compliment, if paid to his general conduct, is rather an offensive measure to me personally." The nation paid its tribute anyway.

Shortly afterward, the king wrote to North, asking, "May not the exit of Lord Chatham incline you to continue at the head of my affairs?" Since the other competent political leaders were almost all open supporters of American independence, they were unacceptable to the king. There was no one but North to head the government. Thus, with Chatham's death, North's thralldom to the king became unbreakable.

In Montreal after the defeat at Saratoga, General Sir Guy Carleton was waiting for "ice out" on the St. Lawrence River so he could return to London. He had sent a caustic letter of resignation to Germain, saying, "An officer entrusted with the supreme command ought, upon the spot, to see what is the most expedient to be done, better than a great General at three thousand miles away." This saber thrust at Germain's military career and his court-martial over Minden could hardly pass unnoticed.

In Cambridge, Major General John Burgoyne was a prisoner of war, living with the freedom of his personal parole but with nowhere to go. He was impatiently petitioning General Washington and the Congress for permission to return to London, where he intended to deal with Lord George Germain over the responsibility for the disaster at Saratoga. Meanwhile, his army, which had been disarmed and marched to Boston, sat in cantonments awaiting transport back to England.

In Philadelphia, General Sir William Howe had disregarded his subordinates' suggestions after Saratoga and refused to venture out in the bitter 1777–78 winter weather to attack Washington's ragged army at Valley Forge. Having failed for more than two years to win a decisive victory over Washington, Howe decided that to attack Valley Forge offered no certainty of success and would be a waste of manpower and supplies. He spent the winter enjoying the comforts of Philadelphia and the hospitality of Loyalists there while he waited for Germain to reply to his request to be relieved of his command.

By the middle of 1778, all three generals would be back in London and unburdening themselves of the iniquities dealt them at the hand of Lord George Germain.

The king, though he refused to consider American independence, was quite realistic about the changed military and strategic dimensions of the war. On January 13, he had sent a memo to Lord North in which he suggested that Lord Jeffrey Amherst, his favorite general,

be examined in the Cabinet . . . he is clear that after the disaster of Burgoyne, not less than an additional army of what is there at present 40,000 men can carry on with any effect as an Offensive Land War; that a Sea War is the only wise plan, and the preventing of the arrival of Military Stores, Clothing, and the other articles necessary from Europe must distress [the Americans] and make them come into what Britain may decently consent to; that at this hour they will laugh at any proposition.

But Amherst firmly declined the king's appeal that he return to America. As an alternative, the king instructed him to sit in on all cabinet discussions of the war, Amherst functioning, in effect, as defense chief of staff.

Four days after receiving this memo, Lord North called a cabinet meeting. It was quickly agreed that "under our present circumstances the future operation must be principally Naval." The army would act defensively, holding Canada, Nova Scotia, Rhode Island, New York, the Floridas, "and if possible Philadelphia." The army would also conduct raids on the smaller ports and coastal towns to stifle commerce and, as King George put it, bring the rebels to their senses. Germain began preparing orders for General Sir Henry Clinton on how he was to conduct the war in 1778.

The new orders were dispatched on March 8, before France entered the war. Clinton was ordered to proceed to Philadelphia and take over command from Howe. (Howe's request to be relieved of command had been granted, and he was to return to London.) Clinton was told that he could not expect any troop reinforcements from England until late in the year. But he was also ordered to bring General Washington's army into battle and defeat it—a success that had eluded Howe for more than two years. If he needed additional troops for this, he was authorized to abandon Philadelphia and withdraw the ten-thousand-man British force to New York. Finally, Clinton was to prepare plans for an attack on Georgia and the Carolinas in autumn 1778, by which time the reinforcements would have arrived from England. He was also to send reinforcements to Canada and Halifax. The orders were, in short, indecisive and called for a strategy of dispersal rather than a concentration for an offensive.

The frigate bearing Clinton's new orders had barely cleared Lands End when the government received the official word of France's treaty with the Americans. The British now faced war with France. An entirely new set of orders was hastily prepared for General Clinton.

England was back on familiar terrain in dealing with France. The English mental and strategic compass needle swung immediately to the West Indies, a rich prize for both nations. England's trade with the West Indies was, at that time, far greater than her trade with India, and it had to be protected.

Even if England could not strike directly at France, she could attack the French possessions in the West Indies. Admiral Lord Howe's fleet was in American waters and could be reinforced and dispatched to the Caribbean. The important thing was to get a naval force into those waters before the French fleet there could be reinforced.

New orders were hastily drawn up for Admiral Howe and General Clinton and sent out on March 21. Clinton was now told to give up Philadelphia, withdraw to New York, and dispatch five thousand of his troops to attack the island of St. Lucia, south of the key French possession, Martinique. Another three thousand troops were to be transferred to St. Augustine and Pensacola, Florida, for possible deployment in the Caribbean. More reinforcements were to be sent by Clinton to Halifax to secure the British fleet's headquarters. Howe was instructed to send four of his heavily gunned ships of the line, three fifty-gun vessels, and four frigates to the Leeward Islands to support the operation to take St. Lucia with the army.

The sweeping change of focus for operations in America would curtail, without actually abandoning, the possibility of the Royal Navy blockading the American coast. Clinton's army would be reduced to limited holding operations, with little or no prospect of engaging Washington's forces. The change would also leave the American coast open to the French fleet.

The orders were prepared in great secrecy by Germain, Sandwich, and Lords North and Weymouth. The king was, of course, fully informed and involved. Sandwich himself wrote out the instructions to Admiral Howe, so not even the supervising Admiralty Board knew what was planned.

In a personal dispatch to Admiral Howe, Lord Amherst elaborated on the new strategy: "The object of the war now being changed, and the contest in America being a secondary consideration, our principle object must be distressing France and defending His Majesty's possessions [in the West Indies]."

Three weeks after the new orders went out, important intelligence from the British ambassador to The Hague reached London. The ambassador had been informed by an Amsterdam banker with good friends in the shipping business that the French fleet at Toulon, under its newly appointed commander, the comte d'Estaing, was preparing to put to sea. Its destination was unknown. London reacted by immediately dispatching the Royal Navy sloop *Prosperine* from Plymouth to Gibraltar, with orders to track the French fleet if it ventured out of the Mediterranean. If the French fleet did leave the Mediterranean, would it turn north toward England or west toward America and the Caribbean? The intelligence would be crucial. If d'Estaing joined up the Toulon fleet with the Atlantic fleet at Brest, the French would have a decisive superiority over the Royal Navy in any action fought in the Channel.

The Toulon fleet sailed past Gibraltar in the first days of May. The *Prosperine* followed the French for several days until, by May 13, its captain was satisfied that d'Estaing was heading toward America. The *Prosperine* crowded on sail to hasten to Plymouth with the news. The Admiralty's relief was superseded by its concern over what Admiral Howe's fleet would have to face when the French reached American waters.

France's alliance with the Americans did not long remain a matter of passive friendship but quickly turned into active cooperation.

About the same time the French were sailing from Toulon, Lord North's second peace commission embarked from England.

Eden, whose influence with North was very strong, organized the commission, of which he was to be a member. To act as head of the commission, he chose an amiable lightweight, the earl of Carlisle. He made a shrewd and serious choice in the third man, Benjamin Franklin's old associate Richard "Omniscient" Jackson. But Jackson, after initially agreeing to serve, changed his mind when he learned of the Franco-American treaty. It would be "idle and ruinous," he said, for England to go to war with France, and the only way to forestall this would be to recognize American independence immediately. In his stead, Eden chose George Johnstone, former governor of East Florida, a liberal who was against independence.

As the commission prepared to sail, Eden, in a sudden display of pomposity, decided to give each of the commissioners ambassadorial rank and salary. He asked that they be made privy councillors, but this the king refused on the grounds that General Clinton, under whose care they would be, was not a privy councillor. A Royal

Navy ship, the *Trident,* was assigned to carry the commissioners. Eden insisted that it carry a commodore's pennant to give it superiority over any other Royal Navy ships it might encounter. Further, he asked for permission for his wife to accompany him. This she did, commandeering two cabins on the crowded vessel for herself and four servants. The king commented on all this, "Parade is not the object of the mission, but business."

While the commission sailed slowly across the Atlantic, the precious leather-bound, signed and sealed, true copy of the Franco-American treaty had been landed secretly somewhere in the Delaware Bay. It was rushed to York, Pennsylvania, where the Continental Congress was sitting while the British occupied Philadelphia, arriving on Saturday, May 2. On the Monday following, excited delegates gathered to acclaim the treaty and unanimously approve ratification. One key clause read:

> Neither of the two Parties shall conclude either Truce or Peace with Great Britain, without the formal consent of the other first obtained; and they mutually engage not to lay down their arms, until the independence of the United States shall have been formally or tacitly assured by the Treaty or Treaties that shall terminate the war.

The peace commission knew nothing of this clause before it sailed aboard the *Trident* on April 16. Even so, only a severe case of political myopia could have induced the faintest belief or hope in the mission. Shortly before sailing, William Eden wrote to his brother, "I am given to speculation upon most occasions, but in this it fails me totally; some cool-headed sensible men are very sanguine; others of the same description are equally positive that we shall totally fail; I know that I am in neither extreme of Confidence or Despondency."

As it neared New York on May 27, the *Trident* made contact with another British warship, and the commissioners learned that Admiral Howe and General Clinton were in Philadelphia. The ship changed course immediately. When they reached the Delaware on June 5, they were stunned by the news that Philadelphia was about to be evacuated. The peace commission's titular head, the earl of Carlisle, wrote to a friend that the news was

> calculated to render the Commission both ineffectual and ridiculous. . . . We found to our great surprise all the naval armament collected with evident preparations for the immediate evacuation of

Philadelphia. Immediately upon our landing, Lord Howe and Sir Henry Clinton lost no time to display the embarrassment they were under & the difficulties that were to attend our undertaking. We were greatly astonished to find that they were both under irresistible influence of positive and repeated orders; which orders had industriously been kept a secret from us, tho' sent out long before our departure.

The evacuation orders came as a double shock for Eden, who considered himself a government insider. He immediately wrote an angry letter to Germain, denouncing "the secrecy in the extraordinary change of measures which makes the river at this moment as vast and mortifying a spectacle as any Englishman ever saw."

Eden pleaded with Clinton and Howe to delay the withdrawal, which he believed would throw away a trump card in enticing the Americans to accept his peace offer. But Clinton and Howe were under orders, and they were adamant that once their preparations were completed, the evacuation would not be delayed by so much as one day. Eden wrote bitterly in his diary:

> I consider the silence of the Ministers [concerning the orders to Clinton and Howe] as a Species of Perfidy, which I shall resent no otherwise than by managing a delay in the intended Evacuation sufficient to enable us to state our Proposals fully to the Congress and to gain an Answer from them before this weak story becomes public. In the course of that delay there may be some fortunate Changes of men or Measures in England or both.

Clinton, in addition to evacuating an army of ten thousand men, had also to contend with some three thousand local Loyalists who were up in arms at this sudden desertion by the English and the prospect of being left to the uncertain mercies of the patriots.

Admiral Howe, who had brought the army to Pennsylvania by sea, had reassembled his transports to ship the Loyalists and some of the troops and bulk stores back to New York. But Clinton's main force, due to leave Philadelphia on June 18, would have to march the length of New Jersey. It would be a long, straggling line of soldiers, wagons, horses, guns, and stores. General Washington's army, now rested and rejuvenated, well fed and much better trained after its wretched winter in Valley Forge, would inevitably attack this vulnerable army.

Eden and the commission had less than two weeks in which to convey England's peace offer. Eden put up as brave a front as possible. He addressed a letter to Henry Laurens, president of the Congress. With deference and politeness, he declared that the one wish of the peace commissioners was to "reestablish on the basis of equal Freedom and mutual Safety the tranquillity of this once happy Empire." The letter promised concurrence in "every just arrangement for the cessation of hostilities" and requested a meeting "so that the British states throughout North America acting with us in Peace and War under one Common Sovereign may have the irrevocable Enjoyment of every Privilege, that is, short of a total Separation of Interests." The commission made no demand that the Declaration of Independence be revoked. The shrewd premise of the Conciliation Plan was that if England and America could reach a new agreement, the Declaration of Independence would expire of its own accord. But an agreement "short of a total Separation of Interests" no longer accorded with the American reality.

The tone of Eden's letter was certainly conciliatory. Eden had even cleverly sought to turn the impending evacuation of Philadelphia into a peace gesture. It represented, he said, their "desire to remove themselves from the scene of war." However, the letter's benevolent tone changed when it referred to "the invidious Interposition" of the French. Henry Laurens and the Congress sent in reply a letter that was vigorous and rather curt:

> Nothing but an earnest desire to spare the effusions of human blood would have induced us to read a letter that so reflected upon our ally, the King of France. We are ready, however, to enter upon the consideration of peace whenever the King of England should show us that he has any sincere disposition for that purpose. The only evidence of that sincerity would be an explicit acknowledgment of the independence of these States, or the withdrawing of his fleets and armies.

This letter was waiting for the commissioners when they arrived in New York. It was, in effect, the end of the commission, which nevertheless stayed on in America until October. The commissioners busied themselves with issuing proclamations and public offers of conciliation, actively contacting Loyalists in an effort to build support for their plan in some of the "softer" parts of the colonies.

George Johnstone then embarrassed the other commissioners by opening a private correspondence with Henry Laurens and attempting private bribes in the form of offers of royal honors and emoluments to two prominent members of Congress, Joseph Reed and Robert Morris. When Johnstone's actions became public, Congress refused to receive any further communications from the commissioners. Johnstone sailed promptly for England. The earl of Carlisle and William Eden soon followed.

Eden did not leave America without some regret. He wrote to his brother:

> It is impossible to give you any adequate idea of the vast scale of this country. I know little more of it than I saw in coming 150 miles up the Delaware, but I know enough to regret most heartily that our rulers instead of making the tour of Europe did not finish their education by a voyage around the coasts and rivers of the Western side of the Atlantic. . . . It is impossible to see even what I have seen of this magnificent country and not go nearly mad at the long train of misconducts and mischances by which we have lost it.

Chapter 18

THE SOUTHERN STRATEGY

General Sir Henry Clinton departed from Philadelphia with ten thousand soldiers and fifteen hundred horse-drawn supply wagons. As soon as he knew Clinton was on the march, Washington left Valley Forge in pursuit. Although Washington's army numbered about the same as Clinton's, his supply train was lighter, and he was able to move faster. He crossed the Delaware River into New Jersey and caught up with Clinton's rear guard at Monmouth Court House on June 28, 1778. In one-hundred-degree heat, the armies fought a day-long battle that ended in heat exhaustion—but no victory for either side. Each army lost three hundred to four hundred men. When night finally came, Clinton managed to slip away and cross the Raritan River to the safety of Staten Island and New York. Washington did not attempt pursuit.

After the Battle of Monmouth Court House, the War of Independence lapsed into a two-year period of stalemate. From June of 1778 to May of 1780, there were no major battles, only sporadic, widely scattered fighting of little significance. Clinton had enough troops to hold New York but not enough to chase after Washington. Washington, whose main strategy was to keep his army intact, had no inclination to attack Clinton's defenses around Staten Island

and New York. Both armies sat tight until Clinton finally launched the full-scale southern strategy in the spring of 1780.

The shift to the southern strategy was virtually inevitable. There was neither the willpower nor the manpower to reignite any military offensive in the northern colonies without major reinforcements from England. The southern states were underpopulated and underdefended, the climate was warmer (which might facilitate military operations), and it was judged in London that the people leaned more toward the Loyalist side. Not least of all, with their large black population and abundant crops of cotton and tobacco, these states represented a considerable economic benefit, traditionally trading heavily with England.

Germain had always been an avid believer in the latent strength of the Loyalist sentiment in America—if only it could be harnessed. After considering all the various arguments that came into play after Saratoga, Germain easily persuaded himself that the southern colonies had never really been given a chance to demonstrate their loyalty. Britain should therefore switch the weight of its war effort to the south.

On the advice of his undersecretary, William Knox, Germain determined that the British Army would advance into the south not to "punish the rebellion" nor to conquer or occupy but to restore benevolent English rule. There is a 1778 memo in Germain's papers that reads:

> The great point to be wished for is that inhabitants of some considerable colony were so far reclaimed to their duty that the revival of the British constitution, and free operation of the laws, might without prejudice be permitted amongst them. A little political management would with ease bring about that which will never be effected by mere force.

Restoring the status quo ante would bring prosperity and the enjoyment of life, liberty, and the pursuit of happiness—under King George III. Such was the rationale in London.

The high point for the Loyalists in America was General Howe's occupation of Philadelphia. This was a social rather than a military success. The Tories of Philadelphia, the wealthy upper crust, welcomed the British. Officers moved into the grander homes of Society Hill and in some cases were welcome guests.*

Philadelphia had modeled itself on English elegance and taste; its wealthy Loyalists were pleased to play host, and the British were pleased to accept. For the British officers, the occupation of Philadelphia was one continual party. They were not very busy with military duties during their ten months in Philadelphia, so life quickly became a round of tavern drinking, dancing, gambling, elegant social events in private homes, and amateur theatricals, all with ample female company. General Howe didn't have Gentleman Johnny Burgoyne's ebullient personality and flamboyant style, but he did like a good dinner party with pretty ladies and young officers serving as acolytes. His own mistress, Mrs. Elizabeth Loring, wife of a commissary officer, kept in close attendance.

But below this level, life was far from pleasurable. Billeting ten thousand troops, plus officers and camp followers, was an enormous strain on the city. Prices skyrocketed, shortages developed, city life grew leaden. As the filth and garbage mounted, for most of the population the occupation became a dirty, sullen, quite literally stinking affair.

The State House, where the Declaration of Independence had been signed, became both a prison for American officers and a barracks for the English troops. So bad was the sanitation that the barracks commander, General Pattison, had to issue this extraordinary general order on February 7, 1778:

Notwithstanding the Great Care and attention that has been paid to Render the Barracks Clean and Comfortable, some of the men have been so Beastly as to ease themselves on the Stairs and Lower area of the House between Doors. The Centry is therefore in future to be very attentive (particularly during the night) to put a stop to such scandalous behaviour and immediately to confine any man who shall presume to make use of any other place whatever than the Privy for his Necessary Occasions.

---

*Franklin's home was taken over by the dashing young Captain John André, best known for his later role in Benedict Arnold's treason.

Along with the filth, there was looting. The Hessian foraging parties, which were supposedly looking for firewood and animal fodder, took to foraging in private homes. Benjamin Franklin lost books, a printing press, and a portrait of himself painted by Benjamin West.

To cope with civilian affairs, Joseph Galloway, Philadelphia's leading Loyalist, was appointed by General Howe as "superintendent general" for the city. A successful lawyer, former speaker in the Pennsylvania Assembly, and one-time friend of Benjamin Franklin's, Galloway had made a full turn from patriot to Loyalist.

General Howe's military occupation of Philadelphia ended in a blaze of social splendor with a dazzling, incredibly lavish farewell party given by his officers. It was styled as a *mischianza,* an Italian term for an extravagant medley of tournament jousting followed by music, entertainment, dancing, and an elaborate banquet. The upper crust of Howe's officers, men of wealth and social standing, each contributed to a handsome fund of three thousand pounds to pay the basic expenses. Merchants added to the bill with the silks and fineries for costuming the guests, both men and women. Captain John André was the key organizer and recorded the affair in detail.

The riverside mansion of Joseph Wharton, on the southern edge of the city, with trees and broad lawns sloping down to the Delaware River, was the site chosen for the *mischianza.* The date was set for Monday, May 18, 1778. Some four hundred guests—officers in dress uniforms and the cream of Philadelphia's Loyalists—made their way to the foot of High Street, where Royal Navy barges provided by Admiral Howe were waiting to row the guests down the river to the Wharton estate. British warships fired their guns in salute as the guests disembarked at midafternoon and passed under two enormous arches to the tournament field. Captain André described the jousters' costumes:

The Knight's dress was that worn in the time of Henry the 4th of France: The Vest was of white Sattin, the upper part of the Sleeves made very full but of pink confined within a row of straps of white sattin laced with Silver upon a black edging. The Trunk Hose were exceeding wide and of the same kind with the shoulder-part of the Sleeves. . . . The Horses were caparisoned with the same Colours, with trimmings and bows hanging very low from either ham and tied round their chests.

After an elaborate equine minuet of challenges, the jousting began. Each rider wore the colors of a favorite lady. When the jousting was over, the "knights" dismounted, and the company passed through an honor guard of soldiers from each of the regiments stationed in the city. Massed regimental bands played as the guests walked leisurely through the formal gardens to the mansion. A faro bank was installed for gambling. The dancing began, only to be interrupted at ten o'clock for a fireworks display.

At midnight came the grand climax. Folding side doors in the garden were opened to reveal a banquet hall built for the occasion, covered with an enormous marquee, 210 feet long and 40 feet wide. Two long tables, lit by three hundred tapers, seated 430. Twenty-four black servants in Oriental costumes led the serving of twelve hundred dishes: tureens of soup; a cold collation of chicken, ham, lamb, beef, and veal; Yorkshire pies; salads; and puddings and sweets. After the supper, the guests returned to the mansion to dance until daybreak.

When accounts of the *mischianza* reached London, the *London Chronicle* criticized it as "nauseous" and a demonstration that General Howe preferred "the pleasure of indolence to a discharge of his duty to the country."

Nor did it sit well with Admiral Howe's private secretary, Ambrose Serle, who wrote, "Every man of Sense, among ourselves, tho's not unwilling to pay a due respect, was ashamed of the way of doing it."

Six days after the party, on May 24, General Howe sailed for England. Captain André pronounced the dockside farewell as "even more flattering testimony of the love and attachment of his Army than all the pomp and splendour of the Mischianza could convey to him."

The day after Howe departed, General Clinton summoned Joseph Galloway to inform him officially that the army would evacuate as soon as it could pack up and go. The Philadelphia Loyalists would be left high and dry, just as the Boston Loyalists had been. Ambrose Serle wrote bitterly: "The contest is at an end. No man can be expected to declare for us when he cannot be assured a Fortnight's protection." A shaken Galloway told Serle, "My fortune is gone, and I will have to wander like Cain upon the Earth without Home and without Property." His prophecy was right. After following the British Army back to New York, he eventually made his way to London. He never saw his native city again.

General Sir Guy Carleton reached London in mid-May of 1778, the first of the three commanders in America to return home. He refused to stand as scapegoat for Germain; to make his position quite clear, he refused even to make an official call on Germain or have anything to do with him. By keeping silent and declining to make any political capital out of the affair, Carleton gained whatever vindication he may have sought from the king himself. The king received him cordially and gave him a sinecure governorship that included a generous stipend. This despite protests from Germain, who told Lord North he would regard it as a personal affront if Carleton received any act of royal favor.

Major General John Burgoyne also returned to London in May. But even though he held a seat in the House of Commons and had many influential friends (including Charles James Fox), he came home under circumstances very different from those of Carleton or Howe—he was a paroled prisoner of war.

Under the terms of surrender signed at Saratoga, the British troops were to be sent home on the government's assurances that they would not return to fight. But the Continental Congress objected, saying that the troops could be used to relieve others who could then be sent to the colonies. Congress therefore refused to approve the convention of capitulation, and the troops remained in Boston as prisoners of war.

Burgoyne, however, fell into a somewhat different category. He applied for a personal parole to return to England so that he might seek a court-martial to establish evidence of responsibility for the defeat at Saratoga. In mid-March 1778, Burgoyne received a personal letter from General Washington indicating that the parole would be approved. Washington declared himself

ever ready to do justice to the gentleman and the soldier, esteem where esteem is due, however the ideas of a public enemy may impose. . . . Viewing you in the light of an officer contending against what I conceive to be the rights of my country, the reverse of fortune you experienced in the field cannot be unacceptable to me; but abstracted from consideration of national advantage, I can sincerely sympathize with your feelings as a soldier—the unavoidable difficulties of whose situation forbid his success; and as a man, whose lot combines the calamity of ill-health, the anxieties of captivity and the painful sensibility of a reputation exposed, where he most values it, to the assaults of malice and detraction. Wishing you a safe and agreeable passage, with a perfect restoration of your health, I have the honor, etc. . . .

                                                        G. Washington

Three weeks later, on April 2, Burgoyne signed a formal parole and sailed for England. When he arrived, he went immediately to call upon Germain, who was far less generous with him than Washington had been. Since Burgoyne was a prisoner of war on parole, he was told not to ask to see the king, who would be unable to receive him. Nor could he have a court-martial; instead, he would be heard by a closed committee composed of senior generals.

Germain had, of course, firsthand familiarity with the risks of courts-martial. All the evidence—the official orders and the dispatches—would be produced, and Germain knew that politics could be as damning as the evidence in the verdict. Thus he had lobbied Lord North, other ministers, even the king himself to deny Burgoyne both the returning commander's traditional audience with the king and the court-martial. A review board, which included General Thomas Gage, met a few days after Burgoyne's return and reached an immediate agreement that as long as Burgoyne was a prisoner of war on parole, he could have neither a court-martial nor an official inquiry into the conduct of the Saratoga campaign. So Germain succeeded in bottling up the evidence and silencing Burgoyne.

Except—Burgoyne was a member of the House of Commons. When Germain tried to have Burgoyne barred from the House on the grounds that he was still a prisoner, he got nowhere. Burgoyne took his seat unchallenged. On May 23, Charles James Fox introduced a motion that allowed Burgoyne to make a major statement on Saratoga, telling all—at least, as he saw it. Burgoyne, avoiding any direct criticism of Generals Howe or Carleton, focused on what he contended was the inflexibility of his orders:

> The plan, as it stood when orders were framed, can with no more propriety be called mine, than others formed by the Cabinet for distant parts of America or any other quarter of the globe where I had no participation or concern. . . . By cutting off every proposed latitude and confining the plan to only one object, the forcing of a passage to Albany, the orders framed upon that plan could in no wise be understood than as positive, peremptory and indispensable.

Burgoyne finished by speaking not only for himself but also for Gage, Howe, and Carleton:

> Let it be for the instruction of all those who might be hazardous enough to attempt to serve their country under the auspices of men who are obliged to cover their ignorance and inability, and screen themselves from ignominy and contempt by throwing blame upon men who were unwise enough to act as they were instructed.

In the uproar that ensued, with other members of the Commons joining in the heated debate, Germain challenged a vociferous Burgoyne supporter to an immediate duel. It took all of Lord North's skill to calm things down. A motion for a parliamentary inquiry into Saratoga was defeated 144 to 92. The popular verdict, however, was that Burgoyne was exonerated from the chief blame for the defeat and that Germain was culpable.

Germain's malevolence persisted. On June 5, two weeks after the debate, Burgoyne received orders, written in the name of the king, to return to his imprisoned troops in Boston. He ignored the order and took off instead for an extended health cure at Bath.

General Sir William Howe returned to London at the height of the rumpus over Burgoyne. Although he too was a member of the House of Commons and though he certainly wished to square accounts with Germain, he preferred to wait until his more astute and influential brother got home.

Admiral Howe reached London in October, but not until May of 1779 did a parliamentary committee of inquiry begin hearings. Germain had even summoned Joseph Galloway to testify against the Howes over the evacuation of Philadelphia, but the inquiry reached

no formal conclusions and petered out when Parliament was pro-
rogued in June.

In June 1778, Clinton, back in New York with his army, was faced
with the prospect of carrying out Germain's hodgepodge of orders,
dispatched from London the previous March. But in July, Admiral
d'Estaing and the French fleet appeared off New York. The strategic
picture of the war abruptly changed. The expedition to St. Lucia had
to be delayed. Next, the French sailed on to Rhode Island to support
the Continental Army against the British at Newport. Then d'Estaing headed for Boston to repair his damaged ships. The Royal
Navy, under Admiral Howe, was hardly strong enough to challenge
the French until more ships arrived from England. When at last Admiral John "Foul-Weather Jack" Byron completed a stormy crossing in October, Admiral d'Estaing returned to the Caribbean.
Clinton finally saw the St. Lucia expedition sail in October. With his
army dwindling, in October Clinton wrote to Germain, asking to be
relieved of his command: "You cannot wish to keep me in this mortifying command, a mournful witness of the debility of an army
whose head, had I been unshackled of instructions, might have indulged expectations of rendering serious service to my country."
    With the imbroglio of Burgoyne, Carleton, and the Howe broth-
ers still fresh, Germain could scarcely afford to have yet another dis-
gruntled general come home. So he replied soothingly to Clinton's
resignation request. He told Clinton that "in view of your great
military talents so discoverable in your movements, the King cannot
at present comply with your request." He went on to reassure Clinton that he would do everything in his power to expedite army replacements but that "intelligence we have received of the intentions
of France . . . would not allow of an alternative, and I am persuaded
you will now join in opinion that these measures were unavoidable."

In December 1778, Clinton turned to Germain's orders to seize
Georgia. As a first test of Loyalist support for the southern campaign, Georgia proved easy. The colony, undisturbed by any military action for more than two years, was protected at Savannah by a
patriot force of barely a thousand almost untrained men.
    Clinton selected Lieutenant Colonel Archibald Campbell, an

able, intelligent young Scottish officer, to lead a small force of fifteen hundred men (including two of his own Highland Light Infantry battalions) to a landing near Savannah. The attack date was set for December 29, and a black slave was recruited to guide the men through the swamps to the city. Campbell had no trouble routing the small band of patriots. In his colorful report to Clinton, Campbell called himself "the first officer taking a stripe and a star from the flag of Congress."

The deposed royal governor of Georgia, Sir James Wright, was reinstated in his post and began the attempt to restore colonial rule to its pre-1775 style of operation. Wright was no more successful at this than his peers in Boston, Philadelphia, and New Jersey: Loyalist roots were very shallow, and only the umbrella of the British Army could keep them from shriveling away.

Nevertheless, London took the reinstatement of a royal governor as a welcome augury that all was not lost in America. James Galloway had arrived from Philadelphia and was actively lobbying for the Loyalist cause. He had prepared several optimistic reports on the Loyalists and had submitted these to John Robinson, an influential undersecretary in North's office. These papers were passed on to General Amherst and eventually reached the king. Galloway contended that the middle colonies were all tired of war, that if Philadelphia had not been abandoned these colonies would have "returned to their allegiance." The Loyalists, Galloway said, were strong enough to disarm the rebels if Washington's army could be "driven away." He suggested that the main effort for the coming year be from New Jersey to Virginia.

This, of course, was just what Lord North, Germain, the king, and others in the government wanted to hear. They began preparing southern-strategy plans for 1779, and in January of that year North wrote the king: "Lord North had a long conversation with Dr. Galloway and some others about the present state of America, and has every reason to believe that a campaign conducted with vigor and ability promises the most happy success in this moment."

The orders that Germain issued to Clinton later in January included a little bit of everything—along with assurances of reinforcements of six thousand troops. Clinton was again told that his first task was either to bring the elusive Washington into pitched battle or else "to chase him into the Highlands of New York." Clinton was ordered to raid the coastal towns of New England and the Chesapeake Bay. He was to raise more troops from among the American Loyalists and to pay officers for recruiting, and he was authorized to offer these recruits British Army rank. Finally, he was to launch a full-scale southern strategy with a seaborne expedition to seize Charleston, South Carolina.

Again, Germain had issued helter-skelter orders. Again, there was no certainty that there would be the manpower to carry them out. In April, Clinton replied to Germain in a restrained tone that he didn't believe all the optimism about a Loyalist welcome in the south:

> I have as yet received no assurances of any favorable temper in the province of South Carolina to encourage me as to an undertaking where we must expect so much difficulty. . . . The small force which the present weakness of General Washington's army would enable me to detach might possibly get possession of Charleston . . . but I doubt whether they could keep it. The move would reduce me to the strictest defense in this country [New York].

Even as Clinton tried to make sense of his orders, the European war took a serious turn. In April 1779, the French signed a secret treaty with Spain, under the terms of which Spain would enter the war with a French guarantee to help her recover Gibraltar from the English. The Royal Navy, already stretched thin from the English Channel to the West Indies, would have to face the combined sea power of France and Spain.

When Spain's entry into the war became public, there was another upsurge of opposition and a demand to abandon the draining war in America and concentrate the fighting on the Bourbon alliance. William Eden, back from his unsuccessful peace mission to the colonies, even proposed a secret visit to Benjamin Franklin in the city of Ghent. In June, Sir William Meredith offered a motion in the House of Commons "for an address to the Throne to direct measures for restoring Peace with America." On the eve of the debate on this motion, the king sent a memo to Lord North, rejecting yet again any ideas of a retreat:

> The present Contest with America I cannot help seeing as the most serious in which any country was ever engaged; it contains such a train of consequences that they must be examined to feel its real

weight. Step by step the demands of the Americans have risen—Independence is their object. . . . Should America succeed in that, the West Indies must follow them, not independence but of its own interest be dependent on North America; Ireland would soon follow the same plan and be a separate State; then this Island would be reduced to itself and soon be a poor Island indeed. Her trade merchants would retire with their Wealth to Climates more to their Advantage and leave this Country for the New Empire; consequently this Country has but one Sensible, one great line to follow, the being ever ready to make Peace when to be obtained without submitting to terms that in that consequence must annihilate this Empire, and with firmness to make every effort to deserve success.

Spain's entry into the war entailed a whole new set of calculations for the Royal Navy and the military commanders. But it did not alter in the least the primary aim of King George—quashing American independence at any cost.

While these events were unfolding in Europe, there occurred in America one of those war incidents that had repercussions well beyond its immediate importance.

To keep Washington on the defensive in the Hudson Highlands, in May of 1779, Clinton seized and fortified a rocky outcropping on the Hudson about twelve miles south of West Point. Called Stony Point, it was an important ferry crossing. Clinton installed a garrison of about seven hundred troops to hold this gateway and block Washington from moving south to threaten New York. But six weeks after Clinton's occupation, the Americans struck.

Following very careful, detailed plans and preparations made by Washington, Major General "Mad Anthony" Wayne led a surprise attack on the night of July 15, and completely wiped out the British garrison. Wayne's forces killed sixty-three British soldiers, wounded another seventy, and took all the rest prisoners—a considerable dent in Clinton's army.

What Washington could not have known was how deeply shaken the English commander in chief was by the defeat at Stony Point. Just before the attack, Clinton had written Germain a bitter protest:

When I was ordered to this difficult command, under circumstances much less eligible than those in which it had been undertaken by my predecessor, I was flattered with the hope of having every latitude allowed me as the moment should require. . . . How mortified then I must be, my Lord, at finding movements recommended to my dehabilitated army which your lordship never thought of suggesting to Sir William Howe when he was in his greatest force without an apprehension from a foreign army.

It is true your Lordship does not bind me down to the plan which you have sketched for the ensuing campaign. Your Lordship only recommends. But by that recommendation you secure the right of blaming me if I should adopt other measures and fail.

I am on the spot; the earliest and most exact intelligence on every point ought naturally, from my situation, to reach me. . . . Why then, my Lord, without consulting me, will you adopt the ill-digested or interested suggestions of people who cannot be competent judges of the subject, and puzzle me by hinting wishes with which I cannot agree yet am loath to disregard? For God's sake, my Lord, if you wish me to do anything, leave me to myself and let me adapt my efforts to the hourly change of circumstances!

After the action at Stony Point, Clinton became even more profoundly depressed and wrote to one of his aides, Colonel Charles Stuart, "Let me advise you never to take command of an army. I know I am hated, nay detested, by this army. . . . The minister [Germain] has used me so ill I can no longer bear with this life."

But Germain was the king's most vigorous and unswerving lieutenant in pursuing the war. He had made himself indispensable to the king, and however much he was disliked, regardless of the confusion he created in conducting the war, it was impossible to remove him.

In July of 1779, one of Germain's favorites, General Lord Cornwallis, arrived in New York to become second in command and successor designate to Clinton.

Clinton and Cornwallis had served together for two years under General Howe, and they had often shared similar frustrations and opinions about Howe's caution and generalship. Cornwallis had been regarded as one of Howe's most aggressive, competent subordinates. But he had been allowed to return to England in 1778 and resign his commission. His wife, to whom he was deeply devoted, was very ill; after six months of failing health, she died in February 1779. Cornwallis was devastated nearly to the point of breakdown. But after a few months, he decided to resume his military career. There was no delay in reinstating him; his relations with Germain were quite amicable.

Cornwallis arrived in New York barely a week after Stony Point. Although Clinton had earlier written to Germain "how happy I am made by his Lordship's indefatigable zeal, his knowledge of the country, his professional ability and the high estimation in which he is held by the Army," cordiality between the two officers did not last long. Clinton, shaken by Stony Point, was suspicious and resentful of Cornwallis.

A month after Cornwallis arrived, Clinton sent off yet another letter of resignation to Germain. He wrote:

> To say the truth, my Lord, my spirits are worn out by struggling against the consequences of so many adverse incidents. . . . Had even the feeble reinforcements which I am still expecting arrived as early as I had thought myself secure . . . I should have found myself enabled to attempt measures perhaps of serious consequences. Under my present circumstances, if I have not fulfilled the expectation which may have been indulged for the army, I trust I shall always find the failure attributed to its just cause, the inadequacy of my strength to its object. . . . Thus circumstanced, and convinced that the force under my command at present, or that will be during the campaign, is not equal to the services expected of it . . . permit me to resign the command of the army to Lord Cornwallis.

Clinton told Cornwallis about the letter of resignation. While they waited to hear from Germain, they had nevertheless to make joint plans and decisions. Cornwallis was Clinton's designated successor, but the war wasn't going to wait for Germain's reply. Charleston was the next strategic objective.

During the second half of 1779, a succession of setbacks dogged the British in the Caribbean. In June, in response to the British seizing St. Lucia, French forces in the Caribbean overran a small English detachment holding the island of St. Vincent. In July, the French captured 159 British regulars and 300 militiamen defending the sugar-producing island of Grenada. Then the French took their biggest prize, landing a force of 2,000 and crushing the English at Dominica. They appeared to be preparing to strike at England's jewel of the Caribbean, Jamaica.

Responding to frantic calls for help from Jamaica's governor, Clinton hastily prepared an expeditionary force of two thousand, led by Cornwallis. But just as the transport ships left New York, a Royal Navy dispatch frigate arrived with word that the French fleet, under Admiral d'Estaing, was heading not for Jamaica but back to North American waters. Clinton hastily recalled Cornwallis, and they waited to see where the French navy would appear.

In September, d'Estaing was sighted off the coast of Georgia, preparing to join his twenty ships and five thousand men with the Americans to attack the English garrison at Savannah. The attack, however, was a failure. On land, the British Army professionals escaped an inexperienced American militia's entrapment. French bombardment from the sea turned out to be a waste of ammunition. The Americans tried to besiege Savannah, but this came to nothing. Admiral d'Estaing decided he had spent enough time off the Georgia coast and headed back to the Caribbean to lay over during the hurricane season.

However, the reappearance of the French in American waters sent a warning signal to Clinton. He decided to withdraw the thirty-five hundred troops holding Newport, Rhode Island, and concentrate them with his forces in New York. While this decision was strategically sound, its consequences favored the Americans. It was another withdrawal that left Loyalists in the lurch. Further, it left Newport wide open to later attack by the French.

In September, thirty-eight hundred troops reached New York from England, the first major reinforcements Clinton had received in more than a year. This was considerably less than the six thousand Germain had promised, but when combined with the troops from Rhode Island and another two thousand returning from St. Lucia, Clinton now had enough men to head for Charleston and still leave behind a force large enough to secure New York.

But both Clinton and Cornwallis were waiting to hear from Lord George Germain as to who was to be the commander in chief.

Chapter 19

THE ROAD TO YORKTOWN

At the end of December 1779, a vast convoy of sails cleared New York Harbor for Charleston. General Clinton's army of eight thousand, plus all its animals and ancillary equipment and baggage, was battered mercilessly by storms and gales, snow and icy rain for more than a month. Masts broke, sails shredded, rigging ripped away in the howling winds. Horses, their legs broken by the ships' pitching, had to be destroyed and thrown overboard. Ships began to leak. Two frigates foundered. Transports sank, one of them with all Clinton's artillery pieces aboard. At dark, captains furled the sails, tied down the ship's wheel, battened everything down tight against the pitching and tossing, and drifted with the wind. At daybreak, they had to find one another.

One transport, dismasted during the night, was blown aimlessly eastward with only a four-week supply of food and water. Eleven weeks later, the ship drifted into port at St. Ives, Cornwall, three thousand miles on the other side of the Atlantic.

The battered fleet finally passed the Carolina capes and moored at the mouth of the Savannah River at the end of January. At Tybee Island, the men spent ten days drying out and repairing vessels. Then they made for Seabrook Island, thirty miles south of Charleston, and began disembarking and preparing for the land operations that finally got under way in mid-February. Foraging parties were sent off into the countryside to purchase or seize food and fresh horses. Clinton sent an urgent message to a supply depot on the Caribbean island of St. Kitts, requesting ammunition and artillery and the loan of forty-five heavy guns from the Royal Navy. He prepared to take Charleston by siege rather than direct assault. This meant encircling the city, cutting off all escape routes for Major General Benjamin Lincoln's fifty-five hundred American defenders.

Infantry and cavalry units moved out through the woods and swamps behind the city, but not until April did the British Army cross the Ashley River and cut off the Cooper River north of the city. Charleston was now completely encircled, and the final stage was set.

In the third week of March 1780, a dispatch had finally arrived from Germain for Clinton. His request to be relieved of his command had been turned down. Both Clinton and Cornwallis were unhappy. Germain had written:

> Though the King has great confidence in his Lordship's abilities, His Majesty is too well satisfied with your conduct to see the command of his forces in other hands. . . . You have had too many proofs of His Majesty's favor to doubt of his royal approbation. The reinforcements sent you have been as ample as could be afforded in the present situation of the country.

So much for Clinton's complaints and attempts to resign.

Thus far, Clinton and Cornwallis had been cooperating closely, although somewhat frigidly, in preparing to take Charleston. But Cornwallis now abruptly informed Clinton that he was withdrawing completely from any further role in the commander in chief's operational planning, and he requested an independent command. Clinton boiled over. He accused Cornwallis of "unmilitary conduct" and of spreading malicious gossip and comments that undermined the confidence of other officers. In his private journal, Clinton charged Cornwallis with "unsoldierly behaviour, neglecting to give orders in my absence." For the three weeks during the final preparations for the siege, Clinton simmered and Cornwallis sulked. Finally, in late April, a month after receiving Germain's dispatch,

Clinton transferred Cornwallis to the command of an army corps blocking an escape route northwest of Charleston—an independent command about as far away from general headquarters as Cornwallis could be and still play a role in the final action. The generals' road to Yorktown had begun.

Major General Benjamin Lincoln, the American commander at Charleston, would have done better if he had followed General Washington's example and pulled out at least his trained soldiers before the British trap was sprung, keeping them alive and free to fight again later. But Charleston citizens were demanding that he stay and fight. Lincoln felt he had no choice.

In mid-April, after the Ashley and Cooper Rivers were closed off, Clinton made his first demand for surrender. Lincoln refused. But two weeks later, he tried to bargain for the withdrawal of part of his army and the surrender of the town. The British refused.

On May 8, the British began firing on the city. The heavy shelling started many fires (Clinton later wrote that "it was absurd, impolitic and inhuman to burn a town you intend to occupy") and brought the Americans down. On May 12, General Lincoln surrendered.

Battle casualties were surprisingly few—89 Americans killed and 138 wounded; 76 British killed and 189 wounded—but the Americans surrendered fifty-five hundred Continentals and militiamen plus equipment, muskets, ammunition, and stores on a scale comparable to Burgoyne's losses at Saratoga. The British, with minimum casualties, had won a substantial victory.

Clinton did not linger in Charleston. Without much confidence, he turned over operations in the south to Cornwallis, admonishing him to act prudently, preserve what had been gained at Charleston, and work to restore Loyalist rule. He particularly warned Cornwallis not to outrun his supply lines if he were to advance north into Virginia. He left Cornwallis with four thousand men and the independent command he had longed for.

Then Clinton withdrew with the rest of the army and returned to New York. He knew the French fleet was still a major presence in the Caribbean, and he feared that it might attack New York during the summer.

*   *   *

At last, in London, there was something to cheer about. Things had been especially gloomy for Lord North: In addition to the war against Spain and France, troubles had boiled up in Ireland. And there was unrest in Parliament, even amongst government support-ers, on the state of the economy and the drain of war. North suffered long spells of despondency and inertia. The earl of Suffolk, head of the Northern Department and an ardent supporter of the American war, had died. It took North five months to decide on a replace-ment. North's able undersecretary and close personal adviser, John Robinson, described this period:

> Nothing done or attempting to be done, no attention to the neces-sary arrangements at home, none to Ireland, nothing to India, and very little I fear to foreign affairs, a Cabinet totally disjointed, *hating* I may say, but I am sure not loving each other; never acting with union even when they meet, looking forward with anxiety to the moment of their parting, can never do, can never direct the affairs of the Kingdom. . . . Indeed it must blow up.

But it did not blow up. The king prevented that from happening by refusing Lord North's repeated attempts to resign. (Biographers haven't even tried to count the number of times North tried, during his twelve long years as prime minister, to quit.) The king knew he couldn't find a replacement without giving in to the opposition and giving way on the American war. This was the price any capable successor to North would demand. It was therefore with some jubi-lation that the king wrote to North when the first reports of the victory at Charleston reached London:

> It is fatal experience that every invitation to reconciliation only strengthens the Demagogues in America in their Arts to convince the Deluded People that a little further resistance must make the Mother Country yield; whilst at this hour every account of the Distress of that country shews that they must sue for peace this Summer if no great disaster befalls us. . . . Letters are arrived with news of the surrender of Charleston, occasioned by a bombardment which had destroyed part of the Town; should this be so, the Congress will soon be set aside by the distress of that Deluded People.

*   *   *

Although the government had held a comfortable majority in the House of Commons, by early 1780 there was rising opposition to the war coupled with a spontaneous outcry for domestic reform. This opposition had sprung up, quite unexpectedly, among the conservative country gentlemen, those hundred or so members who were untitled, independent landowning squires. Most of them lived far from London and were beholden to no one. They were secure in their own land and in their seats in the House of Commons. Although they weren't part of the governing aristocracy, the social elite of England, they normally supported the government. Times were changing, however, after four and a half years of war with America and now war with France and Spain as well. The costs were mounting, and the country gentlemen felt that much of the burden was being paid directly from their pockets.* Whig opponents of the American war made common cause with the new Tory radicals to oppose government spending.

A motion was introduced in the House of Commons for full disclosure and parliamentary scrutiny of how the king spent the enormous sums that were voted every year for all the royal sinecures, appointments, and pensions and of the secret lists of royal perquisites given out each year.

Edmund Burke offered a motion to abolish completely the Board of Trade and the American Department, headed by Lord George Germain. Germain was so unpopular that Burke's motion came within an eyelash of passing. It was defeated by only a vote of 208 to 201. Worse lay ahead for Lord North.

On April 6, 1780, a respected backbencher in the Commons, John Dunning, who had been solicitor general in the 1769 Grafton government, introduced a shrewd and extraordinary motion declaring that "the influence of the Crown has increased, is increasing and ought to be diminished." This motion, which would have been unthinkable only a few months before, suddenly attracted wide support. While it had nothing to do with the American war, it had everything to do with the general domestic unrest. It carried by a

---

*They had good reason to think this: In 1775, when the first shots were fired in America, the government collected £276,000 in land-tax revenues. By 1780, in order to pay for the war, the rates had been increased to yield revenues of £2 million.

startling 233 to 215. For the first time, North's government had been defeated.

Lord North was stunned. The House of Commons was showing an entirely new temper. Of course, the first thing North did was tender his resignation to the king. But because the Dunning motion was not against any specific legislation and was not enough to bring down the government, the king told North that "[it] can by no means be looked upon as personal to Lord North." In a letter, the king added:

> There is no means of letting Lord North retire from taking the lead in the House of Commons that will not probably end in evil; therefore till I see things change to a more favourable appearance I shall not think myself at liberty to consent to Lord North's request. He must be the judge whether he can therefore honourably desert me.

So North continued on. But the motion signaled that a notable shift in allegiances had begun to take place. Lord North decided to call a surprise general election for September.

After General Clinton departed for New York, General Cornwallis took full advantage of his independent command. He had operational freedom; more important, he was soon in direct communication with Germain, bypassing Clinton. This did nothing to improve the trust and understanding among the three men.

Cornwallis was aggressive by nature, a commander who was impatient with defensive warfare and determined to go out and fight. Although not much of a strategist, he was effective in battle. It was written of him that "he was a general among soldiers, but a soldier among generals." Nevertheless, he was the commander upon whom the success of the southern strategy now rested.

Initially, he was less skeptical than Clinton about the Loyalists and ready to embrace the wisdom and enthusiasm of Germain in London. He would have to find out the hard way the futility of trying to crush rebellion on the one hand while attempting to rally Loyalist support on the other. He would learn, as had Gage, Howe, Burgoyne, and Clinton before him, not to count on Loyalists.

Many historians have tried to assess the strength of the Loyalists during the American Revolution. John Adams, a hard-nosed patriot if ever there was one, estimated at one point that probably one third of the colonials were Tories and tacitly loyal.* Later, however, when he was trying to borrow money in Holland for the American cause, he assured Dutch authorities that no more than a tenth of the population was Loyalist. There is a consensus that perhaps half a million Americans, about a quarter of the white population, had Loyalist sympathies. Whether or not they openly committed to working or fighting for the British was another matter. Some historians estimate that from 1775 to 1782, upward of thirty thousand Loyalists actually took up arms. But British Army records indicate that the maximum number at any one time was not more than seven thousand.

As the war moved to its climax during 1780–81, the differences between patriots and Loyalists sharpened almost to the point of a civil war within the Revolution. The more the British tried to recruit Loyalists to take up arms, the more dangerous it became to declare openly for England.

Aggressive military campaigning across the South Carolina countryside was hardly calculated to win the hearts and minds of the citizenry. One British cavalry commander whose swashbuckling successes helped change the supposedly benign political climate was Lieutenant Colonel Banastre Tarleton.

Tarleton's hard-riding, hard-raiding British Legion, while certainly useful to Cornwallis, did much to rouse the fighting determination in the south. His raids were usually short, sharp encounters with small patriot detachments, hit-and-run operations in which no quarter was given by the saber-wielding horsemen. Before the summer was out, American cavalry had emerged, matching Tarleton in their own no-quarter hit-and-run raids against small English detachments deployed to secure the backcountry and encourage Loyalist recruiting. The Swamp Fox, Francis Marion, along with Thomas Sumter, Andrew Pickens, Colonel Elijah Clark of Georgia and Colonel William Washington, became part of the lore. Their cavalry operations did verge on civil war, with summary hangings of Loyalists in English uniform and Loyalist sympathizers.

---

*In 1780, the American population was approximately 2.8 million, of whom 600,000 were black slaves.

During that summer of 1780, Cornwallis had a constant problem with Americans who signed on as Loyalists and after training deserted with their weapons to join the patriots. Sometimes, whole platoons deserted together. By August, Cornwallis was so frustrated that he dictated this instruction to his field commanders:*

> I have given orders that all Inhabitants of this province who have subscribed and have taken part in this Revolt, should be punished with the greatest rigour, and also those who will not turn out that they may be imprisoned, and their whole property taken from them or destroyed. I have likewise ordered that Compensation should be made out of their Effects, to the Persons who have been injured and oppressed by them.
>
> I have ordered in the most Positive Manner that every Militia Man who has borne arms with us and afterwards joined the enemy shall be immediately hanged. I desire you will take the most rigorous Measures to punish the Rebels in the District in which you command, and that you will obey in the Strictest Manner the Directions I have given in this letter relative to the Inhabitants of the Country.

By the end of the summer, his victories were depleting his manpower and supplies but were sounding good in London. Cornwallis was reporting that "our experience is showing that loyalist numbers are not so great as had been represented, and their friendship is only passive."

About the time that Clinton left Charleston to return to New York, a French fleet of warships and transports sailed from Brest under the chevalier de Terney on a voyage that would change the whole complexion of the American war. The French were bringing an army of six thousand men under Lieutenant General Jean-Baptiste de Vimeur, comte de Rochambeau, to join the War of Independence at the side of General Washington.

In early August, the Royal Navy sighted the French off the Vir-

---

*This instruction fell into patriot hands and eventually reached General Washington.

ginia coast, but no naval action ensued, and the French disappeared. Then, on August 18, Clinton, back at his headquarters in New York, suddenly got word that the French convoy had eluded the Royal Navy completely and had slipped past Long Island to land Rochambeau's army unopposed at Newport, Rhode Island—the base that Clinton had evacuated less than a year before. Moreover, they had been digging in on the deserted British fortifications for more than a week when Clinton got the news.

At once, he tried to embark his own army to sail up Long Island Sound and engage the French. But navy transports were slow to assemble, and a shift in the wind prevented prompt sailing. Then the Royal Navy commander, an aging bully, Admiral Marriot Arbuthnot, sent word that the French had been joined by American militias and were too well dug in to be attacked. At the end of August, a frustrated and furious Clinton called off the attempt, and the French were left sitting unchallenged. Rochambeau's arrival was a major turning point in the war for General Washington and for General Clinton.

Clinton and Arbuthnot each vented blame and anger on the other in dispatches to Germain in London. Arbuthnot contended that Clinton shrank from taking risks. Clinton accused Arbuthnot of incompetence, which was largely true. He demanded that the naval commander be replaced, or he would again resign. And he asked for a reinforcement of ten thousand men to meet the new challenge of the French.

With both Washington and the French threatening Clinton's army in New York and New Jersey, England's whole southern strategy was now in question.

But by September of 1780, General Clinton's main preoccupation was Benedict Arnold.

Benedict Arnold was one of the authentic heroes of the early years of the war. In May of 1775, he and his unit joined Ethan Allen and the Green Mountain Boys in the attack on Fort Ticonderoga. That December, he led an American march, under the harshest of winter conditions, from Maine to Quebec. At the Battle of Saratoga, his spectacular charges against the British were crucial to the American victory. He broke a leg badly at Saratoga when his horse fell on him; though unfit for combat, he was with Washington at Valley Forge. Washington then appointed him military governor of Philadelphia when the British left. His loyalty, up to that point, was unquestioned.

Arnold rode into Philadelphia on June 18, 1778. Almost as soon as he took charge, he cut a black-market deal with a Philadelphia merchant to release an embargoed stock of goods to be sold in return for a share of the profits. He began to keep company with Tories in a city where Tory sympathizers were well-known.

In April of 1779, General Arnold, a widower, took as his bride the petite and comely nineteen-year-old Peggy Shippen, daughter of a family with Tory leanings. Peggy had enjoyed the company of Captain John André during the British occupation, and she was one of the young ladies invited to attend Howe's farewell *mischianza*.

About a month after his wedding, Arnold met with John Stansbury, a Philadelphia merchant of Tory Loyalist leanings, and asked Stansbury to make a secret contact with André, who was now a major in rank and adjutant general on Clinton's staff. He was to tell André that Arnold, the husband of Peggy Shippen and military governor of Philadelphia, was prepared to offer his services to General Clinton—for a price. The price was ten thousand pounds. Clinton responded that what Arnold had to offer wasn't worth such a sum. Clinton then departed for Charleston.

In May of 1780, about the same time that Clinton was closing the circle around Charleston, Arnold sent a coded note to André that he was to be given command of the vital American fortifications on the Hudson River at West Point. He would soon be able, he said, "to point out a plan of cooperation by which Sir Henry [Clinton] shall possess himself of West Point." He also asked for an additional ten thousand pounds for his services regardless of the outcome.*

Arnold assumed command at West Point on August 3, 1780, and

---

*The code for Arnold's messages to Clinton was provided by Major André. These messages came to light only in the 1920s, when all of Clinton's papers were purchased by William L. Clements. Clements, a graduate of the University of Michigan, subsequently endowed the magnificent Clements Library at Ann Arbor, where these messages and a wealth of other original material on the Revolution are kept.

immediately began working out the means to betray it. As evidence of his bona fides, he began sending intelligence to Clinton on the newly arriving French forces under Rochambeau and on General Washington's plans for coordinating operations with the French. Clinton began making his plans for a secret "surprise" attack on West Point, which Arnold would arrange to surrender.

The denouement began on September 20. At Arnold's request, Clinton sent Major André up the Hudson on the British sloop *Vulture* for a secret meeting to coordinate the final plans. André arrived late the following day and was met by a friend of Arnold's, Joshua Smith, who was acting as a guide. André was in a British uniform and was using the name John Anderson. Arnold and André sat down together in a clearing in the thick woods well inside the lines near West Point and talked till four o'clock in the morning. By the time they finished, it was too late for André to make his way back under cover of night and be picked up by the *Vulture*. Instead, he and Arnold went to Joshua Smith's home. Here, on the morning of September 22, they parted.

André, with Smith as a guide, had to ride back to New York in civilian clothes, the incriminating West Point information stuffed into the soles of his socks. On Friday night, the twenty-second, they stopped on their way. On Saturday morning, Smith, having guided André to a place he thought was well beyond the range of American patrols, said good-bye. André had only about fifteen miles to ride before he could be safely inside British lines. But at midmorning, at a bridge just outside Tarrytown, Major André was stopped by three men.

The three were operating as volunteer militiamen under a New York law that allowed them to claim the property found on any Loyalist or enemy. Their real interest in stopping André was probably the hope of some loot. In any case, they escorted André to an American post at North Castle, where Lieutenant Colonel John Jameson took charge. When the incriminating papers were found in his socks, André confessed to his identity. Even though he was in civilian clothes, he expected (or hoped) to be treated as a prisoner of war. At no time did he mention or admit to his dealings with General Arnold.

Colonel Jameson made the interesting decision, on Sunday, to send one courier with the papers discovered in André's possession to

General Washington, then somewhere in the Peekskill area, and a second courier to General Arnold to inform him of André's arrest. Washington had, that same day, sent word to Arnold to expect him for breakfast on Monday morning at the Robinson mansion, where Arnold was living, away from West Point.

Arnold spent a quiet Sunday with his wife. He did receive the message from Washington, but the courier from Jameson did not arrive until Monday morning. Washington, meanwhile, was on the move. The courier carrying André's papers could not find him.

On Monday morning, a messenger arrived to inform General Arnold that General Washington would be late for breakfast. While Arnold was breakfasting alone, a second messenger arrived with the dispatch informing him of André's detention. Arnold rushed to his wife's bedroom with the news. He had to run immediately. He rushed downstairs to tell a servant to saddle a horse, that he had urgent business at West Point. The servant was to tell General Washington when he arrived that Arnold would return later that morning.

The escaping traitor plunged down to the river, where his barge was waiting. He ordered the oarsmen to row him out to the *Vulture*, which was still lying at anchor in the river. When he climbed aboard, he made himself and his predicament known and asked that his oarsmen be made prisoners so they could not return and report the whereabouts of their commanding officer.

Barely half an hour after Arnold raced off, Washington arrived with the marquis de Lafayette and Alexander Hamilton. After breakfast, they decided to head for West Point, find Arnold, and carry out an inspection. They were puzzled, but not unduly concerned, that Arnold was not at West Point. It was not until late afternoon that Washington returned to the Robinson mansion and the devastating truth began to unfold.

The courier with the papers found on André had left the papers to await Washington's return. Washington opened the parcel in the presence of Alexander Hamilton. Leafing quickly through the papers, he looked up at Hamilton and exclaimed, "Arnold has betrayed us!"

There was feverish activity during the next few hours. Hamilton galloped down to the Hudson to order immediate reinforcements and to alert the garrison at Kings Point, just in case the British sailed up the Hudson to attack West Point. To guard against the possibility that other officers might be in on the plot with Arnold, command changes were effected immediately.

Major André was brought to the Robinson mansion and then sent on to West Point. On September 29, Washington appointed a board of senior officers to examine André. Major General Nathanael Greene presided; Lafayette and Baron von Steuben took part. André cooperated, resignedly but fully, during the day-long examination. The board recommended unanimously that since André had been captured wearing civilian clothes, he be executed as a spy. Washington ordered the execution for Sunday, October 1, at 5:00 P.M. General Clinton, in a request that arrived under a truce flag, asked for a delay "to receive further facts." André pleaded in a letter to Washington to be executed by firing squad rather than die on the gallows. Despite a certain sympathy for André, the shock, anger, and outrage of the American officers over the treason allowed of no extenuating circumstances. Washington delayed the execution for seventeen hours. André was hanged at noon on October 2, 1780.

Benedict Arnold, safe in New York, had already begun haggling with General Clinton for part payment of the twenty thousand pounds.

Even though the betrayal of West Point had failed, it gave England a national hero. The king awarded André's mother and three sisters a life pension and conferred a baronetcy on his brother. A monument was erected to his memory at Westminster Abbey, where his remains were placed after being returned from America in 1821.

After the capture of Charleston in May of 1780, the southern campaign seemed to go well for the British. Washington sent reinforcements south under General Horatio Gates, who had commanded at Saratoga. On August 16, Cornwallis attacked Gates's forces at Camden, South Carolina, and virtually annihilated them. Only seven hundred men (of a force of four thousand) escaped. Gates fled, riding two hundred miles north on what was described as the fastest horse in the American army. Gates was an overrated commander.

On October 7, however, the Americans triumphed at Kings Mountain, South Carolina. The significance of this victory lay in the fact that it pitted Loyalists under a British commander against patriot militiamen. The commander, Major Patrick Ferguson of the Seventy-first Highlanders, was best-known for having invented the first breech-loading rifle for the British Army. Cornwallis had named Ferguson to the post of inspector of militia and given him the task of building up the Loyalist forces. Ferguson was successful, recruiting four thousand men to the British side, twelve hundred of whom he organized and trained for a battalion of his own. But patriots decided to join forces and hunt down Ferguson's Loyalists. Frontiersmen from North and South Carolina were joined by four hundred troops from Virginia; their colonel, William Campbell, was elected commander of these backwoodsmen, and they set off in pursuit of Ferguson. At this juncture, Cornwallis sent a skeptical report to Clinton: "Ferguson is on the move into Tryon County with some militia, whom he says he is sure he can depend on for doing their duty; but I am sorry to say that his own experience, as well as that of every other officer, is totally against him.

Cornwallis's skepticism was soon justified. Ferguson fell back to Kings Mountain, believing that the rugged terrain would be ideal for defending a strong position on the barren mountaintop. In fact, it favored the backwoods sharpshooters. Having trailed Ferguson to Kings Mountain, they dismounted under cover of the woods and surrounded Ferguson's mountaintop position. They attacked suddenly with a heavy fusillade of accurate fire. Ferguson was killed trying to rally his troops. When a white flag finally went up, 157 Loyalists lay dead and another 163 were so badly wounded that most of them died before they could be evacuated from the mountain. Seven hundred were taken prisoner. Nine were promptly hanged. The frontiersmen lost twenty-nine men.

General Clinton later wrote in his personal memoirs that the Battle of Kings Mountain "was the first link of a chain of evils that followed each other in regular succession until they at last ended in the loss of America."

In December of 1780, Germain, buoyed by the initial victories in the south and Benedict Arnold's near success at West Point, wrote with brimming confidence to Clinton in New York:

So very contemptible is the rebel force now in all parts, and so vast is our superiority, that no resistance on their part is to be apprehended that can materially obstruct the progress of the King's arms in the speedy suppression of the rebellion, and it is a pleasing though at the same time mortifying reflection when the duration of the rebellion is considered . . . that the American levies in the King's service are more in numbers than the whole of the enlisted troops in the service of Congress.

Germain's assessment was specious—but it reflected the way London was thinking. When the House of Commons returned to work in January 1781, Lord North declared, "I am fully convinced that the means possessed by this country, when vigorously exerted, constitute the only mode of obtaining a just and honourable peace."

Despite all the domestic turbulence of the early months of 1780, Lord North had won a solid victory in the general election called in September, and a new House of Commons was sitting. England had even gained enough confidence to declare war on Holland in December 1780. (The king was irked with the open support—smuggled tea, gunpowder, financial help—the Americans were getting from the Dutch.)

There were other signs to bolster North's confidence. He had received a secret personal appeal for peace from none other than the great French finance minister, Jacques Necker. French finances were badly strained by the support given the Americans. Necker wrote, "You desire peace. I wish it also." But when North proposed exploring these peace overtures, the king balked. Soon after, Necker was forced out of office.

In January 1781, mutiny broke out among Washington's troops in New York and New Jersey. Congress was way behind in paying its soldiers, and they perpetually lacked adequate food and clothing. Mass desertions were threatened; for several very anxious weeks, Washington's army seemed to be falling apart. But at least Washington and Major General Anthony Wayne, commander in New York, had loyal officers they could count on. Gradually, the mutineers were isolated. Summary executions of a few brought the rest under control. France produced another cash subsidy to meet the back-pay demands. Washington wrote to Joseph Reed in Philadelphia, "In modern wars, the longest purse must chiefly determine events."

All in all, in London the news from America in the early months of 1781 seemed to augur well for British victory at last.

Cornwallis left his winter quarters in Winnsboro, South Carolina, at the end of January, intending to trap General Nathanael Greene's Continentals in North Carolina. He intended then to move on into Virginia, hopefully to restore a royal governor for King George and end the war. But he was now up against General Washington's most experienced and resourceful field commander. Greene had been with Washington at Valley Forge and was imbued with Washington's strategy of avoiding battles that could result in major strategic loss. The Americans had already suffered heavily at Charleston and at Camden. Greene had no intention of risking his army's being wiped out in a third defeat in the south.

When Cornwallis started north, he had only about three thousand men, and various detachments had to be left behind to secure scattered towns and outposts against deteriorating Loyalist support. He was also moving farther and farther away from his assured supply of ammunition, clothing, and boots at Charleston.

So Greene led Cornwallis on a lengthy and debilitating six-week chase through western North Carolina, even crossing the Dan River into lower Virginia, avoiding battle until he could choose the time and place.

Finally, on March 15, Greene stopped at Guilford Courthouse in North Carolina. By now he had added 2,500 local militiamen to his core force of 1,750 Continentals. Cornwallis's ranks, on the other hand, had been reduced to 2,000 by hard marching, rear-guard skirmishing, illness, and desertion. In the ensuing fight, Cornwallis's trained regulars fought determinedly and skillfully. Greene broke off in the late afternoon and retreated. He had lost 400 men.

Cornwallis did not have the strength to follow. He had lost 532 officers and men. He shepherded a decimated army to the seaport at Wilmington, North Carolina, where he could expect supplies and modest reinforcements by ship from Charleston. He had no intention of continuing to chase Greene. Instead, he planned to move north, into Virginia.

Greene turned south, into the backcountry, to clean out the small English garrisons left behind by Cornwallis. England's southern strategy was beginning to crumble.

Germain had long been enthusiastic about carrying the war into Virginia. Clinton, however, differed. He had written to Germain:

> Experience ought to convince us that there is no possibility of restoring order in any rebellious Provinces on this Continent without the hearty assistance of numerous friends. These, my Lord, I think are not to be found in Virginia, nor dare I say under present circumstances that they are to be found anywhere else.

Clinton by now was very dubious about the chances of subduing the Americans. As far as he was concerned, the strategic key to the colonies was indisputably New York—not Virginia. He had hitherto reluctantly sent light reinforcements to Virginia, but by 1781 his control over his vast command had all but ceased. Cornwallis was running his own campaign in the south, and he had the ear and the support of Germain in London.

While Cornwallis was resting up after Guilford Courthouse and planning his march to Virginia, Clinton received a peremptory order from Germain: "I am commanded by his Majesty to acquaint you that the recovery of the Southern Provinces and the prosecution of the war by pushing our conquests from south to north is to be considered the chief and principal object for the employment of all forces under your command."

Clinton had to reinforce Cornwallis no matter what his doubts. Germain wrote to Cornwallis in kinder, less arbitrary terms:

> I make no doubt your Lordship will, by this time, have had the honor to recover the province of North Carolina to his Majesty; and I am even sanguine enough to hope, from your Lordship's distinguished abilities and zeal for the King's service, that the recovery of part of Virginia will crown your success before the season becomes too intemperate for land operations.

On April 10, before starting out for Virginia, Cornwallis wrote to Clinton:

I am very anxious to receive your Excellency's commands, being as yet totally in the dark as to the intended operations of the summer. I cannot help expressing my wishes that the Chesapeake may become the seat of war, even (if necessary) at the expense of abandoning New York. Until Virginia is in a manner subdued, our hold on the Carolinas must be difficult.

On that same day, Cornwallis wrote a second letter. This he addressed to his friend Major General William Phillips, who had been sent by Clinton to take command of the reinforcements in Virginia. In the letter, Cornwallis expressed his unease and frustration:

Now, my dear Friend, what is our Plan? Without one we cannot succeed, and I assure you that I am quite tired of marching about the country in quest of adventures. If we mean an offensive war in America, we must abandon New York, and bring our whole force into Virginia. . . . If our plan is defensive, mixed with desultory expeditions, let us quit the Carolinas (which cannot be held defensively while Virginia can be so easily armed against us) and stick to our salt pork at New York, sending now and then a detachment to steal tobacco.

Cornwallis started for Virginia on April 25. He marched north unopposed with about fifteen hundred men, crossed the Roanoke River, and reached Richmond on May 20. There he learned that Major General Phillips had died of typhoid just a week before.

Replacing Phillips temporarily was none other than Benedict Arnold, now commissioned as a brigadier general in the British Army. Clinton had selected him to command the further reinforcements for Virginia ordered by Germain. Arnold had been paid £6,315 for "loss of property" after West Point; while he wasn't entirely happy with this sum, Clinton perhaps thought he would nevertheless fight for his life. Whatever the case, Arnold had arrived in Virginia with two thousand men and had joined up with Major General Phillips. When Cornwallis arrived after Phillips's death, Arnold turned over the entire force of forty-five hundred and returned to New York. Cornwallis now had a total force of about six thousand men.

There were no orders from Clinton awaiting Cornwallis, so Cornwallis had to proceed on the orders that had been issued to

Phillips. He was to choose a location on the Chesapeake Bay and fortify a base for the Royal Navy, conduct harassing raids on American supply depots, and cut off supplies heading for Greene in the south. These orders were hardly to Cornwallis's liking.

Not until a month later did Cornwallis hear directly from Clinton about operations in Virginia. A dispatch from Clinton, dated June 11, caught up with Cornwallis two weeks later, while he was inspecting possible sites for the naval base. Its orders were quite unexpected: Cornwallis was to ship six battalions of infantry and all of the light cavalry and artillery that he could spare back to New York as quickly as possible. Clinton's only explanation was a statement that read, "The enemy will *certainly* attack this post."

Why was General Clinton so emphatically certain—and wrong, as it would turn out—that Washington and the French would attack New York instead of Virginia? Because the British had just intercepted a secret letter discussing future operations. The letter was written by none other than General Washington himself, and it was addressed to the marquis de Lafayette, whom Washington had sent to command the forces in Virginia.

Washington had written the letter after an important strategy conference at the end of May 1781 with General Rochambeau at Wethersfield, Connecticut, during which they planned the coordination of joint operations. Washington and Rochambeau had much to talk about. A French fleet carrying more reinforcements was on its way from Brest under Admiral de Grasse. Where should the troops be landed? The decision was crucial.

Rochambeau wanted the reinforcements landed at Chesapeake Bay so they could join Lafayette in Virginia; then he would move the French army south with Washington to trap Cornwallis. Washington, however, argued that a greater victory lay close at hand in New York. If de Grasse brought the troops into New York, then a combined land and sea assault could be mounted against General Clinton. Such an attack could decide the war.

Rochambeau had reservations about an attack on New York. It was a strongly held defensive position, one that the English had amply fortified and stocked for years. It held enough supplies to withstand any siege. But in the end, he reluctantly agreed to go along with Washington—with the proviso that the plans could be changed if later developments so indicated. After the Wethersfield meeting, orders were issued to the French army in Connecticut to join Washington's Continentals at White Plains, about twenty-five miles north of New York.

Washington's letter, which contained a summary of this secret information, was written on May 31 in his own hand and was, surprisingly, not coded:

> Upon full consideration from every point of view, an attempt upon New York with its present garrison, which by estimation is reduced to 4,300 regular troops and about 3,000 irregulars, was deemed preferable to a Southern Operation, as we had not command of the water. The reasons which induced this determination were the danger to be apprehended from the approaching heats; the inevitable dissipation and loss of men by a long march; and the difficulty of transportation— but above all it was thought we had a tolerable prospect of expelling the Enemy, or obliging them to withdraw part of their forces from the southward, which would give the most effective relief to those states.

He continued, "[W]e have Rumours, but I cannot say they are well-founded, that the enemy are about to quit New York altogether. [If this were to happen] we must follow them of necessity."

And there was this curious passage: "As you have no Cypher by which I can write you in safety, and my letters have been frequently intercepted of late, I refrain myself from mentioning many Matters I wish to communicate to you."

If he knew the risk he was taking, then why would Washington put in writing such important information? Was he being deliberately indiscreet? His biographer James Thomas Flexner wrote that "Washington, as he later admitted, was anxious that the information should leak to the enemy . . . to take the pressure off the south by frightening Clinton."

A courier set out with Washington's letter, heading for Lafayette in Virginia. How, when, and where he was intercepted is not known. The letter landed on General Clinton's desk in the first week of June. The British commander sent the original, in Washington's hand, to Germain in London and made a copy for his own files.*

While General Washington would never have planned or in-

---

*These were shipped back to England after the Battle of Yorktown and remained secret until they arrived at the University of Michigan in the Clements Library collection and were opened in the 1930s.

tended that his letter be intercepted, it turned out to be a brilliant ruse to pin Clinton in New York. Instead of sending more troops to Virginia, Clinton's first reaction was to order Cornwallis to send troops back to New York. But Clinton was also under firm orders from Germain in London that the south was to be "the chief and principal object of employment of all the forces under your command." The commander in chief began having second thoughts. What to do? Confusion soon enveloped Clinton's headquarters.

On June 26, he sent fresh orders to Cornwallis. Instead of sending troops back to New York, he was now to send them up the Chesapeake Bay toward Philadelphia. Clinton proposed a raid to destroy military supplies and "distress" that city in a move he hoped would force Washington to divert troops from the expected attack on New York. Cornwallis received these orders on July 8.

But on July 20, yet another set of orders arrived from Clinton. He now told an angry and frustrated Cornwallis that he was to keep *all* his troops in Virginia and recall any that might have sailed for Philadelphia.

Cornwallis was now back to his original orders—to find a naval base for the Royal Navy and use his entire army to secure the Williamsburg-Jamestown area on Chesapeake Bay. Clinton instructed "at all events hold Old Point Comfort which secures Hampton Roads" for the base.

Cornwallis, furious and disgusted with Clinton's confusing and changing orders, grimly complied. He made a quick inspection of Old Point Comfort and sent word to Clinton that it was unsuitable for a Royal Navy anchorage and the ground too swampy for heavy fortifications. He therefore would base at Yorktown, where the York River enters Chesapeake Bay, which was his original choice for a site when he arrived in Virginia in May.

Orders went out to his scattered detachments of British and Hessian troops to converge on Yorktown. Cornwallis surveyed the modest heights with his engineer officers and laid out plans for extensive fortifications and gun emplacements. The first of his six thousand troops began arriving in early August. In intense August heat, the work got under way.

General Cornwallis wrote resignedly to Clinton in New York: "It will be a work of great time and labor, and after all, I fear, not very strong."

Chapter 20

THE KING FIGHTS ON

By the summer of 1781, Lord North's government was again confident and complacent about the war in the colonies. Viewed from London, General Cornwallis's year-long march across the south after the victory at Charleston had been like an English knife through colonial butter. Surely it would now be a matter of only a little time before the colonials would come to their senses and call off the rebellion.

The opposition had grown quiescent after the surprise election in September of 1780. Lord Hillsborough recorded in the spring that "the opposition is at present if not dead at least asleep; since I have been in Parliament I do not recall a session so quiet."

Dr. Samuel Johnson, noted curmudgeon, never concealed his opinions about anything, including his lofty contempt for the Americans. To the faithful James Boswell he said in April:

As to the American war, Sir, the sense of the nation is *with* the Ministry. The majority of those who *understand* is with it; the majority of those who can only *hear* is against it. Opposition is always the loudest, a majority of the rabble will always be for the Opposition.

Boswell begged to differ—at least in his own diary where he commented, "My opinion was that those who could *understand* were against the American war, as almost every man is now."

Boswell was much closer to the mark than the ultra-Tory Johnson. Whatever the government victory in the September election, there was a steady erosion of support for the war. It was not an erosion of great numbers in Parliament, but those "who could *understand*" were sliding away—respected, independent-minded individuals who were going over to the opposition. Whatever the government's complacency, the war had yet to be won; General Cornwallis was successful but not victorious. Until and unless there was a real victory, opposition to the war would continue to grow.

Furthermore, a strong new voice of opposition had emerged from the 1780 elections—that of William Pitt, the twenty-two-year-old son of the earl of Chatham, making his debut in the House of Commons. From the very first, the younger Pitt showed neither diffidence nor hesitancy in following in his illustrious father's footsteps. His intelligence, his grasp of politics and issues, and his leadership qualities all seemed to have been inherited intact from his father. He was mature and ready to soar from the moment he entered Parliament.

Pitt was careful, however, not to offend tradition by rushing to speak or demanding the floor; he had spoken only twice. Then on June 12, 1781, just before Parliament was due to adjourn for the summer, Charles James Fox introduced an opposition motion for "an inquiry into the management of the war in America." This was nothing more than a by now familiar parting shot at North's government, and Pitt had not intended to take part in the debate. But he found some misrepresentations of his father's position on the American question, so he rose to say:

A Noble Lord who spoke earlier has in the warmth of his zeal called this a holy war. For my part, although the Right Honourable gentleman who made the motion, and some other gentlemen, have been more than once in the course of the debate reprehended for calling it a wicked or accursed war, I am persuaded, and I will affirm, that it is a most accursed, wicked, barbarous, cruel, unnatural, unjust and most diabolical war. . . .

The expense of it has been enormous, far beyond any former experience, and yet what has the British nation received in return? Nothing but a series of ineffective victories or severe defeats—victories only celebrated with temporary triumph over our brethren whom we would trample down, or defeats which fill the land with mourning for the loss of dear and valuable relations, slain in the impious cause of enforcing unconditional submission. Where is the Englishman who on reading the narrative of those bloody and well-fought contests can refrain from lamenting the loss of so much British blood shed in such a cause, or from weeping on whatever side Victory might be declared?

When Pitt concluded, the lord advocate, Henry Dundas, rose to reply. He gave the standard defense of the war, but he complimented young Pitt on "so happy an union of first-rate abilities, high integrity, bold and honest independence of conduct, and the most persuasive eloquence."

After the debate, Pitt wrote to his mother that "I expressed as strongly as I could how much my father detested the principle of the war, but avoided saying anything direct on the subject of independence, which at that stage of the business I thought better to avoid."

Fox's motion on the American war was defeated by a vote of 127 to 99. One week later, the House of Commons adjourned until November.

No crisis threatened the North government; no cloud of premonition cast a shadow over the social celebrations of the summer. At their home in Bushey, on the outskirts of London, Lady North gave a ball to celebrate Parliament's vacation.

General Rochambeau had gone along only very reluctantly with General Washington's strategy to attack New York. The French began moving out of their base at Newport and marching from Rhode Island across Connecticut to link up with Washington in early July. But Rochambeau began a secret move to force a change in Washington's strategy. He wrote to Admiral de Grasse, whose fleet had reached the Caribbean, reported his agreement with Washington, but emphasized his own preference for going south to attack the English on Chesapeake Bay. The matter could be resolved if de Grasse would sail for the Chesapeake rather than Sandy Hook.

When Rochambeau reached New York, he and Washington began to examine together the tactical problems and risks of an assault on the well-prepared, strongly held British fortifications. It soon became apparent that even with the combined Franco-American force of ninety-five hundred men—and more reinforcements coming with de Grasse—a battle would be costly and success far from certain.

Washington began to have second thoughts. He wrote in his diary for August 1, "I could scarce see a ground upon which to continue my preparations against New York, and therefore I turned my views more seriously than I had before to an operation to the southward."

On August 14, the situation changed abruptly. Washington received a communication from Admiral comte de Barras, who commanded the French naval forces at Rhode Island. The admiral forwarded news from de Grasse: He was sailing from Santo Domingo with between twenty-five and twenty-nine sail-of-the-line warships and thirty-two hundred troops. He was heading for Chesapeake Bay and expected to arrive there around September 3. He would land his troops, but he could not keep his fleet in American waters past mid-October.

The message from de Grasse came as no surprise to Rochambeau, and it left Washington with no option but to head south. There was no time to lose if he were going to meet the French promptly. He did not hesitate. He had 450 miles to cover. He would have to divide his army, leaving two thousand men behind to guard West Point and the Hudson Highlands and taking twenty-five hundred south. These would combine with Rochambeau's force of five thousand. A week after receiving news from de Grasse, Washington crossed the Hudson and was on his way south. The French army, more numerous and with heavier baggage trains, followed.

Washington's main preoccupation, as he got under way, was to deceive Clinton for as long as possible about the move, to keep him expecting an attack on New York and prevent him from sending reinforcements to Cornwallis. So the American and French troops first marched straight down the Hudson on the New Jersey side, as if they were preparing to outflank the British forces in lower Manhattan and attack Clinton on Staten Island. The French even set up full field kitchens to bake bread for the troops to add to the deception. Washington and the Americans crossed New Jersey to the familiar countryside of Princeton, Trenton, and Philadelphia.

Not until Clinton received intelligence on September 5 that

Washington had arrived in Philadelphia on September 2 did he realize the strategic plan had changed and that the Americans and
French were on their way to Virginia. The deception had worked.

Admiral Sir George Rodney, commander of the Royal Navy in
the Leeward Islands, had arrived in the Caribbean in January. The
French fleet sailed in a few months later. Where would de Grasse sail
next? By July, having watched the French for three months and received Admiralty intelligence from London, Rodney concluded that
de Grasse intended to divide his fleet, sending part of it to transport
French troops to America and part to escort a convoy back to
France. He therefore ordered Admiral Sir Samuel Hood to be prepared to take fourteen ships-of-the-line to American waters as soon
as de Grasse left the Caribbean, to join Admiral Thomas Graves,
Arbuthnot's replacement. This combined force, Rodney estimated,
would be sufficient to deal with de Grasse. Rodney, quite ill, then
sailed for England and a cure.

De Grasse, in early August, left Santo Domingo with his *entire*
fleet and sailed *northeast* toward the Bahamas. The British knew that
he had sailed, but they had no idea of where he was, nor did they
know that he had *not* divided his fleet. Admiral Hood sailed his
fourteen ships *northwest,* toward the American coast, on his way to
join Admiral Graves. Hood looked for de Grasse around the Chesapeake Bay and the Virginia capes but found no sign of him. The
French, in fact, were behind him. So Hood sailed on to Sandy
Hook, linking up with Graves on August 28—just as Washington
and Rochambeau were nearing Philadelphia.

Admiral Barras, in Newport, acting on an urgent message from
Rochambeau, loaded the heavy guns Rochambeau had left behind
in Rhode Island. He sailed from Newport during the last days of
August, managed to slip his squadron past the Royal Navy, and
headed south to Chesapeake Bay.

When the news reached Admiral Graves that the French had
slipped out of Newport, and with no sign of de Grasse in New York,
he and Hood hastily set sail for the Chesapeake on August 31. This
was the only place Barras could be heading. Graves was confident he
could catch the French and, with his joint fleet's superior numbers,
defeat them.

The two British admirals reached the mouth of the Chesapeake on September 5. What they found was not the light squadron from Newport commanded by Admiral Barras but a huge French fleet, the entire sail of Admiral de Grasse. It was a devastating moment.

De Grasse had arrived three days earlier and disembarked the thirty-two hundred reinforcements for Lafayette near Jamestown. When the English sighted him, he already had three warships in the bay, at the mouth of the York River, clearly visible to Cornwallis. Even without these warships, de Grasse had superior numbers: twenty-four ships-of-the-line carrying eighteen hundred guns against England's nineteen ships and fourteen hundred guns.

Admiral Graves had to engage the French, but he could not risk a major battle. The losses that the Royal Navy might incur at this juncture could cripple England's entire war effort. Admiral de Grasse did not need a sea victory. All he needed was temporary control to isolate Cornwallis. So the two fleets engaged in desultory fighting on September 5. De Grasse withdrew at sunset. No colors were struck, no victory obtained. Crews sorted out the damage and made repairs. On September 7 and 8, the two fleets maneuvered and exchanged more gunfire with each other. The French held the advantage of the wind but did not close to attack. On September 9, Admiral Graves decided it would be imprudent to engage any further. He and Admiral Hood sailed north, returning to Sandy Hook for needed repairs.

The French were left in complete control of Chesapeake Bay.

The first two weeks of the march south for General Washington were a period of acute tension and anxiety. Throughout the war, he had gambled his army with caution, but now, in dividing his army, he was going against all his instincts, staking everything on a single throw of the dice. Even though Rochambeau and his army were marching at his side, Washington was well aware that the French had their own agenda. They would make their own decisions. And would de Grasse show up in the Chesapeake as promised? Or would he be intercepted by the Royal Navy, which was surely on the lookout for him. Might Clinton be withdrawing Cornwallis from Virginia to New York? Or could he have discovered what was going on and reinforced Cornwallis?

Washington had planned carefully for the combined army of seventy-five hundred. Below Trenton, he hoped to find riverboats to speed up the movement south. He intended to cross overland south of Philadelphia to the head of the Elk River at the northern end of the Chesapeake. Here he expected to find more boats that could move his troops past Baltimore and all the way to the Potomac.

On September 2, he got a rapturous welcome in Philadelphia. He also got a much needed transfusion of hard cash from the French and from the Revolutionary War financier Robert Morris. He was thus able to pay his troops. Then he headed out with a few of his staff officers to reconnoiter the transport situation.

On September 5, south of Philadelphia at the town of Chester, a courier caught up with Washington. He carried the dispatch Washington had anxiously been waiting for: Admiral de Grasse had reached the Chesapeake and landed Lafayette's reinforcements.

"I have never seen a man more overcome with great and sincere joy than was General Washington," wrote the duc de Lauzun, the French liaison officer who was with him at the time.

At Yorktown, Cornwallis had at first not been unduly alarmed by de Grasse's arrival, the landing of the troops, or the sight of the three French warships riding at anchor in the York River. He fully expected the Royal Navy to deal with the French fleet; the additional troops for Lafayette still left the Americans with inferior numbers against his concentration of six thousand British and German soldiers. Cornwallis was confident that he could hold out well into October, and by that time, he thought, British sea power would control the Chesapeake and Clinton would have sent reinforcements. He did not yet know that Washington was moving south.

Then he received news that Admiral Barras had given the Royal Navy the slip and had safely landed the French siege guns for Lafayette. After that, the Royal Navy had sailed away, back to New York. Cornwallis was left without a Union Jack in sight.

In mid-September, Cornwallis dispatched a solemn assessment to Clinton. He warned that if a relief force did not reach the Chesapeake promptly, then Clinton must be prepared to hear the worst. The dispatch reached New York on September 23.

* * *

The Franco-American army began arriving at the head of the Elk River, north of Baltimore, the second week of September. Many troops marched on to Baltimore and Annapolis to find more boats. Washington, keeping well ahead of his army, rode in frantic haste to his beloved Mount Vernon, which he had not seen in six years.

On September 9, Washington spent the night at Mount Vernon and lingered there for another two days as dispatch riders came and went. He left for the Yorktown area on September 12. By September 26, the concentration of French and American troops was complete. There were now 16,800 men under Washington's command, only 6,000 under Cornwallis's. On September 29, Cornwallis made a first withdrawal from his outer defense ring to his inner fortification line. It was the beginning of the end.

In New York, Clinton had been mesmerized by the expectation that a battle would be fought there and by the assumption that the arrival of Admiral Hood's fourteen warships would assure the superiority of British sea power. Then he received the alarming dispatch from Cornwallis, describing the magnitude of the crisis he faced.

Clinton convened a council of war on September 24. Admirals Hood and Graves had been back for a week, with a number of their ships laid up for repairs in the security of New York Harbor. Although Clinton had taken some steps early in September to prepare reinforcements for Cornwallis, everything depended on the Royal Navy. Yet the repairs on the ships were going very slowly. Major Frederick Mackenzie, an English staff officer who kept a personal diary throughout his time in America, recorded in October that

> If the Navy are not a little more active they will not get a sight of the Capes of Virginia before the end of this month, and then it will be a little too late. They do not seem to be hearty in this business, or to think that the saving of that army is an object of much material consequence. One of the Captains exposed himself as much as to say, that the loss of two line-of-battle ships in effecting the relief of the army is of much more consequence than the loss of the army.

Finally, the navy was ready, and Clinton loaded on October 16 and sailed on October 19. Five days later, the fleet reached the mouth of the Chesapeake. Here they sighted a small sailing dinghy bobbing in the water. Aboard were a white man and two black men.

The three reported that they had come from Yorktown. The fighting was finished; the war was over. Cornwallis had surrendered his entire army to Washington on October 18, 1781.

General Clinton and Admiral Graves turned back to New York without sighting the enemy or firing a shot.

Yorktown represented a major victory for the French in their war with England, and the news reached Paris first. A French frigate made a fast crossing of the Atlantic. On the night of November 19, a messenger arrived at the door of Benjamin Franklin's home in Passy. He carried a note from Foreign Minister Vergennes with the news. In the morning, Franklin hastily copied the bulletin on a little copying press he had invented and sent the copies off by messenger to various friends. The word spread rapidly. It was, in fact, from a source in Paris that the news reached Germain in London, on Sunday, November 25.

Germain at once ordered his carriage and drove to the home of Lord Stormont, head of the Northern Department and former ambassador to Paris. Together, they continued on to find Lord Thurlow, lord chancellor of the government. Together, the trio, all hard-liners on the war, presented themselves at Lord North's door on Downing Street. In Germain's account, Lord North "received the news as he would have taken a ball in the breast. 'Oh God, it is all over!' he repeated as he paced the floor in obvious anxiety."

The news of Yorktown fell on London as a complete surprise. There had been neither warning nor even unheeded signs of what was coming. At least at Saratoga four years before, there had been a chain of events that foreshadowed the surrender. But this time, as far as London knew, General Cornwallis had marched from Charleston to the Virginia coast on a virtually unbroken trail of successes. Further, Germain had enthusiastically urged the march to Virginia. There was no reason to think the British Army might be in grave danger. Nothing was known in London of Washington's march south. English pride in the Royal Navy simply would not allow the preposterous scenario of a French fleet slipping past it into Chesapeake Bay. It seemed as if these events had sprung out of nowhere. The battle was over before General Clinton could even warn London that it was imminent.

Word of the catastrophe spread rapidly. It stunned everyone—

some with dismay, some with resignation, some with relief that the war might at last end. But it would take more than Yorktown to change King George's thinking. That resolute, stubborn monarch would fight on.

Parliament was due to return from recess on Tuesday, November 27. The nation waited to hear what the government would have to say about the loss at Yorktown. But the address from the throne had been written before the news of Yorktown, and it was not changed. The king spoke without mentioning Yorktown or Cornwallis's surrender and made no statement of plans for either war or peace.

In the debate that followed, Lord North, vague as ever, voiced platitudes that seemed to favor both war and peace. He denied that all hope was lost and implied that the war could now be fought at less expense since it would no longer be fought aggressively—but he warned that large sums of money would have to be raised to keep it going. He was vague for good reasons: He knew that it would be impossible for the government to make up its collective mind about either war or peace. The situation precluded trying yet again to tender his resignation to the king. He could do nothing but muddle along until latent political forces in the country coalesced to force a change on the government—and above all, on the king.

On the morning following the opening-day debate in the House of Commons, King George wrote to Lord North:

> It shows the House retains that spirit for which this Nation has always been renowned, and which alone can preserve it in its difficulties. . . . I have already directed Lord G. Germain to put on paper the mode and means most feesible for conducting the war, that every Member of the Cabinet may have his propositions to weigh by themselves, that we may adopt a Plan and abide by it. I do not doubt if measures are well concerted a good end may yet be made to this war, but if we despond, certain ruin ensures.

For Lord North and the government, there was a somewhat hollow quality of déjà vu about this. After the debacle at Yorktown, there was only one man in the government who could even pretend to believe that the war in America should go on, and that was Germain. He was also the most unpopular man in the government.

By rushing to carry the news of Yorktown first to Lord North and then to the king, Germain was able to reassure the stubborn sovereign that he could count on him to continue the war. And he quickly picked out a scapegoat for Yorktown, Admiral Thomas Graves. He blocked (temporarily, at least) the king's choice of a replacement for Clinton, General Sir Guy Carleton, simply because he hated him.

For the next two months, everything—the war (or peace), the future of North's government, even the future of the empire—revolved around getting rid of Germain. He had to go—but how? Germain had cards in his hand that would allow him to extract a price for either his dismissal or his retirement, and he still had the support of the king.

On December 12, 1781, the first of a series of anti-war motions that would force out Germain was introduced in Parliament. Sir James Lowther moved

> that the war has proved ineffectual either to the protection of His Majesty's loyal subjects in the said colonies, or for defeating the dangerous designs of our enemies, that all further attempts to reduce the revolted colonies are contrary to the true interests of this kingdom, as tending to weaken its efforts against its ancient and powerful enemies.

Lowther was one of the independents who had supported the government in the past. His motion made it obvious that the tide of opposition was on the rise. Lord North made a careful response, telling the Commons that "it is not the design to send another army to America to replace that of Lord Cornwallis, but only to retain the same number of men as they have already on foot necessary to keep the present Posts."

Germain intervened with a fire-breathing speech that seemed to contradict Lord North. In the end, the Lowther motion lost, 220 to 179—but this was less than half the government majorities of the past.

To North's intimates, it was clearer than ever that he wanted to end the war. He even talked at the dinner table about the inevitabil-

ity of accepting American independence. He also made another forlorn attempt to open channels with Benjamin Franklin in Paris. This
time, his intermediary was David Hartley, a well-meaning busybody
who had kept up an intermittent correspondence with Franklin. At
North's request, Hartley wrote to Franklin on December 31, asking
if the American commissioners were authorized to discuss peace
terms on their own with England, separate from the French. Franklin sent this reply on January 15, 1782:

> The Congress will never instruct their commissioners to obtain a
> peace on such ignominious terms; and though there can be but few
> things in which I should venture to disobey their orders, yet, if it were
> possible for them to give me such an order as this, I should certainly
> refuse to act, I should instantly renounce their commission and ban-
> ish myself for ever from so infamous a country.

Franklin was incensed because he learned that Lord North had
sanctioned a similar overture to the French about a separate peace.
And he probably assumed that every letter he wrote from Paris was
opened and read. In any case, he wrote a second letter to Hartley
some weeks later:

> You were of the opinion that the Ministry desired *sincerely* a recon-
> ciliation with America and with that view a separate peace with us was
> proposed. It happened that, at the same time, Lord North had an
> emissary here to sound out the French ministers with regard to peace
> and to make them very advantageous proposition in case they would
> abandon America. . . . You may judge, my dear friend, what opinion
> I must have formed of the intentions of your ministers.

Thus ended Lord North's peace overtures.

Within the government, the insidious problem of Germain was
getting worse. Germain could not escape his own responsibility for
the dispatches that encouraged Cornwallis to campaign in Virginia
despite objections and warnings from General Clinton. He had
never got along with the earl of Sandwich, first lord of the Admiralty, and now he enraged Sandwich by proposing that Admiral
Thomas Graves be court-martialed for failing to give proper naval
support to Cornwallis at Yorktown. Sandwich's response was that

the Admiralty would never court-martial Admiral Graves. If Germain insisted, then he must apply to the king to order it.

But Germain was already at odds with the king over the choice of Sir Guy Carleton as Clinton's successor. Carleton could be just as high-handed and caustic as Germain, and the two had exchanged some very bitter communications in 1777 and 1778, when Carleton resigned his command in Canada. Germain wrote the king a "him or me" letter:

> The little confidence which could ever subsist between Sir Guy Carleton and Lord George might, from your Majesty's great condescension and goodness, create some doubt in your mind whether the appointment proposed might not prejudice your Majesty's service, but in the present circumstances there seems to be very little probability that your Majesty may find it convenient to continue the seals of office much longer in Lord George's hands.

The king was beginning to weary of Germain. But instead of replying directly to Germain, he tried to prod Lord North into taking action. The king reiterated his choice of Carleton to go to New York but told North that "on the whole it is best to gratify the wishes of Lord G. Germain and let him retire."

When Parliament returned from Christmas recess, two of North's junior ministers, Henry Dundas and Richard Rigby, made the bold and unusual move of trying to force the prime minister to do something about Germain. They announced that they would no longer attend sessions of the House of Commons as long as Germain remained in office—and then, with great ceremony, they stalked out of the chamber.

The situation could not be allowed to continue. Germain stated his price: After the Battle of Minden, he had been dismissed from the army at the rank of lieutenant general, and in 1760 he had been court-martialed, "adjudged unfit to serve his Majesty in any military capacity whatsoever." As secretary of the American Department, he had presided over, but refused to accept responsibility for, the defeat at Saratoga, and now he was immersed in the defeat at Yorktown. He demanded that he be given a peerage in his own right, and he wanted the king to clear his name completely.*

---

*His adopted name, Lord George Germain, represented neither a peerage nor a seat in the House of Lords.

On February 5, Germain called on King George to turn in his seals of office. He was to be made a baron (the bottom rung of the peerage ladder)—but he had the effrontery to plead with King George that, grateful as he was, this was not good enough. He pointed out that General Lord Jeffrey Amherst had also been made a baron—and Amherst, he said (erroneously), had once been Germain's father's coachman. He asked that the king recognize this difference in social rank and make him a viscount. King George seems to have been as anxious as everyone else to get rid of this impossible man; Germain left the palace, pleased to call himself the Viscount Sackville.

This was not quite the end of the Germain saga, however. The House of Lords was incensed that the king had elevated Germain to the rank of viscount. When the new Viscount Sackville made his first appearance in the Lords a week later, the members turned out in unprecedented numbers to give vent to one of the most vituperative debates ever directed at one member. They very nearly precipitated a constitutional crisis by refusing to accept a peer created by the king. The earl of Abingdon called the new viscount "the greatest criminal this country has ever known." Lord Carmarthen moved that admission to the Lords be refused to a man "stamped by an indelible brand and by a sentence [the Minden court-martial] that has never been cancelled." His motion was supported by an array of twenty-five that included Shelburne, Rutland, Portland, Derby, Devonshire, and Craven.

Viscount Sackville sat through the entire debate, listened to the scorn and insults and denunciations—and then joined the seventy-seven other peers in a successful vote admitting him to the House of Lords.

In its February 23, 1782, issue, *Lloyd's Journal* commented that the change in government "seemed to imply that the ardour for carrying on the American war was beginning to cool in the Cabinet." The new head of the American Department was a totally faceless placeman. Welbore Ellis had plodded the government corridors for nearly twenty years, and he would do whatever he was told.

For a while, the government members had been sounding the bugles of advance while they were actually in retreat. But on February 22, Henry Seymour Conway, who had proposed the repeal of the Stamp Act in 1766, moved an address to the king, asking that "the war in America be no longer pursued for the impracticable purpose of reducing the inhabitants to obedience by force." Lord North waffled—but once again, the country gentlemen deserted him. The Conway motion was defeated by only one vote.

The following week, on February 27, Lord North had to present the House of Commons with a necessary series of budget measures, increases in taxes on tea, beer, salt, tobacco, soap, and public entertainment—and a request for approval of another government loan. He tried to emphasize the fact that England was also fighting France, Spain, and Holland. Conway returned to the attack by moving for an amendment to the budget bill against continuing the war with America. After a lengthy and complex debate, during which North tried some clever but ineffective maneuvers to sidetrack the Conway motion, it was passed, 234 to 215.

To the king, Lord North wrote, "As the House of Commons seems now to have withdrawn their confidence from Lord North, it will be right to see as soon as possible what other system can be found."

The king, regardless of his determination concerning the war and American independence, certainly recognized the seriousness of the House of Commons vote. He adopted a new tone in his reply to Lord North: "I am mortified Lord North thinks he cannot now remain in office." He added that he wished to have Lord Thurlow, the lord chancellor and an ardent supporter of the American war, undertake the soundings "with such others of any party they think right to recommend, the basis of Public Measures being founded on keeping what is in our present possession in North America." Strangely, the king was still determined to fight on. He seemed to believe that England could keep New York, where Clinton's army was still strong, and let the rest of America go.

Lord Thurlow began a round of consultations and quickly found that there were no longer enough diehards left in England to form a government that would carry out the king's wishes. The only solution was a government formed by the opposition, and this meant either the marquess of Rockingham or the earl of Shelburne.

For two weeks, Thurlow conducted intricate conversations back and forth, Rockingham to Shelburne to the duke of Grafton to Lord North to the king and around again. The king stubbornly refused to deal directly with Rockingham, who held the strongest position in the opposition. Rockingham, who had repealed the Stamp Act, was adamant in insisting that he would form a government only after direct personal discussions with the king. Furthermore, he would form a government only if the king would promise not to oppose independence for America if the ministry recommended it to him.

In mid-March, Charles James Fox made it known that he intended to submit a motion of no confidence, which would force Lord North's government from office. On March 18, 1782, the country gentlemen sent word to North that they would support "the sense of the House of Commons that the ministry should resign immediately."

At this point, with North's government about to fall, King George III wrote out, in his own hand, an act of abdication:

> His Majesty during the twenty-one years he has sate on the Throne of Great Britain, has had no object so much at heart as the maintenance of the British Constitution, of which the difficulties he has at times met with from His scrupulous attachment to the Rights of Parliament are sufficient proof.
>
> His Majesty is convinced that the sudden change of Sentiments of one Branch of the Legislature has totally incapacitated Him from either conducting the War with effect, or from obtaining any Peace but on conditions which would prove destructive to the Commerce as well as the essential Rights of the British Nation.
>
> His Majesty therefore with much sorrow finds He can be of no further Utility to his Native Country which drives him to the painful step of quitting it forever.
>
> In consequence of which Intention His Majesty resigns the Crown of Great Britain and The Dominions appertaining thereto to His Dearly Beloved Son and lawful Successor, George Prince of Wales, whose endeavours for the Prosperity of the British Empire he hopes may prove more successful.

For more than a decade, King George had repeatedly lectured Lord North on duty, duty, duty every time North had sought, usually with sensible reasons, to quit his onerous office. Now it was Lord North's turn to lecture the king on duty. In a letter dated March 18, North told the king:

The fate of the present Ministry is absolutely and irrevocably decided. . . . Your Majesty is well apprised that, in this country, the Prince on the Throne cannot, with prudence, oppose the deliberate resolution of the House of Commons.

Your royal predecessors (Particularly King William the Third and his late Majesty George II) were obliged to yield to it much against their wish in more instances than one; they consented to changes in their Ministries which they disapproved because they found it necessary to sacrifice their private wishes, and even their opinions on the preservation of public order, and the prevention of those terrible mischiefs, which are the natural consequence of the clashing of two branches of Sovereign Power in the State. The concessions they made were never deemed dishonourable, but were considered as marks of their wisdom, and of their parental affection for their people.

Your Majesty has firmly and resolutely maintained what appeared to You essential to the welfare and dignity of this Country, so long as this Country itself thought proper to maintain it. The Parliament have altered their sentiments, and as their sentiments, whether just or erroneous, must ultimately prevail, Your Majesty having persevered, as long as possible, on what You thought right, can lose no honour if you yield at length, as some of the most renowned and glorious of your Predecessors have done, to the opinion and wishes of the House of Commons.

King George had no capacity for being gracious in defeat, nor did he know how to accept it. The next day, he replied to Lord North that since

my sentiments of honour will not permit me to send for any of the Leaders of the Opposition and personally treat with them, I could not but be hurt at your letter of last night . . . and whatever you or any man can say on that subject has no avail with me, and if you resign before I have decided what I will do, You will certainly forfeit my regard.

However, North's statesmanlike letter had its intended effect: The king stuffed the act of abdication back into his desk.

On the morning of March 20, Lord North wrote the king: "[T]here is no chance of keeping the present ministry in place any longer, and if there should be anybody who informs Your Majesty that there is the least hope of doing so, he deceives you, himself being misinformed." This message reached the king at Windsor just as he was about to set out on a morning ride. He reined in his horse, read North's letter, and turned abruptly to his companions and said, "Lord North has sent in his resignation, but I will not accept it." But North would not allow the king to refuse his resignation this time.

The House of Commons would meet that afternoon to take up the no-confidence motion as its first order of business. But after twelve years as prime minister, North was determined not to suffer the indignity of dismissal by Parliament. He would quit before he would be voted out.

The no-confidence motion was to be introduced by the earl of Surrey, member for Carlisle, son of the duke of Norfolk. At the same time, Burke had an impeachment motion ready, and Fox was also ready to move for censure.

The House convened at four-thirty, "one of the fullest and most tense that has ever been," said one member. When Surrey rose to present the censure motion, North rose at the same time, asking to be recognized. The speaker quite properly gave recognition to the prime minister.

Pandemonium broke out. Members knew that North, skilled parliamentarian that he was, would try to preempt the motion. Fox shouted that Surrey should speak first. For an hour, the speaker could gain no control over the shouting.

Finally, North was able to be heard. He proclaimed that his ministry no longer existed, that whatever Surrey wished to move for was irrelevant. He then moved that the Commons be adjourned.

A noisy debate on the adjournment motion went on for several hours. North was alert and amiable and even seemed to be enjoying himself. In the early evening, adjournment was voted at last. As he left the Commons, North issued genial invitations to a few friends on the way out: "Come home and dine with me, and have the credit of having dined with a fallen minister on the day of his dismissal."

Lord North has gone down in history as the prime minister who lost England her American colonies, but the responsibility was scarcely his alone. He was not a wartime prime minister, and his weaknesses exceeded his strengths. But no man, whatever his political strengths or strategic genius, could have carried the day for King George III in the American war. At every turn of the way, it was the king who insisted on fighting on. In the words of Charles James Fox, "It was the influence of the Crown in the two Houses of Parliament that enabled His Majesty's ministers to persevere against the voice of reason, the voice of truth, the voice of the people."

In the end, Lord North averted an abdication crisis and refused to act as buffer between the king and the opposition any longer. By stepping down from office, he forced a graceless and ungrateful King George to accept the democratic will of the House of Commons and agree to a government that would end the war with peace and independence for America.

The king, angry with North for quitting and petulant at being forced to swallow more than just his pride, fought at first to deal with the earl of Shelburne and keep Rockingham at arm's length. Shelburne wanted to end the war but believed that it would still be possible to extract a price from the Americans for their independence. Rockingham did not.

Rockingham now headed the strongest opposition bloc. He was supported by Burke, Fox, Conway, Barré, the Old Whigs, and the new independents for reform, all of whom were ready to concede American independence as the price of any agreement to end the war.

But the king still refused to deal with Rockingham—and Rockingham still refused to form a government without first having an appointment with the king. This impasse was finally overcome when it was agreed that Shelburne would give the king a list of proposed cabinet appointments drawn up by Rockingham. The king would then meet with his new prime minister to discuss the new government. Rockingham finally took office on March 28, 1782.

Rockingham and Shelburne lost no time in sweeping clean the officials from Lord North's years in office. The only minister who stayed on was Lord Thurlow as lord chancellor. Dozens of sinecure officeholders and junior ministers were pitched out. The whole patronage system was shaken up and turned inside out, not only by this purging but also by reform measures. Many of the offices were simply abolished—among them, the American Department. Shelburne took over as secretary of state with the combined responsibility for home, Irish, and colonial affairs. Charles James Fox became

England's first secretary of state for foreign affairs. (While this division of duties seemed logical, it put the two of them at odds to direct the peace process. The arrangement didn't last long.)

The duke of Grafton returned to the government as lord privy seal. Edmund Burke became paymaster. Vice Admiral Keppel replaced the earl of Sandwich as first lord of the Admiralty, and Isaac Barré, longtime champion of the American cause, became treasurer of the Royal Navy. General Burgoyne was rewarded with appointment as the military commander in chief in Ireland. General Sir William Howe was given the honor of lieutenant general of ordnance (actually a sinecure), while his brother, the admiral, was raised in the peerage and eventually became commander in chief of the fleet.

Almost the first action of the new government was to dispatch General Sir Guy Carleton to New York to replace Clinton. Carleton was ordered to wind up England's military presence as expeditiously as possible. He was authorized to inform the Americans of his orders, and he was instructed to send out discreet feelers for opening direct peace negotiations. (This backfired quickly, and Carleton gave up on the ill-advised move.)

However, it was easier to issue orders in London than it was for Carleton to carry them out. There weren't enough ships available for any speedy, efficient evacuation of all the men and material involved. It ended up taking a full eighteen months from the time Carleton arrived in New York in May 1782 until the final departure of the British, on November 25, 1783.

Chapter 21

THE PEACE PROCESS

The marquess of Rockingham, less than one hundred days after forming his government, died suddenly, on July 1, 1782, aged only fifty-two, in an influenza epidemic that swept England and all of northern Europe. The peace process in Paris had barely got under way, and a new government had to be formed.

Charles James Fox, as the leader of the Rockingham faction in the House of Commons, commanded a bloc of about ninety votes and would have been the natural successor to Rockingham but for one important obstacle. King George would not have him. The king wrote to John Robinson, one of his confidants, that "every honest man must wish to the utmost to keep Mr. Fox out of power." The king could still choose whomever he wished to be his prime minister, and he sent for the earl of Shelburne. Fox was given a five-minute audience to turn over his seals of office as the first and most short-lived British secretary of state for foreign affairs. Fox was back in opposition, where he was generally more comfortable anyway. Shelburne was delighted to have Fox out of the way.

The two men had been openly at odds over the peace process in the brief period of the Rockingham government, and they thoroughly disliked each other.* Fox had been ready to recognize American independence unequivocally and immediately. Shelburne took the view that conceding American independence at the outset of negotiations for peace would be giving away a major trump card. With Fox now out of the government, the peace process would be entirely in Shelburne's hands.

Shelburne was something of a cold fish, but he was intelligent and hardworking, and he did have vision and was prepared to make hard decisions. He had been briefly responsible for American affairs in the Chatham government in 1766, and like his old mentor Lord Chatham, he was determined to end the war. Like Chatham, he knew from the outset that America could not be kept by force. Now he hoped to offer peace terms that somehow would still preserve some link to the British Empire. His negotiating strategy was peace terms first and independence last.

Shelburne chose an obscure retired diplomat, Lord Grantham, to replace Fox in the foreign affairs post. He named one of his supporters, Thomas Townshend, to be secretary of state for home, Irish, and colonial affairs. Neither of these men would interfere in the peace negotiations, which Shelburne was determined to control himself.

In his most innovative political decision, Shelburne brought the twenty-three-year-old William Pitt into his cabinet as the youngest chancellor of the Exchequer in English history. He included Pitt in an inner circle that he kept small, for he intended to run a very tight ship.

Almost immediately after the new government was formed, Parliament departed for its long vacation. Shelburne, well aware that there would be complications as soon as Parliament returned from recess, was anxious to advance peace negotiations as far and as fast as possible while Parliament was out. After seven years of war with America, four years of war with France, three with Spain, and one and a half with Holland, economic, military, and political exhaustion had set in. Regardless of territorial gains or losses or ancient

---

*When someone referred to Shelburne as "a pious fraud," Fox quipped, "I can see the fraud plainly, but where is the piety?"

enmities that had to be resolved, no matter what King George's will, the wars had to end. The threat of a breakdown in the peace process would have no reality. It was a negotiation that had to succeed.

In June 1782, John Jay arrived in Paris to join Benjamin Franklin as a peace commissioner. Jay, a New Yorker, had been representing the Continental Congress at Madrid for two frustrating, unsuccessful years. The Spanish had deliberately held Jay at arm's length, ignoring and even seeking to humiliate him. He was glad to move to Paris.

Jay was thirty-seven when he went to Paris, nearly forty years younger than Franklin. He had an intense intelligence, an incisive mind, and excellent legal training. The grandson of Huguenot immigrants, he had an innate suspicion of all things Catholic and French. Franklin's intellectual and social style, his readiness to indulge the French, was not to Jay's taste at all. But Jay was openminded enough to appreciate Franklin's many strengths. Despite open arguments and differences, the two men respected each other. Jay was an effective balance to Franklin and provided a valuable counterpoint in the intricate diplomatic game they were playing.

When negotiations reached a decisive stage, in October, Franklin and Jay were joined by a third peace commissioner, John Adams of Massachusetts, who had been representing American interests in Amsterdam, successfully concluding both recognition and loan agreements with the Dutch government.

A fourth commissioner, Henry Laurens of South Carolina, had also been appointed by Congress. But on his voyage to Holland in September 1780, Laurens's ship had been captured off Newfoundland by the Royal Navy. He had been taken to England and imprisoned in the Tower of London on a charge of treason. Laurens's imprisonment and the refusal of the English to recognize his status as a civilian diplomat had incensed the Americans and had been vigorously protested by Congress and General Washington through communications with General Clinton. Laurens was finally released at the end of 1781, after the Battle of Yorktown, in a "peace gesture." He was, however, on parole under a heavy bail provided by a wealthy pro-American merchant and could not leave England. The

English finally allowed him to join his fellow commissioners at the very end of the peace negotiations.

At the outset of the peace talks, the most difficult problem for Franklin and Jay was their instructions from Congress. These had been drafted in Philadelphia under heavy pressure from a French diplomat, the chevalier de la Luzerne. Its language was very severe, very restrictive:

> You are to make the most candid and confidential communications upon all subjects to the ministers of our generous ally, the King of France; to undertake nothing in the negotiations for peace or truce without their knowledge and concurrence; and ultimately to govern yourselves by their advice and opinion, endeavouring in your whole conduct to make them sensible how much we rely upon His Majesty's influence for effectual aid in everything that may be necessary to the peace, security and future prosperity of the United States of America.

This extraordinary instruction seemed very much at odds with the independence the Americans were fighting for. How Franklin and Jay would negotiate under such stipulations was, of course, critical to the outcome. Were the French to dictate the terms of peace with England and recognition of independence?

Until now, Franklin had rebuffed attempts by the English government to open separate peace talks, the most recent of which had been in January 1782. But things had changed. Could they now negotiate separately with England, remain loyal to the French alliance, and follow their instructions from Congress? Franklin knew—they all knew—that France could not make peace with England on America's behalf. In March, acting on the suggestion of one of his many English visitors, Franklin took the initiative to reopen his old contacts, from his London days, with the earl of Shelburne. He gave his visitor a seemingly innocuous letter to carry to London personally (thus avoiding interception by the French). In it, he sent assurances to Shelburne of "continuance of my ancient respect" and congratulations on "the new temper in England." The letter ended: "I hope it will tend to produce *a general peace* which I am sure your Lordship with all good men desires, which I wish to see before I die, and to which I shall with infinite pleasure contribute everything in my power." Shelburne responded soon thereafter by sending a personal envoy for exploratory talks with Franklin.

Shelburne's choice was a shrewd one, an elderly Scottish businessman, a year older than Franklin, who had lived in America for several years before the war. He quickly established a good rapport with Franklin. His name was Richard Oswald.

Oswald's first meeting with Franklin took place in Passy on April 12. Two days later, Franklin, honoring the French alliance, took Oswald to a meeting with Vergennes, the French foreign minister, at Versailles. Franklin wanted no suspicion of double-dealing.

Vergennes wasted no time in telling Oswald that the French would never agree to any separate peace between England and America, that only a general peace that included Spain and Holland could conclude the war. Franklin nodded his assent. Oswald asked for peace proposals from France, but Vergennes told him it was up to the king of England to make such proposals, not the king of France. He pointed out that France had several allies in the war with whom she would have to consult, while England had none. But he was not closing the doors on any peace talks. He suggested that Paris could be the venue for these discussions. Oswald readily agreed.

The following day, Franklin and Oswald had a long discussion about a framework for the settlement to end the war. Then Oswald headed back to London, greatly encouraged by his talks with Franklin. With him, he took a letter to Shelburne in which Franklin had said, "I desire no other channel of communication between us than that of Mr. Oswald, whom I think Your Lordship has chosen with much judgment."

After receiving Oswald's report, the English sent another special envoy to open discussions directly with Vergennes on an overall agreement "with France and her allies." This inadvertently gave Franklin more freedom for maneuvering.

On May 28, after meeting with the English special envoy, Vergennes had dinner with Franklin and told him:

The English wish to treat with us for you, but this the King will not agree to. He thinks it not consistent with the dignity of your state. You will treat for yourselves, and every one of the powers at war with

England will make his own treaty. . . . All that is necessary for common security is that the treaties go hand in hand and are signed on the same day.

Franklin now had Vergennes's blessing to negotiate directly and alone with England. Paradoxically, Vergennes had no qualms about letting Franklin do this because he fully expected that the Americans would adhere to the instructions from Congress and consult with France every step of the way. He could assume, therefore, that France would hold some veto power over the outcome. He was not a little angry when, at the end, he found out that he had been deliberately and decisively outmaneuvered by Franklin, Jay, and Adams.

When John Jay arrived in Paris, the preliminaries were largely over. The next step was to move to formal negotiation. This would require an exchange of "commissions" between the negotiators, the purpose of which would be to establish the negotiating authority on each side, the bona fides to speak for the governments. For older, established governments, this was merely a diplomatic formality. For the fledgling United States, it meant gaining from the British diplomatic recognition of its status as an independent state.

In his early discussions, Franklin had found Oswald positive about this. But Oswald had no authority from Shelburne as to how, when, where, in what form, and on what terms England would finally officially recognize American independence. Franklin wrote to a friend in Philadelphia, "I hope our people will not be deceived by fair words, but be on their guard, ready against any attempt that our insidious enemies may make upon us." This warning seemed justified when he and Jay were handed the terms of the commission that Richard Oswald would carry. Under Shelburne's close scrutiny and meticulous drafting, the language avoided any mention of "the United States of America" or anything that might be even remotely interpreted as immediate recognition of the former colonies' independence. The document empowered Oswald

to treat, agree and conclude with any commissioner or commissioners, named or to be named by the said colonies or plantations, or with any body or bodies, corporate or politic, or any assembly or assemblies, or descriptions of men, or person or persons whatsoever, a peace or truce with the said colonies or any of them or any part or parts thereof.

With this wording, not only had Shelburne avoided "independence" and diplomatic recognition of the United States of America, he seemed to be attempting to divide the colonies against one another. Shelburne also undoubtedly was reflecting the resistance of King George.

Oswald reported to London that when he met with Franklin at Passy on August 6 and showed him the commission, "the Doctor seemed satisfied" and had commented that "I hope we shall agree and not be long about it."

Then Oswald met with John Jay, whose response was entirely different. Why, Jay demanded, did the terms of Oswald's commission not recognize that England was negotiating with the United States of America? Why did England hesitate to concede American independence? Independence should be acknowledged from the outset of the talks, Jay told Oswald, and "should not be granted as the price of peace." Jay continued a long, frosty harangue, very different from the relaxed, avuncular discussions Oswald was used to with Franklin. Oswald retreated to report to London.

On August 10, Franklin and Jay called on Vergennes to discuss the impasse over the "commissions." Franklin was still inclined not to make a sticking point of the wording. Vergennes, the consummate diplomat, attempted to soothe the problem. Why worry about technicalities? he asked. If the English accept *your* commissions to negotiate as plenipotentiaries on behalf of the United States, will they not have recognized your independence? As long as independence is a part of the final treaty, the wording of the negotiating commission is unimportant. Franklin was prepared to accept this view. Jay, however, told Vergennes that he was not satisfied, that he wished to proceed cautiously. This meeting marked a turning point, not only in Franco-American relations but also between Jay and Franklin.

When they got back to Passy, they engaged in a lengthy and somewhat heated argument (which Jay later detailed in letters to New York). Franklin reminded Jay of Congress's instructions to follow closely the advice of the French court. But, Jay countered, they also had instructions from Congress that recognition of American independence was a precondition of any treaty with England. Franklin thought this was consistent with the advice from Vergennes. He asked Jay, "Would you deliberately break Congress's instructions?" Jay responded:

> I do not mean to imply that we should deviate in the least from our treaty with France. Our honor and interests are concerned in inviolably adhering to it, but if we lean on her love of liberty and her affection for Americans, or her interested magnanimity, we shall lean on a broken reed that will sooner or later pierce our hands. If the instructions [from Congress] conflict with America's honor and dignity, Yes, I would break them.

A week later, Franklin was stricken with a severe attack of kidney stones, which intensified his chronic gout. He was a very sick man, and rumors spread that he had been incapacitated by a stroke. Nursed at his home in Passy, it was many weeks before he could resume any active role in the peace diplomacy. So, in September, the conduct of the negotiations shifted entirely to Jay.

Jay was determined to force Shelburne to acknowledge American independence before any negotiations began and change the wording of Oswald's commission. On September 2, he met with Oswald. After much discussion, Jay wrote out what he considered to be acceptable wording of a commission. In Jay's revision, Oswald would be empowered "to treat of Peace or Truce with the Commissioners and Persons vested with equal powers by and on the part of the thirteen United States of America." This was acceptable to Oswald, but he would have to get approval from Shelburne, the cabinet—and the king.

Jay then made another audacious move. He called in Benjamin Vaughan, another of Shelburne's personal envoys in Paris, who was primarily dealing with the French. Vaughan, a man of mildly radical and pro-American sentiments, was anxious to see the issues resolved and the peace obtained. Jay asked Vaughan to travel to London with an oral message for Shelburne—nothing to be put into writing that could be intercepted. He gave Vaughan a number of "talking points," but the basic message was a warning: Without prompt acknowledgment of American independence, "neither confidence nor peace can reasonably be expected." No change in the commission wording, no negotiations, and the war, without fighting, would drag on. Vaughan hastened to London with the message.

Jay neither consulted with Franklin on his sickbed nor informed him of what he had done. He was issuing an ultimatum to the English, and Franklin did not believe in ultimatums.

When Oswald next met with Jay, he brought a simple amendment to the wording of Jay's revision. Would it be acceptable, Oswald asked, if the thirteen colonies were listed individually, by name, after the official designation, "United States of America"? Apparently, the English diplomats believed this would convey that these were not truly *united* states and that England had not yet relinquished those last connections in the capitals once ruled by royal governors.

Now Jay did consult with Franklin. They met on September 9. Franklin was still uneasy about Jay's seeming breach with the French. He urged that no dealings with the English be put into writing. So Jay returned to Oswald and told him orally that if the wording of the commission were revised along the lines they had discussed, then "we would proceed with the Treaty, and should not be long about it."

Oswald had hoped to have something in writing, signed by Franklin and Jay. Nevertheless, he sent off a full report and urged the necessity of revising the wording. He told Shelburne:

> I hope His Majesty will grant it. If it is refused, Mr. Fitzherbert [a fellow diplomat in Paris] as well as me may go home, and it is my opinion it will not be an easy matter for any other to take up the same clue for extracting the nation out of the difficulties which I think is within our reach.

Shelburne was an intelligent man. He knew that American independence was already a fact and that its formal recognition was inevitable. What he wanted to put together was a treaty that would sugarcoat this unpalatable pill and make it easier for the king and the Tories, who had fought the war, to swallow. But he could not prevaricate on or postpone independence any longer. Benjamin Vaughan was urging compromise, Richard Oswald was urging compromise, . . . and it was September, and time was running out. He desperately needed to wind up at least the American negotiation before Parliament returned. If he didn't compromise, then the war would drag on. Shelburne and the English people wanted peace.

Shelburne called a special cabinet meeting for the evening of September 18. The new wording was accepted, reluctantly. For the benefit of King George, the cabinet recorded that it was accepting the changes simply to accommodate the American commissioners "with the title they wished to assume." The new wording, the cabinet stoutly declared, did not constitute "any final acknowledgment of independence." This was all sham, . . . but the bitter pill went down.

The approved revisions were hastily dispatched to Paris. With Oswald's new commission, Great Britain affixed its seal to a document recognizing the United States of America as an independent equal at the negotiating table. John Jay had won the first round.

"I hope we shall agree and not be long about it," Franklin had told the English at the start of the peace process. As soon as Oswald produced his newly worded commission to negotiate, Jay set to work on a provisional treaty draft. There would be much to argue over, Jay knew, and he felt it very important to put the American position on the table first.

The treaty draft outlined American expectations on two central points—national boundaries to be recognized for the United States of America and fishing rights off the Grand Banks of Newfoundland. Jay's treaty draft was handed to Oswald without any discussions or consultations with, or knowledge of, the French.

The draft specified that the western boundary of the United States would be the Mississippi River, with free navigation from its source to its mouth. Jay knew that this would be opposed heartily by both France and Spain. Both wanted to see the western border of the new republic held roughly to the line of the Appalachian mountain range. Spain was particularly vehement about retaining her settlements at the southern end of the Mississippi.

But in demanding the Mississippi as the western boundary, Jay was carrying out a unanimous decision taken by the Continental Congress in 1779, when he himself had been the Congress president.

Whatever the position of France and Spain with regard to the boundary question, the fact remained that the decision was entirely in England's hands. To Jay, therefore, it was all the more important to negotiate with the English without consulting France. If England agreed to the Mississippi boundary, there was nothing the French could do to block it.

France, after all, had relinquished all its claims on American territory east of the Mississippi at the end of the Seven Years' War, in 1763. Further, this was a problem with which Shelburne had some familiarity. He had been in charge of American affairs in 1766–67 and at that time had made a detailed study of the issues concerning the western lands in America. He had formed a liberal view on opening up the area to colonial expansion. It was clear that England could gain nothing by attempting to confine the Americans to the east of the Appalachian Mountains. France and Spain were attempting to perpetuate an imperial role on the American continent, the very role that England was relinquishing.

When Jay's treaty draft reached London, Shelburne decided to send a new emissary to Paris to stiffen the English delegation. He chose Henry Strachey, who had worked with Admiral Howe on the ill-conceived, ill-fated first peace mission to America, in 1776. Oswald would stay, but Strachey would more or less supersede him.

About this same time, John Adams arrived to join the American delegation. He had been serving with great effectiveness in Amsterdam, where Holland, of course, was also at war with England. Adams, however, had an open dislike of Franklin and deliberately delayed for four days before making a personal call on him at Passy. Adams was vain, full of self-importance, envious, prone to personal feuds. But he was possessed of high intelligence, a quick mind, and strong abilities. He grew somewhat more tolerant of Franklin, but he greatly resented being introduced in Paris as "le collègue de Monsieur Franklin."

Jay and Strachey, meanwhile, got down to business on the boundary question and other treaty provisions. Strachey surprised Jay by first producing a counterproposal based on the French and Spanish position—the Appalachian Mountains. Jay's blunt response was "If that line is insisted upon, it is needless to talk peace. We shall never accept it." The English were not going to see the whole peace process snagged or halted to support a French proposal. So Strachey consulted Shelburne and dropped the idea. England accepted the Mississippi boundary. After that, boundaries for Nova Scotia, Maine, and Canada were quickly settled. John Jay had won another round.

*   *   *

Jay had taken the lead on boundaries, and John Adams led on behalf of New England's fishermen. There was much discussion on catching and drying fish on the Newfoundland coast. In the end, it came down to a semantic argument over whether the treaty would state that the Americans had the *right* to fish off the Grand Banks or merely the *liberty* accorded by England. Adams argued vociferously that the Americans had a far greater *right* to fish there than the English or the French, who came from the other side of the Atlantic. The English countered that use of the word *right* would be "unpleasing." In the end, Adams agreed to accept *liberty*.

By the last week of November, final arguments began over British demands for compensation by the American Loyalists and Tories whose property had been seized or destroyed. The venerable Franklin, recovered after more than two months' illness, took on this argument. Compensation, he pointed out, was beyond the competence of the American commissioners and even beyond the American Congress. It was a matter for the individual states.

After listening to repeated English insistence on compensation, Franklin finally pulled from his pocket a piece of paper and began reading. "The principle of peace is equality and reciprocity," he said, "and if you demand compensation from us, then we have some reparations and compensation to demand from you." He went on to review the looting and burning of American homes. He cited the behavior of German troops (somewhat less than exemplary), Gage's troops in Boston, Howe's in Philadelphia, Cornwallis's in Charleston and the south. He even mentioned the loss of his own library in Philadelphia during Major André's occupation.

Eventually, the Americans agreed to a clause "earnestly recommending" the legislatures of the individual American states to provide restitution for "real British subjects" and persons "resident in districts in the possession of His Majesty's arms, who have not borne arms against the said United States." The clause further stipulated that "there shall be no further confiscations made or prosecutions commenced" against Loyalists as a result of the war. The Americans did agree to repay all debts outstanding to British merchants for goods shipped to America since 1775 but not paid for because of the war.

"Dr. Franklin behaved well and nobly, particularly this day," observed John Adams in his diary.

At the end of November, Henry Laurens was at last permitted to join the other commissioners in Paris. There was a mood of satisfaction, exultant but subdued, as the participants prepared for a signing on Saturday, November 30.

On Friday evening, Franklin penned a brief note to Vergennes, advising him that England and America would sign a *preliminary* peace treaty on the morrow and a copy would be forwarded immediately to the French foreign minister. In accordance with the terms of the American alliance with France, the treaty would not be formally concluded or effective until England also made peace with France.

Since it was a "preliminary" treaty, and not the final peace, the signing was not a state occasion. It would be signed by the participants as negotiators, not as ministers or plenipotentiaries.

On Saturday, everyone gathered at the rooms that Richard Oswald had taken at the Grand Hôtel Muscovite. Oswald signed for England. The four American commissioners signed in alphabetical order. John Adams was very pleased to be the first.*

When Benjamin Franklin and Henry Laurens called on Vergennes a few days later, the foreign minister, more than a little irked at the Americans' strategem, remarked coldly that "the abrupt signing of the articles had little in it which would be agreeable to the King." He then made the unusual request that the American commissioners *not* send a copy of the preliminary treaty to America, since it could not be ratified (or effective) until France had concluded a peace treaty with England. "[It] might make the people in America think a peace consummated," Vergennes told Franklin, "and embarrass Congress, of whose fidelity I have no suspicions."

Once again, Vergennes's advice was ignored. The texts were dispatched in mid-December aboard an American vessel suitably named *Washington*. To la Luzerne, the French minister in Philadel-

---

*Two copies were signed and exchanged, but the American copy has since disappeared. The only original of the document is in the Public Records Office in London.

phia, Vergennes complained that "our opinion could not influence the negotiations since we knew nothing of the details because they were completed in a most sudden, unforeseen, and, I might say, extraordinary manner."

La Luzerne soon made the French irritation known to the American secretary of state, Robert Livingston, and to members of Congress. Jay, however, defended the commissioners' actions. He wrote to Livingston, "As we had reason to imagine that the articles respecting the boundaries, the refugees and the fisheries did not correspond to the policy of the Court, we did not communicate the preliminaries to the Minister until after they were signed." The explanation was as simple and as unassailable as that. Franklin and Adams wrote their accounts of the negotiations, and such controversy as there was subsided.

The earl of Shelburne was braced for trouble no matter what his negotiators brought back from Paris. King George wrote to Shelburne:

> I cannot conclude without mentioning how sensibly I feel the dismemberment of America from this Empire. *I should be miserable indeed if I did not feel that no blame on that account can be laid at my door,* and did I not also know that knavery seems to be so much the striking feature of its inhabitants that it may not in the end be an evil that they become aliens to that Kingdom. [Emphasis added.]

The king would take no blame, his only solace the good riddance of his obstreperous, ungrateful American subjects.

Shelburne deliberately kept Parliament in recess until negotiations on the American treaty were finished. Parliament would reconvene December 5, when the king would read a carefully prepared speech; soon after, Parliament would begin its Christmas recess. Shelburne could therefore reasonably hope to avoid a vote of confidence on the treaty for at least a few more months. During that time, he hoped to conclude treaties with France and Spain and end the war completely. (Holland was only marginally important and could wait.)

On December 5, a crowded House of Lords waited two hours for the king to appear. Among those present to record the scene were

Edmund Burke, the French diplomat Gérard de Rayneval, and a visiting American merchant named Elkanah Watson, there by virtue of a letter of introduction to the earl of Stanhope from Benjamin Franklin.

The king, in his traditional speech from the throne, would have to address the English defeat at Yorktown fourteen months previously and the signing of the peace treaty in Paris five days before. The government had composed a speech for him that was intended to make it as easy on him as possible.

He began by asserting that he had lost no time after Yorktown in ending further offensive wars in the colonies. He said that all his views and actions had been directed to "an entire and cordial reconciliation" with the colonies. Then he said, "Finding it indispensable to the attainment of this object, I did not hesitate to go to the full length of the powers vested in me, and offer to declare them . . ." An awkward pause. The king was clearly shaken and embarrassed; the silent audience waited while he composed himself. "[A]nd offer to declare them free and independent states, by an article to be inserted in the Treaty of Peace." At last, he had said the words he had tried so hard to avoid. He went on hastily, closing on a note later characterized by Edmund Burke as "insufferable":

> We offer a humble and ardent prayer to Almighty God that Great Britain will not feel the evils which might result from so great a dismemberment of the Empire, and that America may be free from the calamities which have formerly proved, in the mother country, how essential monarchy is to the enjoyment of constitutional liberty, and that religion, language, interests and affection may yet prove a bond of permanent union between the two countries.

Elkanah Watson wrote that the king "hesitated, choked, and executed the painful duties with an ill grace which does not belong to him." The French diplomat Rayneval wrote to Vergennes that "in pronouncing *independence* the King of England did it in a constrained voice."

By the time Parliament returned in January from its Christmas recess, Shelburne had concluded peace agreements with France and Spain and was ready to present them for approval. But immediately, his government began to fall apart. The duke of Richmond resigned and so did Admiral Keppel, first lord of the Admiralty. Young William Pitt tried his best in the House of Commons to hold things together for Shelburne. But on February 13, Lord North delivered a major attack on the treaties. Edmund Burke, erstwhile champion of American liberty, now wailed about "abandonment" of the Loyalists and England's "surrender" of territories in the American west. Fox joined, condemning concessions to the French. The end was not long in coming.

On February 21, Lord North stunned Parliament and the king by announcing that he and Charles James Fox, hated by the king, would form a new coalition to overthrow Shelburne. The king did everything possible to find someone else to save Shelburne. Young William Pitt, who was by now the most likely candidate on the rise, declined for lack of solid parliamentary support.

When the North-Fox coalition took office, the peace treaties were back in limbo. Fox, once again the foreign minister, had proclaimed that he could do better—but he quickly found that England had no bargaining power to force revisions on France and America on issues that had already been agreed upon. Altogether, Fox wasted six months before the treaties could finally be signed—with only cosmetic changes.

On the morning of September 3, 1783, Adams, Franklin, and Jay took carriages to David Hartley's Paris residence at the Hôtel d'York.* After Hartley signed, the Americans signed, in alphabetical order.

That afternoon, the English ambassador to France, the duke of Manchester, signed England's treaties of peace with France and Spain in Versailles.

A few days later, Benjamin Franklin wrote to his friend John Quincy in Boston: "We are all friends with England and all mankind. May we never see another War! For in my opinion there never was a good war or a bad peace."

* * *

---

*Located in the Latin Quarter, on the rue Jacob, the building is marked today by a simple plaque of the kind identifying historic sites in Paris.

One month before the peace treaties were finally signed, King George wrote a somewhat testy memorandum to Foreign Secretary Charles James Fox:

> As to the question whether I wish to receive a Minister from America, I can certainly never express its being agreeable to me; and indeed I should think it wisest for both parties to have only agents who can settle matters of commerce. But so far I cannot help adding that I shall ever have a bad opinion of any Englishman who would accept of being an accredited minister of that revolting state, and which certainly cannot establish a stable government.

Nor was the American Congress in a rush to open diplomatic relations with the erstwhile rulers in London. There was much antagonism and unfinished business to clear away after the treaties were signed: matters of trade and commerce, discharge of debts, English troops still on American soil. England turned her back, and the mood on both sides was neither friendly nor accommodating.

Nor was King George so very wrong in his judgment of the stability of the new government. The early years of peace were chaotic politically, economically, and governmentally. For eight years, the unifying force for the thirteen colonies had been the war. When it was over, each of the states, bound together only very loosely by the 1777 Articles of Confederation, quickly turned away from any ideas of a strong central government. The Articles united them only in a "firm league of friendship" and specified that each state retained its own "sovereignty, freedom and independence, and every power, jurisdiction and right which is not expressly delegated" to the Continental Congress.

Depression settled over the less-than-united states. Each state dealt on its own with its post-war economic shambles. Overseas trade had virtually collapsed. The sizable British purchases of naval stores, rice, and indigo from the Carolinas and Georgia dried up to almost nothing. New England fishermen, while they could still sail to the Grand Banks to catch cod, could no longer dry their catch in the cold, clear air of Labrador and Newfoundland because these territories flew the English flag. No longer did Britain buy cargo vessels from Massachusetts shipyards, where the average number of vessels built per year dropped from 150 to only 25. England also barred American ships from trading with the English islands in the

Caribbean. While English ships crowded the American ports, the English refused to allow American ships to bring just any cargo into English ports; each ship had to be registered to the state where the cargo originated. (For example, John Hancock's Massachusetts-registered vessels could not carry Virginia tobacco to England, only Massachusetts dried cod, timber, or pig iron.) As a result of all this, American imports, exports, and general shipping all suffered greatly from the exclusion from the British Empire, while British shipping prospered.

As the states squabbled amongst themselves and struggled for survival, the American peace commissioners in Paris continued to work, seeking commercial treaties to break the economic stranglehold imposed by English embargoes and restrictions. Eventually, they were able to do this, but it was a long, slow process.

In December of 1783, King George found a pretext to rid himself of the North-Fox coalition, which had been in power only nine months. William Pitt, at the age of twenty-four, became prime minister of England. Three months later, Pitt boldly called a national election, which produced a resounding victory and consolidated his hold on power for a remarkable, unbroken seventeen years.

A new era began under the younger Pitt, and the floundering new United States of America virtually disappeared from the English mind. Pitt looked firmly toward Europe and the east for England's role as a world power and for its security. As the political follies that produced the American Revolution receded, the English were increasingly content to treat the whole affair as an aberration, a footnote to English history.

By 1785, two years after the signing of the peace treaties, King George was grudgingly prepared to receive an American envoy at the Court of St. James's. In Philadelphia, when the name of John Adams was put forward, there was much objection by members of Congress.

Adams had been overbearing in seeking the appointment and had offended many. His dislike of Franklin was common knowledge, and his co-commissioner in Paris, Henry Laurens, wrote directly to members of Congress against sending Adams to London. Two other candidates were nominated—John Rutledge of South Carolina and

Robert Livingston of New York. But whatever Adams's personality, his abilities and years of experience made him the best man for the job. Finally, in February of 1785, Congress agreed to make John Adams the first American diplomatic minister to England.

Adams wasted no time when the news reached him in Paris. He sought out the British ambassador to take advice on protocol and purchased suitable court dress from a French tailor: formal coat, black silk breeches, silk stockings, buckled shoes, sword, sash, powdered wig, and hat. He arrived in London on May 25 and took an apartment with his wife, Abigail, at the Bath Hotel in Piccadilly.

The king would receive him in a formal ceremony to present his credentials on Wednesday, June 1, 1785. The master of ceremonies at the court, Sir Clement Cotterell, called on Adams to brief him on the etiquette of the audience. It was customary, Adams was told, to address His Majesty in a manner "as complimentary as possible." He was to bow three times to the king on entering the audience room and three times on departure.

Adams promptly memorized and practiced with great care the speech of the first American to address the king.

On the morning of June 1, Sir Clement arrived in a carriage to take Adams to Foreign Secretary Lord Carmarthen's office. Then Adams and Carmarthen rode in an official coach to St. James's Palace. Adams was ushered by Carmarthen through a waiting crowd of peers, ministers, and other foreign ambassadors, the cynosure of all eyes. They reached the door of the audience chamber.

In a letter to John Jay, Adams recounted what happened:

The door was shut, and I was left alone with His Majesty and the Secretary of State. I made the three reverences—one at the door, another about half-way and a third before the Presence—according to the usage established at this and all the northern Courts of Europe, and then addressed myself to His Majesty in the following words:

Sir,—The United States of America have appointed me their Minister Plenipotentiary to your Majesty, and have directed me to deliver to your Majesty this letter which contains the evidence of it. It is in obedience to their express commands that I have the honour to assure your Majesty of their unanimous disposition and desire to cultivate the most friendly and liberal intercourse between your Majesty's subjects and their citizens, and of their best wishes for your Majesty's health and happiness and for that of your royal family.

The appointment of a Minister from the United States to your Majesty's Court will form an epoch in the history of England and of America. I think myself more fortunate than all my fellow-citizens in having the distinguished honour to be the first to attend in your Majesty's royal presence in a diplomatic character; and I shall esteem myself the happiest of men if I can be instrumental in recommending my country more and more to your Majesty's royal benevolence, and of restoring an entire esteem, confidence and affection, or, in better words, the old good-nature and good-humour between people who, though separated by an ocean, and under different governments, have the same language, a similar religion and kindred blood.

I beg your Majesty's permission to add that, although I have some time before been instructed by my country, it was never in my whole life in a manner so agreeable to myself.

Adams continued, reporting that the king "listened to every word I spoke with dignity, but with apparent emotion." Adams told Jay of his own "visible agitation—for I felt more than I did or could express."

The king

was much affected, and answered me with more tremor than I had spoken with, and said:

Sir—The circumstances of this audience are so extraordinary, the language you have now held is so extremely proper, and the feelings you have discovered so justly adapted to the occasion, that I must say that I not only receive with pleasure the assurances of the friendly dispositions of the United States, but that I am very glad the choice has fallen on you to be their Minister. I wish you to believe, Sir, and that it may be understood in America, that I have done nothing in the late contest but what I thought myself indispensably bound to do, by the duty which I owe to my people. I will be very frank with you. I was the last to consent to separation; but the separation having been made, and having become inevitable, I have always said, as I say now, that I would be the first to meet the friendship of the United States as an independent power. The moment I see such sentiments and language as yours prevail, and a disposition to give to this country the preference, that moment I shall say, let the circumstances of language, religion, and blood have their natural and full effect.

Adams related to Jay that the king "was indeed much affected, and I confess I was not less so, and, therefore, I cannot be certain that I was so cool and attentive, heard so clearly and understood so perfectly as to be confident of all his words or sense."

There was a brief, informal exchange between the king and Adams before they parted:

> The King then asked me whether I came last from France, and upon my answering in the affirmative, he put me on an air of familiarity, and, smiling, or rather laughing, said, "There is an opinion among some people that you are not the most attached of all your country-men to the manners of France." I was surprised at this, because I thought it an indiscretion and a departure from dignity. I was a little embarrassed, but determined not to deny the truth on one hand, nor leave him to infer from it any attachment to England on the other. I threw off as much gravity as I could, and assumed an air of gaiety and a tone of decision as far as was decent, and said, "That opinion, Sir, is not mistaken; I must avow to your Majesty, I have no attachment but to my own country." The King replied as quick as lightning, "An honest man will never have any other."

Adams withdrew with the ceremonial three bows. He told Jay he was amused to hear the servants calling out, as he walked down the long corridor with Cotterell, "Mr. Adams's Carriage . . . Mr. Adams's Carriage . . ."

Adams ended his long account to John Jay on a practical, cautious note: "I may expect a residence less painful than I had once ex-pected, as so marked attention from the King will silence many grumblers, but we can infer nothing from all this concerning the success of my mission." His caution was justified. He spent three frustrating, disappointing years in London, returning home in 1788 without having resolved any of the basic problems he had brought with him.

In his official dealings, Adams found himself up against a wall of polite prevarication and determined delay all the way up to a polite but unsuccessful meeting with William Pitt. Adams argued that American debts to Britain couldn't be paid off unless trade restric-tions were eased. And his forceful protests against the continued presence of British troops on American territory drew the constant response, "Well, pay your debts and we will live up to the terms of the treaty."

After attending one opening session of Parliament, Adams re-ported that

The most remarkable thing in the King's speech and the debates is that the King and every member of each house has entirely forgotten that there is any such place on earth as the United States of America. We appear to be considered as of no consequence at all in the scale of the world.

In September of 1787, the convention that had met in Philadelphia to write the Constitution finished its work and sent it to the thirteen states for ratification. In February of 1788, Congress sent Adams a welcome recall from London. In April, he sailed for his home in Boston, to become the first vice president of the United States, alongside George Washington, when the federal government was formed in March of 1789.

Relieved at his recall and anxious to get home, Adams had a farewell audience with King George. With formal but frustrated politeness, he gave King George "assurances of friendly disposition, and continued desire of a liberal intercourse of commerce and good offices with Your Majesty's subjects and states" on the part of the United States of America.

King George replied with sentiments that Adams had heard repeatedly in his three years in London: "Mr. Adams, you may with great truth assure the United States that whenever they shall fulfill the treaty on their part, I on my part will fulfill it in all particulars."

On that note, they parted. A new Anglo-American "special relationship" and understanding would take another 150 years of history to form.

EPILOGUE

In June 1788, just two months after John Adams departed from London, King George, now aged fifty, was stricken with a massive flare-up of porphyria. The attack began with stomach cramps and convulsions while he was out riding in the rain on the grounds of Windsor Castle.

Two weeks later, he began to show the first signs of madness. He was well enough to be at the dinner table, but he began to talk nonstop gibberish. Then he suddenly attacked the Prince of Wales (whom he had come to hate, in the Hanoverian tradition of father-son relationships) and tried to smash the prince's head against the dining-room wall, all the while yelling incoherently, his mouth foaming, and "his eyes so bloodshot they looked like currant jelly," according to one account.

His doctors called in a supposed specialist in mental diseases and insanity, one Dr. Francis Willis. Willis operated a private London lunatic asylum and boasted to the king's equerry that "he broke in patients as horses in a ménage." The doctors, baffled by the up-and-down nature of the king's illness, surrendered his care to the not so tender mercies of this Dr. Willis.

"His Majesty quarrelled with his tea and dinner and was confined," read a typical log by Dr. Willis. "His Majesty threw off His wig and tie and resisted them being replaced and was restrained."

The king would be strapped in a "winding sheet," similar to that used to shroud corpses; or he would be straitjacketed with his legs tied to a bed or strapped to a restraining chair, which he was sane enough to dub "my coronation chair." He was forced to submit, after formidable struggles, to purges, vomits, bleedings, blisterings, cuppings, applications of leeches, and nearly every other medical torture the doctors could invent.

The attacks of madness continued off and on for more than six months. Then suddenly, in February 1789, the porphyria began to recede. By the end of February, the doctors were able to announce the "cessation" of the unknown illness. In mid-March, the king resumed his full duties.

He wrote in his own hand to the bishop of Worcester, "After a most tedious and severe illness I escaped the jaws of death, though I cannot boast of the same strength and spirits I enjoyed before." Nevertheless, the king remained in normal health for another twelve years. Then, in February and March of 1801, the porphyria struck again. And again, in 1804, from January to March. The king was now nearly sixty-six, and each attack took a heavier toll of mind and body.

The king's final decline began in October 1810, and now a regency was declared under the Prince of Wales. In 1812, the year that England went to war with America the second time, the king was removed from London to Windsor Castle.

Once again, on the orders of Queen Charlotte, Dr. Francis Willis was called in to take charge of the case. The other doctors, kept at a distance but fully aware of the treatment the king was receiving, were so appalled by what was going on that they wrote to the archbishop of Canterbury to protest. The doctors, Sir Henry Halford and Dr. Matthew Baillie, told the archbishop, "The King has been kept in unedifying confinement and seclusion which of itself has become a source of irritation and excited a fresh accession of his disorder." They asked for "a milder and more liberal system of management," hoping that the archbishop would intercede on behalf of the king. But their pleas were to no avail.

The king's younger son, the Duke of York, was allowed to visit his father not long before he died. He found the king "amusing himself with playing on the harpsichord and singing . . . [he saw] a look of death about him." At Christmas of 1819, the porphyria flaring, the doctors recorded that the king talked restlessly and incoherently for a period of fifty-eight consecutive hours. He died on January 29, 1820, aged eighty-one years and seven months.

Lord North held no further public office after turning in his seals to the king in December 1783, at the demise of the North-Fox coalition. He did, however, continue in active and popular attendance at the House of Commons until his eyesight failed and his health began to decline. In 1790, on the death of his father, he succeeded to the title of earl of Guilford and entered the House of Lords.

North, in his twelve years as prime minister, had embraced and embodied, with the king, all of the collective mistakes and misjudgments of England's going to war with America. At the end of his life, he also embodied England's determination to dismiss the distress of the past: During his decline, he wondered to a friend how history would judge him; then he added, with a deprecating smile, "I suppose that is a fault, but I cannot help it."

He faded away peacefully, dying of dropsy in 1792. He was sixty.

A friend recorded of North's last days, "His mind is in such a state of mildness and benignity that to see and hear him would disarm the rancour of his greatest enemies." A member of his family wrote of North's last hours:

> When he found that he had but a few hours to live, he desired that all his family be sent for to his bedside. When this had been done, he said that with regard to his political life, though he could not have the presumption to suppose but what there had been much at error in many things he had done, yet it was a satisfaction which none but himself would in that hour conceive, that on no one act of it could he look back with regret.

General Sir Henry Clinton returned to England and wrote a lengthy and irascible memoir of the war.* He was particularly harsh about General Sir William Howe:

---

*This was not published until it was found among the Clinton papers when they were brought to America and placed in the Clements Library.

Had Sir William Howe fortified the hills around Boston, he could not have been driven disgracefully from it; Had he pursued his victory at Long Island, he had ended the rebellion; Had he landed above the lines at New York, not a man could have escaped him; Had he fought the Americans at Brunswick [New Jersey] he was sure of victory; Had he cooperated with the Northern Army, he had saved it, or had he gone to Philadelphia by land, he had ruined Mr. Washington and his forces. But, as he had done none of these things, had he gone to the Devil, before he was sent to America, it had been a saving of infamy to himself and indelible dishonour to this Country.

The king had offered Clinton an Irish peerage on his return. This he brusquely refused because he would have ranked lower than either Admiral Viscount Howe or Lord George Germain, the new Viscount Sackville.

Clinton was appointed governor of Gibraltar in 1794. He died there in 1795, aged fifty-seven.

Lord George Germain had sought to consign Sir William Howe to oblivion when he returned after the British withdrawal from Philadelphia. But as soon as Germain was ousted, following Yorktown, Howe was brought back by the Rockingham government. In 1782, he was named lieutenant general of Ordnance, a post to which he clung for twenty years. He was promoted to full general in 1793, during the Napoleonic Wars, and given successive commands of the British Army to organize land defenses against possible invasions by the French. He resigned his Ordnance post in 1803 for health reasons. He died in 1814, aged eighty-five.

Admiral Viscount Howe also returned to an active naval career when the Rockingham government replaced Lord North's ministry, after Germain's departure. In 1782, he assumed command of the Royal Navy in the English Channel. Later, in 1783, he led the fleet that relieved the siege of Gibraltar and routed the French and Spanish fleets. Howe went on to serve as first lord of the Admiralty for five years. He went back to sea in 1793, aged sixty-seven, to a command in the English Channel in the new Napoleonic War. He died in 1799.

*   *   *

More fortunate in both his abilities and his friendships, Lord Cornwallis had the most successful post-war career of all the senior commanders who fought in America. He became governor general of India in 1786, even then the most exalted post in the British Empire. He served effectively for seven years, responsible for both civil administration and military operations. He returned to England to become governor general of Ireland in 1797 and was sent back to India in 1804. But by this time, he was a sick man. He died in 1805, at the age of sixty-seven.

"Gentleman Johnny" Burgoyne was sent by the Rockingham government to Dublin as commander in chief of the British troops stationed there. He much preferred life in London, and when the North-Fox coalition fell apart, in December 1783, Burgoyne promptly gave up the Irish command and returned to his social life and the theater. He wrote half a dozen plays in his lifetime. The first of them, in 1774, was titled *The Maid of the Oaks*. It ran for enough nights at the Drury Lane to be deemed a success.

His best play, *The Heiress*, was staged at Drury Lane in 1786. It was given thirty performances (the equivalent of a smash hit in those days) and was written up by Horace Walpole: "General Burgoyne's battles and speeches will be forgotten, but his delightful comedy *The Heiress* still continues the delight of the stage and one of the most pleasing domestic compositions."

But the Battle of Saratoga has never been forgotten, and Burgoyne's plays were ultimately forgettable. His place in the theater was subsequently assured by none other than George Bernard Shaw, who made Burgoyne a leading character in his enduring comedy *The Devil's Disciple*.

Burgoyne, a widower, fathered four children between 1782 and 1788 in a liaison with a singer, Susan Caulfield. All the children were reared by Lord Derby, father of Burgoyne's deceased wife.

Gentleman Johnny, in apparent good health, died suddenly of a heart attack in 1792. He was seventy.

Lord George Germain, the newly minted Viscount Sackville, appeared occasionally to speak in the House of Lords. Mainly, he ruled over his country estate, where he died in 1785 at the age of sixty-nine.

Charles James Fox, worn out by pleasure and politics, died in 1806 at the age of fifty-seven.

Edmund Burke kept his oratorical flame alive in the House of Commons with denunciations of the French Revolution and at the great trial of Warren Hastings. He died in 1797, aged sixty-eight.

Could England have won her war for America? With a more far-sighted policy by London, one based on conciliation and compromise, England might well have reached an accommodation that would have kept the American colonies in the British Empire. But she could not win a war based on a policy of full submission, as the king demanded. To that extent, the colonies were lost in London.

Militarily, the odds against conquering America were great to begin with, and they lengthened with each passing year and each successive commander in chief.

The duke of Wellington, master of wars fought in theaters far from home, wrote:

> In such a country as America, very extensive, thinly peopled, and producing but little food in proportion to their extent, military operations by large bodies are impracticable, unless the party carrying them on has the uninterrupted use of navigable rivers, or a very extensive means of land transport, which such a country can rarely provide.

The English never fully controlled the Hudson River, the Delaware River, Chesapeake Bay, or even Long Island Sound. Even if England had managed to destroy the Continental Army, occupy all thirteen colonial capitals, and disperse all rebellious assemblies and local governments—what then? The British Army would still have been operating to control a widely scattered hostile population in a state of rebellion, and the war would have gone on and on.

A French officer of Rochambeau's staff summarized the military problems of war in America more succinctly than Wellington: "No opinion was clearer than that the people of America might be conquered by well disciplined European troops, but the country of America was unconquerable."

SOURCE NOTES

Any author writing about the American Revolution can quickly be swamped by the sheer volume and scope of the detailed writings on the subject. A countless number of historians, biographers, and scholars on both sides of the Atlantic have plowed over this ground.

A bibliography of writings on the American Revolution, compiled by the Library of Congress in Washington, D.C., with titles, authors, and subjects, takes up two large reference volumes of some twelve hundred pages. An upsurge in historical examination of the Revolution has been relatively recent. In the first 150 years after the events, Americans paid little scholarly attention to the origins and details of their independence. This began to change after World War II, partly because of the growth in university attendance and the increase in graduate schools. The result has been a flood of new histories, biographies, and scholarly studies, some of which took on added impetus from the bicentennial celebrations of the Declaration of Independence in 1976.

In focusing the story on England's politics before and during the Revolution and on the conduct of the war from London, I have delved into authors' works that go back to the last century. In the absorbing and distilling of a wide range of historical material, there is no particular author who stands out; I am indebted to all. What follows is a summary of the principal works and research sources from which I formed my narrative framework. I have also noted some titles of subsidiary works.

The starting point for understanding the complexities of internal and external events and the politics of England from 1760 to 1785 is *The Reign of King George III* in the *Oxford History of England* series, written by J. Steven Watson and published in Oxford in 1960. This standard work is rich in scholarly detail and alive with sharp portraiture of an ever-changing cast of political characters.

There are two modern biographies of the king, both published in 1972. They are *George the Third* by Stanley Ayling (London) and *King George III* by John Brooke (New York). Ayling is more interesting in political detail and richer in quotations from source material. I have also used a much earlier biography, *George III as Man, Monarch, and Statesman* by Beckles Willson, published in Philadelphia in 1907. This is amusing for its cloying attempt to humanize and deify a monarch whom the English have treated with as much, if not more, disdain than the Americans. It does, however, include useful documentation and interesting details.

As to the king's reign, *King George III and the Politicians* by Richard Pares (Oxford, 1953) contains a wealth of insights and a lively and stimulating analysis of how this difficult monarch exercised his power. Lewis B. Namier's *England in the Age of the American Revolution* (London, 1930) is a classic of English history, a basic work with a mass of original research into the composition of the House of Commons and the social as well as the political fabric and workings of English democracy in the 1760s and 1770s.

The main source material, however, comes from King George himself—*The Correspondence of King George III,* edited by Sir John Fortescue, takes up six large volumes (London, 1927–28). The quotations I have used from George III have been drawn almost entirely from these Fortescue volumes.

In addition, the early letters from young George to the earl of Bute, which I have quoted, were collected by Romney Sedgwick and published in London in 1939. The more important letters from the king to his ministers, sifted out by Bonamy Debrée and published in London in 1935, added useful background material on the events and political matters involved.

Military History. Two recent general works by American authors that I found useful are *A History of the American Revolution* by John R. Alden, history professor at Duke University (New York, 1969), and *The Glorious Cause: The American Revolution, 1763–1789,* by Robert Middlekauff, director of the Huntington Library in California, published in New York in the *Oxford History of the United States* series in 1982. Alden is concise and academically thorough, while Middlekauff is more discursive, anecdotal and colorful. He also pays more attention to what was going on in England.

The outstanding military history of the Revolutionary War, however, is by the British historian Piers Mackesy: *The War for America, 1775–1783,* first published in 1964 and recently reissued (in 1993) in paperback with a foreword by the American historian John W. Shy. Mackesy is from a British military family, and he brings to the story both the research and the insights into the conduct of the war on the English side that only a writer steeped in English military lore can offer. At the same time, his research on the American side, the result of several years at Princeton University, is formidable in detail and written with an impeccable understanding of America at war. He makes thorough use of material from original dispatches in telling the story.

Military Commanders: Excellent biographical studies of the principal military commanders on both sides will be found in *General Washington's Generals and Opponents,* edited by George Athan Billias, first published in 1964 and 1969 and recently reissued in a one-volume paperback by De Capo Press. A full-length study, *Cornwallis and the War of Independence* by Franklin and Mary Wickwire (Boston, 1970), covers the best of the British generals who fought in America, with valuable source documentation on the feuding among General Lord Charles Cornwallis, General Sir Henry Clinton, and Lord George Germain in London.

General John Burgoyne is the subject of a rather obscure biography by F. J. Hudleston, librarian of the War Office in London, published in Indianapolis in 1927, which contains much valuable documentation of the dispatches and the controversy between Burgoyne and Germain on the Battle of Saratoga. I also found in a copy of Hudleston, picked up at a secondhand shop years ago, the text of

General Washington's personal letter to Burgoyne in 1778, endorsing his parole as a prisoner of war so he could return to England to face Germain and seek a court-martial to clear his name of blame for the defeat. He got more sympathy from Washington than from Germain.

Original papers and dispatches of General Clinton, General Thomas Gage, General Sir William Howe, and much material on Lord George Germain are all to be found in the magnificent William L. Clements Library at the University of Michigan in Ann Arbor. *The Correspondence of General Thomas Gage* was published in New Haven, Connecticut, in 1931, edited by Clarence Edwin Carter. I have consulted these files and documents in checking and selecting various quotations that I have used and am indebted to the hospitality of the Clements Library.

Biographies and Politics: If a British author has written the outstanding military history of the American Revolution, an American has written the definitive biographies of the two central British politicians who shaped the history. Alan Valentine, one-time dean of Swarthmore College and president of the University of Rochester, published *Lord George Germain* in Oxford in 1962 and followed this with a two-volume biography of *Lord North* published in Norman, Oklahoma, in 1967. Both biographies are models of thorough research, full quotations from source material, engaging political anecdotes, and clear and lively writing. Valentine does not conceal his distaste for the egregious character of Germain. He finds Lord North a much more enjoyable personality in the unrewarding role of the king's prime minister for twelve years.

Other biographical material I have used includes O. A. Sherrad's three volumes on the elder *William Pitt, Earl of Chatham,* published in London from 1955 to 1958; biographies of *Charles James Fox* by John Drinkwater (New York, 1927) and by John W. Derry (London, 1972); *The Younger Pitt* by John Ehrman (London, 1983); Henry Brougham's *Historical Sketches of Statesmen in the Time of George III,* published in London closer to events, in 1845; and *Wilkes, Sheridan, Fox: Opposition under George III* by W. Fraser Rae, published in London in 1874, with interesting detail on political opposition to King George III.

The best narrative treatment of English politics from 1765 to

1775 that I have found is Charles R. Ritcheson's concisely written *British Politics and the American Revolution,* published in Norman, Oklahoma, in 1954. The English historian Max Beloff has edited a useful compendium of major parliamentary speeches and other documentary material in *The Debate on the American Revolution, 1761 to 1783,* published in London in 1949.

Benjamin Franklin: The letters, writings, and records that Benjamin Franklin produced in his fifteen years in London are of course an integral and vital element in the story of England and the American Revolution. Years ago, when I was living in London after World War II, I picked up for a few shillings on Charing Cross Road two volumes, published in 1818, of the third edition of *The Autobiography of Benjamin Franklin* plus the first published collection of his papers and correspondence. They were in excellent condition on good paper, and I promptly had them newly bound. They include the full transcript of Franklin's testimony before the House of Commons on the Stamp Act in 1766 and his fascinating but little noticed account of his secret talks with the English in a futile effort to head off the war before it began, in 1775. All of this and much more is now, of course, available in *The Papers of Benjamin Franklin,* published in New Haven, Connecticut, which has reached Volume 30, covering up to 1779, when Franklin was in Paris. Franklin's papers on the peace negotiations in Paris are yet to be published, but these have been researched.

Carl van Doren's massive 1938 life of Franklin has never been equaled and still remains in print and on the shelf at any worthy bookshop. Of course, Franklin's life and activities have been explored by many other authors, and his writings turn up in a variety of other works. In sifting through the many quotations from Franklin that are part of the story in this book, I have gone regularly to the Franklin Papers at the Library Company of Philadelphia to check material and have found useful interpretations in their knowledgeable editing. He was truly one of the wondrous intellects of history.

The Peace Process: The definitive basic historical work on the peace process, unmatched in the quality of its research and the telling of the story, remains *The Peacemakers* by Richard B. Morris, published in New York in 1965. It is a rare combination of a sifting of complex and obscure research matched by superb writing skills. Morris also wrote a notable collection of biographical sketches, *Seven Who Shaped Our Destiny,* published in New York in 1973. *The Diplomacy of the American Revolution* by Samuel Flagg Bemis, first published in Bloomington, Indiana, in 1937 and reissued in 1957 and 1965, contains much solid source material but lacks the narrative style of Morris.

Press and Publication References: A remarkable little volume, *Preliminaries of the American Revolution as Seen in the English Press,* by Fred J. Hinkhouse was published in New York in 1926. This thorough work has many direct quotes from the time of the Stamp Act troubles and much else. Using Hinkhouse as a guide, I drew further material from the microfilm archives at the well-organized British Library publications repository at Colingdale in London. Original copies of the monthly *Gentleman's Magazine* from 1760 to 1785 were fortunately close at hand, at the Library Company of Philadelphia, for on-the-spot perusal.

Specialized Works on Subject Matter: Bernhard Knollenberg's *Origins of the American Revolution, 1759 to 1776* (New York, 1960) is full of fascinating research, including the near hysterical dispatches of General Jeffrey Amherst during Pontiac's War. *With the British Army in Philadelphia, 1777–1778* by John W. Jackson (San Rafael, Calif., 1979) contains original material on Philadelphia Loyalists and details of the occupation, including contemporary accounts of that outlandish farewell *mischianza* given for General Howe.

Special studies have been made of *Lexington and Concord* by Arthur B. Tourtellot (New York, 1959); *The Boston Tea Party* by Benjamin Woods Labaree (New York, 1964); and *Toward Lexington: The Role of the British Army in the Coming of the American Revolution* (Princeton, N.J., 1965) by John W. Shy. Shy's essay collection, *A People Numerous and Armed* (Ann Arbor, Mich., 1990), includes a succinct study of the British shift to a southern strategy. Ira D. Gruber has written a full volume on *The Howe Brothers and the American Revolution* (Chapel Hill, N.C., 1974). The University of South Carolina has published a full-length study of *Lord Dartmouth* and his frustrated efforts at conciliation, by Bradley D. Bargar in 1965. Edmund B. and Helen R. Morgan have made a book-length examination of *The Stamp Act Crisis,* primarily the events in the colonies, published in Chapel Hill, North Carolina, in 1953.

Samuel Eliot Morison assembled and edited *Sources and Documents of the American Revolution,* which includes many important items, such as the John Dickinson *Letters from a Farmer.* The collection was first published in New York in 1929 and has been frequently reprinted since. *Voices of 1776* by Richard Wheeler (New York, 1972) is an exhaustive compendium of political and battlefield quotations and letters. A similar collection, more substantive in political material, *The Fire of Liberty: Letters and Documents* was edited by Esmond Wright and published in London in 1983.

SELECT BIBLIOGRAPHY

SOURCE MATERIAL

Beloff, Max, ed. *The Debate on the American Revolution, 1761 to 1783*. London: Nicholas Kaye, 1949.

Boatner, Mark Mayo III, ed. *Encyclopedia of the American Revolution*. New York: David McKay, 1966.

Carter, Clarence Edwin, ed. *The Correspondence of General Thomas Gage, 1763 to 1775*. New Haven, Conn.: Yale University Press, 1931.

Crane, Vernon W., ed. *Benjamin Franklin's Letters to the Press, 1758 to 1775*. Chapel Hill: University of North Carolina Press, 1954.

Curtiss, Edward H. *The Organization of the British Army in the American Revolution*. New Haven, Conn.: Yale University Press, 1926.

Davies, K. G., ed. *Documents of the American Revolution, 1770 to 1783. Colonial Office Series*. Dublin: Irish University Press, 1976.

Debrée, Bonamy, ed. *The Letters of King George III*. London: Cassell, 1935.

Franklin, Benjamin. *The Papers of Benjamin Franklin*, vol. 8–30. New Haven, Conn.: Yale University Press, 1965–93.

Fortescue, Sir John, ed. *The Correspondence of King George III*. 6 vols. London: Macmillan, 1927–28.

Gentleman's Magazine. Monthly issues, 1760–85. London: Library Company of Philadelphia Collection.

Hinkhouse, Fred J. *Preliminaries of the American Revolution as Seen in the English Press*. New York: Columbia University Press, 1926.

Jensen, Merril, ed. *American Colonial Documents to 1778. English Historical Documents Series.* London: Eyre and Spottiswood, 1955.

Macalpine, Ida, M.D., and Richard Hunter, M.D. "The Insanity of King George III: A Classic Case of Porphyria." *British Medical Journal* (January 1966).

Morison, Samuel Eliot, ed. *Sources and Documents of the American Revolution.* New York: Oxford University Press, 1929.

Peckham, Howard H., ed. *Sources of American Independence.* Chicago: University of Chicago Press, 1972.

Wheeler, Richard, ed. *Voices of 1776.* New York: Crowell, 1972.

Wright, Esmond, comp. *The Fire of Liberty: Letters and Documents.* London: Folio Society, 1983.

HISTORY, BIOGRAPHY, AND GENERAL READING

Alden, John R. *A History of the American Revolution.* New York: Alfred A. Knopf, 1969.

Ayling, Stanley. *George the Third.* London: Collins, 1972.

Bargar, Bradley D. *Lord Dartmouth.* Columbia: University of South Carolina Press, 1965.

Bemis, Samuel Flagg. *The Diplomacy of the American Revolution.* Bloomington: Indiana University Press, 1937; reprint, 1965.

Billias, George Athan, ed. *General Washington's Generals and Opponents.* New York: Da Capo Press, 1994.

Bowen, Catherine Drinker. *The Most Dangerous Man in America.* Boston: Little, Brown, 1974.

Brandt, Clare S. *The Livingstons, An American Aristocracy.* New York: Doubleday, 1986.

———. *The Man in the Mirror: A Life of Benedict Arnold.* New York: Random House, 1994.

Brooke, John. *King George III.* New York: McGraw-Hill, 1972.

Brougham, Henry. *Historical Sketches of Statesmen in the Time of George III.* London: Charles Knight, 1845.

Calhoun, Robert McClure. *The Loyalists in Revolutionary America.* New York: Harcourt Brace Jovanovich, 1973.

Clinton, Sir Henry. *Sir Henry Clinton's Narrative.* Edited by William B. Willcox. New Haven, Conn.: Yale University Press, 1954.

Connell, Brian. *The Plains of Abraham.* London: Hoddard and Stoughton, 1957.

Derry, John W. *Charles James Fox.* London: B. T. Batsford, 1992.

Drinkwater, John. *Charles James Fox.* New York: Cosmopolitan Books, 1927.

Dull, Jonathan R. *A Diplomatic History of the American Revolution.* New Haven, Conn.: Yale University Press, 1985.

Egerton, H. E. *Causes and Character of the American Revolution.* Oxford: Clarendon Press, 1931.

Ehrman, John. *The Younger Pitt.* London: Constable, 1983.

Eyck, Erich. *Pitt versus Fox, Father and Son.* New York: Octagon Books, 1973.

Fleming, Thomas. *1776, Year of Illusions.* New York: W. W. Norton, 1975.

Flexner, James Thomas. *George Washington.* 4 vols. Boston: Little, Brown, 1965–72.

Franklin, Benjamin. *Autobiography of Benjamin Franklin.* London: Henry Colburn, Conduit Street, 1818; Boston: Houghton Mifflin, Bicentennial Limited Edition, 1906.

George, M. Dorothy. *London Life in the Eighteenth Century.* London: Penguin Books, 1965.

Green, V.H.H. *The Hanoverians.* London: Edward Arnold, 1948.

Green, Walford David. *William Pitt, Earl of Chatham.* New York: G. P. Putnam's Sons, 1900.

Gruber, Ira D. *The Howe Brothers and the American Revolution.* Chapel Hill: University of North Carolina Press, 1974.

Guedalla, Philip. *Fathers of the Revolution.* Garden City, N.Y.: Doubleday, 1926.

Hibbert, Christopher. *Redcoats and Rebels: The American Revolution through British Eyes.* New York: W. W. Norton, 1990.

Hudleston, F. J. *Gentleman Johnny Burgoyne.* Indianapolis: Bobbs-Merrill, 1927.

Jackson, John W. *With the British Army in Philadelphia, 1777–1778.* San Rafael, Calif.: Presidio Press, 1979.

Knollenberg, Bernhard. *Origins of the American Revolution, 1759 to 1776.* New York: Macmillan, 1960.

Labaree, Benjamin Woods. *The Boston Tea Party.* New York: Oxford University Press, 1964.

Macauley, Thomas B. *Essays.* 2 vols. London: Longmans, Green, 1908.

Mackesy, Piers. *The War for America, 1775–1783.* London: Longmans, Green, 1964. Reprint. Lincoln: University of Nebraska, Bison Books, 1993.

Middlekauff, Robert. *The Glorious Cause: The American Revolution, 1763–*

1789. Oxford History of the United States. New York: Oxford University Press, 1982.

Miller, John C. *Origins of the American Revolution.* Boston: Little, Brown, 1943.

Morgan, Edmund B. and Helen R. *The Stamp Act Crisis.* Chapel Hill: University of North Carolina Press, 1953.

Morris, Richard B. *The Peacemakers.* New York: Harper and Row, 1965.

———. *Seven Who Shaped Our Destiny.* New York: Harper and Row, 1973.

Namier, Lewis B. *England in the Age of the American Revolution.* London: Macmillan, 1930.

Pares, Richard. *King George III and the Politicians.* Oxford: Clarendon Press, 1953.

Rae, W. Fraser. *Wilkes, Sheridan, Fox: Opposition under George III.* London: W. Izbister, 1874.

Randall, Willard. *A Little Revenge: Benjamin Franklin and His Son.* Boston: Little, Brown, 1984.

Ritcheson, Charles R. *British Politics and the American Revolution.* Norman: University of Oklahoma Press, 1954.

Rutman, Darrett B. *The Morning of America.* Boston: Houghton Mifflin, 1971.

Schlesinger, Arthur M. *Prelude to Independence.* New York: Alfred A. Knopf, 1957. Reprint, Boston: Northeastern University Press, 1980.

Sherrad, O. A. *Lord Chatham.* 3 vols. London: Bodley Head, 1952–58.

Shy, John W. *Toward Lexington: The Role of the British Army in the Coming of the American Revolution.* Princeton, N.J.: Princeton University Press, 1965.

———. *A People Numerous and Armed.* Ann Arbor: University of Michigan Press, 1990.

Smith, Page. *John Adams.* 2 vols. New York: Doubleday, 1962.

Spector, Marion. *The American Department of the British Government, 1768 to 1782.* New York: Columbia University Press, 1940.

Tarleton, Banastre. *Campaigns in the Southern American Colonies.* London: T. Cadell, 1787.

Thomas, P.D.G. *The House of Commons in the Eighteenth Century.* Oxford: Clarendon Press, 1971.

———. *Lord North.* London: Alan Lane, 1976.

Tourtellot, Arthur B. *Lexington and Concord.* New York: W. W. Norton, 1959.

Treese, Lorett. *The Storm Gathering: The Penn Family and the American Revolution*. State College: Pennsylvania State University Press, 1992.

Tuchman, Barbara: *The First Salute*. New York: Alfred A. Knopf, 1988.

———. *The March of Folly: From Troy to Vietnam*. New York: Alfred A. Knopf, 1984.

Tucker, Robert W., and David C. Hendrickson. *The Fall of the First British Empire*. Baltimore: Johns Hopkins University Press, 1982.

Valentine, Alan. *Lord North*. 2 vols. Norman: University of Oklahoma Press, 1967.

———. *Lord George Germain*. Oxford: Clarendon Press, 1962.

Van Doren, Carl. *Benjamin Franklin*. New York: Viking Press, 1938.

Watson, J. Steven. *The Reign of King George III. Oxford History of England*. Oxford: Clarendon Press, 1960.

Willson, Beckles. *George III as Man, Monarch, and Statesman*. Philadelphia: George W. Jacobs, 1907.

Wickwire, Franklin and Mary. *Cornwallis and the War of Independence*. Boston: Houghton Mifflin, 1970.

INDEX

Abingdon, earl of, 353
Adams, Abigail, 197, 378
Adams, John, 39, 58, 141, 178, 197, 222
    as first diplomatic minister to England,
        377–81
    Howe's peace overtures and, 256–57
    Loyalist strength assessed by, 324–25
    as peace commissioner, 362–63, 365,
        370–73, 375
    as vice president, 381
Adams, Samuel, 58, 129, 160, 165, 172,
    177, 192
Administration of Justice Act, 187, 188
Administration of the Colonies (Pownall),
    141
Admiralty Court, 59, 64, 121
Albany, New York, 260, 261, 266, 267,
    268, 273, 310
Allen, Ethan, 222, 223, 229
Amelia, Princess, 6, 7
American colonies:
    British Army permanently stationed in,
        34–35, 37
    billeting and supplying of, 108–09,
        114, 119–20
    Boston Commons taken over by, 133,
        143
    Boston Massacre, 150–52
    evacuation from western frontiers,
        109, 121, 153

Mutiny Act and, 108–09, 119, 120
Pontiac's War and, 35–37
Quartering Act, 187, 188
taxation of colonists for, 35, 52–53,
    56, 57
constitutional rights of, 40–41, 84–87
Continental Congress, *see* Continental
    Congress
embargo of British goods, 132, 133,
    138, 192, 193, 198, 205, 206,
    215
French and Indian War, 4–5, 32
independence:
    Declaration of Independence, *see*
        Declaration of Independence
    England's recognition of, 365–69
    rumblings of desire for, 33–34,
        165–66
    war of, *see* War of Independence
militias, state, 4
Parliament's right to legislate for,
    questioning of, 158–59, 169–71,
    198
Pontiac's War, 35–37, 49, 58
population of, 3, 325*n*.
right to tax property within its
    boundaries, 48
salutary neglect, England's policy of, 3,
    5, 54
when Seven Years' War ended, 2–3

American colonies *(continued)*
taxation imposed by England on, 53–54,
119–27, 188–90, 323n.
distinction between revenue-raising
taxes and trade regulation, 126, 129
opposition of colonists to, 61, 62,
66–68, 71–82, 88
Parliament's views on, 61, 69, 82–105
Pitt's views on, 84–87, 88, 89, 90
rejection by colonists of internal taxes,
76, 97–98, 101
tea tax, *see* Tea tax
see also names of specific acts, e.g. Stamp
Act
tightening of control over, 5, 37, 160,
163
War of Independence, *see* War of
Independence
western expansion, England's policy and,
36–37, 119, 153
see also names of individual colonies
see also United States
American Crisis, The, 262n.
American Department, 152, 323
abolished, 358
creation of, 127–28
earl of Dartmouth as head of, *see*
Dartmouth, earl of
Ellis replaces Germain at, 353
Germain takes over, 236, 238
Hillsborough's resignation from, 161,
162
Amherst, Major General Jeffrey, 5, 12, 36,
80, 182, 206, 234, 239, 245,
296–98, 313, 353
André, Captain John, 306n., 307–08,
328–31
Annemours, chevalier d', 74n.
Arbuthnot, Admiral Marriot, 327, 344
Arnold, Benedict, 222, 223, 229, 243–44,
278, 327–31
as brigadier general in British Army, 336
treason of, 306n., 328–31, 332
Arnold, Peggy (née Shippen), 328, 330
Articles of Confederation, 376
Augusta of Saxe-Gotha, Princess, 8, 9–10,
11, 13, 14, 21, 29, 70–71
Autobiography (Franklin), 44

Bache, Richard, 216
Baillie, Dr. Matthew, 383
Balfour, James, 92
Bancroft, Edward, 284, 285, 286, 288
Bancroft, George, 18
Barclay, David, 202, 203, 205, 208, 209,
213–14, 217

Barras, Admiral comte de, 343–46
Barré, Colonel Isaac, xii, 67–68, 90, 137,
187, 281, 358, 359
Barrington, Viscount, 109, 121, 221
War of Independence and:
naval strategy, 231, 234
reports to, 226, 228, 233n
Bathurst, Lord, 292
Beaver, 177
Bedford, duke of, 29, 30
faction led by, 127, 128, 140, 150
*Benjamin Franklin's Letters to the Press,
1758 to 1775,* 43n.
Bennington, Vermont, 276, 277
Bernard, Sir Francis, 128, 130–31, 133,
143, 154
Board of Commissioners of Customs, 121,
125, 128, 130
Board of Trade, British, 37, 53, 54, 58, 60,
62, 127–28, 323
Boston, Massachusetts, 128, 130, 133,
143, 202, 207
closing of port of, 186–89, 191, 192,
198
motion to withdraw troops from, 209–10
town meetings, 191
during War of Independence, 245, 261,
312
Boston Citizens' Committee, 193
Boston Committee of Correspondence,
174
Boston Gazette, 59, 179
Boston Massacre, 150–52
Boston Port Bill, 186–92, 198, 213
Boston Tea Party, 175–78, 190
English reaction to, 179–81, 184, 186
payment for tea destroyed at, 213, 214,
216
Boswell, James, 340–41
Braddock, Major General Edward, 4, 25
Brandywine, Battle of, 274
British Army, 33, 201–02
fighting of War of Independence, 210,
224
Germain's direction of, *see* Germain,
Lord George, War of Independence
and
problems in, *see* War of Independence,
England's limitations in
shift to naval strategy, 296–97
southern colonies and, 245–46, 247,
318, 319, 325, 331–35
stalemate, 304–05
*see also names of individual battles and
generals*
mercenaries in, 210, 232, 234, 263

peacetime budget for, 32–35
permanently stationed in American colonies, *see* American colonies, British Army permanently stationed in
problems in fighting America, *see* War of Independence, England's limitations in fighting
see also specific battles fought by British Army
British Empire, 32–33, 45, 126*n.*
see also England
British Medical Journal, 18
Bunker Hill, Battle of, 224, 225–28, 229, 230, 254
Burgoyne, Major General John, 120, 210, 224, 239, 244, 261, 266
    Battle of Saratoga and, 277–79, 281, 310–11, 386
    Bunker Hill, 226, 227
    campaign from Canada south, 261, 267–68, 273, 275–79
    described, 225, 276
    junction with Howe, failed, 261, 267, 268, 275, 279–80, 310–11
    post-war career, 359, 386
    as prisoner of war, 296, 309–11
    surrenders to Gates, 279, 280–81
Burke, Edmund, xii, 5–6, 76, 82, 157, 182, 185, 239, 270, 281, 323, 357, 358, 374
    American independence and, 91, 217–18
    Coercive Acts debate and, 188–89
    last years of, 387
    Letter to the Sheriffs of Bristol, 270–71
    on reaction to Boston Tea Party, 179
    recognition of American independence, as proponent of, 291
    Stamp Act repeal and, 90–91
    Townshend's taxes and, 122–23
Bute, earl of, 9–13, 26, 29, 48*n.*, 55, 70, 182, 227, 237, 238
    armed forces and, 32, 34–35, 57
    cabinet seat, 24, 26–27, 30
    correspondence with George III, 11–13, 31–32, 52, 71
    described, 10–11
    foreign policy role, 30–31
    Pitt and, 12, 23, 24, 27, 111–12, 136
    as prime minister, 30, 32–35, 52, 147
    on Privy Council, 21, 23
    Stamp Act repeal and, 89, 104
    as tutor of George III, 11–13, 17
Byron, Admiral John, 312

Camden, Lord, 146
Camden, South Carolina, 331

Campbell, Lieutenant Colonel Archibald, 312–13
Campbell, Colonel William, 332
Canada, 1, 2, 4, 30, 32, 45–46, 121
    American incursion into, 243–44
    attempt to persuade Canadians to join in War of Independence, 244*n.*
    Burgoyne's campaign from, 261, 267–68, 273, 275–79
    Quebec Act, 190–91
Carleton, Major General Guy, 239, 267–68, 272, 277
    American incursion into Canada and, 243, 244, 247
    as Clinton's successor, 350, 352, 359
    described, 244*n.*, 275
    resignation of, 295–96
    return to London, 309
Carlisle, earl of, 299, 300–01, 303
Carlyle, Dr. Alexander, 45
Carmarthen, Lord, 353, 378
Catherine the Great, 114, 115, 210, 232
Caulfield, Susan, 386
Causes for the Present Distractions in America Explained (Franklin), 158–59
Céloron, Commandant, 4
Charles III, King of Spain, 29
Charleston, South Carolina, 245–46, 253, 314, 318, 319–21
    British victory at, 321, 322
Charlotte Sophia, Queen of England, 14, 29, 70, 241, 383
Chatham, earl of, *see* Pitt, William (later earl of Chatham)
Chesapeake Bay, 344–45, 346, 348
Chesterfield, Lord, 10–11
Church of England, 14, 49
Clare, Lord, 142–43
Clark, Colonel Elijah, 325
Clements, William L., 328*n.*
Clinton, Admiral George, 225, 227
Clinton, Major General Henry, 210, 224, 239, 247, 253, 258, 268, 273, 274, 279, 299
    Benedict Arnold and, 327–31
    arrival of French army forces and, 327
    arrives in Yorktown after Cornwallis's surrender, 347–48
    Battle of Monmouth Court House, 304
    Burgoyne seeks assistance of, 277, 278
    Cornwallis and, 316–17, 318, 320–21, 324, 332, 335–36, 337–39, 346, 347
    deceived as to Washington's plans, 337–39, 342–44, 347

Clinton, Major General Henry *(continued)*
  depression, 316
  described, 225
  first Carolinas operation and, 245, 246,
    253–54
  Germain's orders to:
    for 1778, 297, 312
    for 1779, 313–14
    for 1781, 335
    withdrawal from Philadelphia to New
      York, 298, 301, 308
  last years of, 385
  memoirs, 384–85
  in New York, 254, 257, 288, 347
  reinforcements arrive for, 318
  replacement of, 359
  resignation requests, 312, 317, 320
  southern strategy, 305, 314, 318, 319,
    327
  Stony Point defeat and, 315–16
  surrender of Charleston to, 321
  takes command from Howe, 297
Clive, Robert, 182
Coercive Acts, 180–81, 186–94, 200, 213
Colonial Department, *see* American
  Department
Committees of Correspondence, 160, 165,
  171, 172, 192
Connecticut, 62, 66, 72, 131, 193, 210
Constitution, U.S., 38, 381
Continental Army:
  Canadian incursion, 243–44
  defense of Philadelphia, 263, 274
  French forces join, 326–27, 329
  march to Virginia, 343–44, 345–46,
    347
  mutiny among, 333
  New Jersey retreat, 259
  in New York, 247, 252, 254–55, 257
  one-year enlistments, 258–59, 262
  payment of, 333–34, 344
  raising of, 223–24
  stalemate, 304–05
  training of, 229
  at Valley Forge, 274, 296, 300, 328
  see also Washington, George; *specific
    battles*
Continental Congress, 272
  Declaration of Independence, 249
  diplomatic relations with England, 376,
    378
  final peace negotiations and, 363, 367,
    369
  the first, 165, 192–93, 197–200, 203,
    205, 212, 214, 215
  peace overtures to, 302–03

ratification of treaties with France, 288,
  300
  the second, 222–24, 230
Conway, Henry Seymour, 77, 81–82, 84,
  90, 104, 105, 353–54, 358
  as leader of House of Commons, 112,
    115
Cooke, George, 90
Cooper, Grey, 96
Cooper, Samuel, 157, 159, 174
Cornwallis, Major General Charles, 254,
  258, 259, 264, 316–17
  Clinton and, 316–17, 318, 320–21, 324,
    332, 335–36, 337–39, 346, 347
  described, 324
  loyalists and, 324, 326
  North Carolina battles, 334
  post-war career, 386
  South Carolina battles, 331–32
  in Virginia, 336–37, 345, 346
    outnumbered, 347
    realization that French navy controls
      Chesapeake Bay, 346
    surrender at Yorktown, 348, 349
Correspondence of King George III, The, xii
Cotterell, Sir Clement, 378
Crane, Verne W., 43*n.*
Craven, Lord, 353
Creek Indians, 192
Cruger, Henry, 28
Cumberland, duke of, 70, 71, 76, 77,
  109–10
Cushing, Thomas, 167, 169–72, 185, 194
Customs, British, 54, 58–59, 61, 121–22,
  160–61

Dartmouth, 176
Dartmouth, earl of, xii, 80, 164, 210–11
  described, 164
  diplomatic efforts to avoid war, 202,
    203, 205, 208, 213, 214, 235
  heads American Department, 162–65,
    169–71, 172, 179, 200
    Coercive Acts and, 181, 193–94
    tea tax and, 167, 174
  War of Independence and, 220–21, 229,
    230, 245, 248
  as North's confidant, 235, 236
  reports to, 226
Dashwood, Sir Francis, 135
Deane, Silas, 283, 285, 286, 287
Declaration of Independence, 38, 197,
  270, 289, 302, 306
  publication of, 249–50
Declaration of Rights, 179–98, 204, 205,
  207

Declaratory Act, 69, 89–91, 97, 98, 105, 106, 108
de Grasse, Admiral, 337, 342–45
Delaware Assembly, 131
Delaware River, 259, 261–64
Derby, Captain John, 220, 221
Derby, Lord, 353
Derby, Richard, 220
Devonshire, duke of, 29
Dickinson, John, 125–26, 128, 175, 198–99, 224
Digby, Lieutenant, 275, 279
Disraeli, Benjamin, 111
Dominica, 108, 318
Donop, Colonel Karl van, 263, 264
Dowdeswell, William, 167–68, 187
Dudington, Lieutenant William, 160–61, 165
Dundas, Henry, 342, 352
Dunning, John, 182–83, 323–24
Duquesne, Fort, 4, 5, 25

Eagle, 249, 250, 255
East India Company, 114, 115–16, 153*n.*, 166–68, 171, 174, 175, 186, 187, 192
Eden, William, 226, 284–89, 293, 299–303, 314
Egmont, Lord, 56, 110
Eleanor, 177
Ellis, Welbore, 34–35
England:
    declaration of state of war with France, 288
    democracy as practiced in, 16
    diplomatic relations with United States, 376, 377–80, 381
    economy of 1700s, 15–16, 138–39
    Parliament, *see* House of Commons; House of Lords; Parliament, English
    recognizes United States of America, 369
    salutary neglect, policy of, 3, 5, 54
    Seven Years' War, *see* Seven Years' War
    taxes imposed on American colonies, *see* American colonies, taxation imposed by England on
    voting rights in, 16, 27
    War of 1812, 20
    War of Independence and, *see* War of Independence
England in the Age of the American Revolution (Namier), 27–28
Estaing, Admiral comte d', 299, 312, 318

Fauquier, Francis, 76
Ferdinand of Brunswick, Prince, 232, 237

Ferguson, Major Patrick, 332
First Four Georges, The (Plumb), 18
Fitch, Thomas, 66
Fitzpatrick, Richard, 134
Flexner, James Thomas, 338
Fortescue, Sir John, xii, 13, 267*n.*
Fothergill, Dr. John, 202–03, 205, 209, 213–14, 217
Fox, Charles James, xii, 17, 133–35, 188*n.*, 215, 270, 281, 309, 310, 341, 342, 355, 376
    coalition government with North, 375, 377, 384
    death of, 387
    in Rockingham government, 358–59
    Shelburne and, 360–61
France, 4, 33, 37, 45, 231
    alliance with American colonies, 283, 284–88, 302, 322
        Battle of Yorktown, *see* Yorktown, Battle of
        Caribbean successes, 317–18
        coordination of joint operations, 337–38, 342–44
        desire for peace, 333
        effect on England's strategy, 279–99
        English fears of, 271, 280, 286, 289
        financial aid, 333–34, 346
        French army forces join war effort, 326–27, 329
        French fleet, operations of, 312, 317–18, 342–43, 344–45, 346, 348
        peace negotiations and treaties ending the war, 363, 364–65, 366, 369–70, 372–73, 374, 375
        treaties of alliance and commerce, 288, 292, 297, 300
    Franklin's diplomacy with, 38, 39, 288
    French and Indian War, 4–5, 25, 32
    Pitt's foreign policy and, 114–15
    Seven Years' War, *see* Seven Years' War
Franklin, Benjamin, xii, 2, 28, 137*n.*, 153, 272, 374, 377
    accomplishments, 38–39
    Battle of Yorktown victory and, 348
    dismissal from colonial post office, 185–86, 214
    earl of Dartmouth and, 162, 163, 167, 169
    France, diplomacy with, 38, 39, 288
    Grand Ohio Company and, 161, 162
    Hillsborough and, 140–41, 153–57
    home of, 306*n.*, 307
    mail of, tampering with, 172–73, 194
    marriage, 44

Franklin, Benjamin *(continued)*
  on Parliament's power over the colonies, 158–59
  peace commissions and:
    final peace negotiations, 362, 363–67, 369–73, 375
    of David Hartley, 351
    of Lord Howe, 250–52, 256–57
  as Pennsylvania's agent to London, 38, 39–49, 194
  Pitt's meetings with, 195–96, 207–08, 209–10, 211–12
  private letters made public by, 171–74, 181, 183–84
  Privy Council and, *see* Privy Council, Franklin's dealings with
  revolution of American colonies and, 125, 197
    last efforts to prevent war, 202–18
    predictions of, 123–24, 144–45
    views on, 46, 158–59, 195, 207–08
  as scientist, 39, 40
  secret peace overtures to, 283, 284–86, 287, 288, 314
  Stamp Act and, 57–58, 65, 71–72, 73, 78–79, 82, 91–103, 107
    testimony before House of Commons, xi, 92–103
  tea tax and, 149–50, 167
  Townshend duties and, 143–44
Franklin, Deborah, 43–44, 78–79, 102, 107, 216
Franklin, Sally, 216
Franklin, William, 42, 44–45, 47, 48, 58, 78, 80, 137*n.*, 163, 173, 216
Frederick Louis, Prince, 8, 9
Frederick the Great of Prussia, 30, 115, 232
French and Indian War, 4–5, 25, 32
Fuller, Rose, 187, 190

Gage, Major General Thomas, 130, 133, 153, 182, 202, 206, 233*n.*, 310
  advises London to assert its supremacy, 159–60
  billeting of soldiers requested by, 109, 114, 120, 121
    Quartering Act, 188, 189
  Bunker Hill, 225–26, 228
  enforcement of Coercive Acts, 191, 193–94, 200
  instructed to move against the rebellion, 211
  Lexington and Concord, 211, 218, 219–22

  misjudgment of temperament of Americans, 180
  reinforcement of, 210, 224–25
  Stamp Act riots and, 80–82
  strategy of, 227
  turns command over to Howe, 228
Galloway, Joseph, 129, 131, 140, 163, 165, 197, 216, 307, 308, 313
Garth, Charles, 66, 67
Gaspée, 160–61, 162, 164–65, 166
Gates, Major General Horatio, 244, 274, 331
  Battle of Saratoga, 277–79
Gentleman's Magazine, 93, 219, 229–30, 250
George I, King of England, 16, 241
George II, King of England, 16, 237
  death of, 6–7, 21–22, 48
  education of George III and, 8–9, 12
George III, King of England, xii, 5, 11–14, 17, 22, 31–32, 52, 71, 238–39, 292–94, 323
  abdication, considers, 355–56, 358
  accession of, 1, 5, 6–7, 13, 21, 48, 238
  American colonies, policy for, 17, 18, 49, 127, 130, 139, 145, 180, 196–97, 199–200, 205–06
    Coercive Acts and, 187, 188, 190, 191
    failure of, 17
    Olive Branch Petition to, 224, 230, 236
    Stamp Act and, 65, 83, 89, 104–07
    tea tax and, 167
  birth of, 8
  childhood of, 8–9
  Church of England and, 14, 49
  Continental Congress's appeal to, 198–99
  death of, 383–84
  described, 5, 7–8, 13–15
  diplomatic relations with United States, 376, 377–80, 381
  early popularity of, 23
  education of, 8–9, 11–13, 17
  Germain made a viscount by, 353
  Grenville and, 52, 55, 56, 65, 70, 71, 76–77
  as hard working, xii, 13
  as headstrong and opinionated, 9, 17, 55, 250, 349
  historical judgment of, 18
  insanity of, 7, 18–20, 65, 382–83
  marriage, 14, 29
  North resignations and, *see* North, Lord, as prime minister, attempts at resignation

North's carrying out of king's American
  policy, 147, 149, 196, 199, 200,
  205–06, 210, 289–90
Pitt's government formed under,
  111–13, 118
porphyria suffered by, 18–20, 65, 70,
  382–84
reign of, 5, 7
Rockingham and, 76, 77, 104, 358
Shelburne government and, 360, 375
War of Independence and, 201, 202,
  220–21, 227, 232, 235, 248,
  264–68, 271–72, 282, 293–94,
  298, 313, 316, 333, 352, 357–58,
  372
  Benedict Arnold and, 331
  British losses, reaction to, 208, 281,
    283
  Charleston victory and, 322
  early victories, 260, 277
  Franco-American alliance and, 286
  Holland's support for Americans and,
    333
  Lexington and Concord, 220–21
  naval strategy, change to, 296–97
  peace commissions, 247, 290, 299,
    366, 369
  returning generals and, 309, 310
  secret peace overtures and, 284
  Seven Years' War and, 29–31
  after Spain's entry into the war,
    314–15
  speech to House of Lords at
    conclusion of, 373–74
  Yorktown and, 349–50
Whigs and, 5, 13, 16–17
Wilkes and, 136–38, 145–46
George IV, King of England, 8n.
Georgia, 76, 192–93, 312–13, 318
Georgia Assembly, 131
Gérard, Conrad-Alexandre, 284–88
Germain, Lord George, xii
  American Department taken over by,
    236
  background of, 238
  described, 236–37
  last years of, 385, 386–87
  name changed to, 89n., 238
  as Lord George Sackville, 89, 237–38
  as Viscount Sackville, 353, 386–87
  steps down in exchange for peerage,
    352–53
  takes over American Department, 238
  unpopularity of, 323, 349
  War of Independence and, xiii, 236, 289,
    332–33, 338
    blamed for British losses, 281, 292,
      296, 309
    direction of war effort, xiii, 238, 242,
      253, 258, 265–70, 272, 273, 297,
      298, 305, 312, 313–14, 320, 335,
      339, 351
    peace commissions and, 248, 265
    reports from generals in America,
      259–60, 261, 263–64, 266–67,
      269, 272, 276, 277, 280, 282,
      295–96, 315–16, 327
    returning British generals and, 309–12
    southern strategy, 305, 312–13
    Yorktown, after, 348, 349–50, 351–53
Gerrish, Edward, 151
Gibraltar, 314
Gordon, Reverend William, 166
Gower, Lord, 182
Grafton, duke of, 31, 150, 236, 354, 358
  autobiography, 143
  described, 112
  as prime minister, 112, 115–18, 120,
    121, 127–28, 130, 139, 143–44
  resignation of, 146
Grand Ohio Company, 161–62
Grantham, Lord, 361
Granville, Lord, 40–41
Graves, Vice Admiral Samuel, 248
Graves, Admiral Thomas, 344–45, 347–48,
  350, 351–52
Greene, Major General Nathanael, 331,
  334–35, 337
Green Mountain Boys, 222, 327
Grenada, 318
Grenville, George, xii, 19, 58–68, 83, 123
  described, 51–52, 55
  George III and, 52, 55, 56, 65, 70, 71,
    76–77
  on Lord North, 147–48
  Stamp Act and, 51, 62–68, 72, 76–77,
    85, 89, 91, 104, 105, 112, 116
    Franklin testimony and, 96, 99, 102
Guadeloupe, 45
Guilford, earl of (father of Lord North),
  148, 164, 384
Guilford Courthouse, Battle of, 334

Halford, Sir Henry, 383
Halifax, Lord, 63, 127
Hall, David, 92–93, 103
Hamilton, Alexander, 39, 330
Hancock, John, 39, 58, 106, 130, 179,
  377
Harcourt, Lord, 8
Hardwicke, earl of, 29, 31, 83, 90
Hartley, David, 351, 375

Harvey, General Edward, 234
Hastings, Warren, 387
Haydn, Joseph, 14
Hayley, 179
Hayter, Dr., 8
Henry, Patrick, 73–74, 75
Henry VIII, King of England, 181*n.*
Hewitt, James, 94
Hillsborough, Viscount, 128, 129–30, 133,
    140–43, 152, 160, 182, 340
  described, 128
  Franklin and, 140–41, 153–57
  resignation of, 161, 162
  response to Massachusetts Circular,
    129–30, 131
Historical Society of Pennsylvania, 45
History of the British Army (Fortescue),
    267*n.*
History of the United States (Bancroft),
    18
Holderness, Lord, 26
Holland, 206, 325, 333, 370
  peace negotiations and, 362, 364, 373
Holland, Baron (né Henry Fox), 31, 134
Hood, Admiral Sir Samuel, 130, 344–45,
    347
House of Commons, 140, 248
  Americans in, 28, 168
  bribery of members, 28, 31, 89
  Coercive Acts and, 186–90
  Conciliation Plan approved by, 242
  elections, 27–28, 133, 136, 196, 324,
    333, 340, 341, 377
  factional voting in, 28–29
  Howe brothers and, 241, 242
  Massachusetts declared in state of
    rebellion by, 213, 215, 249
  Pitt honored by, 295
  Pitt moves to House of Lords from, 113
  pro-American opposition in, 149*n.*, 167,
    187, 188*n.*
  progress of War of Independence and,
    270–71, 281, 291–92, 314, 333,
    340, 349
    examination of failed strategies,
      310–11
    North's government's loss of
      confidence in, 354–58
    rising opposition to the war in, 323,
      340–42, 350, 353–54
  Stamp Act and, 67–69, 77, 82–105, 107
  tea tax debated in, 167–68
  Townshend's duties and, 122–23, 140,
    149
House of Lords, 29, 31, 68, 77, 80, 90,
    113, 140, 145, 271, 280, 373–74

attempts to prevent war in, 209–10,
    212–13
  motion to recognize American
    independence in, 291, 295
  Viscount Sackville in, 353, 386
Howe, Caroline, 206–07, 208, 214
Howe, Viscount George, 241–42
Howe, Admiral Viscount Richard (Lord
    Howe), 206–09, 214–17, 239–40,
    258, 273, 300, 307
  background of, 240
  blockage of American colonies, 265, 298
  efforts to prevent war, 206, 207, 208–09,
    214–15, 216, 217, 242
  last years of, 385
  new orders after France enters the war,
    298, 299, 301
  as peace commissioner, 240, 242,
    247–49, 250–53, 255–57, 260–61,
    265–66
  reputation of, 230
  return to England, 311–12
  sympathies for Americans, 241–42
Howe, Major General William, 206, 210,
    224, 235, 239–40, 242, 258, 259,
    263, 265, 316, 384–85
  after War of Independence, 359
  background of, 225
  Battle of Brandywine, 275
  Battle of Trenton and, 263–64
  Bunker Hill, 226, 229
  Burgoyne's orders and, 269
  as deputy peace commissioner, 240, 252
  described, 253
  Gage's command turned over to, 228
  in Halifax, 247
  immobilized in Boston, 245, 246–47
  junction with Burgoyne, failed, 261, 266,
    268, 275, 279–80, 310–11
  knighting of, 260
  mistress, 306
  New York operations, 247, 249, 254–55,
    257–58
  offers his resignation, 280, 282
  Philadelphia occupied by, 259–61, 266,
    269, 272–74, 305–07
    party before departing, 307–08
  relief from command, 292, 296, 297
  reputation of, 239
  returns to England, 308
  return to England, 311–12
  strategy of, 227, 259–60, 261, 266,
    269–70
  sympathies for Americans, 241–42
Hughes, John, 72, 73, 78
Hunter, Dr. Richard, 18–19

Huske, John, 28
Hutchinson, Thomas, 61, 72, 73, 78–79,
     152, 154, 155
  on Boston Port Bill, 191
  Gaspée affair and, 161
  as Loyalist, 161, 171
  petition to remove, 172, 181, 182–85
  private letters circulated, 171–74, 181,
     183
  salary paid by Britain, 160
  speech to Massachusetts Assembly,
     168–70
  tea delivery to Boston and, 176–77
     Boston Tea Party, 179, 184
Hyde, Lord, 202, 203, 205, 209, 214, 216

India, 115, 116, 117, 386
Indians, American, 2, 43, 60, 102, 192,
     268
  French and Indian War, 4–5, 25, 32
  Pontiac's War, 35–37, 49, 58
  western territory reserved for, 36–37
Industrial Revolution, 15, 138
Ingenhousz, Jan, 186
Ingersoll, Jared, 66, 68, 72, 73
*Interest of Great Britain Considered with
     Regard to Her Colonies and the
     Acquisition of Canada,* 45–47
Intolerable Acts, *see* Coercive Acts
Ireland, 63, 98, 315, 322, 359, 386

Jackson, Richard, 42, 56–57, 61, 62,
     65–67, 299
Jamaica, 17
Jameson, Lieutenant Colonel, 329–30
Jay, John, 39
  Adam's letters to, 378–80
  as peace commissioner, 362, 363,
     366–73, 376
Jefferson, Thomas, 39, 93, 165
Johnson, Dr. Samuel, 15, 42, 340, 341
Johnstone, George, 168, 299, 302–03
Journal of a French Traveller in the Colonies,
     74n.

Kames, Lord, 45, 124–25
Kembal, Margaret, 80
Keppel, Vice Admiral, 359, 375
Kings Mountain, Battle of, 331–32
Knox, William, 34, 269, 305
Kościuszko, Tadeusz, 277

Lafayette, marquis de, 330, 331, 337
  interception of Washington's letter to,
     337–39
  reinforcements arrive for, 345, 346

Laurens, Henry, 302, 303, 362–63, 372,
     377
Lauzun, duc de, 346
Lecky, William E. H., 18
Lee, John, 183
Lennox, Lady Sarah, 29
*Letters from a Farmer in Pennsylvania to the
     Inhabitants of the British Colonies,*
     125–26, 129
Letter to the Sheriffs of Bristol, 270–71
Lexington and Concord, 211, 218, 219–22
Lincoln, General Benjamin, 320, 321
Livingston, Robert, 373, 377
Lloyd's Evening Post, 78, 88–89
Lloyd's Journal, 353
London, 178
London, England, 15–16, 42–43, 138–39
London Chronicle, 42, 82, 92, 93, 308
London *Daily Advertiser,* 68
London *Evening Post,* 179
London Magazine, 126–27
London Packet, 185
Loring, Elizabeth, 306
Louis XVI, King of France, 284, 287, 288
Lowther, Sir James, 350
Loyalists, American, 247, 251, 260–61,
     302, 318, 371
  British attempt to create Loyalist force,
     245, 246, 314, 325, 332
  Continental Congress's rejection of right
     of Parliament to legislate for
     colonies, 198
  Cornwallis and, 324, 326, 334
  Massachusetts Assembly's resolution on
     lack of sovereignty of, 169–71
  in Philadelphia, 301, 305–09
  in southern colonies, 305, 312, 313,
     314, 321, 332
  strength of, assessments of, 324–25
Luttrell, Henry, 137
Luzerne, chevalier de la, 363, 372–73

Macalpine, Dr. Ida, 18–19
Macaulay, Thomas Babington, 26, 51
Mackenzie, Frederick, 347
Mackesy, Piers, 234–35, 236n., 261
Madison, James, 39
Manchester, duke of, 375
Mann, Sir Horace, 2
Mansfield, Lord, 47
Marion, Francis, 325
Martin, Josiah, 245
Maryland, 66, 80, 82, 215
Maryland Assembly, 131
Massachusetts, 62, 66, 72, 76, 160, 201,
     210

Massachusetts (continued)
  Boston, see Boston, Massachusetts
  declared to be in state of rebellion, 213, 215, 249
  embargo on English goods, 192, 193
  Franklin as agent for, 153–57
  Lexington and Concord, 211, 218, 219–22
  Massachusetts Assembly, 129, 130–32, 133, 160, 172
  Hutchinson's inflammatory speech to, 168–70
  petition to remove Hutchinson and Oliver, 172, 181, 182–85
  resolution asserting Parliament's lack of sovereignty over Massachusetts, 169–71
Massachusetts charter, 187–88, 214
Massachusetts Circular Letter, 129–30, 132
Massachusetts Council, 187, 193
Massachusetts Government Act, 187–88, 200, 242
Memoirs of the Reign of King George III (Walpole), 149
Meredith, Sir William, 314
Minden, Battle of, 237, 238, 296, 352
Molasses Act, 54, 58
  revision of, 57, 59, 60
Monmouth Court House, Battle of, 304
Montagu, Admiral John, 161, 177
Montcalm, Louis Joseph de, 5
Montgomery, Fort, 278
Montgomery, Major General Richard, 243
Montreal, 4, 33, 36, 243, 244
Moore, Sir Henry, 120
Morgan, Colonel Daniel, 274, 278
Morris, Robert, 303, 346
Morris, Staats Long, 28
Mount Vernon, 347
Mozart, Wolfgang Amadeus, 14
Murray, William, see Mansfield, Lord
Mutiny Act of 1765, revision of, 108–09, 119, 120

Namier, Sir Lewis B., 27–28, 29
Napoléon, 20
Navigation Acts, 3, 104, 213
Necker, Jacques, 333
Newcastle, duke of, 15, 22, 24, 29, 30, 76, 89, 104
  background of, 24
  government coalition with Pitt, 25–26
  loss of power, 30–31
New Hampshire, 76, 193
New Jersey, 62, 80, 131, 215
  fighting in, 259, 261, 263–65, 270

Newport, Rhode Island, 318, 327, 344
New York, 192, 215, 222–23, 227, 260
  British control of, 305, 315, 318, 354
  British drive on, 247, 249
  British expectations for attack on, 337–39, 342–44
  fighting in, 254–55, 257, 261, 315–16
  final evacuation of troops from, 359
  Stamp Act and, 62, 82
New York Assembly, 179
  refusal to billet and supply British soldiers, 109, 114, 119–20, 121
New York Committee of Correspondence, 192
New York Gazette, 152
Norris, Isaac, 40, 41
North, Lord, xii, 117, 164
  burned in effigy, 192
  coalition government with Fox, 375, 377, 384
  described, xiii, 147–49
  as Exchequer, 127, 142
  at Franklin's hearing before the Privy Council, 182, 184, 185
  George III's American policy, carrying out of, 147, 149, 196, 199, 200, 205–06, 210, 289–90
  last years of, 384
  as prime minister, 146–53, 322
    attempts at resignation, xiii, 235, 281, 290, 292–95, 322, 324, 357
    cabinet crisis, 292–94
    Coercive Acts and, 180, 186–88, 190, 191
    elections of 1774, 196
    loss of confidence in his government, 354–58
    rearrangement of his government, 236, 238, 289, 290
    tea tax and, 163, 166, 169, 174
    War of Independence and, see War of Independence, North and
  Wilkes and, 136, 137
North Briton, 136
North Carolina, 62, 76, 131, 245, 246, 334
North Carolina Assembly, 131
Northumberland, duchess of, 48
Norton, Sir Fletcher, 90

Olive Branch Petition, 224, 230, 236
Oliver, Andrew, 160, 171
  petition to remove, 172, 181, 182–85
Oswald, Richard, 364–70, 372
Ottoman Empire, 114

Paine, Thomas, 262n.
Palliser, Admiral Sir Hugh, 234
Palmerston, Lord, 227
Palmes, Richard, 151, 152
Parker, Commodore Sir Peter, 246
Parliament, English, 17, 43, 291, 380–81
  Conciliation Plan and, 289, 292
  Franklin's views on, 158–59
  misunderstanding of Americans, 5–6
  progress of War of Independence and,
    270–71, 280, 291, 349
  sovereignty over American colonies,
    refutation of, 169–71, 198
  see also House of Commons; House of
    Lords
Patronage system, British, 28, 31, 34,
  58–59, 358
Pattison, General, 306
Peace commissions, see War of
  Independence, peace commissions
Pelham, Henry, 25
Penn, John, 48–49, 58, 131
Penn, Richard, 230
Penn, Thomas, 40, 41, 49, 131
Penn, William, 39, 41, 48
Penn family, 40–41, 47, 48
Pennsylvania, 62, 72, 94, 95–96, 129, 153,
  165, 215
  Philadelphia, see Philadelphia,
    Pennsylvania
Pennsylvania Assembly, 129, 131
Pennsylvania Chronicle, 125, 131
Pennsylvania Journal, 174–75, 178
Percy, Lord, 220, 221–22
Peters, Richard, 40
Philadelphia, Pennsylvania, 128n., 339
  Battle of Brandywine, 274
  evacuation of British troops from, 288,
    300–01, 302, 304
  evacuation of British troops from,
    party prior to, 307–08
  Howe's occupation of, 259–61, 266,
    269, 272–74, 305–07
  occupied by the British, 296, 297, 300
  Washington's arrival in, 344, 346
Phillips, Major General William, 235,
  336–37
Pickens, Andrew, 325
Pigout and Booth, 175
Pitt, Hester, 117, 270
Pitt, William (later earl of Chatham), xii, 4,
  5, 32, 45, 48, 52, 55, 68, 71, 185
  American policy under, 113–14, 116,
    120
  attempts to prevent war, 209–10,
    211–13

background of, 24–25
becomes earl of Chatham, 113
Bute and, 12, 23, 24, 27, 111–12, 144
coalition government with Newcastle,
  25–26
Coercive Acts debate and, 189–90
death of, 295
death of George II and, 7
forms government at king's behest,
  110–13
Franklin's meetings with, 195–96,
  207–08, 209–10, 211–12
George III's dislike for, 12–13, 23, 26,
  110, 146, 271–72, 295
illness deters his ability to govern, 116,
  117–18, 119, 121, 122, 127, 128,
  139
opposes American independence, 291,
  295
peerage obtained by, 111, 113
resignation of, 30, 139
Seven Years' War and, 22, 23, 27, 29–30
on taxation of American colonies and
  Stamp Act repeal, 84–87, 88, 89,
  90, 104–05
warns of France's entrance into the war,
  271–72, 280
Wilkes affair and, 145–46
Pitt, William, the younger, 7, 295, 341–42
  as prime minister, 377, 380
  in Shelburne government, 361, 375
Plumb, J. H., 18
Poland, 115
Polly, 178
Pontiac, chief of the Ottawas, 36
Pontiac's War, 35–37, 49, 58
Portland, duke of, 353
Pownall, Thomas, 141–42, 149, 155, 174
Preston, Captain Thomas, 151
Priestly, Dr. Joseph, 39, 182, 185, 217
Princeton, Battle of, 264–65, 270
Privy Council, 37, 152, 161–62
  first meeting under George III, 21–23
  Franklin's dealings with, 194
    Cockpit hearing, 181–86, 212
    as Pennsylvania's agent, 39–40, 41,
      47–48, 49
Prosperine, 299
Prussia, 22, 30, 115
Public Advertiser, 56, 59, 173
Pultenney, William, 168
Putnam, Major General Israel, 257

Quakers, 128n., 196–97
  diplomatic efforts to prevent war,
    202–03, 205, 209, 213–14, 217

Quartering Act, 187, 188
Quebec, 243–44, 268
Quebec Act, 190–91
Quebec City, 4, 32, 33, 243
Quero, 220
Quincy, John, 375

Räll, Colonel Johann, 263–64
Randolph, John, 75
Randolph, Peyton, 74–75
Rayneval, Gérard de, 374
Read, John, 79
Reed, Colonel Joseph, 255, 303, 334
Regency Council, 70–71
Reign of George III, The (Watson), 52
Renown, 178
Revere, Paul, 192
Rhode Island, 60, 131, 161, 164–65, 206,
    210, 227, 258, 312
    Stamp Act and, 62, 82
Richmond, duke of, 291, 295, 375
Riedesel, Baroness von, 275
Riedesel, General Friedrich von, 275,
    276
Rigby, Richard, 352
Robinson, John, 313, 322, 360
Rochambeau, comte de (Lieutenant
    General Jean-Baptiste de Vimeur),
    326, 327, 329, 337, 342–43, 344
Rochford, Lord, 205, 236
Rockingham, marquess of, 29, 31, 136,
    238, 270, 281, 291, 354–55
    death of, 360
    described, 77
    as prime minister, 76, 77, 79, 81, 108,
        358–60
    repeal of Stamp Act and, 82–84, 88–91,
        103–04
    unraveling of government of, 107, 108,
        109–10
Rodney, Admiral Sir George, 344
Romney, 130, 133
Ross, John, 138
Rotch, Francis, 168
Royal Academy, 14
Royal Navy, 30, 32, 33, 53, 130, 187,
    201–02, 210, 359
    customs enforcement by, 59, 61
    mercenaries in, 33
    peacetime budget for, 32, 33, 56, 114
    Pitt's rebuilding of, 114
    War of Independence and, 225, 239,
        245–46, 247, 254, 258, 294, 298,
        320, 349
        French fleet and, 312, 326–27,
            344–45, 346, 348

    peace commission and, 299–300
    shift to naval strategy, 296–97
    Spain's entry and, 314, 315
    strategy for, 231
Royal Society, 39
Rush, Benjamin, 186
Russia, 114, 115, 210
Rutland, duke of, 353
Rutledge, Edward, 256–57
Rutledge, John, 377

Sackville, Viscount, *see* Germain, Lord
    George
St. Clair, Major General Arthur, 276
St. Kitts, 320
St. Lucia, 298, 312, 317
St. Vincent, 317
Salem Gazette, 220
Sandwich, earl of, 135–36, 212–13, 231,
    242, 247–48, 281, 298, 351–52,
    359
Saratoga, Battle of, 269, 277–79, 281, 284,
    296, 309, 310–11, 327–28, 386
Savannah, Georgia, 312–13, 318
Savile, Sir George, 270
Schreider (valet), 6–7
Schuyler, Major General Philip, 277
Serle, Ambrose, 308–09
Seven Years' War, 1–4, 22–23, 26, 27,
    29–33, 37, 39, 53, 56, 114, 237,
    242
Sharpe, Horatio, 131
Shaw, George Bernard, 386
Shelburne, earl of, 10, 11, 185, 269, 270,
    353, 354, 358
    in charge of American colonies, 112,
        114, 116, 120, 121, 127–28
    Fox and, 360–61
    as prime minister, 360–75
        fall of his government, 374–75
        peace process under, 361, 363–69,
            370, 372, 374
    resignation of, 139
Sherrard, O. A., 51
Shirley, William, 34
Slave trade, 60
Smith, Charles, 165–66
Smith, Joshua, 329
Smyth, Chief Justice, 165
Sons of Liberty, 77, 80, 106, 130, 174
South Carolina, 198, 215, 246, 325,
    331–32
    Charleston, *see* Charleston, South
        Carolina
    Stamp Act and, 62, 66, 80
South Carolina Assembly, 131, 137

Spain, 4, 32, 114, 283, 285, 286, 287
  entry into the war, 314–15, 322
  peace negotiations and, 362, 364, 369,
    373, 374
  Seven Years' War and, 29, 30
Stamp Act, 18, 19, 27, 43, 51–105
  economic consequences for England of,
    79–80, 88, 103, 107
  events leading to, 52–62
  Grenville and, see Grenville, George,
    Stamp Act and
  opposition of colonists to, 62, 66–68,
    71–82, 88
  Pitt's speech, 84–87, 88, 89
  reaction to American riots, 88–89
  repeal of, 64n., 68–69, 82–84, 86–87,
    88–105, 119, 242
    Declaratory Act accompanying, 69,
      89–91, 97, 98, 105, 106, 108
    effects in England, 107–08
    Franklin's testimony, xi, 92–103
    reaction in America on, 106–08
  writing of, 63–64, 65
Stamp Act Congress, 76, 90
Stanhope, earl of, 195, 212, 374
Stansbury, John, 328
Stark, General John, 276
Sterling, General Lord, 255
Steuben, Baron von, 331
Stony Point, action at, 315–16
Stormont, Lord, 288, 292, 348
Strachey, Henry, 261, 370
Strahan, William, 42, 43–44, 91–92, 143,
    144, 218
  Franklin testimony on Stamp Act and,
    92–93, 103
Stuart, Colonel Charles, 227, 316
Suffolk, earl of, 232, 322
Sugar Act, 61, 62, 92
  revision of, 108, 119
Sukey, 221
Sullivan, General John, 255–56
Sumter, Thomas, 325
Surrey, earl of, 357

Tarleton, Lieutenant Colonel Banastre, 325
Tea tax, 149–50, 160, 163, 166–68,
    174–78, 189–90, 210
  Boston Tea Party, 175–78, 190
Temple, Lord John, 112, 173
Terney, chevalier de, 326
Thompson, Charles, 71
Thurlow, Lord, 348, 354, 358
Ticonderoga, Fort, 222, 223, 229, 244,
    267, 273, 275–76, 277, 327
Townshend, Charles, xii, 67, 89

  death of, 123, 127
  as Exchequer, 112, 113, 115–23
Townshend, Thomas, 361
Townshend duties, 121–23, 124–27, 140,
    142–43
  repeal of, 141, 145, 149
  tea tax, see Tea tax
Trecothick, Barlow, 28, 82–83, 92, 168
Trenton, Battle of, 261, 263–65, 270
Trevelyan, George Otto, 18
Triangular Trade, 60
Trident, 300
Tryon, William, 131, 176, 229–30, 260

United States, 376–77
  diplomatic relations with England, 376,
    377
  recognition by England, 369

Valentine, Alan, 236n.
Valley Forge, 274, 296, 301, 328
Vaughan, Benjamin, 367–68
Vergennes, comte de, 284–86, 348, 374
  peace negotiations and, 364–65, 366,
    372–73
Victoria, Queen of England, 111
Virginia, 198, 215, 223, 230
  House of Burgesses, 131, 165
    rejection of Stamp Act by, 73–75, 78,
      79–80
  tobacco tax and, 54
  during War of Independence, 246, 334,
    335, 336
    confusing orders given by Clinton to
      Cornwallis, 337–39, 345
Virginia Gazette, 106
Vulture, 329, 330

Waldegrave, Earl, 9
Walpole, Horace, 1, 2, 70, 80, 113,
    134–35, 148–49, 277, 386
Walpole, Sir Robert, 3, 24
Walpole, Thomas, 161–62
War for America (Mackesy), 234–35
War of 1812, 20
War of Independence, 2, 6
  arming of America, 206, 223
  blockade of colonies, 247, 248, 265, 298
  Bunker Hill, 224, 225, 228, 230
  Canada, American incursion into,
    243–44
  Conciliation Plan, 289, 292, 302
  Continental Army, see Continental Army
  end of, 230
  England's limitations in fighting,
    230–35, 387

War of Independence (continued)
  knowledge they were fighting
    brethren, 235
  manpower, 230, 231–33, 253–54,
    277, 278, 293–94, 297, 305, 312,
    313, 314, 318
  ships, 230, 294, 347
  supply system, 230, 233–34, 253, 254,
    272, 276, 277
  last efforts to prevent, 201–10, 211–18
  Lexington and Concord, 211, 218,
    219–22
  North and, 210, 211, 229, 235–36, 242,
    264, 271, 281, 293–94, 296–98,
    314, 333
    attempts to prevent war, 201–02, 205,
      208, 215
    Conciliation Pan, 289, 292
    desire to end the war, 350–51, 354
    Franco-American alliance, 286, 289
    military leadership, 210
    peace commissions and, 247, 248,
      265, 289, 290, 292, 299–300, 351
    returning generals and, 309, 310, 311
    secret peace overtures and, 283, 284,
      288
    southern campaign and, 313, 340
    Yorktown, after, 348, 349
  peace commissions, 240, 242, 247–49,
    250–53, 255–57, 261–66, 289,
    290, 292, 299–303, 351, 361–73
    boundary negotiations, 369–71
    demands for compensation, 371
    recognition of American
      independence, 365–69
  peace process ending, 360–75
  peace treaty, signing of, 375
  Proclamation of Rebellion, 230
  secret peace overtures, 283–88
  stalemate in, 304–05
  turning point in, 327
  see also specific battles
Warren, Dr. Joseph, 222
Washington, 372
Washington, George, 38, 93, 228, 229
  chosen as commander in chief, 223
  as commander in chief, 243, 247,
    257–64, 269, 273–74, 309–10, 334
    Benedict Arnold and, 330
    Battle of Monmouth Court House,
      304

Battle of Yorktown, 347
  change of strategy, 342–44
  crossing the Delaware to attack
    Trenton, 261, 263–64, 270
  escape from Brooklyn Heights,
    254–55
  French forces arrive to join, 326–27,
    329
  interception of letter to Lafayette,
    337–39
  march to Virginia, 343–47
  Stony Point, attack at, 315–16
  survival strategy, 255, 304–05, 334
  Valley Forge, winter at, 274, 296, 328
peace overtures to, 255–56
as president, 381
shaping of Continental Army, 229
Washington, Colonel William, 325
Watson, Elkanah, 374
Watson, J. Steven, 52
Wayne, Major General Anthony, 315, 333
Wedderburn, Alexander, xii, 181–85, 248
Wellington, duke of, 387
Wentworth, Paul, 283–87, 288
West, Benjamin, 14, 307
West Indies, 297–98, 315
West Point, 328–31, 332, 343
Weymouth, Lord, 236, 298
Wharton, Joseph, 307
Wharton, Samuel, 161
Whately, Thomas, 63–64, 171, 173, 181
Whately, William, 173
Whigs, 4, 5, 13, 16–17, 26, 35, 52, 291,
    323, 358
  fall from power, 22, 24, 27, 28, 30–31,
    48
  Stamp Act repeal and, 89
  see also names of individuals
White, Hugh, 151
Whitehall Evening Post, 113
White Pines Act, 53
Wilkes, John, 133–34, 135–38, 145–46
Willis, Dr. Francis, 382, 383
Wolfe, Major General James, 5, 225
Wright, Sir James, 313
Wythe, George, 75

Yorke, Charles, 77, 83–84, 89
York River, 345, 346
Yorktown, Battle of, 321, 338n., 339, 347,
    348, 349, 374